Second Edition

JUSTICE ADMINISTRATION
Police, Courts, and Corrections Management

KENNETH J. PEAK

Department of Criminal Justice
University of Nevada, Reno

PRENTICE HALL, Upper Saddle River, New Jersey 07458

6-11-01

Library of Congress Cataloging-in-Publication Data

Peak, Kenneth J. (date)
    Justice administration : police, courts, and corrections
management / Kenneth J. Peak.—2nd ed.
        p.   cm.
    Includes index.
    ISBN 0-13-758772-4
    1. Criminal justice, Administration of—United States.   2. Law
enforcement—United States.   3. Prison administration—United
States.   I. Title.
HV9950.P43 1998
364.973—dc21   97-10406
                                                    CIP

Acquisition Editor: Neil Marquardt
Editorial Assistant: Rose Mary Florio
Managing Editor: Mary Carnis
Project Manager: Linda B. Pawelchak
Prepress and Manufacturing Buyer: Ed O'Dougherty
Cover Director: Jayne Conte
Cover Design: Marianne Frasco/Miguel Ortiz
Cover Art: Suzanne Vincze
Electronic Page Layout: ComCom/RR Donnelley & Sons
Electronic Art Creation: ElectraGraphics
Marketing Manager: Frank Mortimer Jr.
Copy Editing: JaNoel Lowe
Proofreading: Nancy Menges

 © 1998, 1995 by Prentice-Hall, Inc.
Simon & Schuster/A Viacom Company
Upper Saddle River, New Jersey 07458

Printed in the United States of America
10 9 8 7 6 5 4 3 2 1

ISBN 0-13-758772-4

Prentice-Hall International (UK) Limited, *London*
Prentice-Hall of Australia Pty. Limited, *Sydney*
Prentice-Hall Canada, Inc., *Toronto*
Prentice-Hall Hispanoamericana, S.A., *Mexico*
Prentice-Hall of India Private Limited, *New Delhi*
Prentice-Hall of Japan, Inc., *Tokyo*
Simon & Schuster Asia Pte. Ltd., *Singapore*
Editora Prentice-Hall do Brasil, Ltda., *Rio de Janeiro*

Contents

✧ **CHAPTER 3: THE REFORMERS: EVOLUTION OF JUSTICE ADMINISTRATION 55**

✦ PART II: THE POLICE

✦ PART III: THE COURTS

✦ PART IV: CORRECTIONS

✦ CHAPTER 10: CORRECTIONS ORGANIZATION AND OPERATION 210

✦ CHAPTER 13: CORRECTIONS ISSUES AND PRACTICES   281

◆ PART V: SPANNING THE SYSTEM: ISSUES CHALLENGING THE JUSTICE SYSTEM

◇ CHAPTER 14: RIGHTS AND LEGAL RESPONSIBILITIES OF CRIMINAL JUSTICE EMPLOYEES   312

✧ **CHAPTER 17: PEEKING OVER THE RIM:
WHAT LIES AHEAD? 404**

Preface

Thank you for reading this second edition of *Justice Administration*. At the time of its writing, it remains the only book of its kind: a single author's examination of police, courts, and corrections management as well as personnel and financial administration and criminal justice employees' rights. A literal line-by-line analysis of the first edition was performed to provide the most relevant, current material for this edition.

The purpose and organization of this book are discussed in Chapter 1. I would like, however, to add some prefatory comments as well. First, it is still my belief that although the criminal justice system is currently much maligned in many quarters in our society and may well continue to be criticized for many years, it is still the best system in the world. During my 27 years as a police and corrections practitioner and administrator, planner, and educator, I have met hundreds of dedicated practitioners, both administrative and rank and file, and in all sincerity can still profess to my students an abiding conviction that this occupation continues to be a special calling. To be sure, criminal justice administration is more challenging today than ever before.

Criminal justice is a people business, and this book reflects that fact as it looks at human foibles and some of the problems of personnel and policy in justice administration. Thanks to many innovators in the field, a number of exciting innovations and positive activities are highlighted throughout the book. Its general goal is to inform the reader of the primary *people, concepts,* and *terms* of justice administration.

The reader may well disagree with the activities, policies, actions, and my own views presented here. This is not at all bad because in the management of people and agencies, no absolutes exist, only ideas and endeavors to make the system better. The case studies appearing at the end of each part of the book are intended to allow the reader to become familiar with some of the types of problems justice administrators confront daily; with a fundamental knowledge of the system and a reading of the corresponding chapters, readers should be able to develop several feasible solutions to each problem presented.

I would like to thank several people who assisted in bringing this book to fruition: Neil Marquardt, acquisitions editor, and Linda Pawelchak, production editor, at Prentice Hall; JaNoel Lowe, copy editor for this edition whose valuable assistance greatly improved the final product (although any material found wanting is my responsibility alone); and Paul Johnson, distinguished professor at Weber State University in Ogden, Utah, who graciously devoted considerable time to provide helpful comments for the second edition. Case study materials were contributed by the following educators and practitioners, all of whom I am proud to consider friends and thorough professionals (their titles and affiliations are listed in the text, following their respective case study): Ron Angelone, Ron Glensor, Ted Heim, Richard Kirkland, Matt Leone, Catherine Lowe, Dennis Metrick, Burt Scott, Linda Shepard, and Glen Whorton.

Others graciously offered various types of input and/or materials, which are thoroughly appreciated: Clara Kelly and Marie Case, National Judicial College Law Library, Reno, Nevada; and Chuck Campbell, National Center for State Courts, Williamsburg, Virginia. Janice Pettenger, a criminal justice student, assisted in several respects.

I kindly solicit your input concerning any facet of this book's 17 chapters; feel free to contact me if you have ideas for improving it.

Ken Peak
peak_k@unr.edu

About the Author

Ken Peak is professor and former chairman of the Department of Criminal Justice, University of Nevada, Reno (UNR). He entered municipal policing in Kansas in 1970 and subsequently held positions as a criminal justice planner for a nine-county area in southeast Kansas; director of a four-state Technical Assistance Institute for the federal Law Enforcement Assistance Administration; director of university police at Pittsburg State University; assistant professor and outreach coordinator for the Department of Administration of Justice, Wichita State University; and acting director of public safety at UNR. In 1985 he was named Teacher of the Year by the UNR Honor Society. His other books include *Kansas Bootleggers* (Sunflower University Press, Kansas State University); *Policing America: Methods, Issues, Challenges,* 2d ed. (Prentice Hall, 1997); and *Community Policing and Problem Solving: Strategies and Practices* (Prentice Hall, 1996). He has published nearly 50 additional book chapters and journal articles and has consulted with a number of police and sheriff's departments. He served as president of the Western and Pacific Association of Criminal Justice Educators (1995–1996) and as chairman of the 600-member Police Section of the Academy of Criminal Justice Sciences (1997–1999). He holds bachelor's and master's degrees in sociology from Pittsburg State University and a doctorate from the University of Kansas.

Part I

JUSTICE ADMINISTRATION: AN INTRODUCTION

This part, consisting of three chapters, sets the stage for subsequent analysis of criminal justice agencies and their successes and challenges in Parts II through V. In Chapter 1 we examine why we study justice administration and its scope. In Chapter 2 we discuss organization and administration in general, looking at both how organizations are managed and how people are motivated. In Chapter 3 we consider several major reformers in justice administration whose contributions and influence are still evident. Specific chapter content is provided within the introductory section of each chapter.

Chapter 1

The Study and Scope of Justice Administration

[T]he ordinary administration of criminal and civil justice . . . contributes, more than any other circumstance, to impressing upon the minds of the people affection, esteem, and reverence towards the government.

—Alexander Hamilton, *The Federalist* No. 17

If men were angels, no government would be necessary.

—James Madison, *Federalist* No. 51

✦ WHY STUDY JUSTICE ADMINISTRATION?

This book is grounded on the assumption that the reader is an undergraduate or graduate student or an in-service practitioner with a fundamental knowledge of the history and operations of the justice system—the police, courts, and corrections subsystems. Another assumption is that whether you now possess or seek to possess the mantle of leadership, you will one day have thrust upon you additional administrative responsibilities within your organization. To coin a phrase, you may one day be "wearing the gold badge."

Often all of us have difficulty at an early stage in life imagining ourselves assuming a leadership role. As one person quipped, we may even have difficulty envisioning ourselves serving as a captain of our neighborhood block watch program. The fact is, however, that organizations increasingly seek people with a high level of education and experience as prospective administrators. The college experience, in addition to transmitting important and sought-after knowledge, is believed to make a person more tolerant, secure, and less susceptible to debilitating stress and anxiety than those who do not have this experience. We also assume that administration is a science that can be taught; it is not a talent that one must be born with. Unfortunately, administration is an endeavor that is often left to on-the-job training; many of us who have suffered a boss with inadequate administrative skills can attest to that fact.

✧ Purpose of the Book and Key Terms

This book alone, as with any other on the subject of administration, cannot instantly transform the reader into a bona fide expert in organizational behavior and administrative techniques. It alone cannot prepare anyone to accept the reins of administration, supervision, or leadership; formal education, training, and experience are also necessary for those undertakings.

Many good, basic books about administration exist; they discuss general aspects of leadership, the use of power and authority, and a number of esoteric subjects that are beyond the reach of this book. Rather, here we simply consider some of the major theories, aspects, and issues of administration, laying the foundation for the reader's future study and experience.

Many textbooks have been written about *police* administration; only a few have addressed administering courts and corrections agencies. Even fewer have analyzed justice administration from a *systems* perspective, considering all of the components of the justice system and its administration, issues, and practices. This book contributes to the demand for this perspective. Further, most existing books on administration are immersed in "pure" administrative theory and esoteric concepts; in doing so, the *practical* criminal justice perspective is often lost on many college and university students. Conversely, many books dwell on minute concepts, thereby obscuring the administrative principles involved. This book, which necessarily delves into some theory and esoteric subject matter, is intended to focus on the practical aspects of justice administration.

Nor is *Justice Administration* written as a guidebook for major, sweeping reform of the U.S. justice system. Rather, its primary intent is to familiarize the student with the methods and challenges of criminal justice administrators. It also challenges the reader, however, to consider what reform is desirable or even necessary and to be open-minded and visualize where changes might be implemented.

Although the terms *administration, management,* and *supervision* are often used synonymously, it should be noted that each is a unique concept that occasionally overlaps the others. *Administration* encompasses both management and supervision; it is a process by which a group of people is organized and directed toward achieving the group's objective. The exact nature of the organization varies among the different types and sizes of agencies, but the general principles and the form of administration used are similar. Administration focuses on the overall organization, its mission, and its relationship with other organizations and groups external to it.

Management, which is a part of administration, is most closely associated with the day-to-day operations of the various elements within the organization. *Supervision* involves the direction of staff members in their day-to-day activities, on a one-to-one basis. Confusion may arise because a chief administrator may act in all three capacities. Perhaps the most useful and easiest description is to define top-level personnel as administration, mid-level personnel as management, and those who oversee the work as it is being done as supervision.[1]

The terms *police* and *law enforcement* are generally used interchangeably. Many people in the field believe, however, that the police do more than merely enforce laws; they prefer to use the term *police.* Although we tend to think of the chief executive as the administrator, the bureau chiefs or commanders as management, and the sergeants as supervisors, it is important to note that all three of these tasks often are required of one administrator.

✧ ORGANIZATION OF THE BOOK

To understand the challenges of the administrators of justice organizations, we first need to place justice administration within the "big picture." Thus, in Part I, "Justice Administration: An Introduction," we generally discuss organization and administration and the nature of the U.S. justice system; the state of our country with respect to crime and government control; and the evolution of justice administration in all three components: police, courts, and corrections.

Parts II, III, and IV, discussing contemporary police, courts, and corrections administration, respectively, follow the same organization: The first chapter of each part deals with the *organization and operation* of the component, followed in the second chapter by an examination of the component's *personnel roles and functions,* and in the third chapter, a discussion of *issues and practices.* Parts II, III, and IV conclude with several case studies. As indicated in the Preface, these case studies are intended to allow the reader to encounter a few of the types of problems justice administrators confront daily. Several discussion questions follow each case study. With a fundamental knowledge of the system and a reading of the chapters in the respective book part, readers should be in a position to engage in some critical analysis—even, it is hoped, some spirited discussions—and arrive at several feasible solutions to the problems presented.

Part V examines administrative problems and factors that span and influence the entire justice system, including the rights of criminal justice employees, financial administration, technology (in a new and exciting chapter), and the future.

This initial chapter helps to set the stage for later discussions of the criminal justice system and its administration. We first consider whether the justice system composes a *process,* a *network,* a *nonsystem,* or a true *system.* Discussion then ensues about the legal and historical bases for justice and administration, followed by an examination of what some great thinkers have said about governance in general. The differences between public- and private-sector administration are reviewed next, and the chapter concludes with a discussion of policymaking in justice administration. Upon completing this chapter, the reader will have a better grasp of the structure, purpose, and foundation of our criminal justice system.

✦ A TRUE *SYSTEM* OF JUSTICE?

What do justice administrators—police, courts, and corrections administrators—actually *administer?* We will establish that they do not provide leadership over a system that has succeeded in accomplishing its mission. But do individuals within the system work amiably and communicate well with one another? Do they all share the same goals? Do their efforts effectively result in crime reduction? In short, do they compose a *system?* We now turn to these questions, still taking a fundamental yet expansive view of justice administration.

Succinctly, the U.S. criminal justice system attempts to decrease criminal behavior through a wide variety of uncoordinated and sometimes uncomplementary efforts. Each system component—police, courts, and corrections—has varying degrees of responsibility and discretion for dealing with crime. Each system component fails, however, to engage in any coordinated planning effort; hence, relations among and between these components are often characterized by friction, conflict, and deficient communication. Role conflicts also ensure that planning and communication are stifled.

For example, one role of the police is to arrest suspected offenders. Police typically are not judged publicly on the quality of their arrests but on the number of them. A common complaint about police voiced by prosecutors is that they provide case reports of poor quality. Prosecutors, on the other hand, are partially judged by their success in obtaining convictions; a public defender or defense attorney is judged by the success in getting suspected offenders' charges dropped. The courts are more independent in their operation, largely sentencing offenders as they see fit. Corrections agencies are torn between the philosophies of punishment and rehabilitation and, in the view of many, wind up performing neither function with any large degree of success. These agencies are further burdened with overcrowded conditions, high caseloads, and antiquated facilities.[2] Unfortunately, this situation exists today as it has for several decades.

This criticism of the justice system, or process—that it is fragmented and rife with role conflicts and other problems—is a common refrain. Following are several views of the criminal justice system as it currently operates: the process, network, and nonsystem points of view. Following our discussion of those three viewpoints, we consider whether criminal justice truly represents a system.

✦ A Criminal Justice *Process?*

What is readily seen in the foregoing discussion is that our criminal justice system may not be a system at all. Given its current operation and fragmentation, it might be better described as a *process*. As a process, it involves the decisions and actions taken by an institution, offender, victim, or society that influence the offender's movement into, through, or out of the justice system.[3] In its purest form, the criminal justice process occurs as shown in Figure 1.1. Note that the horizontal effects are a result of such factors as the amount of crime, the number of prosecutions, and the type of court disposition affecting the population in correctional facilities and rehabilitative programs. Vertical effects are exemplified by the primary system steps or procedures.[4]

At one end of this criminal justice process are the police, who understandably may view their primary role as getting lawbreakers off the street. At the other end of the process are the corrections officials, who may see their role as being primarily rehabilitative in nature. Somewhere between are the courts, which try to ensure a fair application of the law to each case coming to the bar.

As a process, we assume that the justice system cannot reduce crime by itself, nor can any of the component parts afford to be insensitive to the needs and problems of the other parts. In criminal justice planning jargon, "You can't rock one end of the boat." In other words, every action has a reaction, especially in the justice process. If, say, a bond issue for funds that provide 10 percent more police officers on the streets is passed in a community, the additional arrests of those added police personnel will have a decided impact on the courts and corrections components. Obviously, although each component operates largely in a vacuum, the actions and reactions of each with respect to crime send ripples throughout the process.

Much of the failure to deal effectively with crime may be attributed to organizational and administrative fragmentation of the justice process. Fragmentation exists among the components of the process, within the individual components, among political jurisdictions, and among persons.

✦ A Criminal Justice *Network?*

Still other observers contend that U.S. justice systems constitute a *network*.[5] In the view of Steven Cox and John Wade, for example, the justice system functions much like a television or radio network whose stations share many programs but each station also may present programs that the network does not air to other stations. The network appears as a three-dimensional model in which the public, legislators, police, prosecutors, judges, and correctional officials interact with one another and with others who are outside the traditionally conceived criminal justice system.[6]

Furthermore, the justice system is said to be based on several key yet erroneous assumptions, including the following:

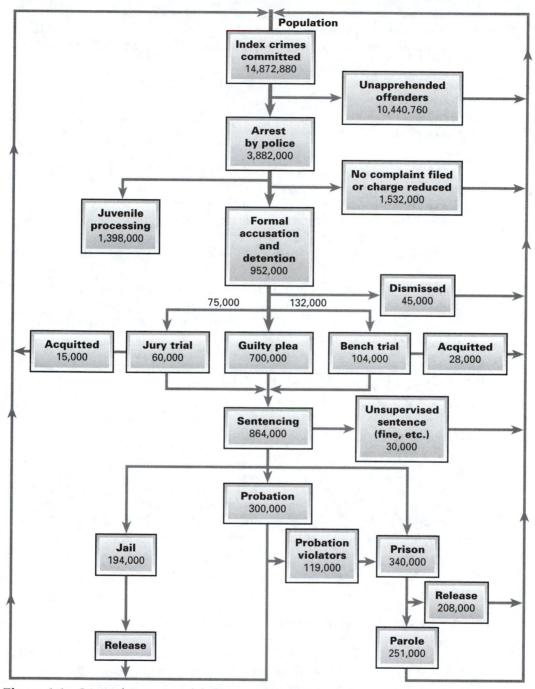

Figure 1.1 Criminal justice model. (*Source:* Adapted from the President's Commission on Law Enforcement and Administration of Justice, *The Challenge of Crime in a Free Society.* Washington, D.C.: U.S. Government Printing Office, 1967, pp. 262–263.)

1. The components of the network cooperate and share similar goals.
2. The network operates according to a set of formal procedural rules to ensure uniform treatment of all persons, the outcome of which constitutes "justice."
3. Each person accused of a crime receives due process and is presumed innocent until proven guilty.
4. Each person receives a speedy, public trial before an impartial jury of his or her peers and is represented by competent legal counsel.[7]

Cox and Wade assert that these key assumptions are erroneous because

1. The three components have incompatible goals and are continually competing with one another for budgetary dollars.
2. Evidence indicates that blacks and whites, males and females, and middle- and lower-class citizens receive different treatment in the criminal justice network.
3. Some persons are prosecuted, but others are not; some are involved in plea bargaining, but others are not; some are convicted and sent to prison, but others convicted of the same type of offense are not. A great deal of the plea negotiation remains largely invisible, such as "unofficial probation" with juveniles (described later). Also, they argue, considerable evidence points to the fact that criminal justice employees do not presume their clients or arrestees to be innocent.
4. Finally, these proponents for a "network" view of the justice process argue that the current tremendous backlog of cases ensures that a speedy trial is more fluff than substance, especially when a vast majority (at least 90 percent) of all arrestees plead guilty prior to trial.[8]

Considering these facts, the adherents to this position are compelled to believe that justice appears to be in the eyes of the beholder and that ours is probably not a just network in the eyes of the poor, the minority group, or the individual victim. Citizens, they also assert, may not know what to expect from the network. Some may believe that the network does not work at all and is not worth their support.[9]

✧ A CRIMINAL JUSTICE NONSYSTEM?

Many observers argue that the three components of the justice system actually compose a *nonsystem*. They maintain that the three segments of the system to deal with criminal behavior used in the United States do not always function in harmony and that the system is neither efficient enough to create a credible fear of punishment nor fair enough to command respect for its values.

Indeed, the theories mentioned are given considerable weight by the President's Commission on Law Enforcement and the Administration of Justice (commonly known as the *Crime Commission*), which made the following comment:

> The system of criminal justice used in America to deal with those crimes it cannot prevent and those criminals it cannot deter is not a monolithic, or even a consistent, system. It was not designed or built in one piece at one time. Its philosophic core is that a person may be punished by the Government, if, and only if, it has been proven by an impartial and deliberate process that he has violated a specific law. Around that core, layer upon layer of institutions and procedures, some carefully constructed and some improvised, some inspired by principle and some by expediency, have accumulated. Parts of the system—magistrates, courts, trial by jury, bail—are of great antiquity. Other parts—juvenile courts, probation and parole, professional policemen—are relatively new. Every village, town, county, city and state has its own criminal justice system, and there is a federal one as well. All of them operate somewhat alike, no two of them operate precisely alike.[10]

Alfred Cohn and Roy Udolf stated that criminal justice "is not a system, and it has little to do with justice as that term is ordinarily understood."[11] Similarly, Burton Wright and Vernon Fox asserted that "the criminal justice system . . . is frequently criticized because it is not a coordinated structure—not really a system. In many ways this is true."[12]

These writers would probably agree that little has changed since 1971, when *Newsweek* stated in a special report entitled "Justice on Trial" that

> America's system of criminal justice is too swamped to deliver more than the roughest justice—and too ragged really to be called a system. "What we have," says one former government hand, "is a non-system in which the police don't catch criminals, the courts don't try them, and the prisons don't reform them. The system, in a word, is in trouble. The trouble has been neglect. The paralysis of the civil courts, where it takes five years to get a judgment in a damage suit . . . the courts—badly managed, woefully undermanned and so inundated with cases that they have to run fast just to stand still."[13]

Unfortunately, as will be demonstrated time and again throughout this book, those words still ring true today. Clearly, the onus on modern-day justice administrators is not to be innovators or reformers but simply to "make do." As one law professor stated, "Oliver Wendell Holmes could not survive in our criminal court. How can you be an eminent jurist when you have to deal with this mess?"[14]

Those who hold that the justice system is in reality no system at all can also point to the fact that many practitioners in the field (the police, judges, prosecutors, correctional workers, private attorneys) and academicians concede that the entire justice system is in crisis, even rapidly approaching a major breakdown. They can cite overcrowding everywhere—police calls for service, court dockets, prison populations—as well as riots (on the streets and within institutions). In short, they contend that the system is in a state of dysfunction, largely as a result of its fragmentation and lack of cohesion.[15]

System fragmentation is largely believed to affect directly the amount and type of crime that exists. The parts of the system are disunified. Contributing to this fragmentation are the wide discretionary powers possessed by actors of the justice system. For example, police officers (primarily those having the least experience, education, and training) have great discretion over whom they arrest and are effectively able to dictate policy as they go about performing their duties. Here again, the Crime Commission was moved to comment that how the police officer moves around his or her territory depends largely on this discretion:

> Crime does not look the same on the street as it does in a legislative chamber. How much noise or profanity makes conduct "disorderly" within the meaning of the law? When must a quarrel be treated as a criminal assault: at the first threat, or at the first shove, or at the first blow, or after blood is drawn, or when a serious injury is inflicted? How suspicious must conduct be before there is "probable cause," the constitutional basis for an arrest? Every [officer], however sketchy or incomplete his education, is an interpreter of the law.[16]

Judicial officers also possess great discretionary latitude. The state statutes require judges to provide deterrence, retribution, rehabilitation, and incapacitation—all in the same sentence. Well-publicized studies of the sentencing tendencies of judges—in which participant judges were given identical facts in cases and were to impose sentences based on the offender's violation of the law—have demonstrated considerable discretion and unevenness in their sentences. The nonsystem advocates believe this to be further evidence that a basic inequality exists—an inequality in justice that is communicated to the offender.[17]

Finally, in corrections—the part of the criminal justice process that the U.S. public sees the least of and knows the least about—fragmentation also occurs, according to some people. Indeed, as the President's Commission noted, the federal government, all 50 states, the District of Columbia, and most of the country's 3,047 counties now engage in correctional activities of some form or another. Each level of government acts independently of the others, and responsibility for the administration of corrections is divided within given jurisdictions.[18]

With this fragmentation comes polarity in identifying and establishing the primary goals of the system. The police, enforcing the laws, seek to protect the community; the courts weigh both sides of the issue—individual rights and community needs; and correction facilities work with the individual. Each of these groups has varied perceptions of the offender, creating goal conflict; that is, the goal of the police is to get the transgressor off the street, which is antithetical to the "caretaker" role of the corrections worker, who often wants to rehabilitate and return the offender to the community. The criminal justice process does not allow much in the way of alternative means to cope with offenders. Eventually, the nonsystem adherent believes that the offender will become a mere statistic that is more important on paper than the person is as a human being.[19]

Because the justice process lacks sufficient program and procedural flexibility, these adherents argue, its workers can either circumvent policies, rules, and regulations, or they can adhere to organizational practices that they know are, at times, dysfunctional. (As evidence, they can point to the many cases of *informal* treatment of criminal cases that occur, such as when a police officer "bends" someone's constitutional rights to return stolen property to its rightful owner; or the "unofficial probation" allowed by a juvenile probation officer who, without a solid case but with strong suspicion, warns a youth that any further infractions will result in formal, court-involved proceedings.)

✧ OR A TRUE CRIMINAL JUSTICE SYSTEM?

That all of the foregoing perspectives on the justice system are grounded in truth is probably evident by now. In many ways, the police, courts, and corrections components work and interact to function as a process, network, or even a nonsystem. Those factors, all of which include the disunity of the justice operation, however, may yet constitute a true system. As Willa Dawson stated, "Administration of justice can be regarded as a system by most standards. It may be a poorly functioning system but it does meet the criteria nonetheless. The systems approach is still in its infancy."[20] J. W. La Patra added that "I do believe that a criminal justice system does exist, but that it functions very poorly. The CJS is a loosely connected, nonharmonious, group of social entities."[21]

To be fair, however, perhaps this method of dealing with offenders is best after all; it may be that having a well-oiled machine—in which all activities are coordinated, goals and objectives are unified, and communication between participants is maximized, all serving to grind out "justice" in a highly efficacious manner—may not be what we truly want or need in a democracy.

We hope that we have not belabored the subject; however, it is important to establish early in this book the type of system and components that you, as a potential criminal justice administrator, may encounter. You can reconcile for yourself the differences of opinion described earlier. In this book, however, we adhere to the notion that even with all of its disunity and lack of fluidity, what criminal justice officials administer in the United States is a system. Nonetheless, it is good to look at its operation and shortcomings and, as stated earlier, force ourselves to confront the criminal justice system (CJS) problems and identify possible areas for its improvement.

Now that we have a systemic view of what criminal justice managers actually administer, we look briefly at how they may go about doing it. To begin in *tabula rasa* fashion, we first consider the legal and historical bases that provide for the United States to be a democracy regulated by a government and a system of justice; we include the consensus-conflict continuum, with the social contract on one end and the status quo/repression on the other. Next we distinguish between administration and work in the public and private sectors because the styles, incentives, and rewards of each are, by their very nature, quite different. This provides the foundation for the final point of discussion, a brief look at the decision-making process in criminal justice agencies.

✦ THE FOUNDATIONS OF JUSTICE AND ADMINISTRATION: LEGAL AND HISTORICAL BASES

Given that our system of justice is founded on a large, powerful system of government, these questions must be addressed: From whence is that power derived? How can governments presume to maintain a system of laws that effectively serves to govern its people and, furthermore, a legal system that exists to punish persons who willfully suborn those laws? We now consider the answers to those questions.

✧ THE CONSENSUS VERSUS CONFLICT DEBATE

U.S. society has innumerable lawbreakers. Most of them are easily handled by the police and do not challenge the legitimacy of the law while being arrested and incarcerated for violating it. Burglars normally do not argue that their arrest is unreasonable or morally wrong. Nor do they challenge the system of government that enacts the laws or the justice agencies that carry it out. The stability of our government for more than 200 years has been a testimony to the existence of a fair degree of consensus as to its legitimacy.[22] Thomas Jefferson's statements in the Declaration of Independence hold as true today as the day when he wrote them and are still accepted as common sense:

> We hold these truths to be self-evident, that all men are created equal, that they are endowed by their Creator with certain inalienable Rights, that among these are Life, Liberty and the pursuit of Happiness—That to secure these rights, Governments are instituted among Men, deriving their just powers from the consent of the governed. That whenever any Form of Government becomes destructive of these ends, it is the Right of the People to alter or abolish it.

The principles of the Declaration paraphrase those in John Locke's *Second Treatise on Civil Government*, which justified the acts of government on the basis of his theory of *social contract*. In the state of nature, according to Locke, people were created by God free, equal, independent, and with inherent inalienable rights to life, liberty, and property. Each person had the right of self-protection against those who would infringe on those liberties. In Locke's view, although most people were good, some would be likely to prey on their fellows, who in turn would constantly have to be on guard against such evildoers. To avoid this brutish existence, people joined together, forming governments to which they surrendered their rights of self-protection. In return, they received governmental protection of their lives, property, and liberty. As with any contract, each side has benefits and considerations; people give up their rights to protect themselves and receive protection in return. Governments give protection and receive loyalty and obedience in return.[23]

Locke believed that the chief purpose of government was to protect the land people occupied and to form the commonwealth from it. Once the people unite into a commonwealth, they cannot withdraw from it, nor can their lands be removed from it. But property holders within a commonwealth cannot be made members of that commonwealth; only their express consent can make them so. They must accept that property only on the condition that they submit to the government of the commonwealth. This is Locke's famous theory of *tacit consent*: "Every Man . . . doth hereby give his *tacit Consent*, and is as far forth obliged to Obedience to the Laws of the Government."[24] Locke's theory essentially describes an association of landowners.[25]

Another theorist connected with the social contract theory is Thomas Hobbes, who argued that all people were essentially irrational and selfish. He maintained that people had just enough rationality to recognize their situation and to come together to form governments for self-protection, agreeing "amongst themselves to submit to some Man, or Assembly of men, voluntarily, on confidence to be protected by him against all others."[26] Therefore, they existed in a state of consensus with their governments, consenting to their existence.

Jean-Jacques Rousseau, a conflict theorist, differed substantively with both Hobbes and Locke, arguing that "man is born free, but everywhere he is in chains."[27] Like Plato, Rousseau associated the loss of freedom and the creation of conflict in modern societies with the development of private property and the unequal distribution of resources. Rousseau described conflict between the ruling group and the other groups in society; Locke had described consensus in the ruling group and the need to use force and other means to ensure the compliance of the other groups.[28]

Thus, the primary difference between the consensus and conflict theorists, with respect to their view of government vis-à-vis the governed, concerns their evaluation of the legitimacy of the actions of ruling groups in contemporary societies. Locke saw those actions as consistent with natural law, describing societies as consensual and arguing that any conflict in them was illegitimate and as such could be repressed by force and other means. Rousseau evaluated the actions of ruling groups as irrational and selfish, creating conflicts among the various groups in society.[29]

This debate is important because it presents the competing views of humankind toward its ruling group; it also has relevance with respect to the type of justice system (or process) we have. The systems model has been criticized for implying a higher level of organization and cooperation among the various agencies of justice than actually exists. The word *system* conjures an idea of machinelike precision in which wasted effort, redundancy, and conflicting actions are nearly nonexistent; our current justice system does not possess such level of perfection. As mentioned earlier, conflicts among and within agencies are rife, goals are not shared by its three components, and the system may move in different directions. Therefore, the systems approach is part of the *consensus model*, which assumes that all parts of the system work toward a common goal.[30] The *conflict model*, holding that agency interests tend to make actors within the system self-serving, provides the other approach. Persons subscribing to this view note the pressures for success, promotion, and general accountability, which together result in fragmented efforts of the system as a whole, leading to a criminal justice nonsystem.[31]

This debate has relevance for criminal justice administrators. Assume a consensus-conflict continuum, with the social contract (the people totally allowing government to use its means to protect them) on one end and class repression on the other. That our administrators of criminal justice agencies *not* allow their agencies to "drift" too far to one end of the continuum or the other is of paramount importance. Americans cannot allow the compliance or conflict that would result at either end; the safer point is more toward the middle of the continuum, where people do not totally depend on their government for protection and maintain enough control to prevent totalitarianism.

✧ CRIME CONTROL THROUGH DUE PROCESS

Both the systems and nonsystems models of criminal justice provide a view of agency relationships. Another way to view U.S. criminal justice is in terms of its goals. Two primary goals exist within this context: (1) to enforce the law and maintain social order and (2) to protect people from injustice.[32] The first, often referred to as the *crime control model,* values the arrest and conviction of criminal offenders. The second, because of its emphasis on individual rights, is commonly known as the *due process model*. Due process—referred to in the Bill of Rights and in the Fourteenth Amendment—is a central and necessary part of our system, requiring a careful and informed consideration of the facts of each individual case. Due process seeks to ensure that innocent people are not convicted of crimes.

These dual goals of crime control and due process are often suggested to be in constant and unavoidable opposition to each other. Many critics of criminal justice as it exists in the world argue that our attempt to achieve justice for offenders too often occurs at the expense of due process. Other, more conservative observers believe that our system is too lenient with its clients, coddling offenders rather than protecting the innocent.

We are never going to be in a position to avoid ideological conflicts such as these. Some observers, such as Frank Schmalleger, believe, however, that thinking of the U.S. system of justice as representative of crime control through due process is realistic.[33] This model of crime control is infused with the recognition of individual rights and provides the conceptual framework for this book.

✦ PUBLIC- VERSUS PRIVATE-SECTOR ADMINISTRATION

That people derive positive personal consequences from their work has long been recognized.[34] Because work is a vital part of our lives and is an activity that carries tremendous meaning in terms of our personal identity and happiness, the right match of a person to a job has for some time been considered as a determinant of job satisfaction.[35] Factors such as job importance, accomplishment, challenge, teamwork, management fairness, and rewards become important.

People in both the public (i.e., government) and private (e.g., retail business) sectors derive positive personal consequences from their work. The means by which they arrive at those positive feelings and are rewarded for their efforts, however, are often quite different. Basically, employees in private businesses and corporations have a panoply of *extrinsic* (external) rewards for motivation, but people working in the public sector must achieve job satisfaction primarily through *intrinsic* (internal) rewards.

Extrinsic rewards include such perquisites as financial compensation, salary, and benefits package; private office; key to the executive washroom; bonuses; trips; company car; awards (including such designations as the employee of the month or membership in the insurance industry's Million-Dollar Roundtable); expense account; membership in country clubs and organizations; and job title. The title assigned to a job can affect one's general perceptions of the job regardless of actual job content. For example, the role once known disparagingly as *grease monkey* in a gasoline service station has commonly become known as *lubrication technician;* garbage collectors have become sanitation engineers. Much of our society's enhancement of job titles is to add job satisfaction and extrinsic rewards to what may often be lackluster positions.

Corporations often devote tremendous sums of time and money to offer extrinsic rewards, incentives, and enhanced job titles to employees to add to their job satisfaction. These rewards, of course, cannot and do not exist in the public sector nearly to the extent that they do in the private sector.

As indicated earlier, public-sector workers must instead seek and obtain job satisfaction primarily from within—through intrinsic means. These workers, unable to become wealthy (in contrast to the Disney executive who in December 1992 cashed in $20 million in stock options) and to be in a position that is filled with perks, instead need jobs that are gratifying and make them feel good about themselves and what they accomplish. Criminal justice work is often characterized by practitioners as intrinsically rewarding, providing a sense of worth in making the world a little better place in which to live. These employees also seek appreciation from their supervisors and co-workers and generally require challenges.

These views can easily be translated to individual views concerning the workplace. In other words, some people work primarily for a paycheck and other external rewards. For example, some police officers merely put in time on the job; they probably would be glad to "patrol" a flagpole all month if such was required to earn their pay.

To be successful, administrators should attempt to understand the personalities, needs, and motivations of their employees and attempt to meet those needs and provide motivation to the extent possible. The late Sam Walton, the multi-billionaire founder of Wal-Mart Stores, provides a unique example of attempting to do this. One night Walton could not sleep, so he went to an all-night bakery (in Bentonville, Arkansas), bought four dozen doughnuts, and took them to a distribution center where he chatted with graveyard shift Wal-Mart employees. From that chat, he discovered that two more shower stalls were needed at that location.[36] Walton obviously solicited—and valued—employees' input and was concerned about their morale and working conditions. Although Walton's business sense was known to be unique, the elements of administration that he used can be applied by public administrators.

✦ POLICYMAKING IN JUSTICE ADMINISTRATION

Imagine the following scenario. Someone in a position having criminal justice operations within his or her purview (e.g., a city or county manager or a municipal or criminal justice planner) is charged with formulating an omnibus policy to reduce crime. He or she might begin by trying to list all related variables as they contribute to the crime problem: poverty; employment; demographics of people residing within the jurisdiction; environmental conditions (such as housing density and conditions and areas where living conditions are at their worst); mortality, morbidity, and suicide rates; educational levels of the populace; and so on.

Next the criminal justice administrator could request from other justice administrators within the jurisdiction specific information to determine where that person believes that problems exist with the police, courts, and corrections subsystems. For example, a police executive could contribute information concerning calls for service, arrests, and crime (including data about offenders and nature of crimes, such as time of day, day of week, methods, locations, and targets). The status of existing programs, such as community policing and crime prevention, could also be provided. From the courts, information could be sought concerning the sizes of court dockets (civil and criminal) and backlogs ("justice delayed is justice denied"). Included in this report could be input from the prosecutor's office concerning the quality and number of police reports and arrests, as well as data on case dismissals and conviction rates at trial. Corrections administrators could provide the average officer caseload and recidivism and revocation rates. Budgetary information could certainly be solicited from all subsystems, as well as miscellaneous data regarding personnel levels, training, and so on. Finally, this person could attempt to formulate a crime policy, setting forth goals and objectives needed to address the jurisdiction's needs.

As an alternative, the policymaker could approach this task in a far less complex manner, simply setting, either explicitly or without conscious thought, the relatively simple goal of "keeping crime down." This goal might be compromised or complicated by only a few other goals, such as a bullish economy. This person could in fact disregard most of the other variables just discussed as being beyond the ken of his or her current needs and interest and could for the time being not even attempt to consider them as being immediately relevant. The criminal justice practitioners need not be pressed to attempt to obtain vast amounts of information and make these critical analyses. If pressed for time (as is often the case in these real-life scenarios), the planner might readily admit to ignoring these variables.[37]

Because executives and planners of the alternative approach expect to achieve their goals only partially, they expect to repeat endlessly the sequence just described as conditions and aspirations change and as accuracy of prediction improves. Realistically, however, the first of these two approaches assumes intellectual capacities and sources of information that people often do not possess; further, the time and money that can be allocated to a policy problem are limited. Public agencies are in effect usually too hamstrung to practice the first method; the second method is the one that is actually practiced. Curiously, however, the literature on decision making, planning, policy formulation, and public administration formalizes and "preaches" the first approach.[38] The second method is much neglected in this literature.

In the United States, probably no area of government has attempted a comprehensive analysis and overview of policy on crime (the first method). Thus, making crime policy is at best an inexact process. For example, without a comprehensive process, we cannot possibly understand how a variety of problems—education, housing, recreation, employment, race, and policing—might encourage or discourage juvenile delinquency. What we normally engage in is a comparative analysis of the results of related past policy decisions. This practice explains why justice administrators often believe that outside experts or academics are not helpful to them, why it is safer to "fly by the seat of one's pants." Theorists often urge the administrator to solve his or her problems the long way, following the scientific method, when the administrator knows that the best available theory does not work. Theorists, for their part, do not realize that administrators are often in fact practicing a systematic method.[39] Thus, what may appear to be mere muddling through is highly praised as a sophisticated form of policy and decision making as well as soundly denounced as being no method at all.

What society needs to bear in mind is that justice administrators possess an intimate knowledge of past consequences of actions that "outsiders" do not. While seemingly less effective and rational, this method, according to policymaking experts, has merit. Indeed, this method is commonly used for personal problem solving in which the means and ends are often impossible to separate, aspirations or objectives undergo constant development, and drastic simplification of the complexity of the real world is urgent if problems are to be solved in reasonable periods of time.[40]

Summary

This chapter presented the foundation for the study of justice administration. We also established the legal existence of governments, our laws, and the justice agencies that administer them. It was demonstrated that each of the three components of the justice system is independent, fragmented, and often working at odds with one another to accomplish the system's overall mission.

Questions for Review

1. What is an organization?
2. Do the three justice system components (police, courts, and corrections) constitute a true system or are they more appropriately described as a process or a true nonsystem? Defend your response.
3. What are the legal and historical bases for a justice system and its administration in the United States? Why is the conflict versus consensus debate important?
4. What are some of the substantive ways in which public- and private-sector administration are similar? How are they dissimilar?
5. Which method—a rational process or one that some view as just muddling through—appears to be used in criminal justice policymaking today? Which method is probably best, given real-world realities?

Notes

1. For a more thorough explication of these terms and roles, particularly as applied in policing, see Richard N. Holden, *Modern Police Management* (Englewood Cliffs, N.J.: Prentice Hall, 1986).

2. Michael E. O'Neill, Ronald F. Bykowski, and Robert S. Blair, *Criminal Justice Planning: A Practical Approach* (San Jose, Calif.: Justice Systems Development, Inc., 1976), p. 5.

3. *Ibid.,* p. 12.

4. *Ibid.*

5. Steven M. Cox and John E. Wade, *The Criminal Justice Network: An Introduction* (2d ed.) (Dubuque, Iowa: Wm. C. Brown, 1989), p. 1.

6. *Ibid.,* p. 4.

7. *Ibid.,* p. 12.

8. *Ibid.,* pp. 13–14.

9. Philip H. Ennis, "Crime, Victims, and the Police," *Transaction* 4 (June 1967): 36–44.

10. The President's Commission on Law Enforcement and the Administration of Justice, *The Challenge of Crime in a Free Society* (Washington, D.C.: U.S. Government Printing Office, 1967), p. 7.

11. Alfred Cohn and Roy Udolf, *The Criminal Justice System and Its Psychology* (New York: Van Nostrand Reinhold, 1979).

12. Burton Wright and Vernon Fox, *Criminal Justice and the Social Sciences* (Philadelphia: W. B. Saunders, 1978).

13. "Justice on Trial: A Special Report," *Newsweek* (March 8, 1971): 16.

14. *Ibid.,* p. 18.

15. Alan R. Coffey and Edward Eldefonso, *Process and Impact of Justice* (Beverly Hills, Calif.: Glencoe Press, 1975), p. 32.

16. The President's Commission on Law Enforcement and the Administration of Justice, p. 5.

17. Coffey and Eldefonso, *Process and Impact of Justice,* p. 35.

18. *Ibid.,* p. 39.

19. *Ibid.,* p. 41.

20. Willa Dawson, "The Need for a System Approach to Criminal Justice," in Donald T. Shanahan (ed.), *The Administration of Justice System—An Introduction* (Boston: Holbrook, 1977).

21. J. W. La Patra, *Analyzing the Criminal Justice System* (Lexington, Mass.: Lexington Books, 1978).

22. Alexander B. Smith and Harriet Pollack, *Criminal Justice: An Overview* (New York: Holt, Rinehart and Winston, 1980), p. 9.

23. *Ibid.,* p. 10.

24. *Ibid.,* p. 366.

25. Thomas J. Bernard, *The Consensus-Conflict Debate: Form and Content in Social Theories* (New York: Columbia University Press, 1983), p. 78.

26. Thomas Hobbes, *Leviathan* (New York: E. P. Dutton, 1950), pp. 290–291.

27. Jean-Jacques Rousseau, "A Discourse on the Origin of Inequality," in G. D. H. Cole (ed.), *The Social Contract and Discourses* (New York: E. P. Dutton, 1946), p. 240.

28. Bernard, *The Consensus-Conflict Debate,* pp. 83, 85.

29. *Ibid.,* p. 86.

30. Frank Schmalleger, *Criminal Justice Today* (2d ed.) (Englewood Cliffs, N.J.: Regents/Prentice Hall, 1993), p. 15.

31. One of the first publications to express the nonsystems approach was the American Bar Association's *New Perspective on Urban Crime* (Washington, D.C.: ABA Special Committee on Crime Prevention and Control, 1972).

32. Schmalleger, *Criminal Justice Today,* p. 16.

33. *Ibid.*

34. Fernando Bartolome and Paul A. Lee Evans, "Professional Lives versus Private Lives: Shifting Patterns of Managerial Commitment," *Organizational Dynamics* 7 (1982): 2–29; Ronald C. Kessler and James A. McRae Jr., "The Effect of Wives' Employment on the Mental Health of Married Men and Women," *American Sociological Review* 47 (1979): 216–227.

35. Robert V. Presthus, *The Organizational Society* (New York: Alfred A. Knopf, 1962).

36. Joseph A. Petrick and George E. Manning, "How to Manage Morale," *Personnel Journal* 69 (October 1990): 87.

37. This scenario is modeled on that set out by Charles E. Lindblom, a Harvard economist, in "The Science of 'Muddling Through,' " *Public Administration Review* 19 (Spring 1959): 79–89.

38. *Ibid.,* p. 80.

39. *Ibid.,* p. 87.

40. *Ibid.,* p. 88.

Chapter 2

Organization and Administration: Principles and Practices

We are born in organizations, educated by organizations, and most of us spend much of our lives working for organizations. We spend much of our leisure time paying, playing, and praying in organizations. Most of us will die in an organization, and when the time comes for burial, the largest organization of all—the state—must grant official permission.

—Amitai Etzioni, *Modern Organizations,* 1964

✦ INTRODUCTION

It is no surprise that "Dilbert"—one of today's most popular cartoon strips, syndicated in more than 1,100 daily newspapers—portrays downtrodden workers, inconsiderate bosses, and dysfunctional organizations. Scott Adams's cartoon "hero," a mouthless engineer with a perpetually bent necktie, is believed by many Americans (1.5 million of whom contact the Dilbert website each day) to be a documentary on today's workplace. They believe that the Dilbert principle—the most ineffective workers are systematically moved where they can do the least damage: management—is alive and well. Although a sizable majority of U.S. workers routinely indicate that their workplace is a pleasant environment, more than 70 percent also experience stress at work because of red tape, unnecessary rules, and poor communication with management, among other causes. Indeed, what gives Adams grist for the Dilbert mill is the way managers mishandle their employees and downsizing.[1] This chapter examines organizations and the employees within them and how they should be managed and motivated.

The chapter offers a general discussion of organizations, focusing on their definition, theory and function, and structure. Included are several approaches to managing and communicating within organizations. We then focus on one of the most important aspects of leadership, personnel administration. We review historical schools of thought concerning management (including analects of Confucius and Machiavelli concerning how to govern) and examine organizational leadership theories. We also review a chronology of management fads that have evolved over the last four decades. We conclude with a discussion of several motivational techniques for employees based on findings by major theorists in the field.

✦ DEFINING ORGANIZATIONS

Like *supervision* and *management,* the word *organization* has a number of meanings and interpretations that have evolved over the years. We think of organizations as entities of two or more people who cooperate to accomplish one or more objectives. In that sense, certainly the concept of organization is not new. Undoubtedly, the first organizations were primitive hunting parties. Organization and a high degree of coordination were required to bring down the huge animals revealed in fossils from as early as 40,000 B.C.[2]

An organization may be formally defined as "a consciously coordinated social entity, with a relative identifiable boundary, that functions on a relatively continuous basis to achieve a common goal or set of goals."[3] The term *consciously coordinated* implies management effort. *Social entity* refers to the fact that organizations are composed of people who interact with one another and with people in other organizations. *Relatively identifiable boundary* alludes to the organization's goals and the public served.[4]

Using this definition, we can consider many types of formal groups as full-blown organizations. Four different types of formal organizations have been identified by asking the question "Who benefits?" Answers include (1) mutual benefit associations, such as police labor unions; (2) business concerns, such as General Motors; (3) service organizations, such as community mental health centers, whose prime beneficiary is the client group; and (4) commonweal organizations, such as the Department of Defense and criminal justice agencies, whose beneficiaries are the public at large.[5] The following analogy to designed to help the reader to understand organizations.

An organization corresponds to the bones that structure or give form to the body. Imagine that the fingers are a single mass of bone rather than four separate fingers and a thumb made up of bones joined by cartilage to be flexible. The mass of bones could not, because of its structure, play musical instruments, hold a pencil, or grip a baseball bat. A police department's organization is analogous. It must be structured properly if it is to be effective in fulfilling its many diverse goals.[6]

It is important to note that no two organizations are exactly alike, nor is there one best way to run an organization.

✦ ORGANIZATIONAL THEORY AND FUNCTION

✧ ELEMENTS OF AN ORGANIZATION

Max Weber (1864–1920), known as the *father of sociology,* explored in depth the organization structure as well as the dynamics related to bureaucracy. He argued that if a bureaucratic structure is to function efficiently, it must have the following elements:

1. *Rulification and routinization.* Organizations stress continuity. Rules save effort by eliminating the need to derive a new solution for every situation. They also facilitate standard and equal treatment of similar situations.
2. *Division of labor.* Labor division involves marking off performance functions as part of a systematic division of labor and providing the necessary authority to perform these functions.
3. *Hierarchy of authority.* The organization of offices follows the principle of hierarchy; each office is under the control and supervision of a higher one.
4. *Expertise.* Specialized training is necessary. It is thus normally true that only a person who has demonstrated an adequate technical training is qualified to be a member of the administrative staff.
5. *Written rules.* Administrative acts, decisions, and rules are formulated and recorded in writing.[7]

Bureaucracies are often criticized for two reasons. First, they are said to be inflexible, inefficient, and unresponsive to changing needs and times. Second, they are said to stifle the individual freedom, spontaneity, and self-realization of their employees.[8] James Q. Wilson referred to this widespread discontent with modern organizations as the "bureaucracy problem," whose key issue is "getting the frontline worker . . . to do 'the right thing.' "[9] In short, then, bureaucracies themselves can create problems.

Another way to view organizations is as systems that take *inputs,* process them, and thus produce *outputs.* These outputs are then sold in the marketplace or given for a charge or free to citizens in the form of a service. A police agency, for example, processes reports of criminal activity and, like other systems, attempts to satisfy the customer (crime victim). Figure 2.1 demonstrates the input/output model for a law enforcement agency and private business. Police agencies have other types of inputs; for example, a robbery might result in an input of newly created robbery surveillance teams, the processing would be their stakeouts, and the output would be the subsequent arrests by the team. Feedback would occur in the form of conviction rates at trial.

✦ ORGANIZATION STRUCTURE

All organizations have an organization structure or table of organization, be it written or unwritten, very basic or highly complex. An experienced manager uses this organization chart or table as a blueprint for action. The size of the organization depends on the demand placed on it and the resources available to it. Growth precipitates the need for more people, more division of labor, specialization, written rules, and other such elements.

In building the organization structure, the following principles should be kept in mind:

1. *Principle of the objective.* Every part of every organization must be an expression of the purpose of the undertaking. You cannot organize in a vacuum; you must organize for something.
2. *Principle of specialization.* The activities of every member of any organized group should be confined, as far as possible, to the performance of a single function.
3. *Principle of authority.* In every organized group the supreme authority must rest somewhere. A clear line of authority to every person in the group should exist.
4. *Principle of responsibility.* The responsibility of the superior for the acts of his or her subordinates is absolute.
5. *Principle of definition.* The content of each position, the duties involved, the authority and responsibility contemplated, and the relationships with other positions should be clearly defined in writing and published for the information of all concerned.
6. *Principle of correspondence.* In every position the responsibility and the authority should correspond.
7. *Span of control.* No person should supervise more than six direct subordinates whose work interlocks.[10]

BUSINESS ORGANIZATION

Inputs	Processes	Outputs
Customer takes photos to shop to be developed.	Photos are developed and packaged for customer to pick up.	Customer picks up photos and pays for them.

Feedback
Analysis is made of expenses/revenues and customer satisfaction.

LAW ENFORCEMENT AGENCY

Inputs	Processes	Outputs
A crime prevention unit is initiated.	Citizens contact unit for advice.	Police provide spot checks and lectures.

Feedback
Target hardening results; property crimes decrease.

COURT

Inputs	Processes	Outputs
A house arrest program is initiated.	Certain people in pre- and post-trial status are screened and offered the option.	Decrease in number of people in jail, speeding up court process.

Feedback
Violation rates are analyzed for success; some offenders are mainstreamed back into the community more smoothly.

Figure 2.1 The organization as an input/output model. (*Figure 2.1 continues on p. 26.*)

PROBATION/PAROLE AGENCIES

Inputs
Parole guidelines are changed to shorten length of incarceration and reduce overcrowding.

Processes
Qualified inmates are contacted by parole agency and given new parole dates.

Outputs
A higher number of inmates are paroled into the community.

Feedback
Parole officer's caseload and revocation rates might increase; less time to devote per case.

Figure 2.1 *(continued)*

A related, major principle of hierarchy of authority is *unity of command,* which refers to placing one and only one superior officer in command or in control of every situation and employee. When a critical situation occurs, it is imperative that someone be responsible and in command. The unity of command principle ensures that multiple and/or conflicting orders are not issued to the same police officers by several superior officers. For example, a patrol sergeant might arrive at a hostage situation, deploy personnel, and give all appropriate orders, only to have a shift lieutenant or captain come to the scene and countermand the sergeant's orders with his or her own orders. This type of situation is obviously counterproductive for all concerned. All officers must know and follow the chain of command at such incidents. Every person in the organization should report to one and only one superior officer. When the unity of command principle is followed, everyone involved is aware of the actions initiated by superiors and subordinates.

An organization should be developed with careful evaluation, or it may become unable to respond efficiently to client needs. For example, the implementation of too many specialized units in a police department (e.g., community relations, crime analysis, media relations) may obligate too many personnel to these functions and result in too few patrol officers. As a rule of thumb for police agencies, at least 55 percent of all sworn personnel should be assigned to patrol.[11]

A simple structure indicating the direct line of authority in a chain of command is shown in Figure 2.2. The classical pyramidal design is shown in Figure 2.3. The pyramidal structure has the following characteristics:

1. Nearly all contacts involve orders going *down* the pyramid and reports of results going *up*.
2. Each subordinate must receive instructions and orders from only one superior.
3. Important decisions are made at the top of the pyramid.

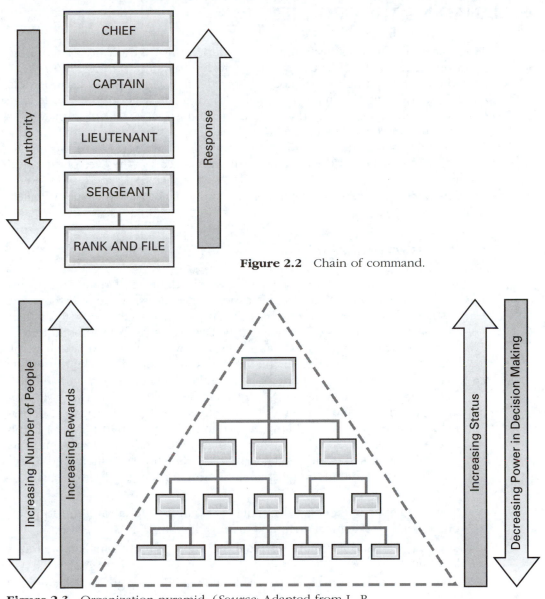

Figure 2.2 Chain of command.

Figure 2.3 Organization pyramid. (*Source:* Adapted from L. R. Sayles and G. Strauss, *Human Behavior Organizations.* Englewood Cliffs, N.J.: Prentice Hall, 1966, p. 349.)

4. Superiors have a limited "span of control," supervising only a limited number of people.

5. Personnel at any level (except at the top and bottom) have contact only with their supervisors above and their subordinates below.[12]

✦ MANAGING THE ORGANIZATION

The success of any organization normally depends on the quality of work life within the agency. Peter Drucker, often referred to as the *business guru,*[13] observed that "nothing quenches motivation as quickly as a slovenly boss. People expect and demand that managers enable them to do a good job. . . . People have . . . a right to expect a serious and competent superior."[14] Unfortunately, as Drucker was implying, leaders are both good and bad because many people—untrained or uneducated, uncaring, unfit, and/or unwilling to have the mantle of leadership thrust upon them—do not succeed (at least in the eyes of their subordinates).

We now look at leaders and what they can do to motivate their subordinates.

✧ WHAT IS MANAGEMENT?

Probably since the dawn of time, when cave dwellers clustered in hunting groups and some particularly dominant person assumed a leadership role over the party, administrators have received, from those around them, advice on how to do their jobs. Even today, manuals for managers, bosses, and upwardly mobile executives abound, offering quick studies in how to govern others. Although many have doubtless been profitable for their authors, most of these how-to primers on leading others enjoy only a brief, ephemeral existence.

To understand management, we must first define the term. This is an important and fairly complex undertaking, however. Perhaps the simplest definition is to say that *management* is "getting things done through people." Ralph Stogdill, in a review of 3,000 leadership studies, noted that "there are almost as many definitions of leadership as there are persons who have attempted to define the concept."[15] Among the most recent definitions are the following:

◊ "The process of influencing the activities of an individual or a group in efforts toward goal achievement in a given situation."[16]
◊ "Working with and through individuals and groups to accomplish organizational goals."[17]
◊ "The activity of influencing people to strive willingly for group objectives."[18]
◊ "The exercise of influence."[19]

Others have said the manager is viewed variously as a

team captain, parent, steward, battle commander, fountain of wisdom, poker player, group spokesperson, gatekeeper, minister, drill instructor, facilitator, initiator, mediator, navigator, candy-store keeper, linchpin, umbrella-holder and everything else between nurse and Attila-the-Hun.[20]

In criminal justice organizations, leadership might best be defined as "the process of influencing organizational members to use their energies willingly and appropriately to facilitate the achievement of the [agency's] goals."[21]

Perhaps, though, a leader, in the purest sense, influences others by example. This characteristic of leadership was recognized in the sixth century B.C. by Lao-Tzu when he wrote:

> The superior leader gets things done
> With very little motion.
> He imparts instruction not through many words
> But through a few deeds.
> He keeps informed about everything
> But interferes hardly at all.
> He is a catalyst.
> And although things wouldn't get done as well
> If he weren't there.
> When they succeed he takes no credit.
> And because he takes no credit
> Credit never leaves him.[22]

We discuss managers in greater length in later chapters.

✧ ANALECTS OF CONFUCIUS AND MACHIAVELLI

The writings of two other major figures have stood the test of time. The analects (or brief passages) of both Confucius (551–479 B.C.) and Machiavelli (A.D. 1469–1527) are quite popular and appropriate today. Many graduate and undergraduate students in a variety of academic disciplines have been compelled to analyze the writings of both, especially Machiavelli's *The Prince*. Both men agree on many points regarding the means of governance, as the following quote demonstrates. After reading some analects of each philosopher, we consider their application to justice administration.

Confucius often emphasized the moralism of leaders, saying

> He who rules by moral force is like the pole-star, which remains in its place while all the lesser stars do homage to it. Govern the people by regulations, keep order among them by chastisements, and they will flee from you, and lose all self-respect. Govern them by moral force, keep order among them . . . , and they will . . . come to you of their own accord. If the ruler is upright, all will go well even though he does not give orders. But if he himself is not upright, even though he gives orders, they will not be obeyed.[23]

Confucius also believed that the persons who the leader promotes is of no small importance: "Promote those who are worthy, train those who are incompetent; that is the best form of encouragement."[24] He also believed that leaders should learn from and emulate good administrators:

> In the presence of a good man, think all the time how you may learn to equal him. In the presence of a bad man, turn your gaze within! Even when I am walking in a party of no more than three I can always be certain of learning from those I am with. There will be good qualities that I can select for imitation and bad ones that will teach me what requires correction in myself.[25]

Machiavelli is often maligned for the philosophy imputed to him that the "ends justifies the means." Even today this philosophy casts a pall over his writings. Although his work is often as biting as the "point of a stiletto"[26] and seemingly ruthless at times ("men ought either to be caressed or destroyed, since they will seek revenge for minor hurts but will not be able to revenge major ones"[27] and "if you have to make a choice, to be feared is much safer than to be loved"[28]), he, like Confucius, often spoke of the leader's need to possess character and compassion. For all of his blunt, management-oriented notions of administration, Machiavelli was prudent and pragmatic.

Like Confucius, Machiavelli believed that administrators would do well to follow examples set by other great leaders:

> Men almost always prefer to walk in paths marked out by others and pattern their actions through imitation. A prudent man should always follow the footsteps of the great and imitate those who have been supreme. A prince should read history and reflect on the actions of great men.[29]

Machiavelli's counsel also agreed with that of Confucius in the sense that leaders should surround themselves with persons both knowledgeable and devoted: "The first notion one gets of a prince's intelligence comes from the men around him."[30]

Again like Confucius, Machiavelli believed that administrators should be careful of their subordinates' ambition and greed:

> A new prince must always harm those over whom he assumes authority. You cannot stay friends with those who put you in power, because you can never satisfy them as they expected. The man who makes another powerful ruins himself. The reason is that he gets power either by shrewdness or by strength, and both qualities are suspect to the man who has been given the power.[31]

On the need for developing and maintaining good relations with subordinates, Machiavelli wrote:

> If . . . a prince . . . puts his trust in the people, knows how to command, is a man of courage and doesn't lose his head in adversity, and can rouse his people to action by his own example and orders, he will never find himself betrayed, and his foundations will prove to have been well laid. The best fortress of all consists in not being hated by your people. Every prince should prefer to be

considered merciful rather than cruel. The prince must have people well disposed toward him; otherwise in times of adversity there's no hope.[32]

In an era of collective bargaining and a rapidly changing workforce, contemporary criminal justice administrators might do well to heed the analects of Confucius and Machiavelli.

✦ COMMUNICATION WITHIN THE ORGANIZATION

✦ DEFINITION AND CHARACTERISTICS OF COMMUNICATION

Communication is one of the most important dynamics of an organization. Mark Twain once said that "the difference between the right word and the almost right word is the difference between lightning and lightning bug."[33] Managers are in the communications business. It has been said that

> Of all skills needed to be an effective manager/leader/supervisor, skill in communicating is *the* most vital. In fact, more than 50 percent of a [criminal justice] manager's time is spent communicating. First-line supervisors usually spend about 15 percent of their time with superiors, 50 percent of their time with subordinates, and 35 percent with other managers and duties. These estimates emphasize the importance of communications in everyday . . . operations.[34]

Communication is the complex process of transmitting information from one person to another through common symbols. These symbols may be written or spoken words or signs and gestures. The communication process involves a message, a sender, a receiver, and an understanding of the idea that is transferred; in other words, successful communication does not occur if one is alone shouting in the middle of a cow pasture or listening to someone speak in a completely foreign language.

We now communicate via facsimile machines, video camcorders, cellular telephones, satellite dishes, and on and on. We converse orally, in written letters and memos, through our body language, via television and radio programs, through newspapers, and in meetings. Even private thoughts—which take place four times faster than the spoken word—are communication. Every waking hour, our minds are full of ideas. Psychologists say that nearly 100,000 thoughts conveyed by a multitude of media pass through our minds every day.[35]

Communication within a bureaucratic organization may be *downward* (including directives from managers and supervisors, either verbal or written), *upward* (including requests from subordinates to their superiors, which may also be verbal or in the form of reports or memorandums), or *lateral* (which includes communication among managers or subordinates on the same level of the hierarchy).

In a criminal justice organization, communication becomes exceedingly important. Criminal justice communication is often sensitive in nature. Criminal justice practitioners, especially police officers, see people at their worst and when they are in their most embarrassing and compromising situations. To "communicate" what is known about these behaviors could be devastating to the parties concerned. A former Detroit police chief lamented several decades ago that "many police officers, without realizing they carry such authority, do pass on rumors. The average police officer doesn't stop to weigh what he says."[36] Certainly, the same holds true today and applies to courts and corrections personnel, especially in view of the high-tech communications equipment now in use.

Most criminal justice administrators prefer a formal system of communication, regardless of how cumbersome it may be, because they can control it and it becomes a record for future reference. Several human factors, however, affect the flow of communication. Employees typically communicate with those persons who can help them to achieve their aims; they avoid communicating with those who do not assist them or may hinder them in accomplishing their goals; they tend to avoid communicating with people who threaten them and make them feel anxious.[37] Other barriers to effective communication are discussed later.

✦ BARRIERS TO EFFECTIVE COMMUNICATION

Many barriers to effective communication exist. Some people, for example, are not good listeners. Unfortunately, listening is one of the most neglected and the least understood of the communication arts.[38] We allow other things to obstruct our communication, including time, inadequate or too great a volume of information, the tendency to say what we think others want to hear, the failure to select the best word, prejudices, and strained sender-receiver relationships.[39]

Several barriers involve the organization itself. Often, the physical distance between superior and subordinate impedes upward communication in several ways. Communication becomes difficult and infrequent when superiors are isolated and subordinates seldom see them. The complexity of the organization may also cause prolonged delay of upward communication. For example, if a correctional officer or patrol officer observes a problem that needs to be taken to the highest level, this information normally must first be taken to the sergeant, then to the lieutenant, captain, deputy warden or chief, and so on. At each level, individuals in these higher positions reflect on the problem, put their own interpretation on it (possibly including how the problem might affect them professionally or even personally), and possibly even dilute or distort the problem. Thus, delays in communication are inherent in a bureaucracy.

Several barriers involve superiors. Their attitude toward subordinates may discourage input; they may appear blasé or annoyed with subordinates during an interview, may develop a "bunker mentality" that completely prohibits input, or

(Copyright © 1994 United Features Syndicate, Inc. Reproduced by permission.)

assume that the messenger who brings bad news should be blamed. Supervisors also may believe that they know and understand what subordinates want and need, and therefore their upward communication or complaints are unnecessary.

Finally, of course, subordinates themselves place barriers. Communication may flow more freely downward than upward because superiors feel free to call in a subordinate and discuss problems at will, whereas subordinates do not have the same freedom. Nor do subordinates always have the same "big picture" viewpoint that superiors must have or have the ability to communicate with someone with a higher position who is more fluent and persuasive than they are. Unless the superior maintains an open door atmosphere, subordinates are often reluctant to bring bad news, unfavorable opinions, and mistakes or failures to the superior or will temper them.[40]

✧ THE GRAPEVINE

Communication also includes rumors, or the so-called grapevine, so termed because information zigzags back and forth like a grapevine across organizations. Students of criminal justice administration should know that probably *no* type of organization in our society has more grapevine scuttlebutt than do police agencies. Departments even establish rumor control centers during major riots. Compounding the usual barriers to communication is the fact that policing is a 24-hour, seven-day-a-week occupation, so that rumors are easily carried from one shift to the next.

The grapevine's communication is fast, operates mostly at the workplace, and supplements regular, formal communication. It can be a tool for management to get a feel for employees' attitudes, spread useful information, and help employees to vent their frustrations. The grapevine can also carry untruths and be malicious; without a doubt, it is a force for administrators to reckon with on a daily basis.

✦ HISTORICAL APPROACHES TO MANAGEMENT

According to Gerald Lynch, the history of management can be divided into three approaches and time periods: (1) scientific management (1900–1940), (2) human relations management (1930–1970), and (3) systems management (1965–present).[41]

✧ SCIENTIFIC MANAGEMENT

Frederick Winslow Taylor, who first emphasized time and motion studies, is known today as the *father of scientific management*. Spending his early years in the steel mills of Pennsylvania, Taylor became a chief engineer and later discovered a new method of making steel; this allowed him to retire at age 45 to write and lecture. He became interested in methods to get greater productivity from workers and was hired in 1898 by Bethlehem Steel, where he measured the time it took workers to shovel and carry pig iron. Taylor recommended giving workers hourly breaks and going to a piecework system, among other adjustments. Worker productivity soared; the total number of shovelers needed dropped from about 600 to 140, and worker earnings increased from $1.15 to $1.88 per day. The average cost of handling a long ton (2,240 pounds) dropped from $0.072 to $0.033.[42]

Taylor, who was highly criticized by unions for his management-oriented views, proved that administrators must know their employees. He published a book, *The Principles of Scientific Management,* on the subject in 1911. His views caught on, and soon emphasis was placed entirely on the formal administrative structure; such terms as *authority, chain of command, span of control,* and *division of labor* were generated.

In 1935, Luther Gulick formulated the theory of POSDCORB, an acronym for planning, organizing, staffing, directing, coordinating, reporting, and budgeting (Figure 2.4); this philosophy was emphasized in police management for many years. Gulick emphasized the technical and engineering side of management, virtually ignoring the human side.

The application of scientific management to criminal justice agencies was heavily criticized. It viewed employees as passive instruments whose feelings were completely disregarded. In addition, employees were considered to be motivated by money alone.

✧ HUMAN RELATIONS MANAGEMENT

Beginning in 1930, people began to realize the negative effects of scientific management on the worker. A view arose in policing that management should instill pride and dignity in officers. The movement toward human relations management began with the famous studies conducted from the late 1920s through the mid-1930s by the Harvard Business School at the Hawthorne plant of the Western Electric Company.[43] These studies, which are discussed in more detail later

PLANNING: working out in broad outline what needs to be done and the methods for doing it to accomplish the purpose set for the enterprise;

ORGANIZING: the establishment of a formal structure of authority through which work subdivisions are arranged, defined, and coordinated for the defined objective;

STAFFING: the whole personnel function of bringing in and training the staff and maintaining favorable conditions of work;

DIRECTING: the continuous task of making decisions, embodying them in specific and general orders and instructions, and serving as the leader of the enterprise;

COORDINATING: the all-important duty of interrelating the various parts of the organization;

REPORTING: informing the executive and his assistants as to what is going on, through records, research, and inspection;

BUDGETING: all that is related to budgeting in the form of fiscal planning, accounting, and control.

Figure 2.4 Gulick's POSDCORB. (*Source:* Luther Gulick and Lyndall Urwick, *Papers on the Science of Administration.* New York: Institute of Public Administration, 1937.)

in this chapter, found that worker productivity is more closely related to *social* capacity than to physical capacity, that noneconomic rewards play a prominent part in motivating and satisfying employees, and that employees do not react to management and its rewards as individuals but as members of groups.[44]

In the 1940s and 1950s, police departments began to recognize the strong effect of the informal structure on the organization; agencies began using such techniques as job enlargement and job enrichment to generate interest in policing as a career. Studies indicated that the supervisor who was "employee centered" was more effective than one who was "production centered." Democratic or participatory management began to appear in police agencies. The human relations approach had its limitations, however. With the emphasis being placed on the employee, the role of the organization structure became secondary; the primary goal seemed to many to be social rewards, with little attention seemingly given to task accomplishment. Many police managers saw this trend as unrealistic. Employees began to give less and expect more in return.[45]

✧ SYSTEMS MANAGEMENT APPROACH

In the mid-1960s, the features of the human relations and scientific management approaches were combined in the *systems management* approach. Designed to bring the individual and the organization together, this approach attempted to help managers use employees to reach desired production goals. The systems approach recognized that it was necessary to have some hierarchical arrangement to bring about coordination, that authority and responsibility were essential, and that overall organization was required.

The systems management approach combined the work of Maslow, who developed his hierarchy of needs, in which he classified the needs of people at different levels;[46] McGregor, who stressed the general theory of human motivation;[47] and Blake and Mouton, who developed the "managerial grid," which emphasized two concerns—for task and for people—that managers must have.[48] (These theories are discussed in greater detail later.) In effect, the systems management approach holds that to be effective, the manager must be interdependent with other individuals and groups and have the ability to recognize and deal with conflict and change. More than mere technical skills and education are required; managers require knowledge of several major resources: people, money, time, and equipment.[49] Team cooperation is required to achieve organizational goals.

Several theories of leadership also have evolved over the past several decades, the most common being trait theory, leadership styles, and situational approaches. Each is discussed briefly.

✦ PRIMARY LEADERSHIP THEORIES

✦ TRAIT THEORY

The *trait theory* was very popular until around the 1950s. This theory was based on the contention that good leaders possessed certain character traits that poor leaders did not. Those who developed this theory, Stogdill and Goode, believed that a leader could be identified through a two-step process. The first step involved studying leaders and comparing them to nonleaders to determine which traits only the leaders possessed. The second step sought people who possessed these traits to be promoted into managerial positions.[50]

A study of 468 administrators in 13 companies found certain traits they had in common. They were more intelligent and better educated; had a stronger power need; preferred independent activity, intense thought, and some risk; enjoyed relationships with people; and disliked detail work more than their subordinates did.[51] Figure 2.5 shows traits and skills commonly associated with leader effectiveness, according to Yuki. Following this study, a review of the literature on trait theory revealed the traits most identified as being associated with leadership ability. Those traits were intelligence, initiative, extroversion, sense of humor, enthusiasm, fairness, sympathy, and self-confidence.[52]

Trait theory has lost much of its support since the 1950s, largely because of its basic assumption that leadership cannot be taught. A more important reason, however, is simply the growth of new, more sophisticated approaches to the study

Traits	Skills
Adaptable to situations	Clever (intelligent)
Alert to social environment	Conceptually skilled
Ambitious and achievement oriented	Creative
Assertive	Diplomatic and tactful
Cooperative	Fluent in speaking
Decisive	Knowledgeable about group task
Dependable	Organized (administrative ability)
Dominant (desire to influence others)	Persuasive
Energetic (high activity level)	Socially skilled
Persistent	
Self-confident	
Tolerant of stress	
Willing to assume responsibility	

Figure 2.5 Traits and skills commonly associated with leadership effectiveness. (*Source:* Gary Yuki, *Leadership in Organizations.* Englewood Cliffs, N.J.: Prentice Hall, 1981, pp. 70, 121–125.)

of leadership. Quantifiable means to test trait theory were limited. What does it mean to say that a leader must be intelligent? By whose standards? As compared with persons within the organization or within society? How can traits such as sense of humor, enthusiasm, fairness, and others be measured or tested? The inability to measure these factors was the real flaw in and reason for the decline of this theory.

When the trait theorists could not empirically document characteristics found in leaders, researchers in the 1940s and 1950s began examining leaders and the situations in which they actually functioned.

✦ STYLE THEORY

A study at Michigan State University investigated how leaders motivated individuals or groups to achieve organizational goals. The study determined that leaders must have a sense of the task to be accomplished as well as the environment in which the followers work. Three principles of leadership behavior emerged from the Michigan State study:

1. Leaders must assume the leadership role and give task direction to their followers.
2. Closeness of supervision directly affects employee production. High-producing units had less direct supervision than highly supervised units. The conclusion was that employees need some area of freedom to make choices. Given this, they produce at an increased rate.
3. Leaders must be employee oriented. It is the leader's responsibility to facilitate employees' accomplishment of goals.[53]

In the 1950s, Edwin Fleishman began studies of leadership at Ohio State University. After focusing on leader behavior rather than personality traits, he identified two dimensions of basic principles of leadership that could be taught: initiating structure and consideration (Figure 2.6).[54] *Initiating structure* referred to supervisory behavior that focused on the achievement of organizational goals; *consideration* referred to a supervisor's openness to subordinates' ideas and respect for their feelings as persons. High consideration and moderate initiating structure were assumed to yield higher job satisfaction and productivity than high initiating structure and low consideration.[55]

The major focus of this, the style theory, is the adoption of a single managerial style by a manager based on his or her position in regard to initiating structure and consideration. Three pure leadership styles were thought to be the basis for all managers: autocratic, democratic, and laissez-faire.

Autocratic leaders are leader centered and have a high initiating structure. They are primarily authoritarian in nature and prefer to give orders rather than invite group participation. They have a tendency to be personal in their criticism. This style works best in emergency situations in which strict control and rapid decision making are needed. The problem with autocratic leadership is the organization's inability to function when the leader is absent. It also stifles individual development and initiative because subordinates are rarely allowed to make an independent decision.[56]

The *democratic,* or participative, leadership style tends to focus on working within the group and striving to attain cooperation from group members by eliciting their ideas and support. Democratic managers tend to be viewed as consideration oriented and strive to attain mutual respect with subordinates. These leaders operate within an atmosphere of trust and delegate much authority. This style is useful in organizations whose course of action is uncertain and whose problems are relatively unstructured. It often taps the decision-making ability of subordinates. In emergency situations requiring a highly structured response,

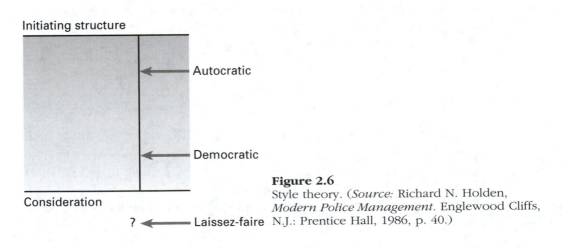

Figure 2.6
Style theory. (*Source:* Richard N. Holden, *Modern Police Management*. Englewood Cliffs, N.J.: Prentice Hall, 1986, p. 40.)

however, democratic leadership may prove too time consuming and awkward to be effective. Thus, although the worker may appreciate the strengths of this style, its weaknesses must also be recognized.[57]

The third leadership style, *laissez-faire*, is a hands-off approach in which the leader is actually a nonleader. The organization in effect runs itself with no input or control from the manager. This style has no positive aspects because the entire organization is soon placed in jeopardy. In truth, this may not be a leadership style at all; instead, it may be an abdication of administrative duties.

✦ SITUATIONAL LEADERSHIP

Style theory assumes that each administrator will adopt one of the three styles just discussed almost exclusively. Further, the style theory assumes that all administrators select a style that they believe works and stay with it because of managerial rigidity. This assumption has led many researchers to abandon its tenets for one that is more flexible: situational leadership.

Early work in *situational leadership* (see Figure 2.7) was conducted by Fred Fiedler. Fiedler held that personality characteristics relevant to leadership are stable over time and across situations. Some personality attributes are believed to contribute to effective leadership in other situations. Through some studies he conducted, Fiedler also concluded that leadership capacity is not likely to be improved through either training or experience.[58]

Fiedler's work was known as *contingency theory* because he argued that there is no single best approach to leadership and that the influence of the situation determined the appropriate leadership style.

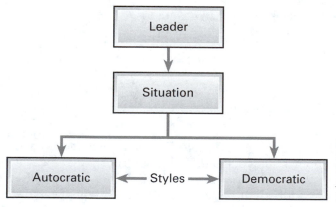

Figure 2.7
Situational leadership. (*Source:* Richard N. Holden, *Modern Police Management.* Englewood Cliffs, N.J.: Prentice Hall, 1986, p. 40.)

✦ THE MANAGERIAL GRID

In 1964 Robert R. Blake and Jane S. Mouton developed their managerial grid based on studies done by Fleishman and others at Ohio State University. The team used two variables, focus on task (initiating structure) and focus on relationships (consideration), to develop a management quadrant describing leadership behavior.

The managerial grid (see Figure 2.8) includes five leadership styles based on concern for output (production) and concern for people. Using a specially developed testing instrument, people can be assigned a numerical score depicting their concern for each variable. Numerical indications such as 9,1, 9,9, 1,1, and 5,5 are then plotted on the grid using the scales on the horizontal and vertical axes. The grid is read like a map, right and up. Each axis is numbered 1 to 9, with 1 indicating the minimum effort or concern and 9 the maximum. The horizontal axis represents the concern for production and performance goals, and the vertical axis represents the concern for human relations or empathy.

The points of orientation are related to styles of management. The lower left-hand corner of the grid shows the 1,1 style (representing a minimal concern for task or service and a minimal concern for people). The lower right-hand corner of the grid identifies the 9,1 style. This type of leader has a primary concern for the task or output and a minimal concern for people. At this point, people are seen as tools of production. The upper left-hand corner represents the 1,9 style, often referred to as *country club management,* with minimum effort given to output or task. The upper right, 9,9, indicates high concern for both people and production—a "we're all in this together," "common stake" approach of mutual respect and trust. In the center—a 5,5, "middle-of-the-road" style—the leader has a "give a little, be fair but firm" philosophy, providing a balance between output and people concerns.[59]

These five leadership styles can be summarized as follows:[60]

◊ Authority-compliance management (9,1)
◊ Country club management (1,9)
◊ Middle-of-the-road management (5,5)
◊ Impoverished management (1,1)
◊ Team management (9,9)

✦ TYPES OF LEADERSHIP SKILLS

In 1974 Robert Katz identified three essential skills that leaders should possess: technical, human, and conceptual. Katz defined *skill* as the capacity to translate knowledge into action in such a way that a task is accomplished successfully.[61] Each of these skills (when performed effectively) results in the achievement of objectives and goals, which is the primary nature of management.

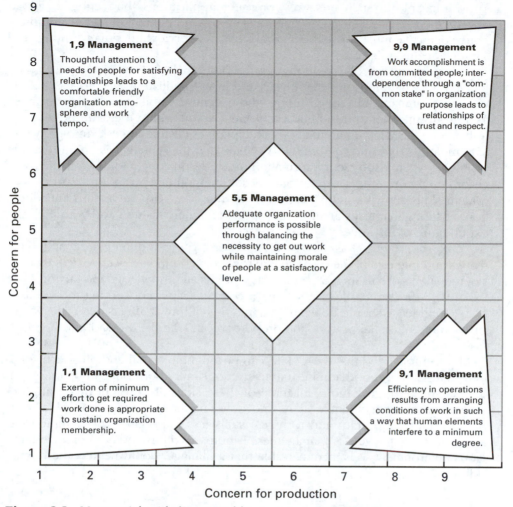

Figure 2.8 Managerial grid. (Reprinted by permission of *Harvard Business Review* [Nov.–Dec. 1964]. An exhibit from "Breakthrough in Organizational Development" by Robert R. Blake, Jane S. Mouton, Louis B. Barnes, and Larry E. Greiner. Copyright 1964 by the President and Fellows of Harvard College; all rights reserved.)

Technical skills are those a manager needs to ensure that specific tasks are performed correctly. They are based on proven knowledge, procedures, or techniques. A police detective, a court administrator, and a probation officer have developed technical skills directly related to the work they perform. Katz wrote that a technical skill "involves specialized knowledge, analytical ability within that specialty, and facility in the use of the tools and techniques of the specific discipline."[62] This skill is the most easily trained. A court administrator, for example, has to be knowledgeable in such areas as computer applications, budgeting, caseload management, space utilization, public relations, and personnel administration; a police detective must possess technical skills in interviewing, fingerprinting, and surveillance techniques.[63]

Human skills involve working with people, including being thoroughly familiar with what motivates employees and how to utilize group processes. Katz visualized human skills as including "the executive's ability to work effectively as a group member and to build cooperative effort within the team he leads."[64] Katz added that the human relations skill involves (1) tolerance of ambiguity and (2) empathy. *Tolerance of ambiguity* means that the manager is able to handle problems when insufficient information precludes making a totally informed decision. *Empathy* is the ability to put oneself in another's place. An awareness of human skills allows a manager to provide the necessary leadership and direction, ensuring that tasks are accomplished in a timely fashion and with the least expenditure of resources.[65]

Conceptual skills, Katz said, involve "coordinating and integrating all the activities and interests of the organization toward a common objective."[66] Katz considered such skills to include "an ability to translate knowledge into action." For example, in a criminal justice setting, a court decision concerning the admissibility of evidence should be examined in terms of how it affects detectives, court cases, the forensic laboratory, the property room, and the work of the street officer.

Katz emphasized that these skills can be taught to actual and prospective administrators; thus, good administrators are not simply born but can be trained in the classroom. Furthermore, all three of these skills are present in varying degrees at each management level. As one moves up the hierarchy, conceptual skills become more important and technical skills less important. The common denominator for all levels of management is human skill. In today's unionized, litigious environment, it is inconceivable that a manager could neglect the human skills.

✦ MANAGEMENT FADS

Paul Whisenand and Fred Ferguson[67] placed much of the theory discussed earlier into a chronology, the result being an interesting history of four decades of management fads. These fads began in the 1950s when "seat-of-the-pants" management was becoming outdated and Frederick Taylor insisted that running a company should be more a science than an art. These four decades of fads are described here. It should be emphasized that several of these so-called fads (such as computerization, Theory X and Y, management by objectives, the managerial grid, and management by walking around) were not short-lived fads at all but have stood the test of time and are still in use today, in differing degrees.

The 1950s

1. *Computerization.* The first corporate mainframes were displayed as proud symbols of success.
2. *Theory X and Y.* Propounded by MIT professor Douglas McGregor, this theory held that workers are more productive if they have an influence in their work.
3. *Quantitative management.* The theory that numbers should be trusted; running a business is more like a science than an art.
4. *Diversification.* The idea that the problem of cyclical ups and downs could be countered by buying other businesses.
5. *Management by objectives.* Peter Drucker popularized the process of setting an executive's goals through negotiation.

The 1960s

6. *T-Groups.* Encounter seminars were used to teach interpersonal sensitivity.
7. *Centralization/Decentralization.* This relates to the concern as to whether headquarters or line managers should make decisions.
8. *Matrix management.* Managers report to different superiors according to the task.
9. *Conglomeration.* Disparate businesses are placed under a single corporation umbrella.
10. *The managerial grid.* This is a process for determining whether a manager's chief concern is people or production.

The 1970s

11. *Zero-based budgeting.* This year's budget is based on throwing out last year's numbers and starting from scratch.
12. *The experience curve.* This method uses past experience to generate profits by cutting prices, gaining market share, and boosting efficiency.

The 1980s

13. *Theory Z.* Japanese management techniques such as quality circles and job enrichment should be adopted.
14. *Demassing.* Trimming the workforce and demoting managers lead to greater efficiency.
15. *Restructuring.* This technique involves sweeping out businesses that don't measure up, often while taking on considerable debt.
16. *Corporate culture.* Attending to the values, goals, rituals, and heroes that characterize a company's style is thought to improve overall performance.
17. *Management by walking around.* By leaving the office to visit the troops instead of relying on written reports, managers obtain more relevant information.

Why did such a proliferation of theories occur? Whisenand and Ferguson speculated the reason to be the intense pressure on managers to perform miracles, resulting in a mad scramble for instant solutions.[68]

Where today's criminal justice administrator is concerned, a return to the basics appears to now be "in," with such values as integrity, innovation, quality, service, and a people orientation. These basics have been practiced for centuries and normally have resulted in successful managers and organizations.[69]

✦ MOTIVATING EMPLOYEES

One of the most fascinating subjects throughout the history of humankind is that of motivating people. Some have sought to do so through justice (Plato), some through psychoanalysis (Freud), some through conditioning (Pavlov), some through incentives (Frederick Taylor), and still others through fear (any number of dictators, czars, pharaohs, and despots). Since the industrial revolution, managers have been trying to get a full day's work from their subordinates; today, this issue remains a primary concern in the workplace.

The flap in the early 1990s caused by Japanese businessmen who stated that U.S. workers were lazy certainly raised our collective ire; nonetheless, many U.S. businesspeople and managers would probably agree that better worker motivation is needed. As Donald Favreau and Joseph Gillespie stated, "Getting people to work, the way you want them to work, when you want them to work, is indeed a challenge."[70]

Many theories have attempted to explain motivation. Some of the best known are those resulting from the Hawthorne studies and those developed by Abraham Maslow, Douglas McGregor, and Frederick Herzberg, all of which are discussed here along with expectancy and contingency theories.

✧ THE HAWTHORNE STUDIES

As mentioned earlier, one of the most important studies of worker motivation and behavior, launching intense interest and research in those areas, was Western Electric Company's study in the 1920s. In 1927 engineers at the Hawthorne Plant of Western Electric Company near Chicago conducted an experiment with several groups of workers to determine the effect of illumination on production. The engineers found that when illumination was increased in stages, production increased. To verify their findings, they reduced illumination to its previous level; again, production increased. Confused by their findings, they contacted Elton Mayo and his colleague Fritz Roethlisberger from Harvard to investigate.[71]

First, the researchers selected several experienced women assemblers for an experiment. Management removed the women from their formal group and isolated them in a room. The women were compensated on the basis of the output of their group. Next researchers began a series of environmental changes, each discussed with the women in advance of its implementation. For example, breaks were introduced and light refreshments were served. The normal six-day week was reduced to five days and the workday was cut by one hour. *Each* of these changes resulted in increased output.[72] To verify these findings, researchers returned the women to their original working conditions; breaks were eliminated, the six-day workweek was reinstituted, and all other work conditions were reinstated. The results were that production again increased!

Mayo and his team then performed a second study at the Hawthorne plant. A new group of 14 workers—all males who worked in simple, repetitive telephone coil-winding duties—were given variations in length of rest periods and workweeks.[73] The men were also put on a reasonable piece rate; that is, the more they produced, the more money they earned. The assumption was that the workers would strive to produce more because it was in their own economic interest to do so.

The workers soon split into two informal groups on their own, each group setting its own standards of output and conduct. The workers' output did not increase. Neither too little nor too much production was permitted, and peers exerted pressure to keep members in line. The values of the informal group appeared to be more powerful than the allure of increased wages. The values were stated as follows:

1. Don't be a "rate buster" and produce too much work.
2. Don't be a "chiseler" by turning out too little work.
3. Don't be a "squealer" to supervisors.
4. Don't be officious; if you aren't a supervisor, don't act like one.[74]

Taken together, the Hawthorne studies revealed that people work for a variety of reasons, not just for money and subsistence. They seek satisfaction for more than their physical needs at work and from their co-workers. For the first time, clear evidence was gathered to support workers' social and esteem needs. As a result, this collision between the human relations school, begun in the Hawthorne studies, and traditional organizational theory sent researchers and theorists off in new and different directions. At least three major, new thrusts evolved: inquiries into (1) what motivates workers (leading to the work of Maslow and Herzberg), (2) leadership (discussed earlier), and (3) organizations as behavioral systems.

✦ MASLOW'S HIERARCHY OF NEEDS

Abraham H. Maslow (1908–1970), founder of the humanistic school of psychology, conducted research on human behavior at the Air University, Maxwell Air Force Base, Alabama, during the 1940s. His approach to motivation was unique in that the behavior patterns he analyzed were those of motivated, happy, and production-oriented people—achievers, not underachievers. He studied biographies of historical and public figures, including Abraham Lincoln, Albert Einstein, and Eleanor Roosevelt; he also observed and interviewed some of his contemporaries—all of whom had no psychological problems and no signs of neurotic behavior.

Maslow hypothesized that if he could understand what made these people function, this information could be applied to others, thus achieving a high state of motivation. His observations were coalesced into a *hierarchy of needs*.[75]

Maslow concluded that because human beings are part of the animal kingdom, their basic and primary needs or drives are physiological: air, food, water, sex, and shelter. These needs are related to survival. Next in order of prepotency are needs related to safety or security: protection against danger, murder, criminal assault, threat, deprivation, and tyranny. At the middle of the hierarchy is belonging, or social needs: being accepted by one's peers and associating with members of groups. The next level on the hierarchy are the needs or drives related to ego: self-esteem, self-respect, power, prestige, recognition, and status. Located at the top of the hierarchy is self-realization or actualization: self-fulfillment, creativity, and becoming all that one is capable of becoming.[76] Figure 2.9 depicts this hierarchy.

Unlike the lower needs, the higher needs are rarely satisfied. Maslow suggested that to prevent frustration, needs should be filled in sequential order. A satisfied need is no longer a motivator. Maslow's research also indicated that once a person reaches a high state of motivation (i.e., esteem or self-realization levels), he or she will remain highly motivated, will have a positive attitude toward the organization, and will have a "pitch-in and help" philosophy.

✦ MCGREGOR'S THEORY X/THEORY Y

Douglas McGregor (1906–1967), who served as president of Antioch College and then on the faculty of the Massachusetts Institute of Technology, was one of the great advocates of humane and democratic management. At Antioch, McGregor tested his theories of democratic management. He noted that behind every managerial decision or action are assumptions about human behavior. He chose the simplest terms possible with which to express his theories, designating one set of assumptions Theory X and the other Theory Y.[77]

Theory X managers hold the traditional views of direction and control, such as the following:

◊ The average human being has an inherent dislike of work and avoids it if possible. This assumption has deep roots, beginning with the punishment of Adam and Eve, their banishment into a world where they had to work for a living. Management's use of negative reinforcement and the emphasis on "a fair day's work" reflect an underlying belief that management must counter an inherent dislike for work.[78]

◊ Because of this human characteristic of dislike of work, most people must be coerced, controlled, directed, or threatened with punishment to get them to put forth adequate effort to achieve organizational objectives. The dislike

Self-Realization Needs	Job-Related Satisfiers
Reaching Your Potential	Involvement in Planning
Independence	Your Work
Creativity	Freedom to Make Decisions
Self-Expression	Affecting Work
	Creative Work to Perform
	Opportunities for Growth
	and Development

Esteem Needs	Job-Related Satisfiers
Responsibility	Status Symbols
Self-Respect	Merit Awards
Recognition	Challenging Work
Sense of Accomplishment	Sharing in Decisions
Sense of Competence	Opportunity for Advancement

Social Needs	Job-Related Satisfiers
Companionship	Opportunities for Interaction
Acceptance	with Others
Love and Affection	Team Spirit
Group Membership	Friendly Co-workers

Safety Needs	Job-Related Satisfiers
Security for Self and Possessions	Safe Working Conditions
Avoidance of Risks	Seniority
Avoidance of Harm	Fringe Benefits
Avoidance of Pain	Proper Supervision
	Sound Company Policies, Programs,
	and Practices

Physical Needs	Job-Related Satisfiers
Food	Pleasant Working Conditions
Clothing	Adequate Wage or Salary
Shelter	Rest Periods
Comfort	Labor-Saving Devices
Self-Preservation	Efficient Work Methods

Figure 2.9 Maslow's hierarchy of human needs. (*Source:* A. H. Maslow, *Motivation and Personality,* 2nd ed. New York: Harper & Collins, 1970.)

(Copyright © United Features Syndicate, Inc. Reprinted by permission.)

of work is so strong that even the promise of rewards is not generally enough to overcome it. People accept rewards and demand larger ones. Only the threat of punishment works.[79]

◊ The average human being prefers to be directed, wishes to avoid responsibility, has relatively little ambition, and wants security above all. This assumption of the "mediocrity of the masses" is rarely expressed so bluntly. Although much lip service is paid to the "sanctity" of the worker and human beings in general, many managers reflect this assumption in practice and policy.

(*Note:* Theory X managers would be autocratic and classified as a 9,1 on the managerial grid.)

Theory Y managers naturally take the opposite view of the worker:

◊ The expenditure of physical and mental effort in work is as natural as play or rest. The average human being does not inherently dislike work; it may even be a source of satisfaction, perhaps performed voluntarily.

◊ External control and the threat of punishment are not the only means to bring about effort to meet organizational objectives.

◊ Commitment to objectives is a function of the rewards associated with their achievement. The most significant of such rewards—satisfaction of ego and self-actualization needs—can be direct products of effort directed toward meeting organizational objectives.

◊ Under proper conditions, the average human being learns not only to accept responsibility but also to seek it. Under this view, the avoidance of responsibility, the lack of ambition, and the emphasis on security are general consequences of experience, not inherent human characteristics.

◊ The capacity to exercise a high degree of imagination, ingenuity, and creativity in the solution of organizational problems is widely, not narrowly, distributed in the population.

◊ Under the conditions of modern industrial life, the intellectual potential of the average human being is only partially utilized.

✧ HERZBERG'S MOTIVATION-HYGIENE THEORY

During the 1950s, Frederick Herzberg conducted a series of studies in which he asked workers, primarily engineers, to describe the times when they felt particularly good and particularly bad about their jobs. The respondents identified several things that were sources of satisfaction and dissatisfaction in their work. Then, from these findings, Herzberg isolated two vital factors found in all jobs: maintenance or hygiene factors and motivational factors.

Maintenance factors are those things in the work environment that meet an employee's hedonistic need to avoid pain. Hygiene factors include the necessities of any job (e.g., adequate pay, benefits, job security, decent working conditions, supervision, interpersonal relations). Hygiene factors do not satisfy or motivate; they set the stage for motivation. They are, however, the major source of dissatisfaction when they are inadequate.[80]

Motivational factors are those psychosocial factors in work that provide intrinsic satisfaction and serve as an incentive for people to invest more of their time, talent, energy, and expertise in productive behavior. Examples include achievement, recognition, responsibility, the work itself, advancement, and potential for growth. The absence of motivators does not necessarily produce job dissatisfaction.[81]

Although these needs are obviously related, they represent totally different dimensions of satisfaction.

✧ EXPECTANCY AND CONTINGENCY THEORIES

In the 1960s, *expectancy theory* was developed, holding that employees will do what their managers or organizations want them to do if the following are true:

1. The task appears to be possible (employees believe they possess the necessary competence).
2. The employees see the reward (outcome) offered as desirable (intrinsic rewards come from the job itself; extrinsic rewards are supplied by others).
3. Employees perceive that performing the required behavior or task will bring the desired outcome.
4. Employees believe there is a good chance that better performance will bring better rewards.[82]

The expectancy theory will work for an organization that specifies what behaviors it expects from people and what the rewards or outcomes will be for those who exhibit those behaviors. Rewards may be pay increases, time off, chances for advancement, a sense of achievement, or other benefits. Managers and organizations can find out what their employees want and see to it that they are provided the rewards they seek.

Walter Newsom[83] said that the reality of the expectancy theory can be summarized by the "nine Cs": (1) capability (does a person have the capability to perform well?); (2) confidence (does a person believe that he or she can perform the job well?); (3) challenge (does a person have to work hard to perform the job well?); (4) criteria (does a person know the difference between good and poor performance?); (5) credibility (does a person believe the manager will deliver on promises?); (6) consistency (do subordinates believe that all employees receive similar preferred outcomes for good performance?); (7) compensation (do the outcomes associated with good performance provide the employee with money and other types of rewards?); (8) cost (what does it cost a person, in effort and outcomes forgone, to perform well?); and (9) communication (does the manager communicate with the subordinate?).

Later, in the 1970s, Morse and Lorsch built on McGregor's and Herzberg's theories with their theory of motivation called *contingency theory*. This theory sought to determine the fit between the organization's characteristics and its tasks and the motivations of individuals. The basic components of the contingency theory are that (1) among people's needs is a central need to achieve a sense of competence, (2) the ways in which people fulfill this need vary from person to person, (3) competent motivation is most likely fulfilled when there is a fit between task and organization; and (4) a sense of competence continues to motivate people even after competence is achieved. In essence, we all want to be competent in our work. Contingency theory contends that people performing highly structured and organized tasks perform better in Theory X organizations and that those who perform unstructured and uncertain tasks perform better under a Theory Y approach. This theory tells managers to tailor jobs to fit people or to give people the skills, knowledge, and attitudes they will need to become competent.[84]

Summary

Most young people entering the labor force would probably like to retain their individuality, feel free to express themselves, have a sense of being an important part of a team, and realize both extrinsic and intrinsic rewards from their work. The reality is, however, that a majority of people entering the job market will work within the structure of an organization that will not meet all of their personal needs.

We have seen that many organizations have a highly refined bureaucracy. Whether an organization meets one's individual needs depends largely on its administrative philosophy. Therefore, our discussions in this chapter covered the structure and function of organizations and, just as important, how administrators and subordinates function within them.

The point to be made above all else is that administrators must know their people. In addition to covering several prominent theories that have withstood the test of time, we pointed out some approaches that have not succeeded. One can learn much from a failed approach or even from a boss who failed to appreciate and understand subordinates and who practiced improper motivational techniques if any.

Questions for Review

1. Define *organization*. What is its function and structure?
2. What are the three historical approaches to management? Distinguish between the historical approach to management and the more "enlightened," contemporary view.
3. How should people be governed in the views of Confucius and Machiavelli?
4. What are some of the skills that strong leaders commonly possess (using the Katz model) and some of the common weaknesses in leadership?
5. What are the major leadership fads from the past decades, beginning with the 1950s?
6. What are three major theories concerning the motivation of employees? Discuss them.
7. What does *communication* mean? What is its importance in organizations? Explain some of the major barriers to effective communication and why they can be particularly problematic in criminal justice agencies.
8. Objectively assess the type of leader you are likely to be (if helpful, use the management grid). Is it an effective style? What are some of the possible advantages and disadvantages of that style (if any)?

Notes

1. Steven Levy, "Working in Dilbert's World," *Newsweek* (August 12, 1996): 52–57.
2. David A. Tansik and James F. Elliott, *Managing Police Organizations* (Monterey, Calif.: Duxbury Press, 1981), p. 1.

3. Stephen P. Robbins, *Organizational Theory: Structure, Design and Applications* (Englewood Cliffs, N.J.: Prentice Hall, 1987).

4. Larry K. Gaines, Mittie D. Southerland, and John E. Angell, *Police Administration* (New York: McGraw-Hill, 1991), p. 5.

5. Peter W. Blau and W. Richard Scott, *Formal Organizations* (Scranton, Pa.: Chandler, 1962), p. 43.

6. Gaines et al., *Police Administration*, p. 9.

7. Max Weber, *The Theory of Social and Economic Organization,* trans. A. M. Henderson and Talcott Parsons (New York: Oxford University Press, 1947), pp. 329–330.

8. James Q. Wilson, *Varieties of Police Behavior* (Cambridge, Mass.: Harvard University Press), pp. 2–3.

9. *Ibid.,* p. 3.

10. Adapted from Lyndall F. Urwick, *Notes on the Theory of Organization* (New York: American Management Association, 1952).

11. Gaines et al., *Police Administration,* p. 9.

12. Leonard R. Sayles and George Strauss, *Human Behavior in Organizations* (Englewood Cliffs, N.J.: Prentice Hall, 1966), p. 349.

13. See, for example, Samuel C. Certo, *Principles of Modern Management: Functions and Systems* (4th ed.) (Boston: Allyn & Bacon, 1989), p. 103.

14. Quoted in Charles R. Swanson, Leonard Territo, and Robert W. Taylor, *Police Administration* (2d ed.) (New York: Macmillan, 1988), p. 127.

15. Quoted in Wayne W. Bennett and Karen Hess, *Management and Supervision in Law Enforcement* (St. Paul, Minn.: West, 1992), p. 61.

16. Paul Hersey and Kenneth H. Blanchard, *Management of Organizational Behavior* (3d ed.) (Englewood Cliffs, N.J.: Prentice Hall, 1977).

17. *Ibid.*

18. Quoted in Bennett and Hess, *Management and Supervision in Law Enforcement,* p. 61.

19. *Ibid.*

20. Roger D. Evered and James C. Selman, "Coaching and the Art of Management," *Organizational Dynamics* (Autumn 1989): 16.

21. Swanson et al., *Police Administration,* p. 61.

22. Bennett and Hess, *Management and Supervision in Law Enforcement,* p. 61.

23. Arthur Waley (trans.), *The Analects of Confucius* (London: George Allen and Unwin, 1938), pp. 88, 173.

24. *Ibid.,* p. 92.

25. *Ibid.,* pp. 105, 127.

26. Robert M. Adams (trans.), *The Prince* (New York: W.W. Norton, 1992), p. xvii.

27. *Ibid.,* p. 7.

28. *Ibid.,* p. 46.

29. *Ibid.,* pp. 15, 41.

30. *Ibid.,* p. 63.

31. *Ibid.,* pp. 5, 11.

32. *Ibid.,* pp. 29, 60.

33. Quoted in Swanson et al., *Police Administration,* p. 161.

34. Bennett and Hess, *Management and Supervision in Law Enforcement,* p. 85. (Emphasis in original.)

35. *Ibid.,* p. 86.

36. Louis A. Radelet, *The Police and the Community: Studies* (Beverly Hills, Calif.: Glencoe Press), p. 92.

37. Charles R. Swanson, Leonard Territo, and Robert W. Taylor, *Police Administration: Structures, Processes, and Behavior* (3d ed.) (New York: Macmillan, 1993), p. 203.

38. Robert L. Montgomery, "Are You a Good Listener?" *Nation's Business* (October 1981): 65–68.

39. Bennett and Hess, *Management and Supervision in Law Enforcement,* p. 101.

40. Swanson et al., *Police Administration* (3d ed.), p. 206.

41. Ronald G. Lynch, *The Police Manager: Professional Leadership Skills* (3d ed.) (New York: Random House, 1986), p. 4.

42. Certo, *Principles of Modern Management and Systems,* p. 35.

43. See Elton Mayo, *The Human Problems of an Industrial Civilization* (New York: Macmillan, 1933).

44. Paul M. Whisenand and Fred Ferguson, *The Managing of Police Organizations* (3d ed.) (Englewood Cliffs, N.J.: Prentice Hall, 1989), pp. 218–219.

45. Lynch, *The Police Manager,* pp. 5–6.

46. Abraham H. Maslow, *Motivation and Personality* (New York: Harper & Row, 1954).

47. Douglas McGregor, *The Human Side of Enterprise* (New York: McGraw-Hill, 1960).

48. Robert R. Blake and Jane S. Mouton, *The Managerial Grid* (Houston: Gulf Publishing Company, 1964).

49. Lynch, *The Police Manager,* pp. 7–8.

50. Richard Holden, *Modern Police Management* (Englewood Cliffs, N.J.: Prentice Hall, 1986), p. 38.

51. Thomas A. Mahoney, Thomas H. Jerdee, and Alan N. Nash, "Predicting Managerial Effectiveness," *Personnel Psychology* (Summer 1960): 147–163.

52. Joe Kelly, *Organizational Behavior: An Existential Systems Approach* (rev. ed.) (Homewood, Ill.: Richard D. Irwin, 1974), p. 363.

53. Bennett and Hess, *Management and Supervision in Law Enforcement,* pp. 65–66.

54. Edwin Fleishman, "Leadership Climate, Human Relations Training and Supervisory Behavior," *Personnel Psychology* 6 (1953): 208–222.

55. Stephen M. Sales, "Supervisory Style and Productivity: Review and Theory," in Larry Cummings and William E. Scott, (eds.), *Readings in Organizational Behavior and Human Performance* (Homewood, Ill.: Richard D. Irwin, 1969), p. 122.

56. Holden, *Modern Police Management,* pp. 39–40.

57. *Ibid.,* pp. 41–42.

58. Fred Fiedler, *A Theory of Leadership Effectiveness* (New York: McGraw-Hill, 1967).

59. Donald F. Favreau and Joseph E. Gillespie, *Modern Police Administration* (Englewood Cliffs, N.J.: Prentice Hall, 1978), p. 80.

60. Bennett and Hess, *Management and Supervision in Law Enforcement,* p. 66.

61. Robert L. Katz, "Skills of an Effective Administrator," *Harvard Business Review* 52 (1975): 23.

62. *Ibid.,* p. 23.

63. Dan L. Costley and Ralph Todd, *Human Relations in Organizations* (St. Paul, Minn.: West, 1978).

64. *Ibid.,* p. 24.

65. James M. Higgins, *Human Relations: Concepts and Skills* (New York: Random House), 1982.

66. *Ibid.,* p. 27.

67. Adapted from Whisenand and Ferguson, *The Managing of Police Organizations,* pp. 4–5.

68. *Ibid.,* p. 6.

69. *Ibid.,* pp. 7–8.

70. Favreau and Gillespie, *Modern Police Administration,* p. 85.

71. W. Richard Plunkett, *Supervision: The Direction of People at Work* (Dubuque, Iowa: Wm. C. Brown, 1983), p. 121.

72. Elton Mayo, *The Social Problems of an Industrial Civilization* (Boston: Division of Research, Graduate School of Business Administration, Harvard University, 1945), pp. 68–86.

73. Favreau and Gillespie, *Modern Police Administration,* pp. 100–101.

74. Frederick J. Roethlisberger and William J. Dickson, *Management and the Worker* (Cambridge, Mass.: Harvard University Press, 1939), p. 522.

75. Favreau and Gillespie, *Modern Police Administration,* p. 87.

76. *Ibid.*

77. *Ibid.,* p. 88.

78. *Ibid.*

79. *Ibid.*

80. Harry W. More and W. Fred Wegener, *Behavioral Police Management* (New York: Macmillan, 1992), pp. 163–164.

81. Frederick Herzberg, "One More Time: How Do You Motivate Employees," in Walter E. Netemeyer (ed.), *Classics of Organizational Behavior* (Oak Park, Ill.: Moore, 1978).

82. Randall S. Schuler, *Personnel and Human Resources Management* (St. Paul, Minn.: West, 1981), pp. 41–43.

83. Walter B. Newsom, "Motivate, Now!" *Personnel Journal* (February 1990): 51–55.

84. Warren Richard Plunkett, *Supervision: The Direction of People at Work,* pp. 131–132.

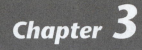

Chapter 3

The Reformers: Evolution of Justice Administration

Man, when perfected, is the best of animals; but if he be isolated from law and justice he is the worst of all. . . .

—Aristotle, *Politics,* Book I, and *Ethics,* Book X

✦ INTRODUCTION

Oliver Wendell Holmes reportedly said that to understand what is, we must understand what has been and what it tends to become. With that philosophy in mind, we highlight the views of several original and distinguished pioneers who were important in the evolution of justice administration. Seeing how these pioneers envisioned the administration of the justice agencies will be instructive. Looking for patterns of thought contained in this overview might also be helpful.

✦ PROFESSIONAL POLICING COMES TO AMERICA

By the 1850s, U.S. police departments had three major responsibilities: maintaining order, preventing and detecting crime, and regulating public morality. Mobs and gangs often controlled the streets of major cities, threatened order, and were connected to numerous crimes.

Several different agencies provided police administration. For example, many cities used an independent board to oversee their police departments. In some cities, city councils made administrative decisions, such as how many police officers would be assigned and who the commander would be.

In 1853 New York City law creating a police board became the national model. The law was an attempt to keep police power limited and divided.[1] By 1873 ten additional cities had followed New York's lead. Corrupt persons found ways to circumvent the boards, however.[2] Eventually, most major cities dropped their independent boards; New York legislation transferred control of the local police to state officials in 1857. In 1901 New York City abolished the state police board and substituted a single police commissioner. Soon other cities followed suit. By 1920 only 14 of 52 cities of more than 100,000 population that at one time had boards had retained them.[3]

Against this backdrop of confusion over how the police were to be administered and organized, several persons began exerting their influence in the early and middle 20th century. This historical foundation was created by Leonhard F. Fuld, August Vollmer, Raymond Fosdick, Bruce Smith, and O. W. Wilson, whose administrative views and accomplishments are discussed here.

✧ LEONHARD F. FULD

In 1909 Leonhard Fuld released *Police Administration,* his critical study of police organizations in the United States.[4] In this book he examined many topics, ranging from the selection of police officers to police organization; he stressed that in all problems of administration, the two factors of efficiency and humanity must be considered.[5]

Fuld criticized the U.S. system of choosing police chiefs and superintendents, noting that in Europe, especially in England and Germany, police administration was an honored and respected career that attracted university graduates and former army officers. Chief executives never came from the rank and file; administration was considered a demanding office that required a broader education and point of view than a patrol officer would have.[6] Fuld wanted police heads to be strong professionals who could command the respect of the community and administer with integrity and impartiality. He was particularly critical of the nonprofessional heads of police departments (such as boards and commissions) and cynically pointed out that to become a chief of police, a person needed political influence, a good physical condition, the ability to pass the civil service examination, seniority, and, in many cities, sufficient money to buy an appointment.[7]

Fuld believed that individual officers should uphold a higher code of conduct and morality than that demanded of other citizens.[8] He pointed out that patrol officers had a need for close supervision because "the authority with which they are invested, and the respect shown them by the citizens, create in them an inordinate desire to shirk their work."[9] Fuld was concerned about the selection and training of police officers, stating emphatically that all political considerations should be eliminated during the selection process.[10] He believed that the ideal police sergeant should be able to write and prepare reports, have a thorough knowledge of police business, be intelligent and capable of being discreet, and have a rudimentary knowledge of criminal law.[11]

Fuld also believed that the most important position within the U.S. police system was that of captain, a position with two broad and important duties: policing and administrative. Police duties included maintaining public peace and protecting life and property; administrative duties included clerical, janitorial, and supervisory functions.[12] Fuld also described the inspector position as a primary one.

✦ AUGUST VOLLMER

August Vollmer's career of more than one-quarter of a century in law enforcement occurred during one of the most important periods in the development of police professionalism. Vollmer became a Berkeley, California, town marshal in 1905. Initially, he commanded a force of only three deputies, but as Berkeley became one of the most progressive and best governed cities in the country,[13] Vollmer quickly expanded the size of his force to form day and night patrols. He soon formed a bicycle patrol (allowing officers to respond to calls three times more quickly than could officers on foot). Then he purchased a $25,000 system of red lights that hung at each street intersection, serving as an emergency notification system for police officers, the first such signal system in the country.[14]

In 1906 Vollmer began questioning the criminals he arrested; he found that nearly all of them used a particular method of operation, or *modus operandi*. He then contacted chiefs of police across the country, requesting information on criminals specializing in specific types of crimes. In 1907 he asked a professor of biology at the University of California to assist in a criminal investigation. This experience convinced Vollmer of the value of scientific knowledge in many cases. By reading several books, he developed a sound knowledge of science.[15]

Vollmer's most daring innovation occurred in 1908, when he created a preservice "police school" that covered a wide variety of subjects for police officers. This initial, formal training program for police officers drew on the expertise of university professors as well as veteran police officers. The school, later expanded to a three-year curriculum, included courses on police methods and procedures, fingerprinting, first aid, criminal law, anthropometry, photography, public health, and sanitation.[16]

Other innovations followed. By 1914 Vollmer had his entire patrol force operating in automobiles; it became the first totally mobile patrol force in the country. In 1916 he persuaded a professor of pharmacology and bacteriology to become a full-time criminalist in charge of the department's criminal investigation laboratory.[17] In 1918, to improve the quality of police recruits in his department, he began to hire college students as part-time officers and to administer intelligence, psychiatric, and neurological tests to all applicants.[18] (From this group of "college cops" came several outstanding police leaders, including O. W. Wilson, discussed later.) In 1921, in addition to experimenting with the lie detector, Vollmer became interested in improving communications among officers on patrol. Each officer soon had a crystal set and earphones in his Model-T touring cars, the first so equipped.

In 1923 Vollmer accepted a one-year appointment as chief of police of Los Angeles, where police corruption, gambling, and the illicit sale of liquor were major problems. He hired ex-offenders to gather intelligence information. He promoted honest officers and required 3,000 line officers to take an intelligence test. Vollmer used the test scores to determine officers to reassign and promote. Already unpopular with crooks and corrupt politicians, he became unpopular within the department as a result of this last action. He returned to Berkeley in 1924, having made many enemies in the LAPD; his attempts at reform had met with too much opposition to have any lasting effect there.[19]

In the late 1920s Vollmer began reorganizing police departments in other cities. Like Fosdick, Vollmer stressed the need for sufficient time and political support for police executives to improve a department; he argued that the single largest drawback to good morale and effectiveness in U.S. policing was the short and uncertain tenure of the chief administrator.[20]

Until his death, Vollmer argued for a liberal education for police officers:

> Obviously, the officer on the beat need not be specially skilled in either the mental, biological or social sciences. But none of these can be overlooked in the training of police officers if they are to have a broad, cultural, scientific, and technical background requisite for the performance of the modern officer's duties.[21]

✦ RAYMOND B. FOSDICK

In 1915 Raymond Fosdick completed a comprehensive study of 72 U.S. cities with populations in excess of 100,000. He shared many of Fuld's views, especially regarding the need for police chiefs to be well educated and politically independent, be given tenure, and be paid good salaries.

Fosdick identified numerous police problems, such as political control of the police, inadequate police leadership, limited tenure of office for chiefs of police, inadequate police techniques, organizational rigidity, and lack of supervision in investigative work.[22] He also found that U.S. police departments had the same basic organization, generally including at least two principal branches: the uniformed force and the detective bureau. Most communities were divided into precincts and were in turn subdivided into beats for patrol purposes.

Fosdick stressed the need for a single police executive; he believed that with more than one police executive, the duties were poorly defined and, consequently, many departments were top heavy with administrators.[23] He found most police departments primitive and crude, having developed without design and with little study given to the relationship between patrol duties and crime conditions.

Fosdick believed that policing essentially had to overcome three major problems. First, many cities had poor police organization, leading to poor relations between supervisors and the patrol force, disharmony between various organization elements, and an inability of the agencies to adapt to their work (their organization having evolved without a plan or design). This, in turn, led to local ordinances and methods of operation that were unsuited to local needs. Second, legislatures had added to policing such extraneous and unrelated jobs as issuing licenses for saloons and other businesses, inspecting steam boilers, supervising the dog pound, providing censorship, and collecting taxes.[24] Finally, he found unskilled, unfit, and unprofessional police executives who had severely harmed their police organizations.[25]

Fosdick believed that in addition to the patrol force, all police departments needed a corps of trained detectives and a crime prevention service. He contended that these three main police functions—patrol, investigation, and crime prevention—were interrelated and that every police force should use these approaches.[26]

✧ BRUCE SMITH

In 1940 Bruce Smith released the first edition of *Police Systems in the United States*.[27] He wrote that administrative problems of police departments had often been neglected or ignored and recommended that the principles of organization commonly found in industry and the military be applied to the structure of police forces.[28]

Smith found that the vast majority of U.S. police agencies continued to function according to patterns set several generations earlier and that the administrative structure had not kept pace with the growth of the departments and the creation of specialized units. This resulted in inadequate controls, and the organizations failed to accomplish the ultimate purpose—unity of action.[29]

Smith often used the term *span of control,* the concept that one supervisor can control only a limited number of subordinates. He pointed out that the actual span of control must be determined for each situation, although no doubt a span of control of five or six is proper in many instances.[30] He identified a broad classification of activities in police organizations: patrol, traffic regulation, criminal investigation, communication and records control, property management, personnel management, crime prevention, and morals regulation.[31]

Smith urged simplicity in the organization of the department by reducing the number of responsible officers whom the administrative head must control for policies to be effective. He was also concerned about overspecialization in policing, although he acknowledged the increase in complexity in some areas of law enforcement and the need for specialization, but he emphasized the importance of maintaining a flexible organization.[32]

✦ O. W. WILSON

In 1950 O. W. Wilson released his seminal work, *Police Administration*.[33] Soon becoming a much used and quoted text, it was comprehensive and included such diverse topics as organization, control, the juvenile offender, public relations, and leadership. Subsequent editions were issued in 1963 and 1977 (the latter editions coauthored with Roy McLaren).

Wilson viewed the primary police objectives as preventing the development of criminal and antisocial tendencies in individuals; repressing criminal activities; arresting criminals, recovering stolen property, and preparing cases for presentation in court; regulating people and their noncriminal activities; and performing a variety of nonregulatory services.[34]

Wilson suggested that the following principles of police organization be considered:

1. Grouping tasks similar or related in purpose, process, or method in one or more units under the control of a single person.
2. Clearly drawing lines of demarcation among the units so that responsibility may be placed exactly.
3. Establishing channels through which information flows up and down and through which authority is delegated.
4. Placing each individual, unit, and situation under the immediate control of one, and only one, person to avoid friction resulting from duplication of direction and supervision.
5. Placing no more units or persons under the direct control of one person than he or she is able to manage.
6. Making each task the unmistakable duty of someone; definitely placing the responsibility for planning, execution, and control on designated persons.
7. Providing supervision for each person at the level of execution regardless of the hour or place.
8. Having each assignment of responsibility carry with it commensurate authority to fulfill the responsibility.
9. Holding accountable for the use of authority persons to whom it is delegated.[35]

✦ DEVELOPMENT OF COURT ADMINISTRATION

As with police administration, there were several prominent individuals who influenced the evolution of court administration, which developed several decades later than police administration and perhaps even centuries after corrections administration.

Although not even beginning to bloom until at least 1940, many people trace the development of court administration to a historic speech in August 1906 by Roscoe Pound, a brash, young law professor from the plains of Nebraska. Pound lashed out at his profession in a speech entitled "The Causes of Popular Dissatisfaction with the Administration of Justice," at the annual meeting of the American Bar Association in St. Paul, Minnesota. This speech, later labeled "the spark that kindled the white flame of progress,"[36] has been reprinted many times since and is now considered a classic on the subject of court reform.

Pound maintained that dissatisfaction with the administration of justice is as old as law, and that there were four basic causes of this dissatisfaction: the dissatisfaction that comes with *any* legal system (including the necessarily mechanical operation of legal rules and the inevitable difference in rate of progress between law and public opinion); causes lying in the peculiarities of the Anglo-American legal system (the "sporting theory of justice" and the absence of any philosophy of law); causes lying in American judicial organization and procedure (uncertainty, delay, and expense); and causes lying in the environment of our judicial administration (popular lack of interest in justice, the strain of law to do the work of morals, also, and public ignorance of the workings of the courts).

Little more would be done to move the courts toward an organized form of administration until 1940. Thus, court administration is actually relatively young, at least in comparison with its cousins, the police and corrections components.

✧ ARTHUR T. VANDERBILT

Arthur T. Vanderbilt, born in 1888 in Newark, New Jersey, attended Wesleyan University in Middletown, Connecticut. He earned his law degree from Columbia University and was admitted to the New Jersey State Bar. He later was dean at the New York University School of Law and chief justice of the New Jersey Supreme Court. A university law center, completed in 1951, is named in his honor. He established the Institute of Judicial Administration at New York University School of Law in 1952 and served as its president from 1952 until his death in 1957.[37] This institute became known nationally and internationally for its services to the improvement of the administration of justice.[38]

During his nearly half-century-long law career, Vanderbilt wrote effusively on the subject of judicial administration. He believed that court administrative reform—as initiated by Pound three decades earlier—was proceeding with the "imperceptible speed of a glacier."[39] He was also put off by the apathy of the legal profession and the roadblocks created by politicians. In 1947, with his guidance, New Jersey adopted a new constitutional article that became the basis for a highly modern state court system.

Vanderbilt's most important writing on court reform was *Minimum Standards of Judicial Administration*[40] in 1949, which has been called an "arsenal of information";[41] it provided the ammunition for the second powerful push for court reform (following that of Pound). Many phrases used in his introductory book have become part of the vocabulary of court administration. Vanderbilt was greatly concerned with the problem of delay and congestion in the courts, as well as the cost of litigation, writing that these problems were "the most reprehensible phase of the disease" that had been allowed to become chronic, "while our judges and lawyers, who are professionally responsible for its cure, and our governors and legislators, a majority of whom are lawyers, sit idly by as if the disease were incurable."[42]

Vanderbilt also chided lawyers for their indifference to the problems of court administration, writing that

> it is a case of the shoemaker neglecting his barefoot children; lawyers are so pre-occupied with the substantive problems of their clients that they have little time to devote to the great problems of ways and means in the law that we call judicial administration.[43]

Vanderbilt believed that the courts administration should use sound business principles; he bemoaned the "almost complete lack of administrative efficiency in most judicial systems" in which courts "have become notorious for their reluctance to accept and put into practice even the most basic and simple principles of business administration."[44] He was quick to quote Chief Justice Taft, who said in 1921 that "each judge paddled his own canoe" under a "go-as-you-please system."[45]

Vanderbilt's work was assisted in 1939, when Congress passed the Administrative Office Act, described by Judge John J. Parker as "the most important piece of legislation affecting the judiciary since the Judiciary Act of 1789."[46] This view was not shared by all, however; one federal judge complained,

> A word of warning is appropriate. It is inevitable that a director will come to feel that he has to direct something. As long as he confines his direction to the staff under him, he is performing his duty, but when he interferes with the work of the judges, he should be promptly and emphatically rebuffed.[47]

Nonetheless, this act soon had a profound effect on the administration of the federal courts. The Administrative Office of the United States Courts established an enviable reputation for efficient service, demonstrating to judges that the courts benefit from modern management methods.

Most states were reluctant to follow the federal example. New Jersey took the lead, with a new state constitution passed in 1947 that designated the chief justice as "the administrative head of all of the courts in the state" and provided that the chief justice could appoint an administrative director of the courts to serve at his pleasure.[48] In the same year, at the urging of the Judicial Administration Section of the ABA, the National Commissioners on Uniform State Laws approved and published a model act to create an administrator for state courts.[49]

The examples set forth in the federal courts and in New Jersey and the support by the ABA, coupled with the growing national concern with rapidly growing volume and cost of litigation and the delays and congestion experienced in the courts, provided the impetus for continued expansion of court administration. In 1951 North Carolina created the position of administrative assistant to the chief justice,[50] followed by the creation of an office of court administrator in Puerto Rico,[51] an administrative clerk to the presiding judge of the Superior Court in Rhode Island,[52] and an executive secretary of the Supreme Court in Virginia.[53] In 1953 Michigan established an office of court administration,[54] Oregon provided for an administrative assistant to the chief justice,[55] and Connecticut expanded the duties of its existing executive secretary to the judicial department.[56]

In 1954 Colorado created the position of deputy clerk of the Supreme Court to assist with administrative matters,[57] Kentucky provided for an administrative director of the courts,[58] Louisiana created the post of judicial administrator,[59] and an administrative assistant was furnished to the presiding judge of the federal district court for the District of Columbia.[60] In 1955 Iowa created the office of statistician of the judicial department.[61] New York established a state administrator and four deputy administrators (one for each department of the Appellate Division of the Supreme Court).[62] Maryland created an administrative office of the courts,[63] and Ohio added the office of administrative assistant to the Supreme Court.[64] Massachusetts followed suit in 1956 with its executive secretary of the Supreme Judicial Court.[65]

In 1957, Vanderbilt wrote with a considerable measure of pride:

> Thus today, twenty years after the creation of the Administrative Office of the United States Courts and ten years after the establishment of the first state Administrative Office of the Courts in New Jersey, a total of fifteen states have given their courts some form of administrative assistance to help the courts manage their own business better. No longer is an administrative organization within the judicial establishment both rare and suspect . . . looked upon as novel experiments.[66]

In the early 1960s probably 30 people in the United States really worked as court administrators; by 1970 there were some 60 to 70. By the 1980s, between 2,000 and 3,000 people had court administrator positions in the United States, in addition to a proliferation of people interested in the courts' activities in budgeting, planning, space management, information systems design, personnel management, public relations, and so on. Some would argue that the pendulum has swung too far, given this influx of administrators into the court system; others argue that the massive caseloads and judicial duties warrant even more such positions. The discussion of three persons who continued Vanderbilt's interest in court reform and management allows us to trace the evolution of court administration further.

✧ A. Leo Levin

Another innovator and reformer was A. Leo Levin, born in New York City in 1919. After receiving his law degree from the University of Pennsylvania, he was admitted to the New York bar and became a law professor at the University of Pennsylvania. He served as director of the National Institute of Trial Advocacy, executive director for the Commission on Revision of the Federal Court Appellate System, and director of the Federal Judicial Center (FJC). A key organizer of the 1976 conference on popular dissatisfaction with the administration of justice, known as the *Pound Conference,* Levin kept Roscoe Pound's name in the limelight, thus keeping the fires of court reform burning.

Justice Holmes once said that "the business of a law school is . . . to teach law in the grand manner, and to make great lawyers."[67] According to Chief Justice William H. Rehnquist, Levin saw the FJC as "a place that pursued its educational and research programs 'in the grand manner' " and where he could pursue his commitment to a judiciary composed of "great judges."[68] Indeed, Levin's greatest contribution to court administration was his support for research in the field. Like Vanderbilt's, Levin's career spanned almost 50 years. He wrote many articles and books on the administration of justice, and he "commanded national recognition and respect as an outstanding teacher, scholar, and administrator."[69] He developed a judicial administration course for the University of Pennsylvania Law School. Upon leaving the law school in 1977 to become the director of the FJC, Levin began traveling to the various U.S. district and circuit courts, teaching judges how to judge, doing important research in a continuing effort to strengthen the federal court system, and constantly introducing new techniques for the courts to use. In 1987 he returned to the University of Pennsylvania Law School as chairman of the task force created by the chief justice of Pennsylvania to make recommendations to the court for improvement of the judicial system.

As director of the FJC, Levin hired a committed cadre of researchers, educators, automation specialists, and support staff. Levin observed in his writings that neither law teachers nor attorneys "have rushed to embrace" the field of court administration; in 1979 he lamented the fact that the Directory of Law Teachers listed only three active professors who were then teaching court administration.[70] Two factors, he believed, contributed to the profession's seeming lack of concern with court administration:

> A rather narrow conception of the field and . . . a failure to appreciate the intellectual challenge, the value judgments, and the ultimate significance to litigants and to society inherent in resolving issues of "mere administration."[71]

Levin defined court administration policies as those "designed to enable courts to dispose—justly, expeditiously, and economically—of the disputes brought to them for resolution."[72] He asserted that court administration policies should guide the mechanics of budget administration; determine the number of personnel needed in a particular court; and define the scope of the rule-making power, the use of staff attorneys to process appeals, the structure of a judicial system, and the processes of ensuring stability in the law of a court system. Levin believed strongly that the "crisis of volume" of case filings is not solved by "the simple expedient of adding resources; resources are too hard to come by."[73] Nor is the problem soluble, Levin argued, by adding more judges—that "in itself creates a new generation of problems."[74]

✧ Edward B. McConnell

Ironically, the person among those who greatly influenced the development of court administration and who is probably its foremost "futurist" once described himself as just the opposite:

> I'm not a futurist and don't feel comfortable trying to "peer over the rim" or to conjure up imaginary visions and scenarios of what might be. I do believe, however, that it is essential for judges, as the primary managers of the court, to plan how to deal effectively with the known.[75]

Edward B. McConnell received his law degree from the University of Nebraska and a master's in business administration with distinction from Harvard. He later taught at the Rutgers University School of Business Administration and became administrative assistant and law secretary to the chief justice of New Jersey (under Arthur T. Vanderbilt), president of the National Center for State Courts, and chairman of the National Conference of Court Administrative Officers.[76]

In a major article, "The Golden Future," McConnell observed in 1984 that many of the problems confronting the courts for the past 25 years—especially that of delay—were still plaguing them. He predicted that state court systems would delegate maximum authority and responsibility to judges and court administrators and that judges and court support personnel would become increasingly professional.

McConnell also echoed Vanderbilt's view that business management techniques should be applied to the courts. He stated that something must be done to stem the flow of litigation and that courts must become tougher in dealing with frivolous lawsuits. He also supported televising court trials to "take away the blindfold" that keeps the average person from understanding court operations.

McConnell saw the relationship of judges and court managers as a close, but not mutually exclusive, one. "The concept that judges should stick to judging and managers to managing is counterproductive," he wrote. "It fails to recognize the independent nature of court management."[77] He viewed the relationship as a team approach but conceded that forging an effective working relationship between judges and court managers—one that does not threaten judges—is one of the major challenges facing the courts: "Judges have the organizational power but lack the operational knowledge, and the court managers have the knowledge but lack the power. The team approach merges these strengths."[78]

McConnell also believed that to be successful as court managers, judges must take the lead in planning; maintain good relations between the courts and the legislative and executive branches of government; better educate the public about the structure, role, and operation of the courts; monitor their own performance and conduct and that of their staff; and improve the quality of service to the public (by reducing the cost and delays, holding court at convenient times and places, and having personnel of the courts reflect the gender and racial composition of their community).[79]

✧ ERNEST C. FRIESEN JR.

Ernest C. Friesen Jr. received his law degree from Columbia University and was then admitted to the New York bar. After stints in private practice and as a trial attorney for the Department of Justice, he taught law at the University of Cincinnati. He then served as an administrator for the ABA, dean of the National Judicial College (Reno), assistant attorney general for the U.S. Department of Justice, director of the Administrative Office of United States Courts, director of the Institute for Court Management, and professor or dean of the law schools at the University of Denver, Whittier College, and California Western.[80]

Friesen possibly provided his greatest contributions to the field by assuming a "devil's advocate" role with court administration. Like those before him, Friesen focused on court delays, writing that neither Vanderbilt's application of Pound's court organization doctrines nor subsequent writings on the subject—although containing thoughtful analyses for court reform—had little practical effect on reducing court delay.

Friesen argued that opponents of the "controlled court management approach" to reduce delays usually argue from one of three premises: first, the problem is one of inadequate resources; second, control is a bad cure; and, third, delay is not bad. He noted that one research project traced delay to the *addition* of law clerks to the staff of trial judges; the clerks took more time to do tasks than the judges did.

✦ DEVELOPMENT OF CORRECTIONS ADMINISTRATION

The philosophy of corrections administration has undergone several changes, from the "slave of the state" view to an individualized treatment-oriented model, to the current punitive ("just desserts") philosophy. Those views and changes in administrative philosophy did not occur by chance; they were espoused by people who either had a personal vision of societal or inmate needs or were compelled by their observations to take a stand on such issues. The following discussion focuses on five such persons: John Howard, Elam Lynds, Mary Belle Harris, Zebulon Brockway, and George Beto.

Some of these five individuals could be deemed harsh, even cruel; others were decidedly compassionate, even friendly with their charges. Surely their disparate methods were not always successful, according to the usual standards of inmate behavior and recidivism. All, however, believed fervently in what they were doing and made a difference in the evolution of corrections administration. In reading of their careers, one might compare and contrast the means they used to accomplish their ends.

✦ JOHN HOWARD

Born in England in 1726, John Howard, a deeply religious person, inherited at age 16 a considerable fortune. He believed strongly in the obligation of people to care for one another; some writers have called him a fanatic.[81] Captured on a ship during hostilities between England and France, he spent several years as a prisoner of war—his first encounter with prisons. In 1773 he was appointed sheriff of Bedford, his primary duty being to visit the three local jails in town. He was shocked by conditions there: inmates had to buy all amenities except a minimum amount of food, brutal jailers sold liquor, and men and women participated in orgies in their cells. Furthermore, prisoners were sometimes chained to walls, and disease was rampant.

Howard tried to convince the courts to force the county to pay for jail improvements; the judges were sympathetic but ordered him to find a precedent in other counties. Thus began a career of sojourns to many penal institutions in England and a number of other European countries; he eventually became a renowned expert on existing conditions. In Gloucester he saw underground prisons and inmates who were half naked and almost dead of starvation; in Plymouth he found several men detained in excruciatingly small cells. After presenting his findings to the English House of Commons, he visited Europe, finding prisons in Paris (except the Bastille) and elsewhere reasonably satisfactory. He then went to Holland and Germany, finding in Mannheim that newly arrived prisoners were fastened by the neck, hands, and feet to a flogging machine and given "the great welcome"—20 to 30 lashes.[82]

On returning to England, Howard wrote and published *The State of the Prisons in England and Wales, with Preliminary Observations, and an Account of Some Foreign Prisons*. He recommended baths, adequate diet, and personal hygiene for prisoners; fire precautions in cells; segregation of women and young offenders from men, abandonment of solitary confinement and the advantages of "trustee" guards, honest and well-paid jailers, and prison infirmaries and doctors. Making a third trip to France in 1778, he still found prisoners treated cruelly, but interest in reforming the prison system was developing. He saw model prisons in Holland and Rome, and in 1784 set off on a tour that included Denmark, Sweden, and Russia. (It should be noted that these were all perilous trips; attacks by pirates were not uncommon, and, indeed, he experienced such attack in 1786 on a voyage to Venice.) Howard constantly wrote of his observations and ideas for model prisons, and by the late 1780s, much was being written about him. In 1790, in the course of making hospital visits to ascertain their conditions following the plague, Howard caught Asiatic fever in Russia and died. His gravestone at Kherson, Russia, bore the following inscription: "Whoever thou art, thou standeth at the tomb of thy friend." Perhaps this sums up his life and philosophy; one author stated that "no man did more to improve the treatment of prisoners than John Howard. He opened the eyes of his contemporaries to elementary human obligations."[83]

✧ ELAM LYNDS

In 1821 Elam Lynds was appointed warden of the Auburn prison system in New York. Lynds believed that the old congregate and solitary confinement systems, attempted earlier at the Walnut Street Jail in Philadelphia and included in a preliminary design at Auburn, had failed. Lynds believed that there was little hope of transforming older criminals into religious and law-abiding citizens and that younger inmates could learn to work in prison and become good craftsmen. He put prisoners to work in small, strictly supervised units in which complete silence was observed; a breach of this rule was punished by flogging (which Lynds believed was the most effective and humane method because it did not affect the offender's physical strength). Inmates were required to keep their eyes cast downward when walking. The "lock step" (walking in single file, with each inmate's hand on the shoulder of the inmate in front of him) was used to move inmates in groups.[84] This "silent" system required inmates to spend their nights in solitary cells with no book other than the Bible. No whisper was permitted while they reflected in silence on their errors.

Lynds also believed that prison wardens must be despised in order to rule with a firm hand.[85] Hearing that an inmate had sworn to murder him, Lynds summoned the offender to his bedroom and ordered him to dress and shave him. The prisoner dared not carry out his threat. Upon dismissing him, Lynds contemptuously said, "I knew you wanted to kill me. But you are too much of a coward . . . alone and unarmed, I am stronger than all of you together."[86]

Meanwhile, the population of New York and its criminal element was growing rapidly. A new prison was needed, and Lynds agreed to have Auburn inmates build one. In 1825 he put about 100 prisoners to work in strict silence, driving them to cut stone from the cliffs and build the first block of cells. A German observer reported that "within three years, these human beasts of burden had built cells for over five hundred prisoners and a chapel for nine hundred."[87]

The result of this toil was Sing Sing (an Indian phrase meaning "stone on stone"), an ugly penal institution built on Mount Pleasant. The same inside cell plan was used as in the Auburn model with high outside walls and dormlike cell blocks inside. Inmates and guards moved about like ghosts, the latter wearing moccasins to muffle the sound of their footsteps. Two French authors wrote that Lynds's successor, Robert Wilste, believed also that "the best prison is the one prisoners consider the worst."[88]

✧ ZEBULON REED BROCKWAY

National discussions on penal problems were very lively during the late nineteenth century, with debate centering on the use of the separate system (prolonged solitary confinement), on the one hand, and the silent system (with inmates congregating) on the other. A new era in penal reform was ushered in by the first National Prison Congress, held in 1870 in Cincinnati, at which the "Declaration of Principles" called for reform based on the progressive Irish system. The "Declaration" was based on a paper written by Zebulon Reed Brockway, who had been employed in prisons as a young man and worked his way up to warden in Detroit. His speech at the congress catapulted him to the leadership of correctional administration.

Brockway believed that the central aim of the prison system was to protect society against crime, not to punish criminals. He believed that sentences should not be determinate but indeterminate (Elmira, New York, became the "cradle" for this concept) and that the true basis for classification of prisoners was character, not conduct. These views signaled the beginning of the reformatory movement in the United States.[89]

The crime rate and population were rising in New York and more prisons were needed. A "reformatory" modeled after Sing Sing was constructed near Elmira, and in 1876 Brockway was hired as its warden. His first act was to build a solid wall around the entire facility. He then planned treatment programs; all inmates coming to Elmira were to be young (16 to 30 years of age) and first-time offenders, but this plan was never fully realized. He regarded vocational training as essential for inmates, along with military drill, occupational therapy, good nutrition, and active moral and religious influences. The institution, he believed, should work "with nature and not against it."[90] He put prisoners to work at 34 major trades and began a prison newspaper, *The Summary*; by 1891 the prison library contained nearly 4,000 volumes. Perhaps his most important innovation was the inmate wage system that compensated prisoners for their work but required them to pay for everything they received except for their first meal and the clothing issued on their arrival at Elmira.[91]

Brockway believed in having personal contact with prisoners. It has been estimated that by interviewing new arrivals and dealing with inmates in the evening, Brockway spoke to between 40 and 50 convicts per day,[92] serving at different times as "friend, minister, and prisonmaster."[93]

After 20 years at Elmira dealing with inmates on an individual basis, Brockway sensed that his life's work had been destroyed by many of his successors who had a more punitive view of treatment and believed in increased use of probation. He wrote in his autobiography that the result would inevitably be prisons that were less correctional institutions and more scientific training centers for degenerate adults.[94]

✦ MARY BELLE HARRIS

One of the foremost proponents of the rehabilitative approach to inmates was Mary Belle Harris, born in 1874 in Pennsylvania. She attended religious schools, earned a doctorate from the University of Chicago in 1900, and then taught school in Kentucky and Chicago, as well as working at the famous Hull House. She soon became known for her high standards and creativity, later to become hallmarks of her administrative career.

Harris's entry into correctional administration was clearly unintended. A New York City commissioner of corrections who had befriended Harris in Chicago took her on a tour of the workhouse for women on Blackwell Island and later offered her a position as its superintendent. Harris, then age 39, accepted, but only temporarily, until "the right person" could be found for the job.[95]

Harris served in this capacity from July 1914 to January 1918. She later confessed that she was in a daze as the ferry took her to the workhouse, considered to be among the worst of the 12 New York institutions. In her 1942 book *I Knew Them in Prison*, she wrote that "it was a depressingly grim place, and I shall never forget the feeling of utter desolation I had when . . . I left . . . there that evening to work out my own salvation, if I could."[96] Harris found the conditions "so unspeakable that abandonment and utter demolition seemed the evident course to recommend."[97] Chaos, in the form of fights, assaults, insubordination, and enforced idleness prevailed.

There she soon revealed her rehabilitative philosophy, which differed with conventional punitive approaches of the day: crime is influenced by social factors, individualized treatment is an appropriate social response for most deviant behavior, and special emphasis should be placed on the person rather than the offense.[98] Over staff protests, Harris emphasized open lines of communication, provided regular table decorations, created outside exercise yards, and scheduled fresh air walks and flower gardening for every woman. She established a separate ward for drug addicts to enhance individualized treatment and introduced Wassermann tests to help free the workhouse of venereal disease. She permitted inmates to play cards and appointed an inmate librarian. For the first time, the women used knives and forks and were served meat on plates instead of in bowls. She advocated inmate classification, individualization, and selective segregation and believed that only a small percentage of all inmates required maximum security.[99]

Because of a change in political administration, Harris's tenure at the workhouse ended in 1918. Having grown accustomed to battling for correctional reform, she sought another tough assignment as superintendent of the state reformatory in Clinton, New Jersey. She served there from February 1918 to April 1919.

She began traveling to other correctional institutions and soon observed considerable disparity between the facilities and programs established for men and women inmates. She began criticizing her female peers as often being too willing to "make things do" and too accepting of leftovers. She enhanced many programs at Clinton, encouraged self-government in the cottages, and discontinued the stigmatizing practice of dressing runaways in red dresses and cutting their hair in "a disfiguring fashion."[100]

After a short stint as assistant director of the War Department's reformatory for women, Harris returned to New Jersey. From May 1919 to January 1925 she was superintendent of the State Home for Girls in Trenton, where she recruited several college students as aides in physical education, music, and domestic science. Because inmate escape attempts were common, she reluctantly authorized spankings as punishment. Later she described this time as the lowest point in her career: "Although I should never wish to be quoted as condoning corporal punishment . . . I profited from this experience. It made me humble and less critical of others who are caught in a situation of a similar nature."[101]

Among other innovations that Harris introduced at Trenton were a "credit card" system whereby at the end of each day, a girl received her "pay" or "credit loss" on the basis of behavior; annual "graduation" ceremonies, with parents and guest speakers, to honor each "class" of departing inmates; a highly successful movie of the Home, which became a public relations bonus; tests for diphtheria and scarlet fever; and special events, such as Harvest Home, when the girls "ran" the institution and had an open house for family, friends, and the press.[102]

From March 1925 to March 1941, Harris served as the first superintendent of the Federal Industrial Institution for Women, Alderson, West Virginia. There she insisted on housing the inmates in cottages rather than cells, discontinued the use of heavily armed guards, enhanced the inmate classification system, offered educational and vocational classes, implemented self-government and religious services, and provided a variety of entertainment, such as clubs, hobbies, special celebrations, contests, and dances. Some believed that Alderson was a model institution; others described it as a fashionable girls' boarding school.[103]

Sanford Bates, the first director of the Federal Bureau of Prisons, summed up Harris's career by saying, "She belonged to that school which believed that there is basic goodness in everyone and if that can be reached and touched, then change will occur."[104]

✧ GEORGE BETO

Known as "Walking George,"[105] Dr. George Beto, a tall, lean, Lutheran minister and college president turned prison director, seemed to personify the essence of the control model of prison administration. Beto, who was himself a party in major inmate litigation,[106] was director of the Texas Department of Corrections (TDC) from 1962 to 1972. Upon his hiring, he promised to leave after 10 years, believing that after a decade, "you lose your courage. You come to know your subordinates too well. You learn too much about the legislature. Fresh ideas and energy fade with time."[107]

Beto's Texas control model involved the strict enforcement of discipline and a daily routine; inmates had virtually no input. It has been suggested that to fully comprehend the philosophical lifeblood of Beto's model, one should read Joseph Ragen's *Inside the World's Toughest Prison* (1962) and Martin Luther's *Secular Authority: To What Extent It Should Be Obeyed,* written in the first half of the 16th century.[108] Luther was not a prison warden, of course, but the German Reformation leader's ideas, set forth in his 95 theses, launched a theological and political revolution throughout Europe. Beto's mentor, Ragen, firmly believed in the need to run a tight ship; Beto also believed that inmates had no right to challenge prison authority, following Martin Luther's writing that "if wrong is to be suffered, it is better to suffer it from rulers than that the rulers suffer it from their subjects."[109] Under Beto at TDC, all inmates wore regulation white uniforms and had short-cropped hair. All who were illiterate attended school at least one day a week. All worked in the fields the first six months and addressed the officers as "boss" or "sir." All privileges had to be earned and could be taken away without a hearing.

Beto believed there existed a moral necessity for seeking and wielding worldly power to protect and guide those who could not follow society's rules, to discipline those who behaved badly, to educate them, and to instill in them a respect for duly constituted authority. His style was unique; one officer recalled that "he could freeze a man—convict or boss—with a stare . . . like he was looking into your heart, finding evil, and putting you back to honesty."[110] Another said, "He was as tough as nails, but he had a big ol' bleeding heart."[111] Under Beto's leadership, prison industries produced everything from food to inmate clothing, and he forged legislation allowing the TDC to sell its industrial goods. He created a work-release program as well. As he walked the institution, any inmate could approach him with a problem or a letter containing information; Beto considered the latter "a source of useful intelligence and a barometer of conditions."[112]

Upon retirement from the prison in 1972 to enter academia, Beto hand picked W. J. Estelle as his successor. In 1983 Beto correctly predicted the demise of the Texas control model. Prison administration rapidly changed, and in 1985 prisons in Texas experienced murder of one inmate by another, gang rapes of young or new inmates, shakedowns of cells turning up hundreds of weapons and contraband, the inability or unwillingness of most staff members to prevent violence, and idle inmate classrooms and workplaces. Three factors helped bring about the Texas control model's death: (1) the cessation of the building tender system (using trustee guards to help control inmates); (2) a class action lawsuit, *Ruiz v. Estelle,*[113] (in which U.S. District Court Judge William W. Justice found that the TDC had violated the rights of inmates in the areas of overcrowding, security, fire codes, medical care, discipline, and access to the court); and (3) changes in personnel and managerial philosophy following *Ruiz*. The Beto era and the Texas control model—for good or bad, depending on one's view of prison conditions—had passed.

✧ OTHER INFLUENTIAL INDIVIDUALS

The methods used by a number of other late 20th century prison wardens have received acclaim. These men include W. J. Estelle and Raymond Procunier, both of the Texas Department of Corrections; Joseph Ragen, of Stateville Penitentiary in Illinois; and Paul Keve from Minnesota. Many prison wardens of this period will live on and be remembered in criminal justice textbooks through the court cases filed against them by inmate litigants. These cases include *Ruiz v. Estelle*,[114] discussed earlier, which took 13 years and $1 billion to resolve and *Estelle v. Gamble*.[115] Inmate Gamble argued that prison administration showed "deliberate indifference" to his medical problems, which constituted cruel and unusual punishment. *Procunier v. Martinez*[116] challenged mail censorship by the California Department of Corrections, and in *Gideon v. Wainwright*,[117] Clarence Gideon, who had been convicted and sentenced for commission of a felony without counsel present, sued Louis Wainwright, director of the Florida Department of Corrections.

✦ DEVELOPMENT OF PROBATION AND PAROLE

Although contemporary probation dates to biblical times, its history in the United States began in the 19th century. "Judicial reprieve" was used in English courts as the temporary suspension of a sentence to allow the defendant to appeal to the Crown for a pardon. In the United States, the suspended sentence was used as early as 1830 in Boston and became widespread in U.S. courts, even though there was no statutory provision for it. By the mid-19th century, however, many courts were using a judicial reprieve to suspend sentences.[118] This posed a legal question: Could judges suspend sentences wholesale after trials that were scrupulously fair simply to give the defendant a second chance?[119]

In 1916 the U.S. Supreme Court, in a decision affecting only the federal courts, held that judges did not have the discretionary authority to suspend sentences. The Court ruled, however, that Congress could authorize the temporary or indefinite suspension of sentences; this led to the development of probation statutes.[120]

✧ JOHN AUGUSTUS

The term *probation* was utilized by John Augustus (1785–1859), a Boston shoemaker who began in the mid-1800s taking people, most of whom were charged with being drunkards, to his home from court. He later wrote that

I was in court one morning . . . in which the man was charged with being a common drunkard. He told me that if he could be saved from the House of Correction, he never again would taste intoxicating liquors; I bailed him, by permission of the court.[121]

During his first year of service as an unpaid, volunteer probation officer, Augustus assisted 10 drunkards; eventually he helped other types of offenders, and of 2,000 cases he handled over an 18-year period, only 10 persons jumped bail or probation.[122] Augustus's work was not viewed favorably, however, by prosecutors (who believed that he clogged court calendars) or by the police and court clerks (who received a fee for each case resulting in a commitment to the infamous House of Correction).[123]

Augustus performed several tasks used in modern probation. He investigated each case—inquiring into the person's character, age, and influences—and kept careful records of each person's progress. His probation work soon caused him to fall into financial difficulties, requiring his friends' monetary assistance.

✦ ALEXANDER MACONOCHIE AND THE PAROLE SYSTEM

The word *parole* stems from the French *parol,* or "word of honor"; it referred to a means of releasing prisoners of war who promised not to resume arms in a current conflict.[124] One writer described 1840 as the year in which "one of the most remarkable experiments in the history of penology was initiated."[125] In that year, Alexander Maconochie (1787–1860) became superintendent of the British penal colony on Norfolk Island, about 930 miles northeast of Sidney, Australia. He implemented his philosophy of punishment to reform offenders: the convict was to be punished for the past while being trained for the future. Maconochie advocated open-ended *(indeterminate)* sentences. His system worked, although it was harshly ridiculed by some Australians as coddling criminals.

Returning to England in 1844, Maconochie began writing and speaking of his experiment. One of those he impressed was Walter Crofton, who in 1854 became director of the renowned Irish System of penal management. Crofton implemented, among many other things, a "ticket of leave" system, allowing inmates to be conditionally released from prison, under police supervision. Crofton recommended a similar system for the United States.

Probably influenced by Maconochie's work in Australia, Zebulon Brockway drafted a statute providing for indeterminate sentences in 1876 when he was appointed superintendent of the Elmira Reformatory in New York. Continued good behavior by inmates resulted in early release—the first parole system in the United States. Paroled inmates remained under the jurisdiction of reformatory authorities for an additional six months, during which the parolee was required to report on the first day of every month to the appointed guardian and provide an account of his or her conduct and situation. This system was copied by other states; it was further expanded during the Great Depression, when the economic exploitation of convict labor was abolished.[126]

Summary

This overview of a number of people who profoundly influenced the development of justice administration demonstrated that change and creativity are possible in criminal justice. It is easy for administrators to become so enmeshed with day-to-day problems that they forget to consider other, more progressive or beneficial ways to accomplish tasks.

Each person discussed in this chapter believed that he or she had something to offer that was better than the existing system. In hindsight, some of their methods were not better but were attempts to improve the situation. Some pioneers, such as Vollmer, Vanderbilt, and Harris, worked from a "clean slate" and thus had the luxury of experimenting with completely new methods.

Questions for Review

1. What significant contributions to police administration were made by 19th century police pioneers? What patterns of agreement exist among the views of these early contributors? Which contributors, if any, appear to have had the largest influence on modern police administration?

2. Clearly, Arthur T. Vanderbilt was a tremendous force on early court administration. What were some of his major contributions? What did each of his followers contribute?

3. The philosophies and approaches to administration of each of the prison reformers discussed differed in some way; some were even quite harsh in their view of offenders. What were each person's contributions, focusing on their influence on current practice? Briefly discuss each person.

4. How did probation and parole evolve? Who were the major actors in their development?

Notes

1. James F. Richardson, *Urban Police in the United States* (Port Washington, N.Y.: Kennikat Press, 1974), pp. 35–37.
2. *Ibid.,* pp. 37–38.
3. Raymond Fosdick, *American Police Systems* (New York: Century Books, 1920), pp. 108–109.
4. Leonhard F. Fuld, *Police Administration* (New York: G. P. Putnam, 1909).
5. *Ibid.,* p. 304.
6. Richardson, *Urban Police in the United States,* p. 70.
7. Fuld, *Police Administration,* p. 41.

8. *Ibid.,* p. 112.

9. *Ibid.,* p. 49.

10. *Ibid.,* p. 153.

11. *Ibid.,* p. 56.

12. *Ibid.,* pp. 59–60.

13. Alfred E. Parker, *Crime Fighter: August Vollmer* (New York: Macmillan, 1961).

14. Nathan Douthit, "August Vollmer," in Carl B. Klockars (ed.), *Thinking about Police: Contemporary Readings* (New York: McGraw-Hill, 1983), p. 102.

15. *Ibid.*

16. *Ibid.*

17. *Ibid.*

18. *Ibid.,* p. 103.

19. Paul Jacobs, *Prelude to Riot: A View of Urban America from the Bottom* (New York: Random House, 1966), pp. 13–60.

20. Richardson, *Urban Police in the United States,* p. 83.

21. Douthit, "August Vollmer," p. 108.

22. Raymond B. Fosdick, *American Police Systems* (Montclair, N.J.: Patterson Smith, 1969), pp. 382–383.

23. *Ibid.,* pp. 189–190.

24. *Ibid.,* p. 213.

25. *Ibid.,* p. 215.

26. *Ibid.,* pp. 268–270.

27. Bruce Smith, *Police Systems in the United States* (New York: Harper and Brothers, 1960).

28. *Ibid.,* p. 208.

29. *Ibid.,* p. 209.

30. *Ibid.,* p. 218.

31. *Ibid.,* pp. 219–220.

32. *Ibid.,* p. 241.

33. O. W. Wilson, *Police Administration* (New York: McGraw-Hill, 1950).

34. *Ibid.,* p. 9.

35. *Ibid.,* p. 17.

36. See *Journal of the American Judicature Society* 20 (1937): 176.

37. Fannie J. Klein and Joel S. Lee (eds.), *Selected Writings of Arthur T. Vanderbilt* (Vol. I) (Dobbs Ferry, N.Y.: Oceana Publications, 1965), p. xv.

38. *Ibid.,* pp. xiv–xvi.

39. Fannie J. Klein and Joel S. Lee (eds.), *Selected Writings of Arthur T. Vanderbilt* (Vol. II) (Dobbs Ferry, N.Y.: Oceana Publications, 1965), p. 37.

40. Arthur T. Vanderbilt, *Minimum Standards of Judicial Administration* (New York: National Conference of Judicial Councils, 1949).

41. *Ibid.,* p. 38.

42. See 39 Mass.L.Q. 9 (1954); 22 J.B.A.D.C. 618 (1955).

43. Vanderbilt, *Minimum Standards of Judicial Administration,* pp. 41–42.

44. *Ibid.,* p. 68.

45. *Journal of the American Judicature Society* 37 (1921).

46. John J. Parker, "The Federal Judiciary," 22 *Tul. L. Rev.* 569, 575 (1948).

47. Quoted in Edward B. McConnell, "What Does the Future Hold for Judges?" *Judges Journal* 30 (Summer 1991): 8.

48. New Jersey Constitution, Article VI, Section VIII, paragraph 1.

49. 9 Uniform Laws 75 (Cum. Supp. 1956).

50. N. Car. Gen. Stat. Sec. 7-29.1 (1953).

51. P.R. Laws Ann. Tit. 4, Secs. 331–334 (1954).

52. R.I. Gen. Laws c. 3030 (1952).

53. Va. Code Ann. Secs. 17-111.1, 17-111.2 (Supp. 1950).

54. Mich. Stat. Ann. Secs. 27.15(1)-27.15(7) (Supp. 1953).

55. Ore. Rev. Stat. Secs. 2.310–2.340, 8.260 (1953).

56. Conn. Gen. Stat. Sec. 7661 (1949); Conn. Practice Book 371–73 (1951).

57. Colo. Rev. Stat. Ann. Secs. 37-10-1 to 37-10-3 (1953).

58. Ky. Rev. Stat. Ann. Sec. 21.220 (Baldwin 1955).

59. La. Sup. Ct. Rev. Rule XXI (1952).

60. No enabling legislation or rule was required.

61. Iowa Code Sec. 685.6 (1955).

62. Laws of 1955 (N.Y.) Ch. 869.

63. Laws of 1955 (Md.) Ch. 343.

64. Ohio Rev. Code Sec. 2503.05; 126 Ohio Laws 51 (1955).

65. Laws of 1956 (Mass.) Ch. 707.

66. See Arthur T. Vanderbilt, *Improving the Administration of Justice: Two Decades of Development* (Cincinnati, Ohio: College of Law, University of Cincinnati, 1957); 26 *Cin. L. Rev.* 155 (1957).

67. O. W. Holmes, "The Use of Law Schools," *Collected Legal Papers* 35 (37) (1920) (oration before the Harvard Law School Association, November 5, 1886).

68. William H. Rehnquist in "Tribute to Leo Levin," 138 *Penn. L. Rev.* 317–318 (1989).

69. See *American Law Schools, Directory of Law Teachers, 1979–80* (St. Paul, Minn.: West, 1979), p. 945.

70. A. Leo Levin, "Research in Judicial Administration: The Federal Experience," 26 *N.Y.L.Rev.* 237 (Winter 1981).

71. Russell Wheeler, "Judicial Reform: Basic Issues and References," 8 *Policy Studies Journal,* 134, 135 (1979).

72. *Ibid.*

73. Levin, "Research in Judicial Administration: The Federal Experience," p. 239.

74. Quoting Judge Harold Leventhal in A. Leo Levin and R. Wheeler (eds.), *The Pound Conference: Perspectives on Justice in the Future* (1979), p. 224.

75. Edward B. McConnell, "What Does the Future Hold for Judges?" *Judges Journal* 30 (Summer 1991): 13.

76. *Who's Who in American Law* (7th ed.) (Chicago: Marquis Who's Who, 1991), p. 603.

77. *Ibid.,* p. 11.

78. *Ibid.*

79. *Ibid.,* pp. 39–40.

80. *Who's Who in American Law, 1992–93,* p. 336.

81. Torsten Eriksson, *The Reformers: An Historical Survey of Pioneer Experiments in the Treatment of Criminals* (New York: Elsevier, 1976), p. 32.

82. *Ibid.,* p. 36.

83. *Ibid.,* p. 42.

84. *Ibid.,* p. 50.

85. G. de Beaumont and Alexis de Tocqueville, *Du Systeme penitentiaire aux Etat-Unis, et de*

son Application en France, suivis d'un Appendice sur les colonies penales et de Notes sta-tistiques (Paris: Fournier, 1833), pp. 281–285.

86. Quoted in Torsten Eriksson, *The Reformers,* pp. 50–51.

87. Nicolaus Heinrich Julius, *Nord Americas Sittliche Zustande nach eigenen Anschauugen in den Jahren* (Leipzig: F. A. Brockhaus, 1839), pp. 470–471.

88. Frederick A. Demetz and Abel Blouet, *Rapports a M. le Comte de Montalivet sur les Peni-tenciers des Etats-Unis* (Paris: Imprimerie Royale, 1837), pp. 10–14.

89. Torsten Eriksson, *The Reformers,* pp. 98–99.

90. *Ibid.,* p. 102.

91. *Ibid.*

92. Herbert A. Johnson, *History of Criminal Justice* (Cincinnati, Ohio: Anderson, 1988), p. 223.

93. Alexander Winter, *The New York State Reformatory at Elmira* (London: Swan Sonnenschein & Co., 1891), p. 37.

94. Zebulon R. Brockway, "The Ideal of a True Prison System for a State," in E. C. Wines (ed.), *Transactions of the National Congress on Penitentiary and Reformatory Discipline, Cincin-nati, Ohio, October 12–18, 1870* (Albany, N.Y., 1871), pp. 38–65.

95. Joseph W. Rogers, "Mary Belle Harris: Warden and Rehabilitation Pioneer," *Criminal Jus-tice Research Bulletin* 3 (1988): p. 2.

96. Mary B. Harris, *I Knew Them in Prison* (New York: Viking, 1942), pp. 6–7.

97. *Ibid.,* p. 8.

98. Rogers, "Mary Belle Harris," pp. 1–2.

99. *Ibid.,* p. 3.

100. *Ibid.,* p. 5.

101. Harris, *I Knew Them in Prison,* p. 42.

102. Rogers, "Mary Belle Harris," p. 6.

103. *Ibid.,* p. 7.

104. H. G. Moeller, *Federal Prison System: Fiftieth Anniversary, 1930–1980* (Springfield, Mo.: U.S. Department of Justice, 1980), p. 7.

105. John J. DiIulio Jr., *Governing Prisons* (New York: Free Press, 1987), p. 195.

106. See *Cruz v. Beto,* 405 U.S. 319 (1972); the inmate-plaintiff, a Buddhist, argued that he was not allowed to use the prison chapel and was placed in punitive segregation for two weeks for distributing religious literature.

107. Quoted in DiIulio, *Governing Prisons,* p. 203.

108. *Ibid.,* p. 175.

109. Duncan B. Forrester, "Martin Luther and John Calvin," cited in Leo Strauss and Joseph Cropsey (eds.), *History of Political Philosophy* (2d ed.) (Chicago: University of Chicago Press, 1981), p. 311.

110. Quoted in DiIulio, *Governing Prisons,* p. 199.

111. *Ibid.*

112. *Ibid.,* p. 202.

113. 503 F. Supp. 1265 (S.D. Tex. 1980).

114. 503 F. Supp. 1265 (S.D. Tex. 1980).

115. 97 S.Ct. 285 (1976).

116. 416 U.S. 396 (1974).

117. 372 U.S. 335 (1963).

118. Howard Abadinsky, *Probation and Parole: Theory and Practice* (3d ed.) (Englewood Cliffs, N.J.: Prentice Hall, 1987), p. 18.

119. Lawrence M. Friedman, *A History of American Law* (New York: Simon and Schuster, 1973), p. 518.

120. Paul F. Cromwell Jr., George C. Killinger, Hazel B. Kerper, and Charles Walker, *Probation and Parole in the Criminal Justice System* (2d ed.) (St. Paul, Minn.: West, 1985).

121. John Augustus, *John Augustus, First Probation Officer* (Montclair, N.J.: Patterson Smith, 1972), pp. 4–5.

122. *Ibid.,* p. 5.

123. Abadinsky, *Probation and Parole,* p. 19.

124. *Ibid.,* p. 143.

125. Torsten Eriksson, *The Reformers,* p. 81.

126. Abadinsky, *Probation and Parole,* pp. 146–147.

Part II

THE POLICE

This part consists of three chapters. In Chapter 4 we examine police organization and operation. Chapter 5 covers personnel roles and functions, and in Chapter 6 we discuss police issues and practices. Specific chapter content is provided in the introductory section of each chapter. Case studies in police administration appear at the end of Chapter 6.

Chapter 4

Police Organization and Operation

Blessed are the peacemakers.
—Matthew 5:8

✦ INTRODUCTION

To perform smoothly (as smoothly as society, resources, politics, and other influences permit), police agencies are organized to enhance the accomplishment of their basic mission and goals. In this chapter we consider first how police agencies are defined and operate as bona fide organizations. We then present the contemporary organization of police departments, including an overview of the bureaucratic model that has evolved and recent challenges to it.

We then discuss the need to develop appropriate policies, procedures, rules, and regulations. Next we examine the influence of recent research on contemporary policing functions to learn what works. We also identify and then debunk myths of police practices. Finally, we explore the "back-to-basics" community-oriented policing and problem-solving concepts being instituted across the country. We define these terms, show how these concepts break from the traditional mode of policing, and examine the roles of chief executives, mid-level managers, and first-line supervisors under this strategy. Essentially, the goal of this chapter is to set the stage for later analyses of personnel and problems in the field.

✦ POLICE AGENCIES AS ORGANIZATIONS

✧ MISSIONS AND GOALS

An *organization* is defined as a group of people working together to accomplish a desired goal.[1] Certainly, police agencies fit this definition. First, the organization of these agencies includes a number of specialized units (e.g., patrol, traffic, investigation, records). The role of chief executives, mid-level managers, and first-line supervisors is to ensure that the different units work together to reach a common goal; allowing each unit to work independently would lead to fragmentation, conflict, and competition and subvert the entire organization's goals and purposes. Second, police agencies consist of people who exist to serve the public; they interact within the organization and with external organizations.

Through mission statements, policies and procedures, management style, among other factors, police administrators attempt to ensure that the organization meets its overall goals of investigating and suppressing crime and that it works amiably with similar organizations. As the organization becomes larger, the need for people to cooperate to achieve the organizational goals increases. The formal organizational charts discussed later in this chapter assist in this endeavor by spelling out areas of responsibility and lines of communication and defining the chain of command.

Police administrators modify or design the structure of the organization to fulfill their mission. The major organizational concerns are (1) identifying what jobs need to be done, such as conducting an initial investigation, performing latent or follow-up investigations, and providing for the custody of evidence seized at crime scenes; (2) determining how to group the areas of responsibility, such as patrol, investigation, and the operation of the property room; (3) forming levels of authority, such as officer, detective, corporal, sergeant, lieutenant, and captain; and (4) equalizing responsibility and authority; for example, a sergeant who supervises seven detectives must have sufficient authority to discharge that responsibility properly, or he or she cannot be held accountable for any results.[2]

✧ SPECIALIZATION IN POLICE AGENCIES

The larger an agency, the greater its need for specialization and the more vertical (taller) its organizational chart becomes. Some 2,300 years ago, Plato observed that "each thing becomes . . . easier when one man, exempt from other tasks, does one thing."[3] *Specialization,* or the division of labor, is one of the basic features of traditional organizational theory.[4] Specialization produces different groups of functional responsibilities, and the jobs allocated to meet these different responsibilities are held by people who are considered to be especially well qualified to perform those jobs. Thus, specialization is crucial to effectiveness and efficiency in large organizations.[5]

Specialization makes the organization more complex, however, by complicating communication, increasing the number of units from which cooperation must be obtained, and creating conflict among different units. Specialization creates an increased need for coordination because it adds to the hierarchy, which can lead to narrowly defined jobs that stifle the creativity and energy of their incumbents. Police departments are aware of these potential shortcomings of specialization, however, and attempt in various ways to overcome them to the extent possible. For example, personnel can be rotated to various jobs and given additional responsibilities that challenge them. In addition, in a medium-size department serving a community of 100,000 or more, a police officer with 10 years of police experience could have had the responsibilities of dog handler, motorcycle officer, detective, and/or traffic officer while being a member of special weapons or hostage negotiation teams. Officers can be empowered through a community policing and problem solving strategy (discussed later) or involved in organizational decision making as part of total quality management (discussed in Chapter 17).

In sum, the advantages to specialization in large police departments include the following:

◊ *Placement of responsibility:* The responsibility for the performance of given tasks can be placed on specific units or individuals. For example, the traffic division investigates all automobile accidents and the patrol division handles all calls for service.

◊ *Development of expertise:* Those who have specialized responsibilities receive specialized training. Homicide investigators can be sent to forensic pathology classes; special weapons and tactics teams train regularly to deal with terrorist or hostage situations.

◊ *Group esprit de corps:* Groups of specially trained persons share a camaraderie and depend on one another for success; this leads to cohesion and high morale.

◊ *Increased efficiency and effectiveness:* Specialized units have a high degree of proficiency in job task responsibility. For example, a specially trained crime unit normally is more successful with complex fraud cases than is a general detective division.[6]

✦ CONTEMPORARY POLICE ORGANIZATION

✧ THE TRADITIONAL BUREAUCRATIC MODEL

By the 1950s some police chiefs began to demonstrate that good administration could make a difference in a police organization's efficiency.[7] These administrators stressed military organization; for them, efficiency meant close supervision and strong internal discipline. This movement improved police service and probably appealed to most police officers, most of whom were military veterans. Given the backgrounds of police recruits and the demands made by communities at the time, the move from political patronage to the military model was probably the wisest change possible.[8]

Frederick Taylor's scientific management theory was in vogue in the 1950s, but its task-oriented approach to worker productivity was not universally popular. Ronald Lynch[9] stated the major criticisms of the scientific management theory as it relates to policing:

1. Officers were considered passive instruments; their personal feelings were completely disregarded. Any differences, especially regarding motivation, were ignored; all officers were basically treated alike.
2. The employee was considered to be an "economic man" who could be motivated through wage incentives or fear of job loss.
3. The focus was on technical efficiency, not on the effectiveness of the organization.
4. The efficiency of operation was to be obtained only through division of labor (breaking the job down into small parts), specialization of police activities, rigid structure of line and staff departments, and the use of a span of control whereby supervisors had only a few subordinates.

The scientific management theory, as many police officers know, is alive and well today in some police agencies where employees are still motivated by fear, and administrators practice a philosophy of "do as I say, not as I do."

A *bureaucracy* is an organization with specialized functions, adherence to fixed rules, and a hierarchy of authority. Police organizations in the United States are *bureaucracies,* as are virtually all large organizations in modern society, such as the military, universities, and private corporations. To a large extent, the structure and management process of most police agencies are similar. The major agency differences result from size, between large and small departments; the former are more complex, reflect more specialization, have a taller hierarchical structure, and use authoritarian style of command to a greater degree.

The administration of most police organizations is based on the traditional, hierarchical, quasi-military organizational structure containing to one extent or another the elements of a bureaucracy just noted. According to Thomas Johnson, Gordon Misner, and Lee Brown (former chief of police in New York City), the appropriateness of the tall hierarchical quasi-military organization structure of bureaucracies is often being challenged, especially by large numbers of college-educated police personnel; indeed, Johnson, Misner, and Brown express surprise at the large numbers of people who are disillusioned with it.[10] The disillusionment with the hierarchical structure of police organizations results from its quasi-military structure; the inability of management to match talent and positions; the organizational restrictions on personal freedom of expression, association, and dress; communication blockage in the tall structure; the outmoded methods of operation that organizations cling to; the lack of management flexibility and real challenge of the job; and the narrow job descriptions in the lower ranks of police organizations.

✧ ATTEMPTS TO REFORM THE TRADITIONAL BUREAUCRATIC MODEL

Attempts to reform the traditional, tall hierarchical structure of police organizations and their inherent rank structure have been described as "attempts to bend granite."[11] Because the rank structure controls the incentives of pay, status, and power, it seriously hinders attempts to provide counterincentives for the officer on the street. Some attempts have been made, however, to soften the effects of the traditional structure, including the following:

1. Using expanded pay scales or salary incentives for the patrol officer (with step or ladder increases).
2. Creating the Master Police Officer designation; recommended in 1967 by the President's Crime Commission, it would afford patrol officers pay and status while working on the street.
3. Adopting skill attainment plans, which provide incentive pay for the patrol officer rank on the basis of longevity, certification in a skill, an academic degree, or a job assignment requiring a particular skill.
4. Separating autonomy from rank to address the current situation in which patrol officers with college backgrounds can be overruled by superiors with less education. The patrol officer with the most knowledge should be in charge of a situation. For example, an evidence technician with the rank of patrol officer should have authority over ranking officers at a crime scene.
5. Implementing a career development plan, a rare system that includes formal job rotation, special assignment to positions that have career value, leaves of absence to pursue education or to obtain experience in other agencies, and exchange programs with other departments.[12]

In the 1940s and 1950s some police departments began to recognize the needs of the employees within the organization; agencies began using such techniques as job enlargement and job enrichment to generate interest in policing as a career. Studies have indicated that a supervisor who is *employee centered* is more effective than one who is *production centered*. Democratic or participatory management theories began to be used by police agencies as private industry began to move from the pyramid-shaped, tall organization structure to a flatter structure.

This human relations approach had its limitations, however. By emphasizing the employee, the organization structure became secondary. The primary goal of this approach seemed to many to be social rewards rather than accomplishing tasks. Employees began to give less and expect more in return.[13]

A number of agencies have experimented with other approaches with mixed results.[14] Indeed, when some police agencies have attempted to flatten the organization structure and then replace paramilitary police uniforms with blazers, they have most often returned to the traditional style. In the late 1960s the military model was replaced by one that stressed bureaucratic accountability. In the 1970s experts on police organization, such as Egon Bittner, contended that the military-bureaucratic organization of the police, emphasizing chain of command, adherence to rules, and unquestioned authority, created obstacles to communication and the development of a truly professional police system.[15] Paul Whisenand listed four reasons that bureaucratic organization has begun to disappear: (1) it is too rigid to adapt to change; (2) it is incapable of meeting the demands of sustained growth; (3) it cannot integrate the increasing diversity of contemporary society; and (4) it is not designed to accommodate "new concepts of man, power, and human values."[16]

Michel Crozier[17] described a four-part "vicious circle" that develops in bureaucracies: (1) bureaucracies require impersonal rules, (2) centralization of decision making limits supervisors in the field (they cannot adjust to problems because they must go "by the book"), (3) often one level of the organization is not aware of what is happening at another level, and (4) unofficial power relationships control areas not covered by rules.

The alternative is to combine a few features of the military model (police officers taking orders from superiors during critical incidents) and a few features of the bureaucratic model with other characteristics to create a reasonably professional organization.[18] Until that occurs, large police agencies will probably continue to experience what a Pennsylvania state trooper described as "being herd-bound."[19]

Disenchantment with the traditional bureaucratic structure of police organizations may exist, but that structure continues to prevail. Many administrators still consider it the best structure when rapid leadership and division of labor are required in times of crises. The traditional structure—assuming each police supervisor can effectively supervise only seven employees—requires this tall hierarchical organization. The traditional structure actually causes a chain reaction in policing: narrow spans of control make police departments taller, and taller organizations are complex and may react slowly during crisis situations because the number of different levels present within the chain of command hampers effective communication. Police agencies with tall hierarchical organization therefore must develop policies and procedures to overcome these problems. Many police departments have redesigned their organizations to reflect larger spans of control or management, resulting in flatter hierarchical structures.[20]

✦ A BASIC POLICE ORGANIZATION STRUCTURE

An organization structure has been developed to help departments carry out the many complex responsibilities of policing. The highly decentralized nature and the different sizes of police departments in the United States, however, cause the structure of police agencies to vary. It is possible, however, to describe the characteristics of most departments and to make certain general statements about all agencies to characterize a "typical" police organization.

As mentioned earlier, the police have traditionally been organized along military lines with a rank structure that normally includes the patrol officer, sergeant, lieutenant, captain, and chief. Many departments, particularly large ones, employ additional ranks, such as corporal and major, but there is a legitimate concern that these departments will become top heavy. The military rank hierarchy allows the organization to designate authority and responsibility at each level and to maintain a chain of command. The military model also allows the organization to emphasize supervisor-subordinate relationships and to maintain discipline and control. We discuss the military model again later.

Every police agency, regardless of size, has a basic plan of organization. In addition, every such agency, no matter how large or small, has an organization chart. A visitor to the police station or sheriff's office may even see this chart displayed prominently on a wall. Even if it is not on paper, such a chart exists. A basic organizational chart for a small agency is shown in Figure 4.1.[21]

Line activities involve policing functions in the field and may be subdivided into primary and secondary line elements. The patrol function—often called the "backbone" of policing—is the primary activity because it is the major law enforcement responsibility within the police organization. Most small police agencies, in fact, can be described as patrol agencies with the patrol forces responsible for all line activities.[22] Such forces provide routine patrol, conduct criminal and traffic investigations, and make arrests. These agencies are basically generalists. In a community that has only one employee—the marshal—he or she obviously must perform all the functions just listed. This agency's organizational chart is a simple horizontal one with little or no specialization.

Figure 4.1 Basic police organization structure.

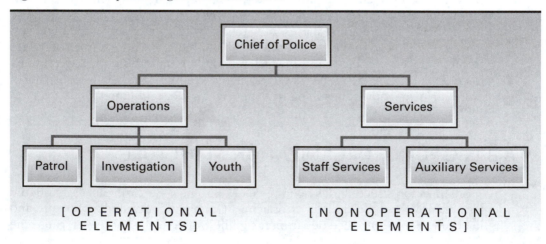

Investigative and youth activities are the secondary line elements. These functions would not be needed if the police were totally successful in their patrol and crime prevention efforts—an obviously impossible goal. Time and area restrictions on the patrol officers, as well as the need for specialized training and experience, require some "spin-off" from the patrol activity.

The nonline functions and activities can become quite numerous, especially in a large community. The nonline functions fall within two broad categories: *staff* (also known as administrative) *services* and *auxiliary* (or *technical*) *services*. The staff services are usually people oriented, including recruitment, training, promotion, planning and research, community relations, and public information services. Auxiliary services involve the types of functions that a nonpolice person rarely sees, including jail management, property and evidence management, crime laboratory services, communications (dispatch), and records and identification management. Many career opportunities exist for persons interested in police-related work but, for some reason, cannot become a field officer or do not want to do so.

The Chicago Police Department's organization structure (Figure 4.2) demonstrates the extent to which specialization exists in a large police department (discussed more fully later) and represents the horizontal and vertical chains of command in a large organization. This organization structure is designed to fulfill five functions: (1) apportion the workload among members and units according to a logical plan; (2) ensure that lines of authority and responsibility are as definite and direct as possible; (3) specify a unity of command throughout so there is no question as to which orders should be followed; (4) place responsibility and authority and hold the delegator responsible if responsibility is delegated; and (5) coordinate the efforts of members so that all will work harmoniously to accomplish the mission.[23] In sum, this structure establishes the so-called chain of command and determines lines of communication and responsibility.

In addition to these generally well-known and visible areas of specialization, other branches involved in policing include crime prevention, drug education, juvenile delinquency, and child abuse units.

✦ POLICIES, PROCEDURES, RULES, AND REGULATIONS IN POLICING

In policing, policies, procedures, rules, and regulations are important to define role expectations for all officers. Police officers are granted an unusually strong power in a democratic society; because they possess such extraordinary powers, police officers pose a potential threat to individual freedom. Thus, because police agencies are intended to be service oriented in nature, they must work within well-defined, specific guidelines designed to ensure that all officers conform consistently to behavior that will enhance public protection.[24]

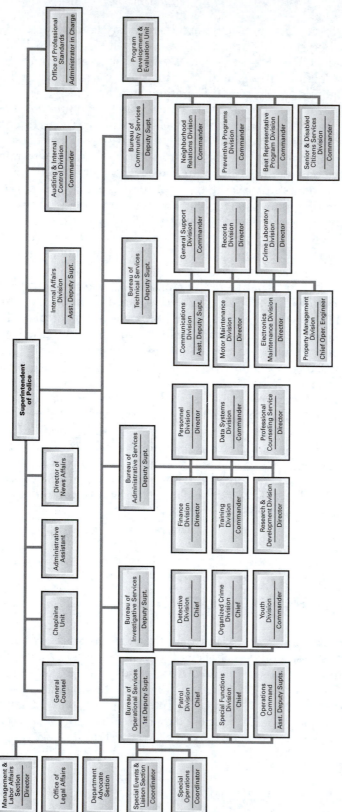

Figure 4.2 Organization for command. (*Source:* Chicago Police Department. Used with permission.)

Related to this need for policies, procedures, rules, and regulations is the fact that police officers possess a broad spectrum of discretionary authority in performing their duties. This fact, coupled with the danger posed by their work and the opportunities to settle problems informally, works against having narrow, inflexible job requirements.

Thus, the task for the organization's chief executive is to find the middle ground between unlimited discretion and total standardization. The police role is much too ambiguous to become totally standardized, but it is also much too serious and important to be left completely to the total discretion of the patrol officer. As Gary Sheehan and Gary Cordner put it, the idea is for the chief executive to "harness, but not choke, their employees."[25]

Organizational *policies* are more general than procedures, rules, or regulations. Policies are basically guides to the organization's philosophy and mission rather than action and help interpret those elements to the officers.[26] Policies should be committed to writing and then controlled, adjusted, and deleted according to the changing times and circumstances of the department and community.

Procedures are more specific than policies; they serve as guides to action. According to Wilson and McLaren, a procedure is "more specific than a policy but less restrictive than a rule or regulation. It describes a method of operation while still allowing some flexibility within limits."[27]

Most organizations are awash in procedures. Police organizations have procedures that cover investigation, patrol, booking, using the radio, filing, roll call, arrest, sick leave, evidence handling, promotion, and others. These procedures are not totally inflexible, but they do describe in rather detailed terms the preferred methods for carrying out policy.

Some procedures have become mandatory as the result of decisions of the U.S. Supreme Court. A good example is the Court's 1985 decision in *Tennessee v. Garner*. This decision resulted in a new policy concerning the use of deadly force. Officers are allowed to use deadly force only when a "suspect threatens the officer with a weapon or there is probable cause to believe that [the suspect] has committed a crime involving the infliction or threatened infliction of serious physical harm."[28]

Some police executives have attempted to run their departments via flurries of temporal memos containing new procedures or rules and regulations. This path is often fraught with difficulty. As Loen observed, an abundance of standardized procedures can stifle initiative and imagination and complicate jobs.[29] On the positive side, procedures can decrease the time wasted in figuring out how to accomplish tasks and thereby increase productivity.[30] As they must with policies, chief executives must seek the middle ground in drafting procedures and remember that it is almost impossible to have procedures that cover all possible exigencies.

Rules and regulations are specific managerial guidelines that leave little or no latitude for individual discretion; they require action (or in some cases, inaction). Some require police officers to wear their hats when outside their patrol vehicle, check the patrol vehicle's oil and emergency lights before going on patrol, and arrive in court 30 minutes before sessions open or at roll call 15 minutes before scheduled duty time. Rules also prohibit smoking in public and consuming alcoholic beverages within four hours of going on duty. These rules and regulations are not always popular, especially if they are perceived as being unfair or unrelated to the job. Nonetheless, these rules and regulations enhance the ability of officers to contribute to the total police mission of community service.

Rules and regulations should obviously be kept to a minimum because of their coercive nature. If they become too numerous, they can hinder action and give the message that management believes that it cannot trust the rank and file to act responsibly on their own. Once again, the middle range is the best. As Thomas Reddin, former Los Angeles police chief, stated,

> Certainly we must have rules, regulations and procedures, and they should be followed. But they are no substitutes for initiative and intelligence. The more a [person] is given an opportunity to make decisions and, in the process, to learn, the more rules and regulations will be followed.[31]

✦ THE INFLUENCE OF RESEARCH ON POLICE FUNCTIONS

✧ THE MID-1970s: CRISES STIMULATE PROGRESS

Little research concerning police functions and methods was conducted until 1964.[32] In fact, little substantive research examining police methods actually occurred until the mid-1970s. Two reasons account for this lack of inquiry into policing. First, the police tended to resist outside scrutiny. Functioning in a bureaucratic environment, they—like other bureaucracies—were sensitive to outside research. Many police administrators perceived research studies as threats to personal careers and to the organization's image, and they were concerned as to the legitimacy of the research. Administrators were naturally reluctant to invite trouble. Given these obstacles, sociologists were often reluctant to attempt to penetrate the walls of what appeared to be a closed fortress.

Second, few police administrators saw any benefit of the research for them. They had no need to challenge traditional methods of operation. The "if it ain't broke, don't fix it" attitude prevailed, particularly among old-school administrators. Some ideas—additional police personnel and vehicles equal increased patrolling and therefore less crime, a quicker response rate, and a happier private citizen—seemed etched in stone. The methods and effectiveness of detectives and their investigative techniques and the old myths of good policing were not even open to debate.

Then, as the police faced crises, things began to change. As Herman Goldstein stated,

> Crises stimulate progress. The police came under enormous pressure in the late 1960s and early 1970s, confronted with concern about crime, civil rights demonstrations, racial conflicts, riots and political protests.[33]

Five national studies investigated police practices, each with a different focus: the President's Commission on Law Enforcement and the Administration of Justice (1967), the National Advisory Commission on Civil Disorders (1968), the National Advisory Commission on the Causes and Prevention of Violence (1969), the President's Commission on Campus Unrest (1970), and the National Advisory Commission on Criminal Justice Standards and Goals (1973). A 1985 national survey probed the effect of budget limits or cuts on police forces in the 1970s and 1980s. It found that 44 percent of police and sheriff's departments had the same number or fewer personnel than they had five years earlier.[34] As a result, police administrators came under increasing pressure to use personnel and equipment in the most efficient fashion—to do more with less. This pressure may explain why police administrators became more willing to challenge traditional assumptions and beliefs and to open the door to researchers. That willingness to allow researchers to examine traditional methods resulted in the growth and development of two important policing research organizations, the Police Foundation and the Police Executive Research Forum (PERF). The results of the research have been significant. As Joan Petersilia of the RAND Corporation observed, "Although systematic research on policing began [only recently], it is already influencing major changes in the way police departments operate and in public perceptions of policing."[35]

George Kelling and a research team at the Police Foundation conducted the best known study of the assumptions concerning patrolling in Kansas City, Missouri, in 1973. The researchers divided the city into 15 beats, which were then subdivided into five groups of three matched beats each. Each group was composed of neighborhoods that were similar in terms of population, crime characteristics, and calls for police services. Patrolling techniques used in the three beats varied: preventive patrolling did not occur in one (police responded only to calls for service); preventive patrol activity in another was two or three times the typical amount; and the third beat used the usual level of activity. Citizens were interviewed and crime rates measured during the one-year period of the Kansas City Preventive Patrol Experiment. The results showed no significant differences in the crime rates or citizen perceptions of safety according to the type of preventive patrol an area received. Similar results were obtained in studies in St. Louis and Minneapolis. These studies also found that the police can stop routinely patrolling their beats for up to a year without necessarily being missed by the residents and without crime rates rising in the beats.[36]

Police response time has also been analyzed. According to the long-standing assumption concerning police response time, the ability to arrest perpetrators decreased proportionately as response time increased. Thus, conventional wisdom held, the more police on patrol in rapid vehicles, the more quickly they can reach the crime scene and make arrests. In 1977 the National Institute of Justice (NIJ) funded a project to analyze the effect of response time on the delivery of police services (making arrests, responding to injured citizens, locating witnesses, and satisfying citizen needs). Again, the site of the research was Kansas City, Missouri. Over a two-year period, the police department collected information on crimes in 56 of its 207 beats; observers rode with police officers and collected travel-time data. The results indicated that police response time was unrelated to the probability of making an arrest or locating a witness and that neither dispatch nor travel time was strongly associated with citizen satisfaction. The time it takes to *report* a crime, the study found, is the major determining factor of whether an on-scene arrest takes place and whether witnesses are located.[37]

✧ RETHINKING "SACRED COW" TRADITIONS

On the basis of these two major studies of patrol methods and effectiveness, many police executives are rethinking their "sacred cow" traditions. For example, one chief of police stated that

> Evidence from the Kansas City study, and others since then, has definitely impacted the way in which I allocate resources. The research findings certainly got me focused on looking at the effectiveness of my own policies and made me do some evaluations of my own. Also, once I understood that preventive patrol does not necessarily reduce crime, I became more flexible in using that manpower in other ways. The Kansas City experiment really opened up the doors for researchers, previously thought to be mostly academic, done for other academics.[38]

Researchers examined another sacred cow—the methods of criminal investigations used by police and their effectiveness. Police departments have always ranked criminal investigation—attempting to link a crime with a suspect—as one of their most critical duties. A mystique—largely perpetuated by the movies—that most crimes can be solved, that most cases involving unknown criminals are solved through good detective work, and that detectives should be assigned to follow up investigations of all but the most minor criminal cases has historically surrounded the area of investigation.[39]

Countless present and former police officers can attest to the elitism and aloofness often displayed by detectives as a result of this mystique. The author learned by personal observation as a patrol officer during the early 1970s that a kind of invisible "leash" was attached to the necks of patrol officers, to be jerked by detectives when a patrol officer unilaterally took an investigation too far. Indeed, a patrol officer trained in criminal investigation who made a felony arrest as the result of good police work was likely to incur the wrath of the detectives, even to the point of being totally ostracized by them. To those of us who incurred that wrath, the recent research on the detective function and the patrol function has been especially rewarding.

Until 1975, however, the criminal investigation function itself had never been investigated. The National Institute of Justice hired the RAND Corporation to penetrate research investigation (sleuthing) by undertaking a national study of the criminal investigation process. The study surveyed 150 large police agencies by interviewing and observing investigators in more than 25 police departments. At about the same time, the Stanford Research Institute (SRI) conducted another study of investigations; it found that in Alameda County, California, in more than 50 percent of the burglaries in which the burglar was arrested, the arrest was made within 48 hours of the report of the burglary. Both the RAND and SRI study results suggested that detectives actually played a relatively minor role in solving burglaries and that the information provided by patrol officers from their preliminary investigations was an important determining factor in whether a follow-up investigation would result in an arrest.[40]

As a result of these findings, NIJ funded additional studies of the investigation process in the late 1970s in Santa Monica, California; Cincinnati, Ohio; and Rochester and Syracuse, New York. Several consistent findings emerged: many serious crimes are not solved; patrol officers are responsible, directly or indirectly, for most arrests (either arresting the suspect at the scene or obtaining helpful descriptions of perpetrators from victims or witnesses); and only a small percentage of all arrests for offenses result from the work of detectives with specialized training and skill.[41]

In 1983 PERF published the results of its own look at the investigative function, including the following:

> Changes have occurred in investigative management as a result of the earlier studies; all of them had a profound influence on investigative management today. For instance, there has been a greater emphasis on case screening and on improving the role of patrol officers in investigations—policy changes that were recommended by many of the earlier studies.[42]

These studies proved that if not all cases can be solved, not all cases should be pursued as vigorously as others. The SRI research produced "predictors of case closure," an index for the police to use to estimate the solvability of burglaries. Included are such elements as the estimated range of time over which the crime occurred and whether a witness reported the offense or an eyewitness was present, usable fingerprints were retrieved, or a suspect was described or named. Using this index, police can better manage the burglary caseload and determine which burglaries have little or no chance of being solved. Obviously, the solvability factors of this predictor prevent the expenditure of tremendous amounts of time and resources on dead-end investigations.

Other major research findings have shaken old assumptions about policing and led to new ones. The following points are now accepted in most quarters as part of the common wisdom of the police:

1. The police deal with much more than criminal activity; they must deal with many forms of behavior that are not defined as criminal.

2. In the past too much emphasis has been placed on the criminal law (using arrests only) to get the police job done; arrest and prosecution are simply not an effective way to handle much of what constitutes police business.

3. Police use a wide range of methods—formal and informal—to do their jobs. Law enforcement is only one method among many.

4. The police (contrary to the desires of earlier advocates of the "professional" model, such as Fuld, Fosdick, Vollmer, and Wilson) are not autonomous. The sensitive functions they perform require that they be accountable, through the political process, to the community.

5. Individual police officers exercise a great deal of discretion in deciding how to handle the tremendous variety of circumstances they confront.[43]

We now know that two-person patrol cars are no more effective than one-person cars in reducing crime or apprehending criminals. Furthermore, police officers in one-person cars are not likely to be injured. And, most officers on patrol do not stumble across felony crimes in progress—only "Dirty Harry" does so.[44]

Although the results of research studies reported here should not be viewed as being conclusive—different results could be obtained in different communities—they do demonstrate that traditional police methods and assumptions should be viewed cautiously. The "we've always done it this way" mentality, still pervading policing to a large extent, may not only provide an ineffective means to organize and administer a police agency but may also cause valuable human and financial resources to be squandered.

A police agency can perform several types of research, provided that the agency has the desire to do it and the personnel to implement it. For example, research into the best way to create a beat could be conducted. Traditionally, many city beats have been configured without any rational basis; boundaries often have been determined by a conveniently located major street or river in town. It would be far better if the geographical boundaries for beats were drawn after analyzing where most crimes have been committed with a view to make high crime areas smaller beats, perhaps with more officers, than low crime areas. In the same vein, it would be a better use of resources to assign personnel according to the time of day and day of week when most crimes and calls for service occur rather than to set the goal as reducing response time, which has not been found to increase arrests. Other types of in-house research that can be performed involve comparing the number of arrests to the number of convictions, the number of personnel hours worked to the number of incidents handled, vehicles used by numbers of personnel, determining the error rate per report.[45] Additional quantitative information that can be obtained includes the number of crimes that result in arrest, the number of officers per 1,000 population, the number of crimes committed by type, the value of items taken in burglaries, and projections of the type of crimes that will occur as well as where and when.

✦ INNOVATION AND VALUES IN POLICE ORGANIZATIONS

Research has shown that neither agency size, technological approach to policing, population variables, nor type of local government substantially constrains the organization structure of police agencies. In other words, none of these factors determines, to any substantial degree, how agencies are structured.[46] This finding is important because it means that police leadership can use innovative approaches to shape police organizations far more effectively than traditional theory allows. Although changing police organizations may sometimes appear to be as difficult as bending granite,[47] as mentioned earlier, it can be accomplished by a leader with vision and the skills to articulate and implement it.

Indeed, Jerome Skolnick and David Bayley examined police departments in six cities, Santa Ana, Newark, Oakland, Denver, Houston, and Detroit.[48] Although some once had reputations for corruption, insensitivity to citizens' needs, gross inefficiency, and even repression and brutality, Skolnick and Bayley reported that innovative administrators kindled the hope that these agencies, despite their past experiences, could be transformed into more responsive servants of their communities.

Skolnick and Bayley undertook this study in part because of the "almost unrelievedly negative findings" about policing methods in the United States.[49] They observed innovations that incorporated community-oriented policing (discussed later). Additionally, they associated successful innovation with four critical ingredients: (1) the chief executive's active commitment to policing for the purpose of preventing crime, (2) the chief's ability to motivate personnel to "enlist in the cause" of new methods, (3) the leadership's commitment to protect the integrity of these innovations and to prevent their decline in quality as the result of everyday demands, and (4) the support and patience of the public.[50]

Also during the course of this study, Skolnick and Bayley identified six obstacles to police innovation: (1) tradition and bureaucratic inertia, (2) public resistance to change and support for traditional police services, (3) resistance by labor unions, (4) the costs of innovation, (5) the lack of vision by police executives, and (6) the inadequate capacity of police departments to evaluate their own effectiveness.[51]

Related to police innovation is the matter of values in police organizations. All organizations have values, which are the beliefs that guide organizations and the behavior of their employees. These values provide the organization a reason for existing.[52] Police departments are powerfully influenced by their values. Policing styles reflect a department's values. Sometimes the values of police organizations are stated publicly. For example, the values for the Houston Police Department under former chief Lee Brown indicated that the department

◊ Will involve the community in all policing activities that directly affect citizens' quality of community life.

◊ Believes that policing strategies must preserve and advance democratic values.

◊ Believes that it must structure service delivery in a way that will reinforce the strengths of neighborhoods.

◊ Believes that the public should have input into the development of policies that directly affect the quality of life.

◊ Will seek the input of employees into matters that affect their job satisfaction and effectiveness.[53]

The growing emphasis on community policing has generated a substantial amount of discussion about values because, by definition, community policing reflects a set of values rather than the technical orientation of the police function. Community policing reflects a service orientation that treats citizens with respect at all times. When riding in patrol vehicles, supervisors and managers must listen for the "talk of the department" to determine whether the values expressed by officers reflect those of community policing.

The values of community policing differ from those held in previous eras. Values are no longer hidden but serve as the basis for citizens to understand the police function and to judge police success, and for employees to understand the police agency's goals.[54]

✦ COMMUNITY-ORIENTED POLICING AND PROBLEM SOLVING

✧ A MODEL FOR PROBLEM SOLVING

A concept representing a return to the basics is now sweeping the country. This concept has been termed *community-oriented policing and problem solving* (COPPS).[55] COPPS breaks from the traditional "professional" era of policing in which police were evaluated on their response time, number of arrests and calls for service, miles driven per shift, and other criteria, which studies indicate have little to do with long-term reduction or elimination of crime and disorder. COPPS is a dynamic and complex process that requires the police to become more customer oriented and employ a logical set of strategies to address neighborhood disorder.

To effect COPPS, police administrators must gradually and thoughtfully implement change in the agency culture, from the top to the bottom of the organization, and with sworn as well as nonsworn personnel. The officers must be trained (see the discussion on COPPS training in Chapter 6) to define more clearly and to understand more fully the neighborhood problems. COPPS also broadens officers' understanding of crime conditions, moving them from viewing incidents separately to recognizing that incidents are often related and symptomatic of deeper problems. Once the root causes are identified, police can develop strategies to attack them.

Under COPPS, the police follow the SARA model,[56] an acronym for scanning, analysis, response, and assessment; this model allows patrol officers to apply problem-solving methods to their daily police practices. A brief explanation of the four model components will help the reader to understand these concepts.

Scanning means identifying problems; officers first determine whether a problem really exists and whether further analysis is needed. To identify problems, police can use data concerning calls for service, citizen complaints, officer observations, and other resources. *Analysis* is the heart of the problem-solving process by which officers gather as much information as possible from sources inside and outside their agency about the scope, nature, and causes of the problem. Dispatch, offense, and other types of data can be sorted to reveal "hot spots"—specific locations from which recurring calls to the police are made. In the *response* stage, officers seek long-term solutions to the problem (a variety of solutions are suggested in the case studies in Chapter 6). Finally, in the *assessment* stage, officers evaluate the effectiveness of their responses and can include before/after comparisons of crime using service data, environmental crime prevention surveys, and neighborhood fear reduction surveys.

✧ THE ROLE OF THE CHIEF EXECUTIVE, MID-LEVEL MANAGERS, AND FIRST-LINE SUPERVISORS

Major change in philosophy and practices is required within a police organization before a major shift such as COPPS can be made. We briefly examine how the chief or sheriff, the captain and lieutenant, and the sergeant are all key figures in effecting such a major transformation.

First, the police organization needs a viable change agent; the person at the top is responsible for setting both the policy and tone of the organization. The chief executive must be both visible and credible and create a climate conducive to change. Employees must be involved in the change process. Gauging the pace and degree of change is also necessary. It is essential, however, that chief executives communicate the idea that COPPS is departmentwide in scope and encourage and guide all officers to engage in problem solving.

Mid-level managers also play a crucial role in the implementation of a COPPS philosophy. They must not view COPPS as a threat to their power. Middle managers (captains and lieutenants, generally) are essential to the process of innovation, much of which only middle management can originate. As George Kelling and William Bratton observed,[57]

> Ample evidence exists that when a clear vision of the business of the organization is put forward, when mid-managers are included in planning, when their legitimate self-interests are acknowledged, and when they are properly trained, mid-managers can be the leading edge of innovation and creativity.[58]

The most challenging aspect of changing the culture of a police agency is believed to lie in changing first-line supervisors. The influence of first-line supervisors is so strong that their role warrants special attention. Herman Goldstein described the critical need to obtain the support of first-line supervisors for COPPS to become operationalized:

> The work of a sergeant is greatly simplified by the traditional form of policing. The more routinized the work, the easier it is for the sergeant to check. [S]ergeants are usually appalled by descriptions of the freedom and independence suggested in problem oriented policing for rank-and-file officers. The concept can be very threatening to them. This . . . can create an enormous block to implementation.[59]

First-line supervisors must be convinced that adopting a different style of supervision makes good sense in today's environment. Another suggestion is that change might be facilitated by allowing the rank-and-file officers to evaluate their supervisors.[60] In an agency fully committed to COPPS, such feedback from street officers would go a long way in helping chief executives to ascertain how well their policies, mission, goals, and objectives are being translated on the streets.

Summary

Today, Robert Peel, the founder of modern policing in England in 1829, would be amazed. His persistent efforts in the mid-1800s to organize and deploy a full-time police force have resulted in a proliferation of police around the globe. In this chapter, we explored the contemporary organization of the police in general; the policies, procedures, rules, and regulations that guide them; and the results of research studies into policing methods. We hope that this body of police research will continue to provide impetus for policing to meet the needs of our shifting society.

Contemporary police organization, an area that presently bears close observation, was also discussed. The organization is an area that needs further research and change. The popularity of community-oriented policing and problem solving (COPPS) is currently causing changes in the traditional administration of police agencies. We expect that careful analysis of the findings of research studies will result in changes to the traditional bureaucratic model of policing as well.

Questions for Review

1. What are the distinctions among policy, procedure, and rules and regulations? Why are they necessary in law enforcement agencies? What are their relationship and role vis-à-vis police discretion?

2. How do law enforcement agencies constitute bureaucracies? Can such a form of organization ever be eliminated?

3. What is the basic police organization structure? Draft an organization chart with the level of specialization you might find in your home town or county police agency.

4. What are some of the major findings of research into policing? How have they affected the field?

5. What role do innovation and values play in police organizations?

6. What is meant by *community-oriented policing and problem solving* (COPPS)? How does this concept differ from past policing methods? What improvements does it offer? Under this strategy, what important roles are played by chief executives, mid-level managers, and first-line supervisors?

Notes

1. Larry K. Gaines, Mittie D. Southerland, and John E. Angell, *Police Administration* (New York: McGraw-Hill, 1991), pp. 5–6.

2. Stephen P. Robbins, *The Administration Process* (Englewood Cliffs, N.J.: Prentice Hall, 1976).

3. Allen Bloom, trans., *The Republic of Plato* (New York: Basic Books, 1968), p. 7.

4. See Luther Gulick and L. Urwick, eds., *Papers on the Science of Administration* (New York: Augustus M. Kelley, 1969).

5. Charles R. Swanson, Leonard Territo, and Robert W. Taylor, *Police Administration* (3d ed.) (New York: Macmillan, 1993), p. 134.

6. Orlando W. Wilson and Roy C. McLaren, *Police Administration* (3d ed.) (New York: McGraw-Hill, 1972), p. 79.

7. Egon Bittner, *The Functions of the Police in a Modern Society,* Public Health Service Publication 2059 (Washington, D.C.: U.S. Government Printing Office, 1970), p. 53.

8. John J. Broderick, *Police in a Time of Change* (Prospect Heights, Ill.: Waveland Press, 1987), p. 231.

9. Ronald G. Lynch, *The Police Manager: Professional Leadership Skills* (3d ed.) (New York: Random House, 1986), p. 4.

10. Thomas A. Johnson, Gordon E. Misner, and Lee P. Brown, *The Police and Society: An Environment for Collaboration and Confrontation* (Englewood Cliffs, N.J.: Prentice Hall, 1981), p. 53.

11. Dorothy Guyot, "Bending Granite: Attempts to Change the Rank Structure of American Police Departments," *Journal of Police Science and Administration* 7 (1979): 253–284.

12. *Ibid.,* pp. 273–274.

13. Lynch, *The Police Manager,* pp. 5–6.

14. Geoffrey P. Alpert and Roger G. Dunham, *Policing Urban America* (Prospect Heights, Ill.: Waveland Press, 1988), p. 71.

15. Bittner, *The Functions of the Police in a Modern Society,* p. 51.

16. Paul M. Whisenand and Fred Ferguson, *The Managing of Police Organizations* (Englewood Cliffs, N.J.: Prentice Hall, 1973), p. 9.

17. Michel Crozier, *The Bureaucratic Phenomenon* (Chicago: University of Chicago Press, 1964), p. 190.

18. Broderick, *Police in a Time of Change,* p. 233.

19. Ray Graham and Jeffrey R. Cameron, "The Integrated Approach to Career Development," *The Police Chief* (June 1985): 26–30.

20. Swanson et al. *Police Administration,* p. 142.

21. For further discussion about basic police organization structures, see George D. Eastman and Esther M. Eastman (eds.), *Municipal Police Administration* (7th ed.) (Washington, D.C.: International City Management Association, 1971), p. 17.

22. *Ibid.,* p. 18.

23. President's Commission on Law Enforcement and Administration of Justice, *Task Force Report: The Police* (Washington, D.C.: U.S. Government Printing Office, 1967), p. 46.

24. Robert Sheehan and Gary W. Cordner, *Introduction to Police Administration* (2d ed.) (Cincinnati, Ohio: Anderson, 1989), pp. 446–447.

25. *Ibid.,* p. 449.

26. *Ibid.*

27. Wilson and McLaren, *Police Administration,* p. 130.

28. 471 U.S. 1 (1985).

29. Raymond O. Loen, *Manage More by Doing Less* (New York: McGraw-Hill, 1971), pp. 86–89.

30. Sheehan and Cordner, *Introduction to Police Administration,* p. 453.

31. Thomas Reddin, "Are You Oriented to Hold Them? A Searching Look at Police Management," *The Police Chief* (March 1966): 17.

32. Peter K. Manning, "The Researcher: An Alien in the Police World," in Arthur Niederhoffer and Abraham S. Blumberg (eds.), *The Ambivalent Force: Perspectives on the Police* (2d ed.) (Hinsdale, Ill: Dryden Press, 1976), pp. 103–121.

33. Herman Goldstein, *Problem-Oriented Policing* (New York: McGraw-Hill, 1990), p. 9.

34. Joan Petersilia, "The Influence of Research on Policing," in Roger C. Dunham and Geoffrey P. Alpert (eds.), *Critical Issues in Policing: Contemporary Readings* (Prospect Heights, Ill.: Waveland Press, 1989), p. 230.

35. *Ibid.*

36. *Ibid.,* pp. 231–232.

37. *Ibid.,* p. 235.

38. *Ibid.,* p. 236.

39. *Ibid.,* p. 237.

40. *Ibid.*

41. *Ibid.,* p. 238.

42. John E. Eck, *Solving Crimes: The Investigation of Burglary and Robbery* (Washington, D.C.: Police Executive Research Forum, National Institute of Justice, 1983), p. xxiii.

43. Goldstein, *Problem-Oriented Policing,* pp. 8–11.

44. Jerome H. Skolnick and David H. Bayley, *The New Blue Line, Police Innovation in Six American Cities* (New York: Free Press, 1986), p. 4.

45. Gaines et al., *Police Administration,* p. 349.

46. Robert H. Langworthy, *The Structure of Police Organizations* (New York: Praeger, 1986).

47. Guyot, "Bending Granite," pp. 253–284.

48. Skolnick and Bayley, *The New Blue Line,* p. 4.

49. *Ibid.*

50. *Ibid.,* pp. 220–224.

51. *Ibid.,* pp. 225–227.

52. Thomas J. Peters and Robert H. Waterman Jr., *In Search of Excellence* (New York: Harper & Row, 1983), p. 15.

53. Robert Wasserman and Mark H. Moore, *Values in Policing* (Washington, D.C.: U.S. Department of Justice, National Institute of Justice, November 1988), p. 4.

54. *Ibid.,* pp. 6–7.

55. See Kenneth J. Peak and Ronald W. Glensor, *Community Policing and Problem Solving: Strategies and Practices* (Upper Saddle River, N.J.: Prentice Hall, 1996).

56. J. Eck and W. Spelman, "Solving Problems: Problem Oriented Policing in Newport News," Research in Brief (Washington, D.C.: U.S. Department of Justice, National Institute of Justice, 1987).

57. Rosabeth Moss Kanter, "The Middle Manager as Innovator," *Harvard Business Review* (July–August 1982): 95–105.

58. Kelling and Bratton, "Implementing Community Policing: The Administrative Problem," p. 11.

59. Goldstein, *Problem Oriented Policing,* p. 29.

60. *Ibid.,* pp. 157–158.

Chapter 5

Police Personnel Roles and Functions

The police are the public and the public are the police.

—Robert Peel

✦ INTRODUCTION

To say that one of the most important and challenging positions one can hold in our society, or in any democratic society, is that of a police administrator, manager, or supervisor is probably accurate. Given the weight of contemporary police decisions and the omnipresent threat of liability in the event of failure to make proper decisions, the administrative role assumes a much higher level of importance than in past decades.

For reasons as much related to the internal aspects of the police organization as to the external factors, changing times have required a higher caliber of leader. The requirements that officers march and salute militarily and refrain from expressing opinions about politics, religion, or police matters—rules found in many departments as late as the 1970s and 1980s—are clearly outmoded today. The Theory X—"do as I say and not as I do"—philosophy of the past engendered many complaints from officers and resulted in the creation of several police unions; thus, the difficult nature of today's police administration is in part due to the iron hand rule of the past. It is also directly a result, however, of a changing, more difficult and litigious society. (Negligence, liability, and other related issues are discussed more thoroughly in Chapter 14.)

This chapter examines today's police executives, beginning by identifying the various roles they fulfill. This is accomplished by adapting Mintzberg's model of chief executive officers. In this section we also consider whether a dominant administrative style exists among police managers and identify the agreed upon observable skills of good police managers. Later we explore the assessment center, which is used as a means for hiring and promoting people into executive and mid-level positions. Several appropriate methods of assessing chief executive performance are described as well.

Then we consider the roles and functions of the various management levels in police organizations: the executives (chiefs and sheriffs), middle managers (captains and lieutenants), and the primary supervisory officers (sergeants). Figure 5.1 shows the hierarchy of managers within the typical police organization and the inverse relationship between rank and number of personnel; in other words, as rank increases, the number of persons at that hierarchical rank decreases. We conclude this chapter by examining methods and considerations that affect the deployment of police personnel.

Figure 5.1 Hierarchy of managers within the typical police organization. (*Source:* Larry K. Gaines, Mittie D. Southerland, and John E. Angell, *Police Administration*. New York: McGraw-Hill, 1991, p. 11.)

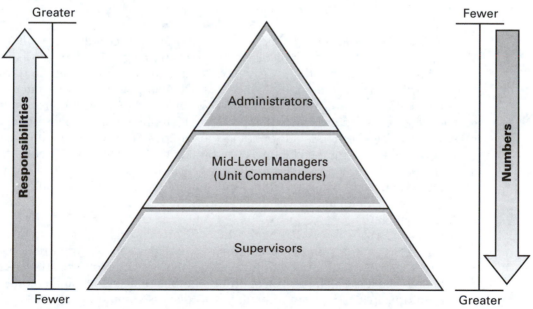

♦ ROLES OF THE POLICE EXECUTIVE: THE MINTZBERG MODEL OF CEOs

A police CEO fills many roles. Henry Mintzberg[1] described a set of behaviors and tasks of chief executive officers in any organization, which can be applied to police organizations. Following is an overview of the role of the chief executive officer (CEO)—that is, the chief of police or sheriff—as adapted to policing, using the Mintzberg model as an analytical framework.

✧ THE INTERPERSONAL ROLE

One role of the chief executive officer is the *interpersonal* role, which comprises (1) the figurehead, (2) leadership, and (3) liaison roles. As a *figurehead,* the CEO performs various ceremonial functions. He or she rides in parades and attends civic events, speaks before school and university classes and civic organizations, meets visiting officials and dignitaries, attends academy graduation and swearing-in ceremonies and certain weddings and funerals, and visits injured officers in the hospital. Like the mayor, whose public responsibilities include cutting ribbons and dedicating buildings, the police CEO performs these duties simply because of his or her title and position within the organization; they come with being a figurehead. Although chiefs or sheriffs certainly cannot be expected to attend the grand opening of every retail or commercial business and other events to which they are invited, they are certainly obligated from a professional standpoint to attend many civic functions and ceremonies.

The *leadership* role requires the CEO to motivate and coordinate workers while having to resolve different goals and needs within the department and the community. A chief or sheriff also may have to take the lead in urging the governing board to enact a code or ordinance that, whether popular or not, is in the best interest of the jurisdiction. For example, a chief in a western state recently led the drive to pass an ordinance that prohibited parking by university students in residential neighborhoods surrounding the campus. This was a highly unpopular undertaking, but the chief was responding to the hardships suffered by and complaints from area residents. The CEO also may provide leadership by taking stands on bond issues (seeking funds to hire more officers or build new buildings, for example) and advising the governing body on the effects of proposed ordinances.

The *liaison* role occurs when the CEO of a police organization interacts with other organizations and coordinates work assignments. It is not uncommon for executives from a geographical area—the police chief, sheriff, ranking officer of the local highway patrol office, campus police chief, and so on—to meet informally each month at breakfast to discuss common problems and strategies. The chief executives also serve as liaison to regional law enforcement councils, narcotics units, crime labs, dispatching centers, and so on. They also meet with representatives of the courts, juvenile system, and other criminal justice agencies.

✦ THE INFORMATIONAL ROLE

Another role identified by the Mintzberg model is the *informational* one. In this capacity, the CEO performs tasks relating to (1) monitoring/inspecting, (2) dissemination, and (3) spokesperson functions. In the *monitoring/inspecting* function, the CEO constantly reviews the department's operations to ensure that they are smooth (or as smooth as police operations can be expected to be). This function is often referred to as *roaming the ship;* many CEOs who isolated themselves from their personnel and the daily operations of the agency can speak from experience of the need to be alert and make their presence felt. For example, a Midwestern sheriff of a small county was voted out of office in part because it was revealed that two deputies on graveyard shift were engaged in a Batman and Robin style of police work that included using an M-16 automatic rifle and a police dog. The sheriff, unaware of departmental operations and preferring the ostrich method of administration, failed to realize that these midnight cowboy stunts and other activities were causing problems that resulted in a tidal wave of opposition. Many police executives use daily staff meetings to acquire information about their jurisdictions, especially criminal and other activities during the previous 24 hours.

The *dissemination* tasks involve distributing information to members of the department via memoranda, special orders, general orders, and policies and procedures described in Chapter 4. The *spokesperson* function is related but is more focused on providing information to the news media. This is a difficult task for the chief executive; news organizations, especially the television and print media, are competitive businesses that seek to obtain the most complete news in the shortest amount of time, which often translates to wider viewership and therefore increased advertising for them. From one perspective, the media must appreciate that frequently a criminal investigation can be seriously affected by premature or excessive coverage. From the other perspective, the public has a legitimate right to know what is occurring in the community, especially related to matters of crime. Therefore, the prudent police executive attempts to have an open and professional relationship with the media in which each side knows and understands its responsibilities. The prudent chief executive also remembers the power of the media and does not alienate them; as an old saying goes, "Never argue with someone who buys his ink by the barrel." Unfortunately, many police executives (a good number who involuntarily have left office) can speak of the results of failing to develop an appropriate relationship with the media.

✧ THE DECISION-MAKER ROLE

In the decision-maker role, the CEO of a police organization serves as (1) an entrepreneur, (2) a disturbance handler, (3) a resource allocator, and (4) a negotiator. In the capacity of *entrepreneur,* the CEO must sell ideas to the members of the governing board or the department—perhaps helping them to understand the need for a new computer or communications system, the implementation of a policing strategy or different work methods, all of which are intended to improve operations. Sometimes the roles blend, as when several police executives band together (in the entrepreneurial and liaison functions) to lobby the state attorney general and the legislature for new crime-fighting laws. As a *disturbance handler,* the executive's tasks range from resolving minor disputes between staff members to dealing with major events such as riots, continued muggings in a local park, or cleaning up the downtown area. Sometimes the executive must solve intradepartmental disputes, which can reach major proportions. For example, the chief executive must intervene when friction develops between different units, as when the patrol commanders' instruction to street officers to increase arrests for public drunkenness causes a strain on the resources of the jail division's commander.

As a *resource allocator*, the CEO must clearly understand the agency's budget and its budgetary priorities. The resource allocator must consider requests for funds from various groups. Personnel, for example, will apply for higher salaries, additional personnel, and better equipment. Citizens may complain about speeding motorists in a specific area, which could require the allocation of additional resources to that area or neighborhood. In the resource allocator role, the CEO must be able to prioritize requests and be able to defend his or her choices.

As a *negotiator,* the police manager resolves employee grievances and is a member of the negotiating team for labor relations. A Police Executive Research Forum (PERF) survey found that 7 of 10 municipal police departments with more than 75 employees now have some form of union representation. This puts the CEO in a negotiating position if the police agency has collective bargaining. In the resource allocator role, the CEO must consider rank and file's requests for raises and increased benefits as part of budget administration. If funds available to the jurisdiction are limited, the CEO must negotiate with the collective bargaining unit to reach an agreement. At times, contract negotiations reach an impasse or deadlock. These situations can become very uncomfortable and even disastrous, leading the rank and file to participate in work stoppages, speedups, or slowdowns or to take other measures.

✧ IS THERE A DOMINANT CEO MANAGEMENT STYLE?

Several studies have attempted to identify the management styles of police executives. An interesting study by Jack Kuykendall and Peter Unsinger[2] involved 155 police executives in California and Arizona, with staffs ranging in number from 3 to more than 1,700; about half of the executives were from agencies with more than 100 employees. The basic purpose of the study was to determine whether the executive emphasized accomplishing *tasks* (therefore using primarily one-way communication with subordinates) or having positive relationships with *people* (with the leader engaging in two-way communication with subordinates).

Executives' styles were measured using a survey instrument to determine whether they fit into one or more of the following four categories: (1) the *telling* style, a high-task, low-people orientation in which the leader uses one-way communication, telling followers what, when, where, and how to do various tasks; (2) the *selling* style, which emphasizes both task accomplishment and people relationships, using two-way communication and emotional support to get workers to "buy into" decisions; (3) the *participating* style, which emphasizes relationships and low-task orientation and involves two-way communication and encourages shared decision making; and (4) the *delegating* style, which has low-task and people orientations, basically letting people "run their own show."[3]

Kuykendall and Unsinger found that police executives used the selling style more frequently than others but tended to be flexible as to style. None of the managers used all four styles, however. The delegating style was used least often. Data showed that about 80 percent of the executives tended to be effective, shifting to a particular style that suited a specific situation. Police executives commonly used two styles with great frequency; more than three-fourths (78 percent) of the executives tended to use participating-selling or telling-selling combinations.

Today the management process in a police setting is affected by the administrator's management style, the people being managed, and the situation. Therefore, one's management style must be flexible. The style a commander uses at the scene of a hostage situation should be much different from that used by a supervisor at a shoplifting scene. A less experienced employee requires a more authoritarian style of management than does a more experienced employee. Management style is always contingent on the situation and the people being managed.[4]

✦ OBSERVABLE SKILLS OF GOOD MANAGEMENT

In addition to assuming several roles and using several management styles, the police executive must develop certain basic management skills. First is *technical* skill, which involves specialized knowledge, analytical ability, and facility in the use of tools and techniques of the specific discipline. This is the skill most easily trained for. Examples in policing include budgeting, computer usage, and fundamental knowledge of some specialized equipment, such as radar or breathalyzer machines. Second is the *human* skill, which is the executive's ability to work effectively as a group member and build cooperation; this includes being sensitive to the needs and feelings of others, tolerating ambiguity, and being able to empathize with different views and cultures. Finally, *conceptual* skills involve coordinating and integrating all the activities and interests of the organization into a common objective: in other words, being able to translate knowledge into action.[5]

These skills can be taught just as other skills can. This proves that good administrators are not simply born but can be trained in the classroom and by practicing the skills on the job.

✦ POLICE EXECUTIVES

Prior to examining the role and functions of contemporary police executives, we digress a bit and consider how persons are selected for these positions. Given the obvious responsibility put on those occupying these positions, the means employed to test applicants or to promote individuals into them become important.

✧ PROMOTING AND HIRING THE BEST: THE ASSESSMENT CENTER

Because a person has been functioning effectively at one level in the organization does not guarantee that he or she will perform effectively at a higher level. For several reasons, many excellent "street cops" have been unsuccessful after being promoted to higher positions. Perhaps they wanted to remain one of the troops and could not maintain the personal distance, perspective, or disciplinary authority needed at times. Or perhaps they could not see the big picture but still identified most strongly with a favorite assignment (for example, after being promoted to deputy chief, an officer who had worked in and strongly identified with the investigative division wanted to provide disproportionate resources to this division). For these reasons, every reasonable means must be utilized to select the best person for the job while identifying those who do not have the ability, temperament, or desire for it.

To obtain the most capable people for executive positions in policing—and to avoid personnel, liability, and other problems that can arise from poor personnel choices—the assessment center method has surfaced as an elaborate yet efficacious means of hiring and promoting personnel. This method, which originated in Germany during World War I and is now used increasingly to select people for all management or supervisory ranks, may include interviews; psychological tests; in-basket exercises; management tasks; group discussions; simulations of interviews with subordinates, the public, and news media; fact-finding exercises; oral presentations; and written communication exercises.[6]

First, behaviors important to the successful performance of the position are identified. Job description listing responsibilities and skills should exist for all executive, mid-management, and supervisory positions (such as chief, captain, lieutenant, sergeant, and so on). Then each candidate's abilities and skill levels should be evaluated using several of the techniques mentioned. (*Note:* Unlike local police chiefs, sheriffs are normally elected, not hired or promoted into their position; thus the assessment center is of little use for that position.)

Individual and group role-playing provides a hands-on atmosphere during the selection process. For example, candidates may be required to perform in simulated police-community situations (such as having candidates conduct a "meeting" to hear concerns of local minority groups), react to a major incident (candidates explain what they will do and in what order in a simulated shooting or riot situation), hold a news briefing, or participate in other such exercises. They may be given an in-basket situation in which they take the role of the new chief or captain who receives an abundance of paperwork, policies, and problems to be prioritized and dealt with in a prescribed amount of time. Writing abilities may also be evaluated. For example, candidates may be given 30 minutes to develop a use-of-force policy for a hypothetical or real police agency; this type of exercise not only illustrates candidates' written communications skills and understanding of the technical side of police work but also shows how they think cognitively and build a case.

During each exercise, several assessors analyze candidates' behavior and perform some type of evaluation; and when the assessment center process ends, they submit their individual rating information to the person making the hiring or promotional decision. Typically selected because they have held the position for which candidates are now vying, assessors must not only know the types of problems and duties incumbent in the position but also should be keen observers of human behavior.

Although operating assessment centers is obviously more costly than using conventional testing procedures, they are well worth the extra investment. As with other occupations, in policing "what goes around, comes around." Monies invested at the early stages of a hiring or promotional process to avoid selecting the wrong person can save untold dollars and problems for many years to come. Good executives, mid-managers, and supervisors make fewer mistakes and are likely to be sued less often.

✦ THE RESPONSIBILITIES OF THE POLICE MANAGER

What are the actual duties of a contemporary police manager? Ronald Lynch stated the manager's primary tasks simply yet directly, saying that police managers

> listen, talk, write, confer, think, decide—about men, money, materials, methods, facilities—in order to plan, organize, direct, coordinate, and control their research service, production, public relations, employee relations, and all other activities so that they may more effectively serve the citizens to whom they are responsible.[7]

Contemporary police managers certainly are not without their problems. Many police administrators see their primary duties as involving internal personnel matters, and themselves as being a personnel manager who happens to wear a uniform. Many such managers forgot long ago how to process a DUI arrest, but they know quite well how to investigate and discipline an officer.

Chiefs or sheriffs in a 10-person agency face the same problems and expectations as their big-city counterparts. The difference between managing large and small departments is a matter of scale. Executives of large departments have many of the same problems that executives of small departments have—just more of them. Yet the chief of a small department must perform the managerial duties as well as those of a working officer.

✦ CHIEFS OF POLICE

✧ POLITICAL AND COMMUNITY EXPECTATIONS

The *chief of police* (also known as *commissioner* or *superintendent*) is generally considered to be one of the most influential and prestigious persons in local government. Indeed, in earlier times chiefs often amassed great power and influenced the level of crime in a community. The use of participatory management, the advent of city managers and public safety directors, the attrition rate of police chiefs, the increased power of local personnel departments, and the influence of police unions, however, have eroded much of this traditional power in recent times. Furthermore, mayors, city managers and administrators, members of the agency, citizens, special interest groups, and the media all have different role expectations of the chief of police that often conflict.

The mayor or city manager likely believes that the chief of police should be an enlightened administrator whose responsibility is to promote departmental efficiency, reduce crime, improve service, and so on. Other, wiser mayors and managers appreciate the chief who simply keeps the lid on while keeping morale high and citizen complaints low. All too many mayors and managers view the police chief in much the same way that owners of professional football teams view their coaches: as scapegoats for not solving problems beyond their control.[8]

The mayor or city manager also may properly expect the chief to communicate with city management about police-related issues and be part of the city management team; to communicate city management's policies to police personnel; to establish written agency policies, goals, and objectives; to develop an administrative system of managing people, equipment, and the budget in a professional and businesslike manner; to set a good example, both personally and professionally; to administer disciplinary action consistently and fairly; and to select personnel whose performance will ably and professionally adhere to the organization's objectives.

Members of the agency also have expectations of the chief executive; these expectations may differ from those of the mayor or manager. The rank and file may be less concerned with the city's wish for an efficient chief concerned about cost-effectiveness than with a chief who will be their advocate, supporting them when necessary and representing the agency's interests when dealing with judges and prosecutors who may be indifferent or hostile. Citizens tend to expect the chief of police to provide efficient and cost-effective police services while keeping crime and tax rates down (often an area of built-in conflict) and preventing corruption and illegal use of force.

Special interest groups expect the chief to advocate policy positions that they favor. For example, Mothers Against Drunk Driving (MADD) insists on strong anti-DUI measures by the police and opposes any movement to reduce expenditures related to enforcing these measures. Finally, the media expect the chief to cooperate fully with their efforts to obtain fast and complete crime information; some media organizations (in the author's personal experience and observation) have participated in a human version of a "feeding frenzy" for news at times, which can involve the chief in a lively or controversial news story when the opportunity presents itself.

✦ QUALIFICATIONS, SELECTION, AND TENURE

Qualifications for the position of police chief vary widely, depending on the size of the agency and the region of the country. Small agencies, especially those in rural areas, may not have a minimum educational requirement for the job. In the early 1970s the National Advisory Commission on Criminal Justice Standards and Goals surveyed police chiefs and their superiors to determine qualities that it believes are essential for the job. Education was found to be an important consideration; many agencies' common requirement today for a police chief is a high school education plus several years of experience as a police supervisor. Large agencies frequently require a college education plus several years of progressively responsible police management experience.[9] In 1985 Don Witham surveyed 493 police chiefs in agencies with more than 75 employees. He found that the typical police chief was 49 years old, had 24 years of police experience (17.7 of which were with the present department), and worked 56.6 hours per week; about 57 percent had earned a baccalaureate degree and 25 percent had a graduate degree.[10] (This compares with this author's 1985 survey of campus police chiefs that found that 48 percent had a baccalaureate degree and 24 percent had graduate degrees.[11])

Police chief executives also need several types of important management skills. The National Advisory Commission asked police chiefs and their superiors to rate, on a scale of 1 to 10, the importance of 14 desirable management skills. The ability to motivate and control personnel and relate to the community ranked highest. A survey today would probably yield similar results. In fact, PERF asked almost 500 police chiefs to indicate the areas in which they needed more training for better decision making; they listed management, legal issues, personnel management, the use of computers, and strategic planning as their priorities.[12]

Although it is perhaps more economical to select a police chief from within the organization, the debate as to whether it is better to promote from within or hire from outside will probably not be resolved soon; each method has obvious advantages and disadvantages. A recent study of western police chiefs both promoted from within and hired from outside indicated only one significant difference in qualification: educational attainment. The outsiders were more highly educated. No difference was found as to background, attitudes, salary, tenure in current position or in policing, or size of agency, community, and current budget.[13]

Job security for police chiefs ranges from full civil service protection in a small percentage of agencies to appointment and removal at the discretion of the mayor or city manager. Increasingly, a term of office is fixed, such as in four- or five-year contracts. Traditionally, however, the tenure of police chiefs has been short. A federal study in the mid-1970s found that the average length in office by chiefs of police was 5.4 years.[14] Another PERF study in the mid-1980s found the average to be practically unchanged, 5.5 years. The average tenure of a metropolitan police chief has dropped from 5.5 years to between 3.5 and 4.5 years.[15] Those who are appointed from within the agency tend to have longer tenure than those appointed from outside.

This short tenure of police chiefs has several negative consequences; it prevents long-range planning, results in frequent new policies and administrative styles, and prohibits the development of the chief's political power base and local influence. In addition, the agency must expend financial and time resources to hire a new chief.

Across the country, police executives are in the eye of the storm. Rising crime, limited budgets, unionization, and conflicting public demands have caused many U.S. police executives to be carefully scrutinized. The toll has been high. For example, from mid-1991 to mid-1992, 8 of the 15 largest city police departments faced turmoil or turnover at the top. As noted, the length of tenure for metropolitan chiefs has dropped.

✦ THE DEPARTURE OF REFORM-MINDED CHIEFS

William Bratton, former police commissioner in New York City, became an international spokesman for crime fighting while being one of the most high-profile police chiefs this country has seen. Bratton disputed experts' claims that crime is outside the control of the police, who claim that it is determined largely by such forces as poverty and racism. He dismissed supervisors who believed they could cut crime by only 2 or 3 percent and fired others who worked bankers' hours. Bratton subscribed to community policing and problem solving (discussed in Chapter 4) and required officers to get out of their cruisers and walk their beats. Bratton's community policing style, however, was "in your face," with officers poured into high-crime areas.

Bratton's tenure resulted in remarkable results. New York City's crime plummeted to its lowest levels in 25 years. Rudy Giuliani, the city's mayor, reported to have national political aspirations, was unable to conceal his resentment of Bratton and ordered him to fire one-half of his public relations staff and cancel a police parade the commissioner had scheduled on his birthday. The mayor's office denies that Bratton was forced out of office, but Bratton maintains that the basic tension with the mayor over press coverage led to his dismissal.[16] In any case, Bratton resigned, and the citizens of New York may well be the big losers.

In recognition of the influence and control that politicians have had on police chiefs over the years, many cities amended their charters in the last several decades in attempts to insulate the chiefs from the politicians. The current emphasis shifts control from politicians to civilians. "There has to be civilian control of the police," asserted Patrick V. Murphy, director of the policy board of the U.S. Conference of Mayors and a former New York police commissioner.[17]

This situation leaves chiefs with little job protection, however. Few chiefs are willing to battle various constituencies—city councils, unions, and various local organizations—to implement changes such as community policing without some job protection.

The various community constituencies battle more viciously when chiefs attempt to implement major change, such as community policing, which unions often resist. The message being sent from chiefs is that without some job protection, do not expect too much real reform or many long-tenured chiefs.[18]

✦ THE SHERIFF

✧ CONTEMPORARY NATURE AND FUNCTIONS

Unfortunately, because of television and movie portrayals, much of the public perceives the county sheriff as a stupid, cruel, overweight, corrupt person wearing a Stetson hat and sunglasses and speaking with a Southern drawl (e.g., see *Smokey and the Bandit, Mississippi Burning, The Dukes of Hazzard,* and *Walking Tall*). This image is both unfair and highly inaccurate; county sheriffs and their offices are dedicated to maintaining order while providing valuable services to unincorporated areas, operating detention facilities, and performing important civil process functions and other duties as delineated later.

The position of sheriff has a long tradition. Because sheriffs tend to be elected, most of them are aligned with a political party. Therefore, it is possible that the only qualification a person brings to the office is the ability to get votes. (Indeed, the author once met a sheriff who was approximately 60 years old and taking a course at the state police academy; his only qualification for being elected was his popularity—he had owned and operated a beer hall in his home town practically all his life.) In some areas of the country, the sheriff's term of office is limited to two years with successive terms prohibited (thus, the office has been known to be rotated between the sheriff and undersheriff). In most counties, however, the sheriff has a four-year term of office and can be reelected. The sheriff enjoys no tenure guarantee, although the federal study referred to earlier found that sheriffs (averaging 6.7 years in office) had longer tenure in office than chiefs of police (5.4 years).[19] This politicization of the office of sheriff can obviously result in high turnover rates of personnel who have civil service protection. The uncertainty as to tenure is not conducive to long-range (strategic) planning.

Largely due to the political nature of the office, sheriffs tend to be older, less likely to be promoted through the ranks of the agency and less likely to be college graduates, and to have less specialized training than police chiefs have. Research has also found that sheriffs in small agencies have more difficulty with organizational problems (field activities, budget management) and that sheriffs in large agencies find dealing with local officials and planning and evaluation to be more troublesome. Because of the diversity of sheriff's offices throughout the country, describing a "typical" sheriff's department is difficult; those offices run the gamut from the traditional, highly political, limited-service office to the modern, fairly nonpolitical, full-service police organization. It is possible, however, to list functions commonly associated with the sheriff's office.

1. Serving and/or implementing civil processes (divorce papers, liens, evictions, garnishments and attachments, and other civil duties, such as extradition and transportation of prisoners).
2. Collecting certain taxes and conducting real estate sales (usually for nonpayment of taxes) for the county.
3. Performing routine order-maintenance duties by enforcing state statutes and county ordinances; arresting offenders and performing traffic and criminal investigations.
4. Serving as bailiff of the courts.
5. Maintaining and operating the county correctional institutions.[20]

Other general duties are found, of course, from one region to another.

Sheriffs often see themselves as police officials, not as jail administrators; they consider duties related to the jail as liabilities. Sheriffs are frequently untrained and uninterested in corrections management, although that is one of their primary functions. This lack of training and interest has resulted in major scandals and problems in jail administration in this country. Some sheriffs tolerate the jail function, however, because of its financial opportunities. One sheriff, allowed a certain amount of money per day to feed each prisoner, told the author that he fed inmates cheap TV dinners and pocketed the savings—a very handsome annual profit.

Sheriffs must respond to numerous problems. An example is the problem of what to do with prisoners released because jails are overcrowded. One sheriff released panhandling inmates from the overcrowded jail. He was criticized because they then bothered area residents by begging for money and transportation and shoplifted at nearby quick-stop establishments. Had the sheriff proposed mandatory transportation of prisoners to another area, he would certainly have been involved in civil rights suits.

✦ RATING CHIEF EXECUTIVE PERFORMANCE

How good is your police chief or sheriff (hereafter referred to as the *chief executive officer* or *CEO*)? The answer probably depends on whom you ask. To some, the CEO is the best thing that ever happened to the community or county; to others, he or she is the worst thing. Rating the CEO's performance in this complex job involves several potential "traps." CEOs are human; they do make mistakes, but citizen perceptions of them and their performance are often wrong. Therefore, it is difficult to assess accurately how the CEO is performing; no litmus test or simple fill-in-the-boxes exercise exists. Several broad, general guidelines can be applied, however, when evaluating these CEOs. We first discuss inappropriate criteria used in evaluation and then discuss the appropriate traits to consider.

✧ INAPPROPRIATE EVALUATION CRITERIA

As pointed out by Jerald Vaughn, former police chief and author of a report for PERF,[21] inappropriate criteria can be used to evaluate CEOs, such as the following:

1. *Personal popularity.* The longer the CEO's tenure, the higher the likelihood that people within and without the department will have complaints about something the CEO did or did not do.

2. *Department morale.* Morale is a fragile thing; it requires a collective effort rather than an individual one. Peter Drucker wrote that *morale* does not mean that "people get along together"; the test is performance, not conformance.[22] Like soldiers and other workers in bureaucratic organizations, police officers can become chronic and notorious complainers; the "grapevine" normally keeps people stirred up, and a certain amount of griping occurs even when things are running smoothly. Thus, the morale of a department is not necessarily the result of the CEO's leadership.

3. *Controversy surrounding the CEO.* Some CEOs may become involved in controversial local issues. This should not necessarily cause the CEO to be evaluated negatively. Controversy and conflict can be productive, causing people to challenge old ideas and methods. CEOs are highly visible and influential; they should be allowed to speak out and provide leadership on matters that concern the public safety.

4. *Rising crime rates.* The former chief of Madison, Wisconsin, David Couper observed that social and economic factors have a large influence on community crime levels.[23] To blame the chief executive for the crime rate is to miss the point. However, when a serious crime rate or public concern about crime exists, the chief executive should develop programs and strategies to combat it rather than merely watch crime statistics soar and engage in mere bean counting.

5. *Single issues: "Run the bum out of town."* Occasionally, a single, critical event or issue (such as the Rodney King incident in Los Angeles in 1991) arises that can result in the call to oust the CEO. Sometimes the chief executive survives the incident if his or her total performance is objectively reviewed. On other occasions, the passion of the moment may prevail, resulting in the loss of years of dedicated service. Indeed, in some incidents the chief may deserve to be relieved of command; however, more often a multidimensional review of the chief's total performance should be made. The ouster of the chief does not ensure that the basic problem causing the upheaval will be eliminated.

✧ APPROPRIATE TRAITS TO EVALUATE

A police executive's evaluation should focus only on qualities, characteristics, and behavior required to perform the job. Honesty and integrity are probably the chief's most important qualities, followed by leadership effectiveness. The direction of the department, its commitment to professional and ethical standards, and its basic values emanate from the chief's leadership role. The chief's ability to motivate people without shoving them and to inspire people both inside and outside the department should also be considered. Any assessment of the chief executive must consider leadership effectiveness. The chief's ability to take a subordinate position to the mayor and city manager/council must also be reviewed; it is important that the chief know where the lines are drawn and when it is time to quit leading and start following.

The management skills of CEOs should be considered in an evaluation. CEOs manage a significant amount of resources—human and financial, equipment, and physical facilities. CEOs must make timely and responsible decisions, as well as realize the impact and legal ramifications of those decisions. The chief executive also must delegate authority and decision making to others rather than taking on too much, which often results in a sluggish operation. Finally, a chief must be innovative and creative in planning and decision making. Today's chief executive must be willing to keep up with the challenges to police work and may need to move the agency into a new era of research, experimentation, and risk taking.[24]

Several other areas of the chief executive's performance must be evaluated.

The first relates to the department's values. Under the CEO's leadership, do the department's values reflect a commitment to the rights of individuals and its employees? The department's view toward the use of force should be considered. Does the CEO manage force carefully and aggressively to ensure that the public is not subjected to unlawful or unwarranted physical force by the police? Written directives are a key to the organization's foundation. Does the CEO require the agency to have clear policies, rules, and procedures to guide employees? Does the CEO see that those directives are constantly updated and enforced fairly and consistently? Has the CEO required that the department be accredited, which reflects the importance he or she places on professional standards? Has the CEO introduced or implemented specific strategies to make the community safer?

The labor climate of the organization is another valid area for consideration when evaluating the chief's performance. This is a very difficult area for today's police executive; civil service regulations, unions, appeal boards, the courts, and the changing profile of today's police officer have made managing labor relations a constant challenge.[25]

Finally, the CEO's understanding of where the department stands with the community and the public's major concerns should be evaluated. Knowing community perceptions should be a paramount concern of the chief executive. No other sector of government in our society has more frequent and direct contact with the public than do the police. As Darlene Walker and Richard Richardson observed,

> Whatever the citizen thinks of the police, they can hardly be ignored. Whereas other police bureaucrats are often lost from the public's view, locked in rooms filled with typewriters and anonymity, police officers are out in the world—on the sidewalks and in the streets and shopping malls, cruising, strolling, watching, as both state protectors and state repressors.[26]

Public opinion surveys provide vital information and feedback to the police executive concerning public perception of officer performance and the department's standing and communication with the public. The mood of the public should be a vital consideration when the CEO makes public policy decisions.[27]

✦ MID-LEVEL MANAGERS: CAPTAINS AND LIEUTENANTS

Few police administration books contain information about the middle-management members of a police department, the captains and lieutenants. This is unfortunate because they are too numerous and too powerful within police organizations to ignore. Opinions about these mid-management personnel vary, however, as we discuss later.

Leonhard Fuld, one of the early progressive police administration contributors, said in 1909 that the captain is one of the most important officers in the organization. Fuld believed that the position had two broad duties, policing and administration. The captain was held responsible for preserving the public peace and protecting life and property within the precinct. Fuld defined the captain's administrative duties as being of three types: clerical, janitorial, and supervisory.[28]

Normally, captains and lieutenants are commissioned officers, with the position of captain being second in rank to the executive managers. Captains have authority over all officers of the agency below the chief or sheriff and are responsible only to those higher ranking officers. Lieutenants, who report to captains, are in charge of sergeants and all officers within assigned responsibility. Captains and lieutenants may perform the following duties:

◊ Inspect assigned operations.
◊ Review reports and make recommendations.
◊ Help develop plans.
◊ Prepare work schedules.
◊ Oversee record keeping and equipment maintenance.
◊ Oversee recovered or confiscated property.
◊ Enforce all laws and orders.[29]

One problem of police organizations is that they tend to become top heavy. Such organizations, having too many leaders and not enough followers, often do not function well because this structure can generate autocracy in its worst form, stifle creative thought or suggestions from the lower ranks, frustrate communication and hinder the accomplishment of goals and objectives. Top administrators, the people who make the key decisions, must be close to the point at which the job is accomplished. Middle management, including captains and lieutenants, often poses a major barrier between the administrator and the officer in the field.

Too often, middle managers become glorified paper pushers, especially in the present climate that requires a myriad of reports, budgets, grants, and so on. The agency should determine what managerial services are essential and whether lieutenants are needed to perform them. Some communities, such as Kansas City, Missouri, have eliminated the rank of lieutenant; they found that this move had no negative consequences and some positive effects.[30]

Obviously, when a multilayered bureaucracy is created, a feudal kingdom and several fiefdoms also exist. As Richard Holden observed, however, "if feudalism was so practical, it would not have died out in the Middle Ages."[31] It is important to remember that the two crucial elements to organizational effectiveness are (1) top administrators and (2) operational personnel. As stated, middle management can pose a threat to the agency by creating a barrier between these two primary elements. Perhaps a lesson may be learned from the Roman Catholic Church, which serves many millions and employs many thousands of people with only five levels in its hierarchy.[32] Research has shown an inverse relationship between the size of the hierarchy in an organization and its effectiveness.[33] Normally, the closer the administrator is to the operations, the more effective the agency is.

◆ FIRST-LINE SUPERVISORS: THE ROLE OF PATROL SERGEANT

◇ SEEKING THE GOLD BADGE

Sometime during the career of a patrol officer (provided that he or she acquires the minimal years of experience), the opportunity for career advancement is presented, to become a three-striped sergeant—to wear the "gold badge." This is a difficult position to occupy because at the mid-administrational level, it is caught between upper management and rank-and-file officers; people who can successfully work with yet command people are in short supply and long demand.

Because most rank-and-file officers will retire with the same rank—patrol officer—at which they entered the occupation, the initial promotional opportunity to attain the rank of sergeant is normally attractive. Practically no lateral entry from agency to agency exists at the lower ranks; therefore, patrol officers are not able to transfer to another police agency with a promotion. Their promotional opportunities are limited to their present agency, and the waiting period for sergeant's vacancies to occur through retirement or otherwise—especially in smaller agencies—can seem interminable.

Intracity and departmental politics certainly influence the promotional process; mayors, city managers, and police administrators have been known to predetermine who will be promoted even before testing and interviewing begin. Another administrative consideration that affects promotion decisions is the knowledge that good patrol officers do not automatically become good mid-level supervisors. Many good patrol officers promoted to the rank of sergeant cannot divorce themselves from being one of the troops and are unable to flex their supervisory muscles when necessary. In short, a good sergeant must wear two hats, one as a people-oriented, democratic leader with concern for subordinates and the other as a task-oriented and authoritarian leader who must make decisions to which subordinates may object. Unfortunately, many supervisors (within and without the police field) today believe that their subordinates are motivated more by the desire for financial rewards than anything else; over the years, however, a number of studies, including the Hawthorne studies mentioned previously, have shown that intrinsic rewards, such as appreciation, sympathetic help, and being made to feel a part of the organization, take precedence over income.

Fuld argued in 1909 that when considering the first-line supervisor, the ideal sergeant needs to possess four qualifications: (1) the ability to write and prepare reports, (2) a thorough knowledge of police business, (3) a capacity for being discrete and intelligent, and (4) a rudimentary knowledge of criminal law.[34]

✧ GETTING THAT FIRST PROMOTION

It is not uncommon for 60 percent to 65 percent or more of those who are eligible to do so take the test for promotion, and it is common for more than half of all persons hired as sergeants in agencies to be working outside the patrol division and not as patrol officers at the time. Senior administrators believe that this is better than bringing the patrol officer's mentality to the sergeant role. Competition for the sergeant openings in most departments is obviously quite keen, but the material rewards are actually slight. Those who are promoted lose opportunities for overtime and court time compensation that are available to patrol officers. Conventional wisdom among many officers is that their immediate supervisors take home less money than they do. Still, the opportunity to test for sergeant normally draws a crowd. Many officers test simply for the experience, because of pressure from peers, out of curiosity, or just to get off the streets for a short while.

Placement as a sergeant in a good-sized U.S. police agency is governed by departmental and civil service procedures that are intended to guarantee legitimacy and impartiality in the process. As mentioned earlier, sponsorship or political pull may still have some influence, although it may not be the blatant hook of past decades.[35] Officers are often told it is best to rotate into different assignments to gain exposure to a variety of police functions and supervisors before testing for sergeant. The promotional system, then, favors officers who are skilled at test taking as well as those skilled at cultivating relationships outside the patrol division.[36]

Sergeants are chosen from a final, rank-ordered list of names often based on scores from written and oral tests as well as factors such as years of experience, minority status, supervisory ratings, military experience, and departmental commendations. The testing process often is regarded by officers as a capricious gauntlet that tests inappropriate skills and knowledge and gives unfair advantage to certain groups (e.g., women, minorities, college graduates, veterans) and emphasizes "trick" or subtle questions. The test is also seen as being a mildly embarrassing process that dishonors more candidates than it honors. As Van Maanen observed, however, "One could hardly expect a favorable impression of a testing procedure that screens out over 95 percent of its takers."[37]

✧ TRANSITION TO SERGEANT

After becoming a sergeant, several dynamics at work make the transition difficult. The new sergeant confronts a solitary process with little, if any, formal training in the new position and must therefore seek advice and counsel. New sergeants are often given unpopular and relief assignments with few officers that the sergeant knows and no officers permanently assigned to him or her. Thus, the sergeant is able to develop little loyalty in subordinates.

The new sergeant eventually adapts to the role and develops individual characteristics that the officers he or she supervises come to know well.

✦ DISTRIBUTION AND DEPLOYMENT OF PATROL FORCES

✧ EVALUATING THE NUMBER OF OFFICERS NEEDED

Once police officers have been hired, the decision of how to deploy them in the best, most advantageous manner must be made. Every modern police department has a patrol unit; even in large specialized departments, patrol officers constitute up to two-thirds of all sworn officers. In small communities, police operations are not specialized, and the patrol division—full of generalists who perform a wide range of duties—includes the entire department.

Approximately five police officers are required to provide one officer around the clock, 7 days per week, 365 days per year. This occurs because days off, vacations, sick leave, training, holidays, and other forms of leave must be covered. Thus, deploying one patrol officer on the street permanently can often cost more than $150,000. From a different perspective, an officer working eight-hour shifts, five days on duty, and two days off per week is available for about 1,760 hours, or 220 shifts per year, or 60 percent of the time.

Given the expense and limited resources available for policing the crime and drug problems in the United States today, every possible consideration should be given so that personnel can be deployed properly. Police agencies need more hard data on what occurs during patrol so that they can determine how to assign patrol officers to obtain maximum benefit. Unfortunately, as we will see, patrol assignments are not often based on documented need.

Essentially, the "appropriate" number of police personnel that a department needs is determined in three ways. One is the intuitive approach, which is basically an educated guess. This method, probably used with considerable frequency in the United States, especially in most small jurisdictions, is obviously not based on any rational scheme. As mentioned previously, conveniently intersecting streets or highways often are used to create permanent beat sectors without regard to an analytical determination of when, where, or how crime occurs.

The second method, the workload approach, requires the organization to identify precisely what the community expects the police to do, which calls must be processed, and an expected level of service. This method is rarely used because it requires an elaborate information system, standards of expected performance, and prioritization of police activities—as well as agreement and understanding of the local police role.

The last approach, the comparative method, is becoming more widely used. It involves comparing one or more communities using the ratio of police officers per 1,000 population as a standard; it attempts to justify additional personnel.[38] According to the FBI's *Uniform Crime Reports,* the national average currently is 2.3 full-time sworn officers for every 1,000 inhabitants (ranging from 1.8 for cities with populations of 25,000 to 99,000 to 3.1 in cities with 250,000 or more inhabitants).[39]

The two most important variables in allocating police personnel, as suggested earlier, are location and time. Knowing the *location* of problems assists the police in dividing a community into geographic beats or sectors of approximately equal workload. Knowing *time of occurrence* is important because it can determine how to group personnel into working time periods or shifts. *Mobility* is also an important consideration; police officers travel by several means; therefore, speed, density of population, and visibility (deciding where officers are to make a stronger presence) need to be taken into account.[40]

Summary

Clearly, police management carries tremendous responsibility. Our initial discussion of the roles and functions of police managers has noted the awesome trust and challenges inherent in this position. Police managers must decide what the best leadership method is, how to perform each role in the best way, and whether to recruit more women and minority officers. Managers are concerned with their standing with the governing board and the rank and file. They must decide how best to deploy and evaluate the officers. Police managers face these issues daily.

Questions for Review

1. What are some of a police executive's primary roles? (Use the three major categories of the Mintzberg model of chief executive officers in developing your response.)
2. Is there a dominant management style of police executives? If so, is it the best style? Defend your responses.
3. What are some elements of the police chief's position that make it attractive or unattractive? Are contemporary hiring requirements adequate?
4. How do chiefs and sheriffs differ in role and background?
5. How is the performance of chiefs and sheriffs evaluated? Are there other, better criteria that could be used? What personal traits are most important for persons occupying or seeking these offices?

6. How do the role and function of sergeant differ from those of upper or middle management?

7. What criteria should be used to determine the distribution and performance of street officers?

Notes

1. Henry Mintzberg, "The Manager's Job: Folklore and Fact," *Harvard Business Review* 53 (July/August 1975): 49–61.

2. Jack Kuykendall and Peter C. Unsinger, "The Leadership Styles of Police Managers," *Journal of Criminal Justice* 10 (1982): 311–322.

3. Paul Hershey and Kenneth H. Blanchard, *Management of Organizational Behavior* (Englewood Cliffs, N.J.: Prentice Hall, 1977), pp. 161–172.

4. Larry K. Gaines, Mittie D. Southerland, and John E. Angell, *Police Administration* (New York: McGraw-Hill, 1991), pp. 10–11.

5. Robert Katz, "Skills of an Effective Administrator," *Harvard Business Review* (January/February 1955): 33–41.

6. R. J. Filer, "Assessment Centers in Police Selection," in C. D. Spielberger and H. C. Spaulding (eds.), *Proceedings of the National Working Conference on the Selection of Law Enforcement Officers* (Tampa, Fla.: University of South Florida, March 1977), p. 103.

7. Ronald G. Lynch, *The Police Manager* (3d ed.) (New York: Random House, 1986), p. 1.

8. Clemens Bartollas, Stuart J. Miller, and Paul B. Wice, *Participants in American Criminal Justice: The Promise and the Performance* (Englewood Cliffs, N.J.: Prentice Hall, 1983), p. 35.

9. *Ibid.*, p. 42.

10. Donald C. Witham, *The American Law Enforcement Executive: A Management Profile* (Washington, D.C.: Police Executive Research Forum, 1985).

11. Ken Peak, "Campus Policing in America: The State of the Art," *The Police Chief* 54 (June 1987): 22–24.

12. Witham, *The American Law Enforcement Chief Executive*, p. xii.

13. Janice K. Penegor and Ken Peak, "Police Chief Acquisitions: A Comparison of Internal and External Selections," *American Journal of Police* 11 (1992): 17–32.

14. National Advisory Commission on Criminal Justice Standards and Goals, *Police Chief Executive* (Washington, D.C.: U.S. Government Printing Office, 1976), p. 7.

15. Gordon Witkin, "Police Chiefs at War," *U.S. News and World Report* (June 8, 1992): 33.

16. Gregory Beals and Evan Thomas, "A Crimebuster's Fall," *Newsweek* (April 8, 1996): 42.

17. Witkin, "Police Chiefs at War," p. 33.

18. *Ibid.*

19. National Advisory Commission on Criminal Justice Standards and Goals, *Police Chief Executive*, p. 7.

20. Bartollas et al., *Participants in American Criminal Justice*, pp. 51–52.

21. Jerald R. Vaughn, *How to Rate Your Police Chief* (Washington, D.C.: Police Executive Research Forum, 1987), pp. 7–14.

22. Peter Drucker, *Management, Tasks, Responsibilities, and Practices* (New York: Harper & Row, 1974).

23. David C. Couper, *How to Rate Your Local Police* (Washington, D.C.: Police Executive Research Forum, 1973).

24. Vaughn, *How to Rate Your Police Chief,* pp. 15–20.

25. *Ibid.,* pp. 23–29.

26. N. Darlene Walker and Richard J. Richardson, *Public Attitudes Toward the Police* (Chapel Hill, N.C.: Institute for Research in Social Science, 1974), p. 1.

27. Mervin F. White and Ben A. Menke, "On Assessing the Mood of the Public Toward the Police: Some Conceptual Issues," *Journal of Criminal Justice* 10 (1982): 211–230.

28. Leonhard F. Fuld, *Police Administration* (New York: G. P. Putnam's Sons, 1909), pp. 59–60.

29. Wayne K. Bennett and Karen M. Hess, *Management and Supervision in Law Enforcement* (St. Paul, Minn.: West, 1992), pp. 44–45.

30. Richard N. Holden, *Modern Police Management* (Englewood Cliffs, N.J.: Prentice Hall, 1986), pp. 294–295.

31. *Ibid.,* p. 295.

32. *Ibid.,* p. 117.

33. Thomas J. Peters and Robert H. Waterman Jr., *In Search of Excellence* (New York: Warner Books, 1982), pp. 306–317.

34. Fuld, *Police Administration,* p. 56.

35. Arthur Niederhoffer, *Behind the Shield* (New York: Doubleday, 1967), p. 79.

36. John Van Maanen, "Making Rank: Becoming an American Police Sergeant," in Roger G. Dunham and Geoffrey P. Alpert (eds.), *Critical Issues in Policing: Contemporary Readings* (Prospect Heights, Ill.: Waveland Press, 1989), pp. 146–161.

37. *Ibid.,* p. 151.

38. Roy R. Roberg and Jack Kuykendall, *Police Organization and Management: Behavior, Theory, and Processes* (Pacific Grove, Calif.: Brooks/Cole, 1990), p. 284.

39. U.S. Department of Justice, Federal Bureau of Investigation, *Uniform Crime Reports for the United States, 1995* (Washington, D.C.: Author, 1996), p. 278.

40. *Ibid.*

Chapter 6

Police Issues
and Practices

*Since this is a time of increasing crime, increasing social unrest and
increasing public sensitivity to both, it is a time when police work is
peculiarly important, complicated, conspicuous, and delicate.*
> —The President's Commission on Law
> Enforcement and Administration of Justice, 1967

✦ INTRODUCTION

It has been stated that in the infancy of policing, a size 3 hat and a size 43 jacket
were the only qualifications for entering police work. Given the nature and responsibilities of the job, that description certainly does not apply today.

This chapter begins with a look at community-oriented policing and problem solving (COPPS), which was introduced in Chapter 4. Two case studies review formal COPPS. The chapter also examines the need for policy development
regarding the use of force (including warning shots, weapons, pursuits, and special weapons and tactics), and special operations (including crowd control,
hostage negotiation, and disasters) in which police engage. Then we discuss a
growing trend for *national accreditation* of law enforcement agencies, which is
similar to a report card. We next explore the effect of technology, including video
camcorders, on policing. After discussing options administrators may consider
when measuring officer productivity and the increasingly important administrative

function of providing adequate training for officers, we conclude with a brief look at police stress and burnout.

In this chapter, unlike the two chapters preceding it, we address administrative matters that are literally life and death in nature, again underscoring the extremely challenging nature of contemporary police administration. Grave issues such as those discussed in this chapter require policies and procedures that are well thought out, written, explained, and implemented.

Several case studies concerning problems of police administration are provided at the end of the chapter.

✦ WHAT WORKS: COMMUNITY-ORIENTED POLICING AND PROBLEM SOLVING IN ACTION

The COPPS concept is being used in communities of all sizes. Following are two case studies, one from San Diego, California, and the other from North Tulsa, Oklahoma, demonstrating that a return to the basics—taking the police officers out of their patrol vehicles and placing them in closer contact with members of their communities to enable the officers and citizens to solve problems—has paid huge dividends.

Note that both the case studies use a common approach, the SARA model (scanning, analysis, response, and assessment, all of which were discussed in Chapter 4) and a core theme (working with the community to identify and address problems). In both cases, the police responded to community needs and took advantage of opportunities to collaborate with individuals and groups in the community. The case studies also demonstrate the rich variety of police problem-solving strategies that can be employed to address various types of problems. These techniques go far beyond the traditional reactive, incident-driven police responses.

✦ CASE STUDIES

✧ DRUGS AND GUNS ON MAPLE AVENUE IN SAN DIEGO

Located in the southeast section of San Diego in a residential neighborhood of mostly apartment buildings, the privately owned three-story complex at 5678 Maple Avenue contained more than 75 units. The complex was divided into four buildings with a small, grassy commons area between them. An on-site manager,

employed by the building management company, was responsible for maintenance. Shortly after the complex opened, serious drug use and sales became evident there.

Scanning. Combatting narcotics activity in this area proved difficult for patrol officers. Initially, the officers focused on making arrests, but suspects often
evaded police by running into the apartments or through a canyon on the north
side, an open field on the east side, or a row of apartments on the west side. Police determined that drug users and dealers congregated in and around two laundry rooms in the complex after finding small plastic bags, glass pipes, and used
matchbooks—all signs of crack cocaine use—in these rooms. Police considered
each location an easy place to make an arrest because someone who either possessed drugs or was under their influence was usually around.

Gunfire and gang-related violence became common occurrences during
evening hours at the complex. Police records indicated nightly shootings during
a single three-week period. Police learned through an informant and confirmed
through undercover surveillance that the complex had become a major supply
source of crack cocaine for several area gangs. Two beat officers applied selective enforcement in the area, making arrests with large groups of officers at random intervals. Because this approach provided only temporary relief, however,
the officers decided to implement a problem-oriented approach.

Analysis. Officers first determined that they needed additional information.
Knowing that apartment managers sometimes are coerced into helping drug dealers or even volunteer to assist traffickers in exchange for money and drugs, the
officers spoke with the apartment manager and suggested that he place locks on
the laundry room doors and install additional lighting in the center of the complex. Two weeks later, the manager had not made the suggested improvements.

Next the officers evaluated their arrest and field interview data. From this information, which included suspect interviews, the officers could identify a number of dealers, gangs, and tenants who were collaborating with drug dealers. Evidence indicated that the manager had been dissuading residents from contacting
police, saying that he would deal with the problem.

The officers then contacted the complex's management company and requested a key to a vacant apartment so they could observe drug dealers. Noting
that some dealers carried guns, the officers later uncovered a gun-running operation and in a subsequent investigation seized a large weapons cache of handguns primarily, an Uzi machine gun, a MAC-10 automatic pistol, and several
sawed-off shotguns.

Response. Officers obtained search warrants for the apartments where they
had observed drug dealing. When they informed the management company of
their findings, its representatives offered to cooperate, agreeing to evict problem

tenants and install security doors on the laundry room. Then with the assistance of the Special Weapons and Tactics (SWAT) unit, five search warrants were executed simultaneously in the complex. Numerous guns and large quantities of drugs and drug paraphernalia were seized and numerous eviction notices were immediately served on the problem tenants. During the legal eviction process, officers continued to work with the private management company and maintain their surveillance, but drug users and sellers continued to congregate on the apartment grounds and in the general vicinity.

The patrol officers went directly to the owner of the complex and learned that he was unaware of the situation. Once informed, he fired the apartment manager and subsequently replaced the management company. The new company hired security guards, improved the apartment grounds, and initiated a new tenant screening process.

Assessment. An after-action assessment revealed that the complex was virtually drug free; security guards reported no drug or gang activity.[1]

✦ PUBLIC HOUSING PROBLEMS IN NORTH TULSA, OKLAHOMA

North Tulsa experienced consistently higher crime rates than the rest of the city. Nearly half of the violent crimes reported occurred in this section of the city, which for a long time had been a depressed, low-income area, lacking in adequate services. The Tulsa Housing Authority was established to support the city's low-income public housing.

Scanning. In an attempt to determine the nature of the crime problem in North Tulsa, a special management team of Tulsa police officials conducted a study and decided to concentrate on five public housing complexes with high crime rates and blatant street drug dealing.

Analysis. With crime statistics in hand, officers conducted a resident survey in each housing complex and learned that 86 percent of the occupants lived in households headed by a single female. Officers assigned to the target area noticed large groups of school-age youth in the housing complexes who appeared to be selling drugs during school hours. A comparison of the dropout and suspension rates in North Tulsa schools with those in other areas of the city indicated that the city's northernmost high school, serving most of the high school–age youths in the five complexes, had the highest suspension (4.4 percent) and dropout (10 percent) rates of any school in the city. This area also reported the highest number of pregnant teenagers in the school system. Officers knew that few of the juveniles observed in the complexes had legitimate jobs and that most of them appeared to be attracted to drug dealing by the easy money. One youth commented, "Why should I work for minimum wage at McDonald's when I can make $400 to $1,400 a day selling dope?"

Supervisors at Uniform Division North arranged volunteers into two-officer teams assigned to the complexes on eight-hour tours. The teams were expected to visit and establish a rapport with residents to assure them that police were present to ensure their safety. Within a month, officers verified juvenile involvement in drug trafficking. As officers approached drug hangouts within the complexes, young lookouts (age 12 to 16) called out "rollers!" to alert the dealers to discard their drugs and disperse. Youth arrested often reappeared in the complex the next day. A strategy was needed to provide programs to deter youth from selling or using drugs.

Response. Officers assigned to one of the complexes believed that the youths needed programs that would help to improve their self-esteem, teach them values, and develop decision-making skills. Eighty-six percent of the boys came from homes without fathers. To provide positive role models for them, the officers started a Boy Scout troop in the complex for boys between 11 and 17 years of age. Two officers, one a qualified Boy Scout leader, began meeting with the boys on Saturdays in a vacant apartment.

In addition, officers initiated a group called SHARE (Stand, Help, and Rid Evil) to raise money for needy residents and police-sponsored youth activities. One officer spoke at civic group meetings and local churches throughout the city to solicit donations and increase awareness of the needs of young people on the city's north side. Those receiving help from SHARE agreed to participate in programs geared to improving life and job skills. Volunteers came from the churches and the civic groups where the officer had spoken.

Officers working at another complex developed plans for unemployed young people. One officer organized The Young Ladies Awareness Group, which hosted weekly guest speakers invited to come and teach different job-related skills. Programs instructed young women on how to dress for job interviews and employment with role-playing officers demonstrating proper conduct during interviews. The women were also instructed in resume writing and makeup, hair care, and personal hygiene. An officer also worked with the Private Industry Training Council (PITC), a government program that sponsored sessions on setting goals and building self-esteem to prepare young people to enter job training programs. The officer also arranged for volunteers from the Oklahoma Highway Patrol and a local school to help teach driver's education.

The officers then became involved in a day camp project conducted at the Ranch, a 20-acre northside property confiscated by police from a convicted drug dealer. Disadvantaged youth recruited from the target projects attended the camp. Tulsa's mayor and chief of police came to the Ranch to meet with the youth, as did psychologists, teachers, ministers, and celebrities. Guests tried to convey the advantages of productive and drug-free lives, among other values.

Assessment. The police noted a decline in street sales of illegal drugs in the five target complexes. Youth reacted positively to the officers' efforts to help them, and the programs seemed to deter them from becoming involved with drugs. The police department continued to address the problems of poor youth in North Tulsa. Social service agencies began working with the police department, establishing satellite offices on the north side of the city, scheduling programs, and requesting police support for their efforts.[2]

The typical (perhaps stereotypical) police response to most problems is to report an offense, leave the site or identify the offenders, and use the criminal justice system to control them. By focusing attention on the most frequent or dangerous offenders, limited police resources can be used more effectively. Note that different solutions are required for different problems; a "cookie cutter" approach will not do. The SARA process allows for the development of multiple options—a list of opportunities that can be discussed and modified—rather than creating a single best solution.

✦ SUPERVISING THE LEGITIMATE USE OF FORCE

✦ VIOLENCE IN OUR SOCIETY

The beating of Rodney King by several Los Angeles police officers occurred in March 1991. That event, which has been described as a "landmark in the recent history of law enforcement,"[3] was later witnessed by the world in an 82-second videotape by citizen George Holliday.

If any good came from the King incident, it perhaps was the realization by the public and police leadership that they must be aware of the potential for excessive force by officers. The riot resulting from the King beating and the police response to it provided police administrators across the country with a crowd control guide. Many people believe that the understanding the police learned from this event—another lesson from Los Angeles—may soon be needed to handle similar riots because the potential for conflict remains in Los Angeles and in other major cities across the country.

The United States, especially from the point of view of its police officers, is a mean and dangerous place. As William A. Westley wrote in 1969 in *Violence and the Police,* "The policeman's world is spawned of degradation, corruption and insecurity. He sees man as ill-willed, exploitative, mean and dirty; himself a victim of injustice . . . he walks alone, a pedestrian in Hell."[4] The job for many U.S. police officers is like a daily foray into a combat zone. Indeed, the inner-city streets have been called a "domestic Vietnam."[5] Instead of facing Viet Cong or some other foreign enemy, however, the foes of these officers include gangs, homicidal killers, and drug addicts. Police adversaries are more heavily armed and have become more arrogant than ever. About 80 police officers are killed each year in the line of duty.

✦ LEVELS OF FORCE

Police officers in the United States are allowed to do three things in performing their jobs that no civilian can do: (1) use deadly force, (2) restrain the freedom of others, and (3) engage in high-speed pursuits.

Police can exercise several forms of force ranging from a simple verbal command, a light touch on the arm to encourage someone to move along or comply with an order, the use of the baton or Mace to control someone, to the use of the lateral-vascular neck restraint (the so-called chokehold or sleeper hold that has been criticized following several deaths when it was applied), to the use of lethal or deadly force. These levels of legitimate force are especially important in policymaking and on the street; as stated in police circles, "You don't bring a baton to a knife fight, and you don't bring a knife to a gunfight."

Prior to the 1970s, police officers had tremendous discretion regarding the use of firearms; police departments often had poorly defined or nonexistent policies regarding this issue. Investigations into police shootings were sometimes conducted in a half-hearted manner, and police agencies did not always keep records of all firearm discharges by officers.[6]

In 1985, the U.S. Supreme Court ruled that shooting any unarmed, nonviolent fleeing felony suspect violated the Fourth Amendment to the Constitution.[7] As a result, almost all major urban police departments enacted restrictive policies regarding the use of deadly force. Supreme Court decisions also made it easier for a private citizen to sue and collect damages as a result of a questionable police shooting.[8]

A study concerning justifiable homicides by the police in 57 cities conducted by the International Association of Chiefs of Police (IACP) was instructive on the use of weapons. Certainly, police administrators need to consider these findings when they develop policy as to who is allowed to carry weapons, the caliber of weapon to be used, the training required before an officer can use weapons, and any rewards given for outstanding marksmanship. The following variables were associated with higher than average justifiable homicide rates: awarding incentives for firearms marksmanship, in-service officer survival training, the issuance of on-duty weapons larger than .38 caliber and shotguns, a high supervisory/officer ratio, the use of semiautomatic handguns by SWAT units, in-service SWAT training, the absence of policy for the management of stakeout and decoy units, and exertion-type pre- and in-service firearms training.[9] What these variables appear to demonstrate is that homicides by police occur with more frequency when organizational and peer support—a hardware milieu—exists for firearms use and training.

✧ Warning Shots, Weapons, and Pursuits: Policy and Procedure

We now consider several specific types of uses of force and whether policy is needed to provide instruction and uniformity in their use.

◊ A department policy on high-speed pursuits definitely should exist. This is a commonly overlooked form of force used by the police, one that many believe will soon be controlled as the result of some future Supreme Court decision. Many people believe that propelling a 5,000-pound vehicle down a public street at 80 miles per hour to attempt to catch someone who may have committed a misdemeanor is overkill and requires regulation. Such pursuits present a tremendous danger to the public and have already caused numerous deaths and injuries and have resulted in lawsuits and settlements.

◊ Most police department policies prohibit firing warning shots in the line of duty because officers can't control where they will end up. In some situations, however, the use of a warning round—into a tree or the dirt—may be necessary to halt a serious brawl or disturbance.

◊ Police policy does not allow officers to attempt to shoot to wound an assailant or other persons they must fire upon. Only Roy Rogers and his peers always managed to wing their adversaries. The police technically do not shoot to kill, however; rather, policy requires them to direct their fire with the expressed purpose of stopping aggressive behavior—normally into an assailant's "center of mass." Only snipers operating at a considerable distance from their targets must actually shoot to kill.

◊ Department policy should absolutely mandate that all officers be qualified to use their off-duty weapons. Furthermore, experts suggest that the same policy should prohibit them from carrying off-duty low-caliber weapons, which are often ineffective and cause more problems than they solve.

◊ Department policy should not allow officers to carry and use lead-filled, hand-held objects for striking people, such as "slappers" and blackjacks. These tools have historically been intended to inflict considerable damage to the head. Finding an "expert" to train officers to certify their abilities is extremely difficult if not impossible.

◊ Department policy should provide for disciplinary action when accidental discharges of police weapons occur. Few truly accidental discharges of weapons happen; most are the result of officer negligence. The problem with such discharges is that no one knows where the bullet is going. When such policies exist and are enforced, they normally reduce the number of occurrences greatly.

To develop policy and procedures for the use of force by police officers, administrators should consider the information presented in Figure 6.1. The high incident (HI) police activities and behaviors indicated in the upper-left quadrant of the figure occur with a considerable degree of frequency and result in a high

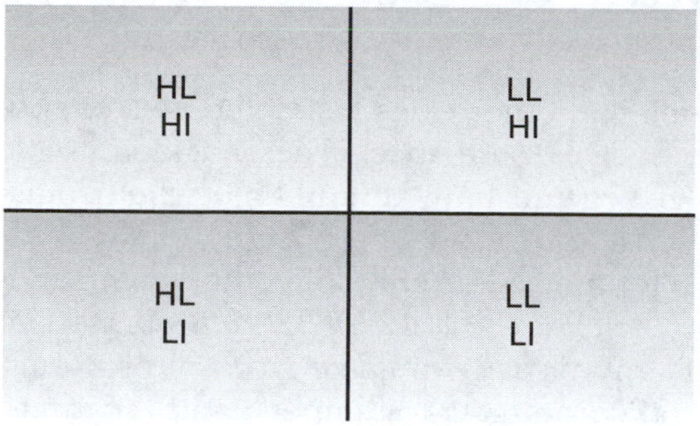

"HL" = high liability
"HI" = high incident of occurrence
"LL" = low liability
"LI" = low incident of occurrence

Figure 6.1
Guidelines for developing use-of-force policies.

liability (HL) factor. The two combined result in the high probability of legal problems for the individual officer, the supervisor, the department, and the employing jurisdiction. Such activities or behaviors include the use of high-speed pursuits, lateral-vascular neck restraint, drug raids, and the execution of felony warrants.[10]

Administrators must be alert to recent court decisions affecting police practices and undertake annual reviews of the policies to update them or develop new ones in response to current rulings.

Police administrators should consider the creation of a red flag warning system to alert them when an officer receives three citizen complaints within a one-year period. This system should cue the administration to review the officer's personnel file closely and possibly to have the officer seek counseling or take other measures to address the problem. Other actions may indicate the need for inquiry and intervention, for example, an officer who makes numerous arrests following routine stops for traffic violations rather than issuing tickets.

✦ MANAGING SPECIAL OPERATIONS: STRATEGIES AND TACTICS

Several unique types of incidents tend to test the mettle of police administrators. Examples of such problems include crowd and riot control, hostage situations, special weapons and tactics teams, and major disasters. These types of occurrences thoroughly challenge administrators' ability to analyze problems and react to them rapidly. In police organizations, leadership qualities are often measured by a person's reaction under duress. In this section we consider briefly these types of situations and some of the important elements of each as they affect the administrators.

✦ CROWD AND RIOT CONTROL

As recent rioting in Los Angeles, Miami, and other cities has demonstrated, police executives must be prepared for such civil disturbances. These incidents serve as constant reminders that the powder keg can blow at any time when something happens to kindle a flame.

Seeing that officers were trained in forming a line and doing the "stomp-and-drag" maneuver, also known in police circles as the *hat and bat routine,* worked well in the 1960s and 1970s and is still appropriate for some types of problems. This formation, however, makes the officers targets for snipers, and they must quickly disperse if fired on. Today's field force plan calls for greater use of small-unit tactics, with a sergeant commanding only five or six officers. Spotters are placed high on building tops to observe citizen activities. The teams take control of and occupy areas of the city as they move. Meanwhile, some officers must be available for other duties because a police agency's calls for service ("I want to see an officer" type of communication) commonly triple during a major disturbance.

When such incidents occur, the first step in mobilizing personnel is to discontinue all nonessential police tasks, such as routine patrolling and response to miscellaneous calls for service. Off-duty and reserve officers should be called to duty quickly. Many jurisdictions have mutual aid agreements and compacts that allow officers from contiguous jurisdictions to respond and assist, and military and federal law enforcement personnel may also be needed. Normally, the decision to involve military personnel is a serious one; our system of government eschews a military state. Thus, requests for the imposition of martial rule must come from the chief executive of the local government or from some other official source, such as a magistrate or sheriff. The governor may make the decision to send military support independently.[11] This course of action is one of last resort; local policing has long been recognized as the primary law enforcement body in the country, and laws have been passed with that concept in mind.

✦ HOSTAGE SITUATIONS

One of the most difficult incidents for police executives to plan and train personnel for is the hostage situation. Of all the problems the police confront, few are as emotionally charged or psychologically complex as incidents in which hostages have been taken. The barricade-and-hostage incident presents a no-win situation in which the media and the public will carefully scrutinize police strategies, procedures, and competence.[12] B. Grant Stitt defined *hostage situation* as "when one or more persons seize another person(s) by force and hold them captive against their will for the purpose of bargaining to have certain demands met by authorities."[13] Hostage takers may be divided into four categories: (1) traditional criminals (those trapped at the scene of a crime or during an escape from a crime scene), (2) terrorists, (3) prisoners, and (4) people who are mentally disturbed.

The police have several available options when facing hostage situations. They can assault or attack without attempting to negotiate; they can neither attack nor assault but attempt to wait out the situation; they can negotiate but make no concessions to demands; they can negotiate and give in to demands; or they can negotiate and lie about giving in to demands.[14]

The job of the specially trained hostage negotiator is to seek the peaceful resolution of a dangerous situation by talking and listening. The negotiator attempts to engage in a dialogue with the hostage taker, barricaded suspect, or person threatening suicide. The purpose of the dialogue is to calm the person, become a sympathetic listener, determine the person's motivation, and negotiate a peaceful solution.[15] The negotiator must obviously be a patient person who can ferret out relevant information about hostages, weapons, and conditions and pass it on to the SWAT team in the event that negotiations fail.

The success rate of skillful hostage negotiators is high. Negotiations often take hours, sometimes days, but eventually most hostage takers and barricaded suspects are convinced to surrender, rewarding the negotiator's patience and skills.

✦ SPECIAL WEAPONS AND TACTICS TEAMS

Since the 1970s, a large number of police departments have developed special weapons and tactics (SWAT) teams to cope with a variety of special problems. According to a report by the Los Angeles Police Department (LAPD), the SWAT concept was initiated there in late 1967[16] in response to the increased incidence of urban violence by snipers, political assassins, and urban guerrillas. Indeed, LAPD's SWAT team was activated almost 200 times from 1967 to 1974.[17]

Special weapons teams are trained to protect police officers from sniper attack while performing crowd control, to provide high ground and perimeter security for visiting dignitaries, to rescue hostages, to use nonviolent techniques to apprehend desperate barricaded suspects, to provide control assault firepower in certain nonriot situations, to rescue officers or citizens endangered by gunfire, and to neutralize guerrilla or terrorist operations directed against government personnel or the general public.

The special weapons team often wears distinctive clothing (black overalls and baseball caps) and is well equipped with automatic rifles, shotguns, flash bang grenades (emitting a loud bong and a bright flash), gas masks and canisters, smoke devices, ropes, pry bars, and walkie talkies. Members of teams often have different position designations, such as leader, scout, marksman or sniper, observer, and rear guard. In large cities, they are accompanied by a mobile command post that carries communications systems, armored vests, steel helmets, ballistic shields, extra ammunition, battering rams, and other provisions including robots equipped with cameras.[18]

Given the tremendous firepower and aggressive behavior of these assault teams, their operations must be supervised with great care. As former police chief and author Anthony Bouza said, "Operations that use dynamite, 'thunderflash stun grenades,' and aggressive SWAT teams can experience spectacular failures. There are the thumpers and Rambos who must be controlled, especially in such popular operations as drug raids, where they like to think they've been granted *carte blanche*." [19]

✧ MAJOR DISASTERS

Almost every citizen of the United States, regardless of the geographical area of his or her residence, lives under threat of some act of nature: a tornado, flood, earthquake, hurricane, or a fire of enormous proportions. In addition, disasters such as plane/train crashes, chemical spills, power plant explosions, structural collapses, major auto accidents, and terrorist attacks result from human action. Many police officers may never encounter such disasters personally during their career, but all must be prepared for whatever befalls their jurisdiction. Because such events occur so infrequently, police may be unprepared when they do take place.

The administrator is responsible for ensuring that an adequate disaster plan is developed and kept current. Many jurisdictions stage mock disasters to give their personnel experience in coping with them; these mock exercises also teach them to establish a command post and communications networks, use first aid techniques, and coordinate interagency logistics and mobilization.

✦ ACCREDITATION OF POLICE AGENCIES

Police executives have long been criticized for resisting outside examination and generally being reluctant to change. In this section we see, however, that this is not necessarily the case. We now review police accreditation, a movement that has begun sweeping the country.

The Commission on Accreditation for Law Enforcement Agencies (CALEA), a private, nonprofit organization located in Fairfax, Virginia, was formed in 1979. Today its policy manual contains 436 standards organized into 40 chapters or topic areas. Each standard has three parts: the standard statement, the commentary, and the levels of compliance (see Table 6.1, pp. 140–141, which presents examples of CALEA standards on the use of force). The levels of compliance denote the relative importance assigned to each standard based on agency size: A (1–24 personnel), B (25–74), C (75–299), and D (300 or more). For each of these four agency size categories, the levels of compliance indicate whether a given standard is mandatory (M), other-than-mandatory (O), or not applicable (N/A). [20]

Today more than 600 police agencies in the United States are CALEA accredited; 18 percent of the full-time police officers in the nation are involved in the CALEA program, as are 10 percent of all cities with populations of 10,000 or more; 90 percent of all accredited agencies seek reaccreditation. [21]

For two reasons, many police agencies have felt impelled to devote personnel and financial resources to seek accreditation during the last decade. First, most accrediting organizations provide standards concerning topics and issues that must be covered by written policies and procedures. Therefore, successful accreditation provides a "liability shield" against litigation.[22] Second, the process provides a nationwide system for change.[23]

One of the most important parts of the accreditation process is self-assessment. Each agency undergoes a critical self-evaluation and is later assessed by an on-site team of law enforcement professionals to determine whether it has complied with the applicable standards for a department of its size.[24] The accreditation process is voluntary for all agencies (although in this era of increased police accountability, many believe that the public will soon demand their local agencies to be accredited or will want to know why they are *not* accredited).

✦ TECHNOLOGICAL DEVELOPMENT: THE VIDEOTAPE

Videotape technology, especially the use of camcorders, has had a major impact on policing and its administration, particularly since the Rodney King incident; "video vigilantes" now abound.[25] The increased use of camcorders by the general public and the benefits of their utilization as tools for police activities have not gone unnoticed by police administrators, many of whom now equip their agency's patrol vehicles with videocameras. Police videos have been particularly useful in recording drunk-driving arrests and crime-scene and traffic accident investigations. Videocameras also are used to record eyewitness testimony and in-progress events, such as robberies and building checks. With little investment in money or personnel, in-house tapes can be made for police roll-call training and for public relations.[26] Many agencies videotape all of their press conferences.

A recent study found that one-third of all police and sheriff's departments serving populations of 50,000 or more in the United States are videotaping at least some interrogations.[27] The likelihood of videotaping interrogations increases as the severity of the felony increases. Thus, agencies are more likely to videotape interrogations in homicide, rape, and armed robbery cases. These cases are videotaped to avoid defense attorneys' challenges of the accuracy of audiotapes and to jog detectives' memories when testifying.[28]

Clearly, the use of videotaping in the United States has changed policing. This high-tech procedure has raised some troubling issues, however. Administrators must decide, for example, whether everything that occurs anywhere and anytime is fair game for someone with a camcorder. At this time, the police and other Americans have no legal protection against being pursued by videotape vigilantes. In general, anything that occurs in public or can be seen from a public place can be videotaped. Oddly, the use of a person's voice has greater protection than the use of his or her videotaped actions; federal law requires a warrant for secret wiretaps but is silent on videotaping. What appears to be occurring on tape may not be what is actually happening at all

TABLE 6.1   EXAMPLE OF A CALEA STANDARD ON THE USE OF FORCE

1.3 Use of Force

1.3.1 A written directive states personnel will use only the force necessary to accomplish lawful objectives.

Commentary: None (M M M M)

1.3.2 A written directive states that an officer may use deadly force only when the officer reasonably believes that the action is in defense of human life, including the officer's own life, or in defense of any person in immediate danger of serious physical injury. Definitions of reasonable belief, serious physical injury, or similarly used terms that are used to qualify the directive, shall be included.

Commentary: The intent of this standard is to establish a clear-cut policy on the use of deadly force that is consistent with applicable law, and which provides officers with guidance in the use of force in life-and-death situations and to prevent unnecessary loss of life. (M M M M)

1.3.3 A written directive governs the use of "warning" shots.

Commentary: None (M M M M)

1.3.4. A written directive governs the use of authorized less-than-lethal weapons by agency personnel.

Commentary: None (M M M M)

1.3.5 A written directive specifies procedures for rendering appropriate medical aid after use of lethal and less-than-lethal weapons.

Commentary: None (M M M M)

1.3.6 A written report is submitted whenever an employee:

a. discharges a firearm for other than training/recreational purposes.

b. takes an action that results in, or is alleged to have resulted in, injury or death of another person.

c. applies force through the use of lethal or less-than-lethal weapons.

d. or applies physical force as defined by the agency.

Commentary: An agency should carefully examine all incidents wherein its employees have caused or are alleged to have caused death or injury to another. (M M M M)

1.3.9 A written directive requires that only weapons and ammunition meeting agency-authorized specifications be used by agency personnel in law enforcement responsibilities, both on or off duty.

Commentary: The intent of this standard is to establish strict agency control over all firearms, weapons, and ammunition. (M M M M)

1.3.10 A written directive requires that only employees demonstrating proficiency in the use of agency-authorized weapons be approved to carry such weapons.

Commentary: The intent of this standard is to cover the carrying and use, both on and off duty, of all weapons, such as handguns, shotguns, chemical sprays, or striking weapons.

TABLE 6.1 *(continued)*

1.3.11 At least annually each employee is required to receive in-service training on the agency's use of force policies and demonstrate proficiency with any approved weapon that the employee is authorized to use.

Commentary: None (M M M M)

(*Source:* Manual of CALEA Standards, Commission on Accreditation for Law Enforcement Agencies, used with permission. Some nonessential parts of some standards have been edited for brevity. *Courtesy* CALEA.)

(e.g., money innocently changing hands may appear to be a bribery transaction).

The law is lagging behind the technology with respect to the use of videotaping.[29] To protect their officers, police administrators may need to consider policy issues related to videotaping. They may want to lobby legislators to pass laws regulating the use of videotapes.

✦ EVALUATING PATROL OFFICER PERFORMANCE

Under the professional model of policing that prevailed in the first half of the 20th century, emphasis was placed on quantifiable activities such as the numbers of arrests, traffic citations, citizen contacts, buildings inspected, and miles driven per shift. However, several new trends have gradually evolved for evaluating police performance. The assessment of police personnel has become more concerned with specific performance requirements other than attitudinal and appearance measurements. Another trend in evaluation is a movement away from listing evaluative criteria to identifying and evaluating performance based on goals and objectives. Goals are usually broad, general statements of purpose that identify an organization's mission, such as to prevent or reduce or control crime. Objectives are quantifiable, measurable, and time-bound, if possible. For example, the patrol division might have the objective of reducing the number of traffic accidents in a certain sector of the city or county by 10 percent in a six-month period. With this system, officers are rated by category, either a general one or in comparison with other officers. For example, in terms of driving skills, an officer could be rated as "excellent," "good," "average," or "below average."[30]

But it should be noted that because of the varying nature of the work done by police officers, depending on such variables as the use of COPPS, the duty shift and location worked, and a variety of other factors, any attempt to evaluate the performance of officers, especially using a quantitative instrument, is difficult. Should the officers, as tradition holds, be judged on number of felons arrested or traffic citations issued? If so, those officers engaged in problem solving and those working the graveyard shift would suffer; if finding open doors and windows of businesses is a criterion, the day shift is at a disadvantage. What criteria, if any, should administrators use to fairly assess the productivity of police officers? Should there be a quota system at all?

One way to develop and retain information on the productivity of individual officers in a traditional agency is through a standardized reporting system. Figure 6.2 is an example of an officer's daily report as used by the Englewood, Colorado, police department. This form, which can be modified for use with the COPPS philosophy, contains a compilation of the officer's activity for the day; it also contains a weighting system (see the three columns at the right side of the figure) whereby each category of activity is given a certain number of points (e.g., DUI arrests are given 5 points). The Englewood police manager examines an officer's total points. The Kentucky State Police use a similar scheme, but it is based on the average time it takes an officer to accomplish a given task; the manager there examines the percentage of an officer's time working in relation to patrol time.

Other criteria used for evaluating officer performance include their orientation (such as use of common sense), knowledge (of agency policies and procedures, laws, and so on), performance (in such areas as driving skills, use of the radio, report writing, managing calls for service), and relationships (with citizens and other police personnel).[31]

Many police administrators see several distinct advantages to these types of productivity monitoring systems. First, they cause officers and supervisors to focus on the complete range of police activities and responsibilities as opposed to one or two categories of police work. By having all types of activities on the form, it serves as a reminder of the range of police responsibilities. Second, it allows managers to exert a degree of control over officers through the examination of periodic summaries.[32]

As noted earlier, an agency that has adopted COPPS must utilize a different set of officer performance standards. COPPS initiatives greatly change the officers' activities during the workday (such as leaving their vehicles for greater periods of time to talk to citizens, performing surveys, and so on), and far less emphasis is placed on quantitative outcomes (such as miles driven per shift, numbers of arrests made). Because officers are given far greater latitude to solve neighborhood problems, it is necessary that different criteria be employed for evaluating officers' efforts, such as the following:

◊ How has the department identified the need for COPPS? Some motivations for its implementation include crime level, resources, police–community relationship, and public concerns.

◊ What goals and objectives has the department set in this initiative? The goal that is most often found among COPPS agencies relates to the need to get the community more involved in decision making about police action.

◊ What structure has been put in place to implement COPPS? Some organizations have established a community policing unit, while others adopt the much preferred method of adopting this concept agencywide.

DAILY FIELD ACTIVITY REPORT

Englewood, Colorado, Police Department

1. OFFICER'S NAME, RADIO NUMBER	2. DATE	3. DAY	4. VEHICLE	5. TTL HRS	6. REMARKS
KING R.R. 202	11.14.78	TUE	6876	11	NO SPARE TIRE — VEHICLE NOT SERVICED

	7. TIME REC.	8. TIME CLEAR	9. MIN USED	10. SRC	11. LOCATION	12. TYPE OF ACTIVITY	NAME	OR SUMMONS
A		1700	15		GCPD	ROLL CALL / VEHICLE INSPECTION		
B	1710	1750	40	DIS	411 S. BANNOCK	PRIOR BURGLARY OFFENSE REPORT	JONES	OR 791 316472
C	1803	1812	09	OFF	TABOR AND CHEROKEE	TRAFFIC STOP / COLO LIC # PP6171 IMPROPER TURN SUMMONS	KESSLER	TS T1001
D	1825	1840	15		LAMPLIGHTER	CODE 7 COFFEE		
E	1908	1920	12	OFF	3500 S. DELAWARE	SUSPICIOUS SUBJECT F.I. CARD	BARNES	I F.I.
F	1935	2010	45	DIS	701 W. KANSAS KING SOOPERS	ADULT SHOPLIFTER O.R. PENAL SUMMONS MISDM ARREST	WALLACE	22631 79-31650
G	2025	2137	70	F	GCPD JAIL	BOOKING PRISONER	WALLACE	
H	2230	2245	15	DIS	ST. CATHERINES HOSPITAL E.R.	DISTURBANCE ASSIST UNIT 201		
I	2250	0010	80	DIS	4219 S. 4TH	DISTURBANCE – MENTAL CASE STOOD BY FOR AREA MENTAL HEALTH WORKER – INCIDENT RPT	SHERWOOD	I.R. 79-31680
J	0015	0025	10	I	MENTAL HEALTH CENTER	TRANSPORT SUBJECT TO MENTAL HEALTH CENTER	SHERWOOD	I.R. 79-31681B
K	0105	0115	10	SPV	STEVENS PARK	MEET SGT. JONES / CK REPORTS 2 - O.R.1-I.R. I - P.S.1-T.S. I-F.I.I-M.A.	JONES _Jones_	ASSIST 791
L	0120	0200	40	DIS	MAIN AND PINE	PROPERTY DAMAGE ACCIDENT (SPU ASSISTED) DUI ARREST – ACCIDENT REPORT-SUMMONS	WELLS	572632 79-31695
M	0200	0205	5	L	TO G.C.P.D.	TRANSPORT PRISONER	WELLS	
N	0205	0400	175	L	G.C.P.D.- JAIL	BOOKING AND PROCESSING PRISONER	WELLS	
O		0400				END OF WATCH		
P								

	SOP	WT	TTL
13. OFFENSE RPT	2	5	10
14. INCIDENT RPT	1	3	3
15. H&R ACCIDENT RPT	0	5	5
16. P.P. ACCIDENT RPT	0	3	3
17. ACCIDENT RPT	1	4	4
18. ACCIDENT SUMMONS	0	4	4
19. RADAR SUMMONS	0	3	3
20. TRAFFIC SUMMONS	1	4	4
21. PENAL SUMMONS	1	3	3
22. PARKING SUMMONS	0	1	1
23. WARNING SUMMONS	0	1	1
24. WARRANT ARREST	0	5	5
25. FELONY ARREST	0	20	20
26. MISDMR ARREST	1	4	4
27. PETTY ARREST	0	3	3
28. D.U.I. ARREST	1	5	5
29. DETOX	0	4	4
30. MISC. DETENTION	0	4	4
31. F.I.	1	2	2
32. DEF VEHICLE	0	2	2
33. TOTAL			35
34. ASSIGNED CALLS	4	1	4
35. ASSIGNED ASSISTS	1	1	1
36. OFF. INITIATED	2	3	6
SPV. NAME	_Sgt. Jones_		

R.R. King

Figure 6.2

◊ What form(s) of evaluation is (are) being used to determine whether the goals and objectives are being met? Some evaluation methods are residential and business surveys, crime rate monitoring, and field experiments.[33]

✦ ISSUES RELATED TO POLICE TRAINING

Given public concern about police use of force, the dramatic increase in liability lawsuits, the expanded use of the COPPS system, the popularity of videotaping police activities, and other developments, police training has come under the spotlight. In this section we examine how police administrators may be deemed negligent for failure to train their officers adequately to provide on-going training.

✧ LIABILITY AND NEGLIGENCE

The serious implications that the training function has for police is perhaps best demonstrated by a very unfortunate incident in Colorado, which points out how administrators can be found negligent in the supervision and training of personnel. While holding a shotgun in one hand and attempting to handcuff a prisoner with the other, a police officer accidentally killed the person when the shotgun he was pointing at the prisoner's head discharged. At trial, the officer stated that he had seen the technique demonstrated in a police training film. The training officer, however, testified that the film was intended to show how *not* to handcuff a prisoner; unfortunately, no member of the training staff made that important distinction to the training class. In *Sager v. City of Woodlawn Park*,[34] the court ruled that improper training had resulted in the prisoner's death.

Another case involving training negligence is *Popow v. City of Margate*.[35] In this situation, an innocent bystander was killed on his front porch at nighttime by a police officer in foot pursuit. The court held the city negligent because the officer had had no training on night firing, shooting at moving targets, or use of firearms in a residential area. In *Beverly v. Morris*,[36] a police chief was held liable for improper training and supervision of his officers following the blackjack beating of a citizen by a subordinate officer.

These cases are but a few of the body of legal precedent related to inadequate police training that now exists. The need for police agencies to provide adequate training for its officers to safeguard both the officers and the public is evident. The cost of negligence in training can be quite high in both human and financial terms.

✧ ONGOING TRAINING

Once police officers leave the basic training academy, it is critical for administrators to see that these neophytes continue to receive adequate annual, in-service training throughout their careers. This training can be accomplished in several ways. News items, court decisions, and other relevant information can be discussed daily at roll call prior to the beginning of each shift. Short in-service courses are available for officers, ranging from a few hours' to several weeks' duration, in such areas as the history of policing, evolution of COPPS, problem-solving techniques, community engagement, and the management and supervision of COPPS initiatives. Computer-assisted training modules, videotapes, and even laser disc training formats are now available.

✦ STRESS AND BURNOUT IN POLICE ORGANIZATIONS

Much has been written about the causes and management of stress in individuals employed in the criminal justice system, particularly in policing.[37] The ways that administrators can assist stressed individuals by understanding and recognizing the symptoms of stress and then helping them to deal with this ominous problem has received far less attention.

Police officers have comparatively high levels of stress and burnout; for these individuals, many of whom often deal with people who are at their worst, no retreat or "fight/flight" choice is available. Police are on the firing line, so to speak, and they need to understand the causes of stress, paying particular heed to the emotional and physical signals they experience and what they can do to manage stress.

Stress and burnout are often related to problems *within* the organization. Therefore, the administrator's management style can have a direct impact on the stress problem. For example, it is well known that the lack of opportunity to participate in the decision-making processes that affect one's job is a major source of stress and eventual burnout.[38]

✧ IMPLICATIONS FOR ADMINISTRATORS AND SUPERVISORS

Much of the stress that patrol officers suffer results from the fact that doing a good job on the street does not necessarily bring departmental rewards and praise. The street officer finds that his or her performance evaluation is often based on a search for failure to follow department rules or negative reports from citizens. Thus, officers may believe that they are being penalized for mistakes but not rewarded for being effective law enforcers and providing service to the community.[39]

Advanced training for administrators and first-line supervisors on how to supervise, which included understanding how employees are motivated, provided positive reinforcement for good behavior, and described the causes and prevention of stress, would be a major contribution to improving the morale of the officers. Furthermore, administrators and supervisors should also strive to act as educators and advisors to the officers who work under them, especially in ways of relating to the public. Finally, the most important role of the supervisor could be that of a role model. Modeling appropriate behaviors is one of the most effective ways of teaching behaviors. Rookie officers are likely to treat people in the manner that they see their supervisors treating them.[40]

Administrators and supervisors must also recognize that the number of situations officers deal with—especially those that place them in contact with death and brutality—will likely result in all officers at one time or another having very strong emotional reactions that interfere with their performance. Besides acute symptoms that arise from traumatic events, such as shootings and disasters, day-to-day stresses build up and result in adverse consequences such as divorce, substance abuse, and even suicide. These are all symptoms of stress that push the officers beyond their zone of stability.[41]

If a professional such as a psychiatrist, psychologist, or counselor is made available, officers may well resist discussing their personal problems, for a number of reasons: they have an image of strength to protect, and admitting to problems they cannot handle might hurt this image; and outsiders do not understand what it is like to be a police officer and cannot be of much help. Therefore, much remains to be done in providing counseling services for police officers. An alternative choice is to provide peer counseling.[42]

Police psychologists recommend that systematic programs to combat stress should minimally (1) develop a behavioral profile of each officer to indicate different reactions or patterns—"red flags"; (2) train supervisors to recognize early warning signs (e.g., withdrawal, accidents, drinking, depression) and to know when to intervene; (3) provide a flexible counseling program for groups as well as for families and individuals (utilizing the peer counseling method); (4) train employees to use biofeedback, relaxation, and other methods of handling stress; and (5) encourage the police organization to reduce department-induced stress, for example, by changing to the use of objective performance criteria and decreasing busywork.[43]

Summary

This chapter opened with a discussion of the COPPS strategy, which seeks to proactively improve the quality of life in communities.

The chapter also explored the issues of the use of force by the police, the effect of videotaping on policing, accreditation, adequate training, and the debilitating effects of stress.

Questions for Review

1. What types of issues involving the use of force should be addressed in policy? What are some essential considerations for each policy?

2. What are some of the major ramifications of the currently available technology on policing? What might police administrators do to address these issues?

3. Why are police accreditation and training important and worth the time and money invested?

4. What are sound methods for evaluating police productivity?

5. Why is the issue of police training particularly important at present? Give examples of problems and consequences if training is inadequate.

6. What can police administrators do to recognize and treat officer stress?

Notes

1. U.S. Department of Justice, Bureau of Justice Assistance, *Comprehensive Gang Initiative: Operations Manual for Implementing Local Gang Prevention and Control Programs* (draft version) (Washington, D.C.: U.S. Government Printing Office), pp. 4-10–4-14.

2. U.S. Department of Justice, Bureau of Justice Assistance, *Problem-Oriented Drug Enforcement: A Community-Based Approach for Effective Policing* (Washington, D.C.: Author, 1995), pp. 45–47.

3. Independent Commission on the Los Angeles Police Department, *Report of the Independent Commission on the Los Angeles Police Department* (Los Angeles: Author, 1991), p. i.

4. William A. Westley, *Violence and the Police: A Sociological Study of Law, Custom, and Morality* (Cambridge, Mass.: MIT Press, 1970).

5. Gordon Witkin, Ted Gest, and Dorian Friedman, "Cops under Fire," *U.S. News and World Report* (December 3, 1990): 32–44.

6. Mark Blumberg, "Controlling Police Use of Deadly Force: Assessing Two Decades of Progress," in Roger G. Dunham and Geoffrey P. Alpert (eds.), *Critical Issues in Policing: Contemporary Readings* (Prospect Heights, Ill.: Waveland Press, 1989), pp. 442–464.

7. In *Tennessee v. Garner,* 471 U.S. 1, 105 S.Ct. 1694, 85 L.Ed.2d 1 (1985).

8. *Monell v. Department of Social Services,* 436 U.S. 658, 98 S.Ct. 2018 (1978).

9. International Association of Chiefs of Police, *A Balance of Forces: A Study of Justifiable Homicide by the Police* (Gaithersburg, Md.: Author, 1981).

10. John Sullivan, personal communication, May 20, 1993.

11. Thomas F. Adams, *Police Field Operations* (Englewood Cliffs, N.J.: Prentice Hall, 1985), pp. 310–311.

12. B. Grant Stitt, "Ethical and Practical Aspects of Police Response to Hostage Situations," in Roslyn Muraskin (ed.), *Issues in Justice: Exploring Policy Issues in the Criminal Justice System* (Bristol, Ind.: Wyndham Hall Press, 1990), pp. 20–45.

13. *Ibid.,* p. 21.

14. Joseph Betz, "Moral Considerations Concerning the Police Response to Hostage Takers," in Frederick Elliston and Norman Bowie (eds.), *Ethics, Public Policy and Criminal Justice* (Cambridge, Mass.: Oelgeschlager, Gunn & Hain, 1982), pp. 110–132.

15. Robert Sheehan and Gary W. Cordner, *Introduction to Police Administration* (2d ed.) (Cincinnati, Ohio: Anderson, 1989), p. 387.

16. Los Angeles Police Department, *Special Weapons and Tactics,* p. 101.

17. Center for Research on Criminal Justice, *The Iron Fist and the Velvet Glove: An Analysis of the U.S. Police* (Berkeley, Calif.: Author, 1975), p. 49.

18. *Ibid.,* pp,. 48–49.

19. Anthony V. Bouza, *The Police Mystique* (New York: Plenum Press, 1990), p. 277.

20. Commission on Accreditation for Law Enforcement Agencies, Inc., *Standards for Law Enforcement Agencies: The Standards Manual of the Law Enforcement Agency Accreditation Program* (3d ed.) (Fairfax, Va.: Author, 1994), pp. xiii–xv.

21. Commission on Accreditation for Law Enforcement Agencies, "CALEA Facts," p. 1.

22. Gary W. Cordner, "Written Rules and Regulations: Are They Necessary?" *FBI Law Enforcement Bulletin* 58 (1988): 18.

23. Russell Maas, "Written Rules and Regulations: Are They Necessary?" *Law and Order* (May 1990): 36.

24. Charles R. Swanson, Leonard Territo, and Robert W. Taylor, *Police Administration* (3d ed.) (New York: Macmillan, 1993), p. 51.

25. Melinda Beck, "Video Vigilantes," *Newsweek* (July 22, 1991): 42–47.

26. *Ibid.*

27. U.S. Department of Justice, National Institute of Justice Research in Brief, *Videotaping Interrogations and Confessions* (Washington, D.C.: Author, March 1993), p. 2.

28. *Ibid.,* p. 3.

29. Beck, "Video Vigilantes," p. 45.

30. Roy R. Roberg and Jack Kuykendall, *Police Organization and Management: Behavior, Theory, and Processes* (Pacific Grove, Calif.: Brooks/Cole, 1990), pp. 256–257.

31. Larry K. Gaines, Mittie D. Southerland, and John E. Angell, *Police Administration* (New York: McGraw-Hill, 1991), p. 285.

32. *Ibid.,* p. 423.

33. Kenneth J. Peak and Ronald W. Glensor, *Community Policing and Problem Solving: Strategies and Practices* (Upper Saddle River, N.J.: Prentice Hall, 1996), p. 293.

34. 543 F.Supp. 282 (D.Colo., 1982).

35. 476 F.Supp. 1237 (1979).

36. 470 F.2d 1356 (5th Cir. 1972).

37. See Kenneth J. Peak, *Policing America: Methods, Issues, Challenges* (Englewood Cliffs, N.J.: Regents/Prentice Hall, 1993), Chapter 11; W. Clinton Terry III, *Policing Society: An Occupational View* (New York: Wiley, 1985), Part 7; Roger G. Dunham and Geoffrey P. Alpert, *Critical Issues in Policing: Contemporary Readings,* Section VIII; Harry W. More Jr., *Critical Issues in Law Enforcement* (Cincinnati, Ohio: Anderson, 1985), Chapter 8.

38. Paul W. Brown, "Probation Officer Burnout: An Organizational Disease/An Organizational Cure," *Federal Probation* 50 (1986): 4–7; Cary Cherniss, *Professional Burnout in Human Services Organizations* (New York: Praeger, 1980).

39. Wayne Anderson, David Swenson, and Daniel Clay, *Stress Management for Law Enforcement Officers* (Englewood Cliffs, N.J.: Prentice Hall, 1995), p. 283.

40. *Ibid.,* pp. 283–284.

41. *Ibid.,* p. 289.

42. *Ibid.*

43. Ben Daviss, "Burnout," *Police Magazine* (May 1982): 58.

CASE STUDIES

Intruding Ima and the Falsified Report

An eight-year employee of your police agency, Officer Ima Goodenough, is a patrol officer who often serves as field training officer. Goodenough is generally capable and experienced in both the patrol and detective divisions. She takes pride in being of the "old school" and has developed a clique of approximately 10 people whom she gets along with while mostly shunning other officers.

As an officer of the old school, she typically handles calls for service without requesting cover units or backup. She has had six complaints of brutality lodged against her during the past three years. For Ima and her peers, officers who call for backup are "wimps." She has recently been involved in two high-speed pursuits where her vehicle was damaged when she attempted to run the offender off the road.

Ima will notify a supervisor only when dealing with a major situation. She is borderline insubordinate when dealing with new supervisors. She believes that, generally speaking, the administration exists only to "screw around with us"— the field officers. You, her shift commander, have been fed up with her deteriorating attitude and lackadaisical performance for some time and have been wondering if you will soon have occasion to take some form of disciplinary action against her.

You have also learned that Ima has a reputation among her supervisors as being a "hot dog." Some of her past and present supervisors have even commented that she is a "walking time bomb" that is unpredictable and could "blow" at any time.

One day while bored on patrol, Ima decides to go outside her jurisdiction, responding to a shooting call that is just across the city limit and in the county. She radios the dispatcher that she is out "assisting" and then walks into the home where paramedics are frantically working on a man with a head wound lying on the floor. Nearby on the floor is a large, foreign-made revolver; Ima holds and waves the revolver in the air, examining it. A paramedic yells at her, "Hey! Put that down, this may be an attempted homicide case!" Ima puts the revolver back on the floor. Meanwhile, you have been attempting to contact Ima via radio to get her back into her jurisdiction. Later, when the sheriff's office complains to you about her actions at its crime scene, you require her to write a report of her actions. She completes a report describing her observations at the scene but denies touching or picking up anything.

Looking at Ima's personnel file, you determine that her performance evaluations for the past eight years are "standard"—average to above average. She has never received a suspension from duty for her actions. While verbally expressing their unhappiness with her for many years, it appears that Ima's supervisors have not expressed that disdain in writing.

Questions for Discussion

1. What are the primary issues involved in this situation?
2. Do you believe that there are sufficient grounds for bringing disciplinary action against Goodenough? If so, what would be the specific charges? What is the appropriate punishment?
3. Do you believe that this is a good opportunity for termination? Do grounds exist?
4. Does the fact that her supervisors have rated her as standard have any bearing on this matter or create difficulties in bringing a case for termination?

"Racin' Ray," the Graveyard-Shift Gadabout*

Members of the Hooterville County sheriff's department have been involved in several vehicle pursuits within the past year. One such incident resulted in the death of a 14-year-old juvenile who crashed during a pursuit in which he was joyriding in his parents' vehicle. This tragedy sparked a massive public outcry and criticism of the police department for using excessive force. A lawsuit against the department and individual officers involved in the pursuit is pending.

The sheriff immediately changed the department's policy regarding pursuits. The policy now requires a supervisor to cancel any pursuit that does not involve a violent felony crime or other circumstances that would justify the danger and potential liability. All officers have been trained in the new policy. A separate policy prohibits the firing of warning shots unless "circumstances warrant."

Last night at 1 A.M., Deputy Raymond "Racin' Ray" Roadhog was patrolling in an industrial park in his sector. Deputy Roadhog, recently graduated from the state police academy and field training, engages in pursuits at every opportunity; also, unbeknown to the sheriff and other supervisors, he occasionally takes along his personal German Shepherd dog to help with building checks and has an M-16 automatic rifle in his trunk. He was providing extra patrol because of

---

*Contributed by Deputy Chief Ronald W. Glensor, Reno, Nevada, Police Department.

reports of vandalism and theft of building materials in that area of the county. Generally, after 6 P.M., no one should have any reason to be in any industrial area. A parked vehicle attracts his attention because private vehicles are not normally parked in the area at this time.

As Roadhog approaches the vehicle with his cruiser's lights off and spotlight on, he notices that the brake lights on the vehicle flash on and off. Immediately getting out of his vehicle for a better view, Roadhog calls dispatch for backup assistance in the event that there is a burglary or theft in progress.

At this point, the vehicle takes off at a high rate of speed in Roadhog's direction. Roadhog, being out of his vehicle and seeing that the vehicle is coming at him from about 30 yards, fires a warning shot into the ground. When about 15 yards away, the vehicle veers away from him and then leaves at a high rate of speed. As the escaping vehicle crosses the path of his spotlight, Roadhog sees that there are two young people inside, a male driving and a female in the passenger's seat. Roadhog yells for the driver to halt and then lets loose another warning shot, this time into a nearby fire hydrant. He then takes off in pursuit of the vehicle.

The officer radios to the dispatcher to inform her of his observations and of his present pursuit. You, the shift commander—a patrol lieutenant—hear this radio transmission.

Questions for Discussion

1. What are the central issues involved?
2. Is the deputy in compliance with the use of force policy?
3. Are you going to "shut down" Roadhog's pursuit? Explain.
4. Should the deputy have fired warning shots?
5. Assuming that all of the preceding information comes to light, will the sheriff be likely to begin disciplinary action against Roadhog?
6. Do the policies appear to be sound as written? Are additional policies needed?

Dismal City P.D.'s Command to "Do More With Less"*

Dismal City, USA, is a rapidly growing community of 50,000 residents located in the southern part of the state along the ocean. The city population increases by 10,000 to 20,000 visitors a day during the summer months when ocean recreation is a popular activity.

---

*Contributed by Deputy Chief Ronald W. Glensor, Ph.D., Reno, Nevada, Police Department.

The city's demographics are changing rapidly. Its Hispanic and Asian populations are growing at a tremendous rate. Most of these new residents work outside the city, however. The downtown area has slowly degenerated over the past few years, resulting in increased crime and disorder.

A property tax cap has resulted in reduced revenues to local jurisdictions, and the recent recession has also taken a substantial toll on the city's budget. The result has been significant reductions in staffing. The city's two attempts to have voters approve bond issues for increased taxes and police officers have failed. The police department has experienced its share of budget cuts and reduced staffing levels. The chief recently retired due to continued problems with the city council, the budget, and low morale in the agency. As a result of these matters, relations between the community and the department have been tense at best.

The police department has experienced a continued reduction in staffing over the past five years. It is not expected to continue, but increases are also not expected. The morale of the department is at its worst and is fueled by the increase in workload and what has been perceived as an uncaring chief. The increase in violent crime only aggravates the problems because officers believe that their safety is in jeopardy as a result of the lower staffing levels. Furthermore, the increase in Hispanic and Asian residents creates an additional burden because the department consists largely of white male officers. The department has no bilingual officers.

You have been hired as the new chief and will begin work in two weeks. The city manager and council have asked for a meeting with you to discuss the future of the department. At this meeting they explain the situation to you and request a staff report within one month of your reporting to work. The manager and several council persons recently attended a conference that presented several workshops on the implementation of community policing. They are convinced that this trend, now apparently sweeping the nation, would result in a more efficient police department.

The manager and governing board enthusiastically seek your views on community policing, its potential for Dismal City, and how you might approach its implementation. They inform you that the police officers' union has heard rumors of this idea and has made it clear that it probably would not want anything to do with changing the organization at a time when resources are strained.

Questions for Discussion

1. In your report, how will you respond concerning whether or not community policing is the panacea for the city's financial and demographic woes? Will it help the department?
2. Do you envision any problems with "traditional thinking" supervisors and community policing? If so, how will you handle their concerns?
3. What would you do to mend the poor relations between labor and management?

4. Would the community need to be involved in the program's design and implementation? If so, how?
5. How might community policing provide more effective delivery of services?
6. Would you anticipate that the officers' workload would be reduced or increased under this program?
7. What types of information would you use to evaluate the progress of your program for city hall?

Part III

THE COURTS

This part consists of three chapters, all of which focus on the courts. In Chapter 7 we examine court organization and operation, in Chapter 8 we focus on personnel roles and functions, and in Chapter 9 we discuss court issues and practices. Specific chapter content is described in the introductory section of each chapter. Case studies in court administration appear at the end of Chapter 9.

Court Organization and Operation

The place of justice is a hallowed place.

—Francis Bacon

Courts and camps are the only places to learn the world in.

—Earl of Chesterfield

✦ INTRODUCTION

Courts have existed in some form for thousands of years. Indeed, the ancient trial court of Israel, and the most common tribunal throughout its biblical history, was the "court at the gate," where elders of each clan determined controversies within the kin group. Then, in the fourth century B.C., courts in Athens, Greece, dealt with all premeditated homicides and heard constitutional cases. Since then, the court system has survived the dark eras of the Spanish Inquisition and the Star Chamber (which, in England during the 1500s and 1600s, without a jury enforced unpopular political policies and meted out severe punishment, including whipping, branding, and mutilation). The U.S. court system developed rapidly after the Revolution and attended to the establishment of law and justice on the western frontier.

Federal, state, and local courts in the United States employ about 373,000 judicial and legal personnel; the annual payroll for these workers is about $12 billion. The largest percentage of payroll expenditures is made at the local level (30.4 percent is at the state level and 13.6 percent is at the federal).[1]

We will examine the courts from several perspectives. First we address the question of whether courts are organizations in the usual sense of the term with a bureaucratic structure and function. Then we examine typical courtroom decor and decorum. Next we discuss whether the adversary system and other procedural mechanisms of our courts create serious impediments to finding the truth. Then we consider the courts in general as policymaking bodies. We next ponder the effects of today's litigious society, which foists on the courts a veritable avalanche of suits, petitions, writs, briefs, and motions.

We examine a relatively new and promising concept, alternative dispute resolution, that has developed to counter the escalating court dockets. Finally, we look at the citizen or "consumer" relationship with our court system and then consider court administration and reform, which serve as a bridge to the following chapter.

✦ COURTS AS ORGANIZATIONS

✧ A NONBUREAUCRATIC WORK GROUP

In the view of Edward Clynch and David Neubauer, many academics have erroneously characterized courts as bureaucracies.[2] Bureaucracies have differentiated and separate divisions tied together by a distinctive authoritarian structure, or hierarchy. They also have well-defined organizational rules governing the disposition of particular tasks, including individually defined, specialized ones.[3] These characteristics do not apply to courts.

Here we examine how courts are very different from the typical organization and how court administration is made more complex because of this uniquely informal structure and organization. Indeed, courts are relatively autonomous single work units that do not function in a bureaucratic manner. A court is an entity that does not report to a single authority figure in a chain of command. It often ignores formal rules in favor of shared decision making among judges, prosecutors, and defense attorneys.[4] Rather than being bureaucracies, trial courts are informal work groups in which interaction among members occurs on a continuing basis. Court participants have discretion in carrying out their tasks; they are mutually interdependent but have the independent ability to modify formal rules and procedures so that people can complete their assignments successfully. A common professional bond exists because most of the participants are lawyers.

A bureaucratic management style generally would be inappropriate for the courts, which are professionally dominated organizations. In fact, the more a judge insists on being treated with great deference, the more that work group's cohesion diminishes. More important, participants' roles are interchangeable: defense attorneys may become prosecutors or judges, and so on.[5]

Formal authority is modified in trial courts in many ways. For example, although the judge has the power to make the major decisions—setting bail, determining guilt, and imposing sentence—he or she often relies on input from others. Because they know more about cases coming to court, a judge's subordinates (prosecutors and defense attorneys) can influence his or her decisions by using selective information flow.[6]

For these informal work groups to be effective, group members must comply with the norms of behavior. If they do, they are rewarded, and if not, they are subject to being sanctioned. Defense attorneys who do not file unnecessary motions or avoid pushing for "unreasonable" plea bargains may be rewarded by receiving more information, such as being allowed to read the police reports of their cases. Prosecutors who abide by these norms may receive more time to talk with witnesses or defense counsel. Conversely, sanctions for defense attorneys who violate group norms may include restricting access to case information, not appointing them to represent indigents in future cases, or having their clients receive harsher sentences. Prosecutors may not receive requested continuances, most of which come from the district attorney's office.[7] In sum, it is important to remember that "courts are not an occasional assemblage of strangers who resolve a particular conflict and then dissolve, never to work together again."[8]

✧ Unifying Court Names and Functions

Turning now to the *functional* organization of the courts, Figure 7.1 shows an organization structure for a county district court serving a population of 300,000. Note the variety of functions and programs that exist and the ones that are in addition to the court's basic role of hearing trials and rendering judgments.

Overall, court organization has "demonstrated little logic or planning, because adding certain new courts serves various political goals."[9] States that do not have a unified court system often have a confusing maze of overlapping courts and jurisdictions, which can cause considerable confusion for litigants, victims, witnesses, and lawyers alike. Figure 7.2 shows the various names of state courts of last resort and the numbers of judges for each, Figure 7.3 presents the same types of information for state intermediate courts of appeals, and Figure 7.4 shows the names for major trial courts in different states.

Perhaps the best example of how courts should be organized statewide is by looking at a system that has become unified on a statewide basis. Kansas, which unified its court system in 1977, provides this example. Kansas has a supreme court (7 justices) with exclusive appellate and original jurisdiction; an intermediate court of appeals (7 justices) that hear appeals from district courts; a district court (70 district judges, 64 associate district judges, and 76 district magistrate

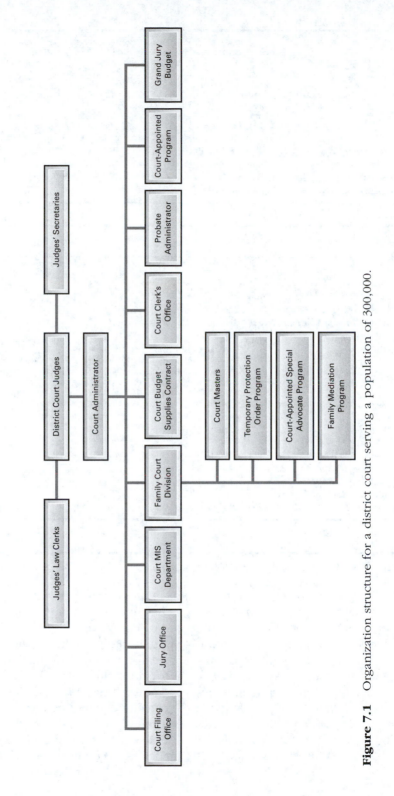

Figure 7.1 Organization structure for a district court serving a population of 300,000.

Supreme Court	Alabama (9), Alaska (5), Arizona (5), Arkansas (7), California (7), Connecticut (7), Delaware (5), Florida (7), Georgia (7), Hawaii (5), Idaho (5), Illinois (7), Indiana (5), Iowa (9), Kansas (7), Kentucky (7), Louisiana (8), Michigan (7), Minnesota (9), Mississippi (9), Missouri (7), Montana (7), Nebraska (7), Nevada (5), New Hampshire (5), New Jersey (7), New Mexico (5), North Carolina (7), North Dakota (5), Ohio (7), Oklahoma[a] (9), Oregon (7), Pennsylvania (7), Rhode Island (5), South Carolina (5), South Dakota (5), Tennessee (5), Texas[a] (9), Utah (5), Vermont (5), Virginia (7), Washington (9), Wisconsin (7), Wyoming (5)
Court of Appeals	District of Columbia (9), Maryland (7), New York (7)
Supreme Judicial Court	Maine (7), Massachusetts (7)
Court of Criminal Appeals	Oklahoma (3),[a] Texas (9)[a]
Supreme Court of Appeals	West Virginia (5)

[a]Two courts of last resort in these states.

Figure 7.2   Courts of last resort in the states.

Appeals Court	Massachusetts (14)
Appellate Court	Connecticut (9), Illinois (42)
Appellate Division of Superior Court	New Jersey (28)
Appellate Divisions of Superior Court	New York (48)
Appellate Terms of Supreme Court	New York (15)
Commonwealth Court	Pennsylvania (9)
Court of Appeals	Alaska (3), Arizona (21), Arkansas (6), Colorado (16), Georgia (9), Idaho (30), Indiana (5), Iowa (6), Kansas (10), Kentucky (14), Michigan (24), Minnesota (16), Missouri (32), Nebraska (6), New Mexico (10), North Carolina (12), North Dakota (3)[b], Ohio (65), Oklahoma (12)[a], Oregon (10), South Carolina (6), Tennessee (12)[a], Utah (7), Virginia (10), Washington (23), Wisconsin (15)
Court of Appeal	California (88), Louisiana (55), Texas (80)
Court of Civil Appeals	Alabama (3)
Court of Criminal Appeals	Alabama (5), Tennessee (9)
Court of Special Appeals	Maryland (13)
District Court of Appeals	Florida (57)
Intermediate Court of Appeals	Hawaii (3)
Superior Court	Pennsylvania (15)

[a]Civil only
[b]Temporary

Figure 7.3   Intermediate courts of appeal.

judges) with general original jurisdiction in all civil and criminal matters, hearing appeals from lower courts; and municipal courts (384 judges) that handle trials related to violations of city ordinances without juries.[10]

This is actually about as simple as court unification can be. Witness the Kansas court system *prior to* unification in 1977: a supreme court; 29 district courts (no intermediate court of appeals); 93 county courts handling civil cases involving less than $1,000, felony preliminaries, misdemeanors, traffic cases involving damages of less than $2,500, and jury trials; 8 city courts handling civil matters of less than $3,000, felony preliminaries, misdemeanors, traffic cases involving less than $2,500 in damages, and jury trials; 5 magistrate courts hearing civil cases involving less than $3,000 in damages, felony preliminaries, misdemeanors, and traffic cases

Circuit Court	Alabama, Arkansas,[a] Florida, Hawaii, Illinois, Indiana,[b] Kentucky, Maryland, Michigan, Mississippi,[a] Missouri, Oregon, South Carolina, South Dakota, Tennessee,[a] Virginia, West Virginia, Wisconsin
Court of Common Pleas	Ohio, Pennsylvania
District Court	Colorado, Idaho, Iowa, Kansas, Louisiana, Minnesota, Montana, Nebraska, Nevada, New Mexico, North Dakota, Oklahoma, Texas, Utah, Wyoming
Superior Court	Alaska, Arizona, California, Connecticut, Delaware,[a] District of Columbia, Georgia, Maine, Massachusetts, New Hampshire, New Jersey, North Carolina, Rhode Island, Vermont,[a,d] Washington, New York[c]
Supreme Court	New York

[a]Arkansas, Deleware, Mississippi, and Tennesse have separate Chancery courts with equity jurisdiction.
[b]Indiana uses Superior and Circuit Courts.
[c]New York also uses county courts.
[d]Vermont also uses District Courts.

Figure 7.4 Major trial courts in different states.

involving less than $2,500; 109 probate courts; 109 juvenile courts; 4 common pleas courts hearing civil cases involving less than $3,000, felony preliminaries, misdemeanors, traffic cases involving less than $2,500; and 384 municipal courts, hearing city ordinance violations, including traffic, resulting in less than one-year imprisonment.[11]

Note the several different titles and types of courts in the pre-1977 Kansas court system, with similar yet different roles and jurisdictions. Imagine the confusion, redundancy, and fragmentation that a nonunified system would have for a much larger population and geographic area. It is obvious that the problems of fragmentation, duplication, and confusion of the previous Kansas system were solved by the creation of a unified system. No matter where in the state a citizen resides, he or she is able to understand what the local "district" court does.

Court unification involves three components: (1) a simplified state trial court structure; (2) judicial system policy- and rule-making authority vested in the supreme court or judicial council, with overall system governance vested in the state supreme court chief justice; and (3) state funding of all or a substantial portion of the judicial system, with the budget prepared by the administrative office of the courts. The American Bar Association endorses such a unified court structure, which characteristically has uniform jurisdiction and standards of justice (such as rules of procedure, management systems, education and training), clearly vested policymaking authority (preferably in the state supreme court), and clearly established administrative authority (normally by the chief justice as the administrative head of the state court system).[12]

✦ COURT DECOR AND DECORUM

Practically everything one sees and hears in a U.S. courtroom is intended to convey the meaning that it is a hallowed place in our society. Alexis de Tocqueville, in his study of the United States more than a century ago, observed the extent to which our legal system permeates our very lives:

> Scarcely any political question arises in the United States that is not resolved, sooner or later, into a judicial question. Hence all parties are obliged to borrow, in their daily controversies, the ideas, and even the language, peculiar to judicial proceedings. . . . the spirit of the law, which is produced in the schools and courts of justice, gradually penetrates beyond their walls into the bosom of society, where it descends to the lowest classes, so that at last the whole people contract the habits and the tastes of the judicial magistrate.[13]

The physical trappings and demeanor one finds in the courts convey this sense of importance. Normally, citizens are struck by the unique decor commonly found in the courtroom: high ceilings, ornate marble walls, and expensive furnishings.

Citizens who observe court proceedings will note the traditional decorum that is accorded this institution. All people must rise when the judge enters the courtroom; permission must be granted before a person can approach the elevated bench; and a general air of deference is granted the judge. A vitriolic message that could lawfully be directed to the President of the United States will result in the utterer's being jailed for contempt of court when directed toward a judge.

The design of the courtroom, although dignified and intended to convey a message of singularity, provides a safe, functional space that is conducive to efficient and effective court proceedings. The formal arrangement of the participants and furnishings reflects society's view of the appropriate relationships between the defendant and judicial authority. The courtroom must accommodate judges, court reporters, clerks, bailiffs, witnesses, plaintiffs, defendants, attorneys, juries, and spectators, as well as police officers, social workers, probation officers, guardians ad litem, interpreters, and the press. Sometimes space must be allotted to evidence, exhibits, recording equipment, and computers.[14]

The trend during the past 20 years has been to build smaller, more specialized courtrooms such as traffic and drug courts; however, in recent years, several large and complex civil cases have highlighted the need for extremely large courtrooms to accommodate as many as 250 participating attorneys and to seat several judges. Criminal trials, such as those involving multiple drug defendants, can be quite large in size as well.

Judges and court staff now may require audiovisual equipment and computer terminals to access automated information systems. The latter are becoming increasingly important to trials and caseload management. A computer equipped with a keyboard tray and a silent printer is often placed at the court clerk's station for typing the transcript. Provision must also be made for the projection of slides, movies, X rays, and overhead materials. A telephone and silent alarm are almost indispensable, especially for emergency communications.

✦ COURTS: SEEKERS OF TRUTH
OR IMPEDIMENTS TO THE TRUTH?

Ralph Waldo Emerson stated that "every violation of truth . . . is a stab at the health of human society."[15] Certainly, most people would probably agree that the traditional, primary purpose of our courts is to provide a forum for seeking and obtaining—through the adversarial process—the truth. Indeed, the U.S. Supreme Court declared that fact in 1966 in *Tehan v. United States ex rel. Shott,* stating that "the basic purpose of a trial is the determination of truth."[16]

Today, however, the perception of our court system, in the words of a state supreme court justice, as a "domain of fiddlers preoccupied with dissonance while citizens' houses are threatened by fire"[17] is held by more and more people. Increasing numbers of Americans have the impression that truth is being compromised and even violated with regularity during the trial, plea bargaining, and appellate stages of our justice system, thereby stabbing at the health of human society, in the words of Emerson.

These observers see many impediments to truth in the judicial process that should be eliminated. High on their list is the adversary system itself. Under this system, the courtroom becomes a battleground where participants often have little regard for guilt or innocence; rather, their concern centers on whether the state is able to prove guilt beyond a reasonable doubt. To many people, this philosophy flies in the face of what courts were intended to accomplish; for example, former Chief Justice Warren Burger has stated that "the responsibility of an ethical lawyer . . . is essentially the same [to search for the truth] whether the client announces an intention to bribe or threaten witnesses or jurors or to commit or procure perjury. No system of justice worthy of the name can tolerate a lesser standard."[18]

In the adversarial system, the desire to win can become overpowering. As one state supreme court justice put it, prosecutors "are proud of the notches on their gun."[19] Defense counsel enjoy winning equally. The attention of both the defense and the prosecution can shift from finding the truth to being effective game players.

Who will foster change in the adversary system? That is an important and difficult question. As one law professor observed, "Lawyers are simply not appropriate to correct the defects of our adversary system. Their hearts will never be in it; it is unfair to both their clients and themselves to require them to serve two masters."[20]

Other impediments to finding the truth must be rooted out of the system. It has been argued that activities prohibited under both the Fourth and Fifth Amendments to the Constitution—the exclusion of evidence and the right against self-incrimination, respectively—should be restrained to assist the courts in getting at the truth. Rules of discovery should be modified so that they no longer are "lawyer's favorite weapon in jousting for a position of trial advantage."[21] The battle between expert witnesses that often develops into a circus atmosphere must be eliminated as well.

These changes may come sooner rather than later. In the words of one jurist

The public ox will not be gored indefinitely. The criminal justice system as we know it today is simply too costly, too cumbersome, too protracted, and most importantly, too compassed with truth retardants. The predominant master must be the truth.[22]

✦ THE INFLUENCE OF COURTS IN POLICYMAKING

The judicial branch has the responsibility to determine the legislative intent of the law and to provide public forums—the courts—for resolving disputes. This is accomplished by determining the facts and their legal significance in each case. If the court determines the legal significance of the facts by applying an existing rule of law, it is engaging in pure dispute resolution.[23] "But if to resolve the dispute the court must create a new rule or modify an old one, that is law creation."[24]

Determining what the law says and providing a public forum involve the courts in policymaking. *Policy* can be defined as choosing among alternative choices of action, particularly in the allocation of limited resources "where the chosen action affects the behavior and well-being of others who are subject to the policymaker's authority."[25] The policy decisions of the courts affect virtually all of us in our daily living. In recent decades the courts have been asked to deal with issues that previously were within the purview of the legislative and judicial branches. Because many of the Constitution's limitations on government are couched in vague language, the judicial branch must eventually deal with potentially volatile social issues, such as those involving the prisons, abortion, and prayer in the schools.[26]

U.S. Supreme Court decisions have dramatically changed race relations, resulted in the overhaul of juvenile courts, increased the rights of the accused, prohibited prayer and segregation in public schools, legalized abortion, and interpreted the Constitution to permit destruction of the American flag. State and federal court decisions have overturned minimum residency requirements for welfare recipients, established standards for prison life, equalized school expenditures, and prevented road and highway construction from damaging the environment. They have eliminated the requirement of a high school diploma for a firefighter's job and ordered increased property taxes to desegregate public schools.[27] The only governmental area that has not been subject to judicial policymaking since the Civil War is foreign affairs.[28] Cases in which courts make policy determinations usually involve government, the Fourteenth Amendment, and the use of equity—the remedy most often used against governmental violations of law. Recent policymaking decisions by the judicial branch have not been based on the Constitution but on federal statutes concerning the rights of the disadvantaged, consumers, and the environment.[29]

The courts have become particularly involved in administrative policy as the result of public interest–group litigation. For example, legislation was enacted by Congress to allow citizens to sue certain federal regulatory agencies, such as the Environmental Protection Agency (EPA), when they failed to perform certain duties as required by statute. Thus, a citizens' environmental group was allowed to sue the EPA.

It may appear that the courts have gone overboard in their review of issues. Remember, however, that judges "cannot impose their views . . . until someone brings a case to court, often as a last resort after complaints to unresponsive legislators and executives."[30] Plaintiffs must be truly aggrieved, or have *standing* to bring suit. The independence of the judicial branch, particularly at the federal court level where judges enjoy lifetime appointments, allows the courts to champion the causes of the underclass: those with fewer financial resources, votes, or who do not have a positive public profile.[31] The judiciary is the "least dangerous branch" because it has no enforcement powers, and its decisions can be overturned by legislative action.[32] The Congress can even overrule decisions based on the Constitution by amending the Constitution. Thus, the judicial branch depends on a perception of legitimacy surrounding its decisions.

✦ AN (OVER)ABUNDANCE OF LAWYERS

Today the United States has about 780,000 lawyers, one for every 307 people (the highest ratio in the world). This ratio has tripled since 1971, and the ranks of lawyers is expected to continue to increase, reaching 1 million by the year 2000. The number of civil suits in federal courts has soared 300 percent since 1960 and in the state courts has increased by more than 4 million. Currently, nearly 20 million lawsuits are filed in state courts alone each year. The fear of being sued has become almost endemic to our society, changing the way we interact and do business.[33]

Contrast this with the situation in Japan, which has just 14,336 *bengoshis,* or lawyers, for a population that is half that of the United States. The Japanese have a distaste for confrontation; their legal system therefore discourages litigation, and litigious persons are not held in high esteem. Barriers exist to litigation there. For example, to become a lawyer, one must win a spot in the Legal Training and Research Institute, which accepts only 2 percent of its applicants each year. Thus, only 400 lawyers are added to the system annually.

◆ OUR NEW NATIONAL PASTIME: LITIGATION

✧ GREED RESULTS IN FRIVOLOUS LAWSUITS

Many Americans are greedy. Egged on by similarly avaricious attorneys and the prospect of hugh financial windfalls, we are suing one another with unprecedented frequency. Many of today's cases would have been laughed out of court not long ago. Following are some of the types of actions that have been taken to the door of our courts by people seeking to obtain "justice":

◊ Two fans of the Washington Redskins filed a suit to overturn a loss by the team, contending that a crucial call by a referee violated the rules and robbed them of their "right" to see a victory.

◊ A young Colorado man sued his parents for $350,000, charging that they gave him inhumane and inadequate care as a child, making it impossible for him to fit into society as an adult.

◊ A 41-year-old California man, upset at being stood up on a date, sued his would-be companion for $38 to compensate him for getting dressed up and driving 40 miles for nothing.

◊ A young Portland man (the plaintiff), employed as a checkout clerk in a grocery store, sued another young man for $100,000; the suit charged that the defendant "continually and repeatedly" sought out the plaintiff on the premises of the grocery store and after locating him, directed his "gas" toward plaintiff, humiliating the plaintiff and inflicting severe mental stress upon him.[34]

We who think of ourselves as rational can only hope that few or none of these litigants prevailed at the bar. Lawsuits of this ilk—smacking of blatant frivolity—do not always fail, however. Following are some examples of jury awards in cases of this nature.

◊ A jury awarded $200,000 to a Chicago couple who were "bumped" from a flight to Florida, causing the "humiliation, indignity, and outrage" of missing the birth of a horse.

◊ A 36-year-old Philadelphia real estate manager who spent 11 years as a student and teacher in transcendental meditation groups sued his teachers because he was never able to achieve the "perfect state of life" they promised. He alleged that he had been told he would learn to "fly" through self-levitation, but he learned only to "hop with the legs folded in the lotus position." A jury awarded him nearly $138,000 in damages.

◊ In New Hampshire, the parents of a nine-year-old won $3,020 from their 88-year-old neighbor who refused to return their son's ball after it rolled into her yard.[35]

We can hope that at least some of these verdicts were overturned or reduced on appeal. Nonetheless, jurors today are often sympathetic with "aggrieved" individuals, especially when the defendant is a large corporation with "deep pockets." In 1962 only one personal injury suit resulted in damages of more than $1 million; now it is not uncommon to have more than 500 such awards each year.[36]

✦ PROPOSED SOLUTIONS TO DECREASE LITIGATION

Several methods are now being proposed to reduce the number of lawsuits in this country. One is to place a cap on punitive damages; such awards could be limited to the amount of compensatory awards, with only the judge being allowed to assess them. Another is to force losers to pay the winners' legal fees. This proposal draws the most resistance because many people with legitimate claims would not sue because of the risk involved.

The process of discovery also warrants examination. This process involves the pretrial, formal and informal exchange of information—test results, statements, confessions and other evidence, witness lists, and police reports—between prosecutors and defense attorneys. It seeks to ensure that the adversary system does not give one side an unfair advantage over the other.

Many knowledgeable people believe that the process of discovery wastes much time and money and could be revamped, requiring both sides to disclose core information in discovery. As a response to the increase in the number of trials that become contests between well-paid "experts" using "junk science," a proposal would require that expert testimony be based on "widely accepted" theories and would ban payments to experts whose side wins.[37]

Another proposal that is already widely used involves the use of alternative dispute resolution (ADR). Realizing that the growing backlog of both criminal and civil cases pushes business cases to the back of the queue, many private corporations are attempting to avoid courts and lawyers by using alternative means of resolving their legal conflicts. Such innovative techniques include "rent-a-judge" services and minitrials. One utility company even pays for its opponents to sit down with a mediator. Some corporations have opted out of litigation completely; about 600 top corporations have signed pledges with other companies to consider negotiation and other forms of ADR prior to suing other corporate signers. It is estimated that in 1990, 142 of these corporations saved more than $100 million in legal costs.[38]

The leading ADR firm is Judicial Arbitration & Mediation Services, Inc. (JAMS), based in Orange, California. Washington-based Endispute, Inc., and the Philadelphia-based Judicate, Inc., are rapidly becoming leaders in the field. These private arbitration and mediation firms charge $300 to $350 per hour, a huge savings from the $300 an hour that each member of a battery of lawyers might charge litigants.[39]

Given the increasing number of lawsuits in this country, ADR may be the wave of the future; as one law professor noted, "in the future, instead of walking into a building called a courthouse, you might walk into the Dispute Resolution Center."[40]

✦ CITIZENS AND THE COURTS

One survey found that far more Americans knew Judge Wapner (of the former television program "The People's Court") than could identify the Chief Justice of the United States. Nonetheless, judges define justice by interpreting and enforcing laws, thus handing out justice.

Whether justice is done depends, however, on the interests or viewpoints of the affected or interested parties. A victim may not agree with a jury's verdict; a "winner" in a civil case may not believe that he or she received an adequate sum of money for the suffering or damages involved. Thus, in light of the fact that everyone does not always agree on what justice is, we must make another distinction and say that the courts must *appear* to be handing out justice. The court's responsibility is to provide a fair hearing, to accord all parties the right to speak or not to speak, to have the assistance of counsel, to cross-examine the other side, to produce witnesses and relevant documents, and to argue their viewpoint. This process, embodied in the due process clause of the Constitution, must appear to result in justice.[41]

The low esteem in which the public regards the courts diminishes the cooperation required from the public in reporting crime and in testifying as witnesses. Certainly, many people in today's society are fed up with accounts of corrupt judges, with what they perceive as coddling offenders, and with the ravages of the "law's delay," which often allows convicted murderers to spend more than a decade awaiting final judgment. People tell their neighbors about long waits at the courthouse after having been summoned for jury service or while trying to take care of legal business. They hear victims and witnesses talk of having been treated badly at the hands of the justice system.

Citizen groups interested in reforming the system have undertaken studies of the courts. Leading this court-watching effort have been such organizations as the Mothers Against Drunk Drivers, the League of Women Voters, and the National Council of Jewish Women. They observe court hearings, examine state juvenile codes, interview justice personnel, and publish their findings. Many times these groups have probably had unrealistic expectations because courts do not prevent crime or enact legislation and see only but a small fraction of offenders (see the discussion of the crime control model in Chapter 1). These groups may also have an insufficient understanding of the problems or operations of the courts.

Americans complain about trial delays, high court costs, and what they consider to be unjust decisions. They want to know what judges are doing about these problems. Americans are asking themselves, "Do we have enough people power in this country? Or have the public officials, including judges, stopped listening to the people?"[42] Americans will increasingly judge their judges. They are going to want the courts to circulate questionnaires concerning how to solve problems such as overloaded dockets and listen to local groups that have concerns about such problems. One person has even suggested that judges must begin looking at judging from the perspective of the consumer.[43] Still, it is important that courts not be swayed by public opinion.

Summary

In this chapter we have reviewed the distinctive nature of the courts. Courts, which have thus far resisted attempts to be bureaucratized, have comparatively little formalized, hierarchical structure or chain of command but are composed of informal work groups and are largely autonomous.

Several areas of concern were highlighted as well. One increasing concern, even among jurists, is whether several elements of due process afforded the accused, the adversarial system itself, and the omnipresent will to win by some court participants are affecting the courts' historical search for truth. Another growing dilemma, because of the litigious proclivity permeating our country, concerns how long the courts will be able to cope with the increasing civil and criminal litigation. A final concern relates to citizens' knowledge of court operations. The mystique surrounding the courts and the fear of being involved with court processes that has been engendered in citizens, and their perception of "justice delayed" indicate a need for improved community relations.

Questions for Review

1. Discuss how the courts differ from other traditional bureaucracies in their organization. How and why do courts not have the usual characteristics found in a bureaucracy?
2. What are the effects of society's litigious nature on court administration?
3. What possible solutions hold promise for reducing the current avalanche of lawsuits?
4. How does the public view the courts today? What specific areas does the public believe need improvement?
5. In what ways are courts unique in terms of their decor and decorum?

Notes

1. Kathleen Maguire and Ann L. Pastore (eds.), *Sourcebook of Criminal Justice Statistics 1995.* U.S. Department of Justice, Bureau of Justice Statistics (Washington, D.C.: U.S. Government Printing Office, 1996), p. 20.

2. Edward J. Clynch and David W. Neubauer, "Trial Courts as Organizations: A Critique and Synthesis," in Stan Stojkovic, John Klofas, and David Kalinich (eds.), *The Administration and Management of Criminal Justice Organizations: A Book of Readings* (Prospect Heights, Ill.: Waveland Press, 1990), pp. 43–61.

3. Peter M. Blau and Marshall W. Meyer, *Bureaucracy in Modern Society* (New York: Random House, 1971), Chapter 2.

4. Clynch and Neubauer, "Trial Courts as Organizations," p. 43.

5. *Ibid.,* pp. 46–48.

6. *Ibid.,* pp. 49–50.

7. *Ibid.,* pp. 51–52.

8. James Eisenstein and Herbert Jacob, *Felony Justice* (Boston: Little, Brown, 1977), p. 20.

9. Henry R. Glick, *Courts, Politics, and Justice* (New York: McGraw-Hill, 1983), p. 41.

10. William E. Hewitt, Geoff Gallas, and Barry Mahoney, *Courts That Succeed* (Williamsburg, Va.: National Center for State Courts, 1990), p. vii.

11. *Ibid.,* p. vii.

12. American Bar Association, Judicial Administration Division, *Standards Relating to Court Organization,* Vol. 1 (Minneapolis, Minn.: Author, 1990), pp. 6–7.

13. Alexis de Tocqueville, *Democracy in America,* Vol. 1 (H. Reeve, trans.), 1875 (New York: D. Appleton, 1904), pp. 283–284.

14. Don Hardenbergh, "Planning and Design Considerations for Trial Courtrooms," *State Court Journal* 14 (Fall 1990): 32–38.

15. Stephen Whicher and R. Spiller (eds.), *The Early Lectures of Ralph Waldo Emerson* (Philadelphia: University of Pennsylvania Press, 1953).

16. 382 U.S. 406 (1966), at 416.

17. Thomas L. Steffen, "Truth as Second Fiddle: Reevaluating the Place of Truth in the Adversarial Trial Ensemble," *Utah Law Review* 4 (1988): 799.

18. In *Nix v. Whiteside,* 475 U.S. 157 (1986), at 174.

19. Steffen, "Truth as Second Fiddle," p. 821.

20. W. Alschuler, "The Preservation of a Client's Confidences: One Value among Many or a Categorical Imperative?" 52 U.Colo.L.Rev. 349 (1981), at 354.

21. *Ibid.,* p. 835.

22. *Ibid.,* pp. 842–843.

23. Howard Abadinsky, *Law and Justice: An Introduction to the American Legal System* (3d ed.) (Chicago: Nelson-Hall, 1995), p. 131.

24. Richard A. Posner, *The Federal Courts: Crisis and Reform* (Cambridge, Mass.: Harvard University Press, 1985), p. 3.

25. Harold J. Spaeth, *Supreme Court Policy Making: Explanation and Prediction* (San Francisco: W. H. Freeman, 1979), p. 19.

26. Jethro K. Lieberman, "What Courts Do and Do Not Do Effectively," in Sheldman Goldman and Austin Sarat (eds.), *American Court Systems: Readings in Judicial Process and Behavior* (New York: Longman, 1989), pp. 18–32.

27. Abadinsky, *Law and Justice,* p. 132.

28. Spaeth, *Supreme Court Policy Making.*

29. Abadinsky, *Law and Justice,* p. 132.

30. Stephen L. Wasby, *The Supreme Court in the Federal System* (3d ed.) (Chicago: Nelson-Hall, 1989), p. 5.

31. Abadinsky, *Law and Justice*, p. 141.

32. *Ibid.,* p. 131.

33. Michele Galen, Alice Cuneo, and David Greising, "Guilty!" *Business Week* (April 13, 1992): 62.

34. David F. Pike, "Why Everybody Is Suing Everybody," *U.S. News and World Report* (December 4, 1978): 50–54.

35. Bob Cohn, "The Lawsuit Cha-Cha," *Newsweek* (August 26, 1991): 58.

36. Galen et al., "Guilty!" pp. 62, 64.

37 Cohn, "The Lawsuit Cha-Cha," p. 59.

38. Galen et al., "Guilty!" p. 63.

39. *Ibid.*

40. *Ibid.,* p. 64.

41. H. Ted Rubin, *The Courts: Fulcrum of the Justice System* (Santa Monica, Calif.: Goodyear, 1976), p. 3.

42. Shirley S. Abrahamson, "The Consumer and the Courts," *Judicature* 74 (August/September 1990): 93–95.

43. *Ibid.*

Chapter 8

Court Personnel Roles and Functions

The justice or injustice of the cause is to be decided by the judge.
—Samuel Johnson

✦ INTRODUCTION

The administration of the judicial process is probably the least known and understood area of justice administration. Therefore, in this chapter we examine the role of judges and other court staff members in processing cases in a timely manner.

We base this discussion on the general observation, supported by relevant literature,[1] that judges and lawyers are normally not well trained to handle the administrative tasks of their courts, and they seldom have the time required to perform them. Furthermore, few judges today would probably "like to spend all day or most of the day handling union grievances or making sure that employees know what their benefits are."[2] Most, instead, would prefer to be on the bench, dealing with cases.

A major function of the courtroom work group is to ensure that cases flow smoothly through the courts. To meet this goal, we consider case management as an administrative function in this chapter.[3]

We begin by defining and distinguishing the terms *judicial administration* and *court administration* and then examine the roles of judges as administrators, court clerks, and court administrators, to include conflicts among these three functionaries. The chapter focuses on the relatively new position of the specially trained court administrator. We also review some criteria that judges can employ to determine whether their court administrators are functioning effectively and efficiently. We close the chapter with a description of an actual court that has used the principles of administration discussed here to revise its operations successfully.

✦ DEFINING JUDICIAL ADMINISTRATION

Judicial administration is difficult to define. This difficulty became obvious during the 1970s when the field became vocationally attractive. Various people and commissions tried to define it but instead seemed capable only of listing the duties of the office. For example, the National Advisory Commission on Criminal Justice Standards and Goals stated in 1973 that "the basic purpose of court administration is to relieve judges of some administrative chores and to help them perform those they retain."[4] Furthermore, in 1974 the American Bar Association specified a variety of functions for the court administrator to perform "under the authority of the judicial council and the supervision of the chief justice."[5]

The problem of definition continued into the 1980s; one law professor who had done a large amount of research in the field stated in 1986 that the safest approach was "not . . . to attempt a definition" but simply "to accept that it is a sub-branch of administration—more precisely of public administration."[6]

To assist in solving this dilemma and to provide more clarity, Russell Wheeler and Howard Whitcomb proposed a good working definition of *judicial administration:* "The direction of and influences on the activities of those who are expected to contribute to just and efficient case processing—except legal doctrinal considerations, insofar as they dispose of the particular factual and legal claims presented in a case."[7]

This definition implies that a *set* of people share a role norm and that judicial administration constitutes *all* of the factors that direct and influence those people.[8] Consequently, as Russell Wheeler noted, "Many court administrators today find themselves under the inevitable strain of not knowing for certain what their purpose is."[9]

Most works on judicial administration consider Roscoe Pound to be an early proponent of the field as a result of his 1906 essay, "The Causes of Popular Dissatisfaction with Administration of Justice" (discussed in Chapter 3). A major essay, "The Study of Administration," by Woodrow Wilson 19 years earlier (in 1887) stressed that the vocation of administration was a noble calling, not one for which every person was competent.[10] With great foresight, Wilson wrote that judges were responsible for judging and "establishing fundamental court policy," and the task of a "trained executive officer, working under the chief judge or presiding judge" was to "relieve judges generally" of "the function of handling the numerous business and administrative affairs of the courts."[11]

✧ COURT ADMINISTRATION

The term *court administration* might be considered loosely as the specific activities of those persons who are organizationally responsible for manipulating the various judicial administration directions and influences.[12] This term is more commonly used in this chapter because we focus on the development of the role and functions of the *individual trial court administrator.*

✦ JUDGES AS ADMINISTRATORS

Our Constitution intended the judiciary to play a key role in the application of its provisions; the overriding duty of judges is to protect the individual from the state. Our courts were created to provide the final defense of freedom: to be, in the words of James Madison, "an impenetrable bulwark against every assumption of power in the legislative or executive."[13] For this reason, our society for the most part accords its jurists a high level of esteem, as noted in Chapter 7.

✧ FACTORS THAT SHAPE JUDGES' ATTITUDES

What makes judges behave and decide matters as they do? What elements of their education and experience might affect their views of judicial administration? A considerable body of literature has investigated the forces that shape the attitudes of judges prior to their election or appointment.[14] One study reported that most judges were recruited from the locality in which they serve, bringing to the bench certain biases, values, and perceptions peculiar to their own locality.[15] A judge's experience *after* his or her appointment may also have a significant bearing on the decision-making process, including both the sentencing and judicial administration functions.

Adapting to the Judgeship. Judges are required to be competent administrators, a fact of judicial life that comes as a surprise to many new judges. One survey of 30 federal judges found that 23 (77 percent) acknowledged having major administrative difficulties upon first assuming the bench. Half complained of heavy caseloads, stating that their court had accumulated backlogs and that other adverse conditions compounded the problem. One federal judge maintained that it takes about four years to "get a full feel of a docket."[16]

Most trial judges experience psychological discomfort upon assuming the role. Seventy-seven percent of new federal judges acknowledged having psychological problems in at least one of five areas: maintaining a judicial bearing both on and off the bench, adapting to the loneliness of the judicial office, sentencing criminals, forgetting the adversarial role, and experiencing local pressure. One aspect of the judicial role is assuming a proper demeanor or learning to act like a judge. One judge remembered his first day in court: "I'll never forget going into my courtroom for the first time with the robes and all, and the crier tells everyone to rise. You sit down and realize that it's all different, that everyone is looking at you and you're supposed to do something."[17]

Like police officers and probation and parole workers, judges complain about having to maintain a proper demeanor at all times, stating that it's not possible to "go to the places you used to. You always have to be careful about what you talk about. When you go to a party, you have to be careful not to drink too much so you won't make a fool of yourself."[18] As stated, the position can be a lonely one:

> After you become a . . . judge some people tend to avoid you. For instance, you lose all your lawyer friends and generally have to begin to make new friends. I guess the lawyers are afraid that they will some day have a case before you and it would be awkward for them if they were on too close terms with you.[19]

Judges frequently describe sentencing criminals as the most difficult aspect of their job. A federal judge reported that

> Sentencing criminals is another problem which often troubles me. I have often said to the other judges that this is the hardest part of being a judge. You see so many pathetic people and you're never sure of what is a right or a fair sentence.[20]

Judges often meet on a regular basis, and, in matters involving sentencing criminals, may frequently guide a new judge. In contrast, most jurisdictions have almost no exchange of information between the novice trial judge and appellate judges. Novice trial judges typically believe that discussing a judicial problem with an appellate judge may be improper; furthermore, trial judges often presume that there is nothing appellate judges can do to help them with their day-to-day problems.[21]

Consequently, many new judges rely on their court staff—particularly their court administrators—to assist them with the difficult early tenure of their judgeship. Another possible source of socialization for novice judges is local lawyers. When the case subject matter is new to them, judges frequently ask opposing lawyers for information about "what the law says." Or when they have a case that involves a new or difficult point of law with which they need help, they occasionally contact a local attorney who specializes in that particular subject matter. Seminars are also helpful in assisting the judge to adapt to life on the bench.[22]

✧ Judges as Court Managers

The Administrative Office of the United States Courts coordinates and administers the operations of federal courts. In the states, judges assume three types of administrative levels: statewide jurisdiction, held by state supreme court chief justices; jurisdictions that include only one court, held by a local trial judge responsible for the operations of his or her individual court; and the jurisdiction of a specific judicial district held by a presiding or chief judge.

Having a judge preside over several courts within a district developed as early as 1940 when Dean Roscoe Pound recommended that a chief or presiding judge of a district or a region be responsible for and have the authority for case and judge assignment.[23] Today these judges assume "general administrative duties over the court and its divisions" and are typically granted authority over all judicial personnel and court officials.[24] Presiding judges have numerous duties including managing personnel and dockets and assigning cases and judges; developing and coordinating all judicial budgets; convening *en banc* court meetings; coordinating judicial schedules; creating and using appropriate court committees (to investigate problems, handle court business, etc.); dealing with outside agencies and the media; drafting local court rules and policies; maintaining the courts' facilities; and issuing orders for keeping, destroying, and transferring records.[25]

A basic flaw in this system is that the chief or presiding judge is actually a first among equals with his or her peers. The title of chief judge is often assigned according to seniority; therefore, there is no guarantee that the chief judge will have the interest, temperament, or skills needed to manage a large court system.

From a court administrator's standpoint, the office of and the person serving as presiding judge are of utmost importance. As one judge put it, "The single most determinative factor of the extent of the administrator's role, aside from his personal attributes, is probably the rate of turnover in the office of the presiding judge."[26] As we will see later, the method of selecting judges is also an important process and consideration.

As mentioned, although judges are ultimately responsible for court administration, they have historically been ineffective managers. Judges are often confronted with issues about which they have little knowledge or experience. As one author stated

> Until recently, judges typically proceeded without the advice of professional managers or the benefit of modern techniques of careful research, planning, evaluation and training. Even today, with court administrators having served for over 10 years in many courts, judges are often slow to heed their advice and continue to rely on intuitions and predilections born of legal training and disposition to follow precedents.[27]

Much of this lack of knowledge of behind-the-scenes court processes can be explained by the environment in which courts function. Judges primarily exist to hear cases and typically are not trained in court management. Furthermore,

Judges Must Train to Take the Bench

At the National Judicial College (NJC) in Reno, Nevada, classroom bells—not gavels and bailiffs—rule the day. The underlying message rings loud: Wearing a black robe alone does not a judge make. In times when the legal profession and the courts are coming under increased scrutiny and public criticism, the weight of judicial robes can be heavy.

At the judicial college, the goal is not only to coach lawyers on how to be judges, but to teach veteran judges how to be better arbiters of justice. For many lawyers, the move to the other side of the bench is an awesome transition. "Judges aren't born judges," said U.S. Supreme Court Justice Sandra Day O'Connor, who attended the NJC upon her election as an Arizona Superior Court judge in 1974. She recalled her anxieties the first time she assumed the bench. "It was frightening, really. There was so much to think about and to learn."

Justice Anthony M. Kennedy, who is on the judicial college's faculty, described the college as "an institutional reminder of the very basic proposition that an independent judiciary is essential in any society that is going to be based on the rule of law. Judicial independence cannot exist unless you have skilled, dedicated, and principled judges. This leads to so many different areas—judicial demeanor, how to control a courtroom, basic rules of civility, how to control attorneys. These are difficult skills for judges to learn. They're not something judges innately have. Judges have to acquire these skills."

Founded in 1963, the college offered its first course the following year in Boulder, Colorado. It is the only full-time institution in the country that provides judicial training primarily for state judges. It is affiliated with the American Bar Association, which pays about 10 percent of the college's annual budget. Other money comes from an endowment fund, donations, and program tuition and fees.

Courses run two days to three weeks. Tuition and fees range from $480 to $1,815. Since its inception, the college has issued more than 60,000 certificates to judges from all 50 states and 136 foreign countries. Regular curriculum includes courses on using courtroom technology; dealing with jurors; handling courtroom disruptions; dealing with domestic violence; managing complex cases; understanding death penalty issues; using mediation; learning family law; using forensic, medical, and scientific evidence; and writing opinions.

As legal issues become increasingly complex and courts become overloaded with cases, judicial training becomes more critical. As Joseph R. Weisberger, chief justice of the Rhode Island Supreme Court and an NJC instructor for 30 years stated, "It is the judiciary that transforms constitutional rights and liberties from a piece of parchment and printed words into living, breathing reality."

Adapted from Sandra Chereb, "Judges Must Train to Take the Bench," *Reno Gazette-Journal* (May 28, 1996): pp. 1B, 5B. Used with permission of the Associated Press.

judges are often not given the necessary authority to administer all court operations. Lawyers learn early in law school training to treat each case individually; when they become judges, they are unaccustomed to handling a large number of cases or analyzing caseloads or patterns of dispositions. However, as we discuss in Chapter 9, case management is a judge's primary duty.

✦ COURT CLERKS

Not to be overlooked in the administration of the courts is the court clerk, also referred to as *prothonotary, registrar of deeds, circuit clerk, register of probate,* and even *auditor*. Most courts have de facto court administrators in these clerks, regardless of whether they have appointed administrators. Court clerks are key individuals in the administration of local court systems; they docket cases, collect fees and other monies, oversee jury selection, and maintain court records. These local officials, elected in all but six states, can amass tremendous power.[28]

From the beginning in English North America, court clerks were vital members of society. The position of clerk held considerable power and respect during the colonial and post-Revolutionary times. Duties included summoning the grand jury, recording bills of indictment, providing for the security and comfort of the jury, conducting the court's business smoothly during arraignments, swearing in the jury, and ensuring the smooth flow of criminal trials. At the end of the trial, the clerk polled the jury and then summoned the gaoler to take the prisoner into custody. Pregnant women convicted of capital offenses were given stays of execution until the birth of the child; the court did not want the blood of innocent children on its hands. In these cases, the clerk was responsible for having the sheriff bring in 12 women to examine the prisoner to determine whether she was in fact pregnant.[29] Clerks charged twopence for a summons, threepence for an attachment or replevin (the recovery of wanted persons or stolen goods), and fourpence to take bond to prosecute a suit.

During the late 17th century, colonial courts became more structured and formalized. Books that explained English court usage in the colonies were available, and clerks, judges, and attorneys were provided proper English forms to use. In fact, the forms used by clerks 200 years ago are very similar to those in use today.[30]

Clerks have traditionally competed with judges for control over local judicial administration. In fact, one study found that the majority (58.9 percent) of elected clerks perceived themselves as judges' colleagues, thus being coequal with them.[31] Court clerks have not as a rule been identified with effective management, however.

Generally they are conservative in nature and reflect the attitudes and culture of the community. Their parochial backgrounds coupled with their conservative orientation, in part accounts for this resistance to change. This resistance often compels judicial systems to retain archaic procedures and managerial techniques.[32]

Much of the United States is rural in nature. Approximately 2,450 general jurisdiction and 14,100 limited jurisdiction courts exist in the United States;[33] nearly four-fifths of them exist in rural counties. These courts serve about 46 million people. A *rural court* is any trial court in a jurisdiction with one full-time judge.[34] An enormous difference in court administration exists between urban courts and rural courts.

The small scale of rural areas affects the type of person who serves as clerk. Urban courts pay high salaries to obtain specially trained and educated court clerks, but rural clerks usually have less training and education and receive lower salaries.[35] Many court observers believe that rural clerks are not adequately trained to manage courts as required in modern times, although they do not indicate that all rural clerks' offices are "parochial" and "archaic."

While ultimately accountable for caseflow management, the clerk actually has little power to control the calendar. In most rural courts, lawyers actually review the proposed calendar before it is final. These clerks are challenged by such conditions as having a single court reporter who is responsible for courtroom work in a large area, the lack of a local crime laboratory, having to bring expert witnesses from outside, and the limitation of the trial judge being available only a few days each month.

Other duties of rural court clerks include keeping tradition by maintaining records concerning the land grants of the town ancestors, the naturalization of the people who broke the sod, and of births, deaths, marriages, and divorces in the community.

Nearly all rural clerks view management information systems and the reports they generate as of no use in managing their courts (thus, one must wonder about the accuracy of statistical information that rural clerks provide to the state, and, consequently, the validity of statewide court information that state offices generate). Nevertheless, many people believe that rural court clerks provide their greatest service in maintaining the history and tradition of their cities and counties.

✦ COURT ADMINISTRATORS

✧ DEVELOPMENT AND TRAINING

One of the most recent and innovative approaches to solving the courts' management problems has been the creation of the position of court administrator. This relatively new criminal justice position began to develop during the 1960s; since that time, the number of practicing trial court administrators has increased tenfold and continues to increase. Actually, the court administrator concept has its roots in early England where judges have historically abstained from any involvement in court administration. This fact has not been lost on contemporary court administrators and proponents of this occupation: "It seems to be a very valuable characteristic of the English system that the judges expect to *judge* when they are in the courthouse . . . it does not allow time for administrative distractions."[36]

The development of the position of court administrator has been sporadic. Approximately 30 people in the United States really worked as court administrators in the early 1960s. By 1970 fewer than 50 such employees were in the system.[37] Estimates differ concerning the expansion of the administrator's role during the 1980s. One expert maintained that by 1982 probably between 2,000 and 3,000 people were working as court administrators,[38] but another expert put that number at only about 500.[39] At any rate, most estimators agree that more than twice as many of these positions were created between 1970 and 1980 than in the preceding six decades.[40]

We also know that by the 1980s every state had established a statewide court administration position that normally reported to the state supreme court or the chief justice of the state supreme court. State court administrators' primary functions may be categorized into three areas: preparing annual reports that summarize caseload data, preparing budgets, and troubleshooting.[41]

Today few, if any, metropolitan areas are without full-time court administrators.[42] (The court organization chart shown in Figure 7.1 demonstrates the breadth of responsibilities held by court administrators.) The underlying premise and justification for this position is that having a trained person perform court management tasks leaves judges free to do what they do best: decide cases.

As court reformers have called for better trained specialists (as opposed to politically appointed persons) as court administrators, the qualifications required for these persons has come under debate. The creation of the Institute for Court Management in 1970 was a landmark in the training for this role, legitimizing the standing of this position in the legal profession. Many judges still believe, however, that a law degree is essential, but others prefer a background in business administration. There will probably never be total agreement concerning the skills and background necessary for this position, but the specialized training that is offered by the institute and a few graduate programs in judicial administration across the country seem ideal to provide the education needed.

Court administrators are trained specifically to provide the courts with the expertise and talent they have historically lacked. This point was powerfully made by Bernadine Meyer:

> Management—like law—is a profession today. Few judges or lawyers with severe chest pains would attempt to treat themselves. Congested dockets and long delays are symptoms that court systems need the help of professionals. Those professionals are managers. If court administration is to be effective, judicial recognition that managerial skill and knowledge are necessary to efficient performance is vital.[43]

✧ GENERAL DUTIES

A recent survey of trial court administrators revealed that they actually perform six major duties:

1. *Generating reports:* Eighty percent of all trial court administrators reported primary responsibility for preparing and submitting to the judges reports or the activities and state of business of the court for specified periods.

2. *Serving as personnel administrator:* Seventy-nine percent of all court administrators have a primary duty as personnel officer for court's nonjudicial personnel.

3. *Preparing research and evaluation:* These duties were performed by 78 percent of all respondents to improve court business methods.

4. *Managing equipment:* Three-fourths of all administrators procure, allocate, and control the inventory and replacement of furniture and equipment.

5. *Preparing the court budget:* This major task is done by 74 percent of all administrators.

6. *Providing personnel training:* About 73 percent of trial court administrators surveyed provide training for nonjudicial personnel.[44]

Other duties of the trained court administrator include jury management (reported as a primary duty by 42 percent of trial court administrators), case-flow or calendar management (42 percent), public information management (56 percent), and management of automated data processing (59 percent).[45]

A few critics of this judicial reform movement believe that trial court administrators have in fact made little difference in the courts' efforts to function more effectively and dispense a higher quality of justice.[46]

✦ CONFLICT BETWEEN JUDICIAL ADMINISTRATORS

✧ A DIFFICULT DICHOTOMY

The nature of the administrative relationship between the court administrator and the clerk has been an area of concern. Administrators often view clerks as a threat and as an intrusion into their business. Clerks therefore have assumed a central role in resisting the creation of a court administrator position, but the court administrator often depends on receiving information that only the clerk can provide.[47]

Some conflicts occur between the judge and the court administrator. Sometimes the judge usurps the administrator's role and makes most management decisions unilaterally, defeating the purpose of having an administrator. Judges should delegate sufficient responsibility to the administrator to do what he or she was trained to do and so that the court receives proper service for the salary being paid. At the other extreme, judges sometimes totally abdicate their responsibilities and delegate too much of the court's work to the administrator without exercising oversight of the latter's performance. Abdication occurs particularly when judges and administrators are in separate buildings or cities. In this instance, the court administrator will in effect not be supervised.

Tension and conflict may arise between the judge and the court administrator because some judges are reluctant to delegate responsibility over major aspects of court operations, such as budgeting and case scheduling. In fact, some studies have shown that because of conflicts with clerks and judges, court administrators have not been given full responsibility over court duties of a nonjudicial nature; they are often allowed to perform only minor tasks.[48] Unfortunately, substantial confusion still exists over the proper role of the court administrator.[49] And in practice, the line separating the administrative and the adjudicatory functions of the courts has not been well established.

The rift that can exist between judges and court administrators is also related to the fact that judges and courts resist bureaucracy; Thomas Leitko stated the problem in general terms:

> The integration of professionals into a professional bureaucracy has always been problematic. Because professionals identify more with their occupations than with their organizations, because they often control their own certification and performance standards, and because they have separate sources of legitimacy within their organizations, they often have functioned somewhat autonomously from and at odds with administrators.[50]

Judges resist measures of performance; their productivity is an intensely personal and private matter to them. The ultimate, and perhaps only, test of judicial performance is when the public must vote to elect, retain, or reject them or during the appointment process. Not even other judges evaluate their performance. No merit salary programs or incentive or performance appraisal systems exist. Judges need autonomy and discretion, but for the court administrator, accountability is the bottom line. Evaluating performance is part of administrators' roles; they evaluate their subordinates and hire, fire, and promote people with accountability in mind.[51]

Nonetheless, judges and court administrators must support and cooperate with one another and even mesh together. The concept that judges should judge and administrators should manage is counterproductive. Each must be committed to three fundamental values: the importance of joint policy formulation, respect for individual expertise, and mutual trust and support for achievement.[52]

In an ideal situation, the administrative and judicial activities should be coordinated and balanced equally between the judge and the administrator. Some activities are clearly administrator centered, others are judge centered, and still others involve joint decision making or information sharing. Figure 8.1 depicts a continuum of all court activities and indicates where collaboration between judge and administrator would be required.

Administration		Adjudication
Administrator makes the decisions without consulting the judge	Joint decision-making or information-sharing; "a shared role"	Judge makes the decisions without consulting the administrator

Examples of Activities

Budgeting	Agency relationships	Case decisions
Training for non-judicial personnel	Legislative relationships	Directing meetings of judges
Purchasing	Public information	Assigning judges
Accounting	Planning committees	Training for judges
Statistics	Research on rules and procedures	Selecting law-trained support personnel
Report preparation	Probation	Supervising screening and instructing of jurors
Systems analysis and research	Case processing	
Record keeping	Financial policy	Record creation
	Personnel rules	

Figure 8.1 Continuum of administrative-judicial activities. (*Source:* E. Keith Stott Jr., "The Judicial Executive: Toward Greater Congruence in an Emerging Profession." *The Justice System Journal* 7[2] [1982]: pp. 152–179.)

Unfortunately, the relationship between court administrators and judges can involve a clash between two cultures. Judges and administrators not only differ in background, education, and training but also approach their jobs from very different perspectives. Obviously, if judges and court administrators can develop a team approach, they will merge these two strengths.[53]

✦ SOURCES OF DISAGREEMENT

Larry Mays and William Taggart conducted a study of court administrators' perceptions of the sources of conflict in managing the courts. First, they asked respondents to indicate on a questionnaire whether a court administrator or a judge had primary responsibility for performing four administrative functions: budgeting, personnel, case scheduling, and jury management. At least half of the managers reported having the primary responsibility for each. The degree of managerial control was not uniform across functions, however. The function most assigned to court administrators concerned the budget, for which nearly 90 percent of respondents claimed responsibility. Fewer than 66 percent claimed primary responsibility for jury management and case scheduling.

The major source of conflict for court administrators was case-flow management (also known as *calendar management*), a crucial element in the functioning of any court. Respondents commented on postponement of cases, judges rescheduling the calendar, docketing, judicial assignments, and backlogs.[54] Mays and Taggart's findings that case-flow management was one of the 10 least delegated duties of presiding judges and that case-flow management ranked last in a list of the 10 administrative duties most often mentioned in conjunction with court administration is confirmed by other researchers.[55] One explanation for this finding is that case-flow management has been considered one function that "judges would be reluctant to delegate" because it is a duty that "might be considered judicial in nature."[56] At the same time, however, Mays and Taggart found that case-flow management was one of the areas giving court administrators the most problems. Thus, it seems ironic that although case-flow management is described by many authors[57] as one of the primary functions of court managers, it is also one that is grudgingly delegated by judges and is a leading source of conflict within the courtroom work group.

Mays and Taggart found that two of the five major areas of judge-administrator conflict in court management revolved around financial issues and personnel matters. Financial issues included accounting problems and methods, unbudgeted expenditures, procurement policies, and budget cutbacks. Among the personnel issues most often cited by respondents were employee evaluations, salary disputes, lack of adequate staffing, and staff competency.[58]

Court administrators must live by rules not of their own making. Internal court procedures and policies allow judges and others to hire, fire, direct, and compensate the administrator's own employees. Both internal and external sources of conflict are evident in the areas of budgeting and personnel. Mays and Taggart learned that court administrators appear to feel constrained by legislative control, by the state administrative offices of the courts, and by the power judges wield, which court administrators often perceive as interference.[59]

Finally, other sources of conflict between judges, court administrators, and clerks were policy and planning issues and what may be called *authority to administer*. In this regard, court administrators mentioned issues such as not having clearly defined authority, being delegated responsibility without authority, lacking major policymaking authority, and being prevented from making changes that only the judge can initiate. The latter concern is understandable. Court administrators do not enjoy constitutional status; most are appointed to their positions by a judge or a panel of judges and serve at the pleasure of their appointer(s). Thus, their authority is derived from or is an extension of the judge's powers. This "reflected glory" can leave an appointed administrator unsure of his or her power base and direction.[60] They must constantly "check with judges" to determine their wants and needs.[61] In fact, only 37.1 percent of court administrators perceive themselves as colleagues with the judges.[62]

Several court administrators have expressed that their judges either failed to provide support or leadership or, at worst, questioned the need for a court administrator position. Many administrators sense that their relationship is tenuous; 41.4 percent consider their position as that of a court employee as opposed to an executive position.[63] Other researchers have concluded that judges view their court administrators as administrative aides,[64] an attitude that could easily result in the discontinuation of such positions in tight fiscal times.

It is perhaps ironic that the more court administrators attempt to control the administrative processes, the wider the gap may become between themselves and judges. They can have widely divergent perspectives on *what* is to be done and *how* it is to be accomplished.[65]

✦ HOW JUDGES EVALUATE ADMINISTRATORS

Like other mortals, judges often see the world from their own perspective. As one Arizona judge observed:

> Judges and court administrators are not likely to view themselves in a negative light. As part of an organization that creates a certain amount of respect and awe for itself, it is not surprising that the [judge] and the court administrator may believe that they are better than they actually are. As a result, their top members frequently believe that the awe displayed toward them is intrinsic to their person, and not to the office.[66]

This view of the world is a pervasive impediment to objective assessment and clear decision making. The judge needs to be able to determine whether his or her court administrator is performing competently and effectively.

According to John Greacen,[67] judges can follow five basic strategies in determining the quality of work performed by their court administrators:

1. *The judge should look for indications of good management.* A good court administrator has implemented a number of plans and procedures, including personnel policies, recruitment and selection procedures, an orientation program for new employees, performance evaluation procedures, a discipline and grievance process, case management policies, financial controls, and other administrative policies (such as facilities and records management).

2. *The judge should be receiving regular information.* The court administrator should provide the judge with critically important reports and data on the court's performance, plans, activities, and accomplishments, as well as the number of case filings and terminations, pending cases, financial information, staff performance, long- and short-range plans, and other statistical data.

3. *The judge should be watching carefully.* The judge observes many of the court staff's activities and so he or she alone can assess the court administrator's strengths and weaknesses. How does he or she respond to problems and crises? Does he or she show initiative?

4. *The judge must often ask others about the court administrator's performance.* This includes soliciting input from lawyers, other judges, and other court staff members.

5. *The judge would be well advised to watch for danger signs.* The judge should be aware of signs of trouble: the administrator's communication is less frequent or less informative, his or her energy level dwindles, or he or she contributes fewer new ideas.

✦ COURT ADMINISTRATION REFORM: A MODEL PROGRAM

Imagine that you are in a crowded main lobby of a courthouse in sweltering heat. Others' tempers are short, lines are long, and people appear frustrated; some are even angry. Many have been waiting several hours simply to pay a traffic violation fine.

Inside the courtrooms, matters are little better. Cases are dismissed because trials are not speedy because records have been lost; continuances abound for the same reason. A large backlog of criminal cases exists. The calendar is in a shambles. In the office areas, problems also abound. Large sums of money frequently disappear; boxes of money orders, checks, and even cash are piled up because no one knows what they are intended to pay or where they go. Case files are stacked high in 20 or more locations around the courthouse; dozens of cubic feet of warrants are stacked in boxes in bathrooms and closets because they cannot be matched to case files. The data entry section is at least 5,000 cases behind. The court has no written procedures, formal management program, training program, or employee performance reviews. Turnover is 50 percent, and absenteeism is rampant. Public relations is a disaster, and complaints about the situation to the mayor and city council abound. This court does not work.[68]

Imagine that you return to the same court on a sweltering summer day three years later. The lobby where citizens wait for an average of 15 minutes before being served by well-trained, motivated court staff members is cool. Citizens give these staffers a 90 percent favorable rating. An express box now allows many to pay fines without waiting. In the courtrooms, action is fast paced but smooth flowing. The calendar is prompt and accurate; missing files now average less than 1 in 1,000. Dismissals for failing to bring defendants to trial speedily are now rare, and continuances are under control. No funds have disappeared from court offices in years, and cash security is tight. All payments are deposited within 24 hours; computer case records are updated within 48 hours. Loose paperwork is no problem, and each section has written procedures, lines of authority, flowcharts, and job standards. Comprehensive training is now provided to employees, who leave at an annual rate of only 4.5 percent, and absenteeism has declined significantly. The public, attorneys, and media recently gave the court high marks for efficiency, and complaints about the court system to the politicians are nominal. The court now works very well.[69]

How has the total program of court administration turned around? The court in Tucson, Arizona, has experienced this dramatic change. Several elements have been involved in this transformation. First, an atmosphere of trust and confidence between the administration and the judiciary exists. The presiding judge delegated sufficient authority to Ron Zimmerman, the court administrator, to begin the reform. In turn, Zimmerman respected the ultimate authority of the presiding judge. Second, the leadership recognized that filing cases is *the* priority for a high-volume court. They acted on all case files processed (computer update, manual logging, mailing distribution, calendaring) on one day and filed the next.[70]

Third, all judicial administrators and staff understand the fundamentals of court productivity. Zimmerman observed that "it makes no difference how many competent, hard-working judges a court may have if it does not have enough clerks to process the cases arriving daily from the bench." Zimmerman further noted that nine support staff for each full-time judge seems appropriate. The daily productivity of judges is quantified according to the types of cases handled; then the number of hours to complete each case is recorded to determine how many hours of required clerical time will be needed to process the actual actions received daily. With this information, the number of clerk positions are calculated. Another factor contributing to court productivity is the ratio of total filings (complaints) per operations clerk. Zimmerman determined that a clerk can be expected to handle no more than 3,000 case filings per year. Thus, if each judge is found to handle all work derived from 15,000 complaints, each judge needs 4.66 clerical staff members to handle his or her work output.[71]

In Tucson totally reorganizing court operations meant revamping a large, open bay of desks into three operating divisions and a support branch:

◊ *Court services* (including calendaring, motions, records, and domestic violence).

◊ *Public services* (counter transactions, mail and insurance, public telephones, and case initiation).

◊ *Case management* (warrant team, misdemeanor team, traffic team, arraignment team).

◊ *Administrative support branch* (bonds, restitution, enforcement team, fiscal/audit, and appeals).[72]

The supervision of court staff had been lacking, but more people were elevated to supervisory positions, allowing for greater decentralized decision making.

Following the implementation of this structure, Tucson courts reduced their case-processing backlogs from 25,000 to 40,000 cases to zero; the number of dismissals for lack of a speedy trial became statistically insignificant; and judicial backlogs were reduced from several thousand to zero. Furthermore, the average time required to service a person at the counter dropped from more than 10 minutes to 2.5 minutes. The court calendar was reformatted for easier readability and maintenance. A new case-tracking and management system, including automatic reporting to the state motor vehicle division, automatic surcharge calculation, revenue distribution, and court scheduling was installed.[73]

These changes required more than four years to accomplish. More changes are planned. Many years of failure to plan have caused this long-term effort; the benefits of bringing order from chaos are obvious. The message provided by a program of reform is that planning and, perhaps just as important, simplification are needed.[74]

Summary

The evolution of judicial administration is not simply the history of the court administrator's office. Conversely, the appointment of the first court administrator did not establish the beginning of judicial administration. This chapter has demonstrated that several elements—judges who have historically possessed the ultimate responsibility for administration of the courts, and court administrators and clerks who blazed new trails as nonlawyers in a field historically dominated by attorneys—had to combine in order for this discipline to develop to its current state. This chapter focused on the role of the court administrator, the important role that he or she can play to make the courts run smoothly, and methods for determining whether the administrator is assisting the court in being effective and efficient.

It was also shown that several obstacles still exist in the total acceptance of court administration as an integral part of the judiciary. The extent of actual and potential areas of conflict between judges and administrators was seen as a major source of problems.

Court administration is a rapidly developing field. While it still has its detractors, it is apparent that it has come far from its roots and is at least evolving into a *bona fide* element of the American justice system.

Questions for Review

1. Why is the term *judicial administration* multifaceted? Provide a good working definition for this term.
2. Why do judges need assistance in keeping the courts' processes flowing smoothly? Include in your response a consideration of the accountability of judges.
3. What are some criteria to be used for evaluating judges? How might you set up an evaluation process?
4. How have court clerks traditionally assumed and performed the role of court administrator?

5. What are some of the problems of being a court clerk in a rural area?

6. Why does the debate concerning the efficacy of court administrators continue? Discuss whether, given their history and relationships with judges, they have been completely successful or need to improve.

7. What are some common areas of conflict between judges and court administrators?

8. What criteria may judges employ to evaluate the effectiveness of their administrators?

Notes

1. See, for example, Edward B. McConnell, "What Does the Future Hold for Judges?" *Judges Journal* 30 (Summer 1991): 11; Russell R. Wheeler and Howard R. Whitcomb, *Judicial Administration: Text and Readings* (Englewood Cliffs, N.J.: Prentice Hall, 1977), p. xiii; and Edward C. Friesen Jr., Edward C. Gallas, and Nesta M. Gallas, *Managing the Courts* (Indianapolis, Ind.: Bobbs-Merrill, 1971), p. 13.

2. Robert C. Harrall, "In Defense of Court Managers: The Critics Misconceive Our Role," *Court Management Journal* 14 (1982): 52.

3. James Eisenstein and Herbert Jacob, *Felony Justice: An Organizational Analysis of Criminal Courts* (Boston: Little, Brown, 1977).

4. National Advisory Commission on Criminal Justice Standards and Goals, *Courts* (Washington, D.C.: U.S. Government Printing Office, 1973), p. 171.

5. American Bar Association, *Standards on Court Organization,* Standard 1.41 (Washington, D.C.: Author, 1974).

6. Ian R. Scott, "Procedural Law and Judicial Administration," *Justice System Journal* 12 (1987): 67–68.

7. Wheeler and Whitcomb, *Judicial Administration,* p. 8.

8. *Ibid.*

9. Russell Wheeler, *Judicial Administration: Its Relation to Judicial Independence* (Williamsburg, Va.: National Center for State Courts, 1988), p. 19.

10. Woodrow Wilson, "The Study of Administration," *Political Science Quarterly* 2 (1887): 197; reprinted in *Political Science Quarterly* 56 (1941): 481.

11. Quoted in Paul Nejelski and Russell Wheeler, *Wingspread Conference on Contemporary and Future Issues in the Field of Court Management* (Phoenix, Ariz., 1980), p. 15.

12. Wheeler and Whitcomb, *Judicial Administration,* p. 8.

13. Quoted in Doug Bandow, "Making Judges Accountable," *USA Today Magazine* (January 1988): 55–57.

14. See, for example, Joel B. Grossman, "Social Backgrounds and Judicial Decision-Making," 79 Harv.L.Rev. 1551 (1966); Walter F. Murphy and Joseph Tanenhaus, *The Study of Public Law* (New York: Random House, 1972), Chapter IV.

15. Robert Carp and Russell Wheeler, "Sink or Swim: The Socialization of a Federal District Judge," *Journal of Public Law* 21 (1972): 359–393.

16. *Ibid.,* p. 370.

17. *Ibid.,* p. 372.

18. *Ibid.*

19. *Ibid.*

20. *Ibid.,* p. 373.

21. *Ibid.,* p. 378.

22. *Ibid.,* pp. 382–383.

23. Roscoe Pound, "Principles and Outlines of a Modern Unified Court Organization," *Journal of the American Judicature Society* 23 (April 1940): 229.

24. See, for example, the Missouri Constitution, Article V. Sec. 15, paragraph 3.

25. Forest Hanna, "Delineating the Role of the Presiding Judge," *State Court Journal* 10 (Spring 1986): 17–22.

26. Robert A. Wenke, "The Administrator in the Court," *Court Management Journal* 14 (1982): 17–18, 29.

27. Mark W. Cannon, "Innovation in the Administration of Justice, 1969–1981: An Overview," in Philip L. Dubois (ed.), *The Politics of Judicial Reform* (Lexington, Mass.: D. C. Heath, 1982), pp. 35–48.

28. Marc Gertz, "Influence in the Court Systems: The Clerk as Interface," *Justice System Journal* 2 (1977): 30–37.

29. Robert B. Revere, "The Court Clerk in Early American History," *Court Management Journal* 10 (1978): 12–13.

30. *Ibid.,* p. 13.

31. G. Larry Mays and William Taggart, "Court Clerks, Court Administrators, and Judges: Conflict in Managing the Courts," *Journal of Criminal Justice* 14 (1986): 1–7.

32. Larry Berkson, "Delay and Congestion in State Systems: An Overview." In Larry Berkson, Steven Hays, and Susan Carbon (eds.), *Managing the State Courts: Text and Readings* (St. Paul, Minn.: West, 1977), p. 164.

33. Kathryn L. Fahnestock and Maurice D. Geiger, "Rural Courts: The Neglected Majority," *Court Management Journal* 14 (1982): 4–10.

34. *Ibid.,* p. 6.

35. *Ibid.,* pp. 6, 8.

36. Ernest C. Friesen and I. R. Scott, *English Criminal Justice* (Birmingham, England: University of Birmingham Institute of Judicial Administration, 1977).

37. Harvey E. Solomon, "The Training of Court Managers," in Charles R. Swanson and Susette M. Talarico (eds.), *Court Administration: Issues and Responses* (Athens, Ga.: University of Georgia, 1987), pp. 15–20.

38. Ernest C. Friesen, "Court Managers: Magnificently Successful or Merely Surviving?" *Court Management Journal* 14 (1982): 21.

39. Solomon, "The Training of Court Managers," p. 16.

40. Harrall, "In Defense of Court Managers," p. 51.

41. David W. Neubauer, *America's Courts and the Criminal Justice System* (5th ed.) (Pacific Grove, Calif.: Brooks/Cole, 1996), p. 384.

42. *Ibid.*

43. Bernadine Meyer, "Court Administration: The Newest Profession," *Duquesne Law Review* 10 (Winter 1971): 220–235.

44. Geoffrey A. Mort and Michael D. Hall, "The Trial Court Administrator: Court Executive or Administrative Aide?" *Court Management Journal* 12 (1980): 15.

45. *Ibid.*

46. *Ibid.,* p. 12.

47. Neubauer, *America's Courts and the Criminal Justice System,* p. 385.

48. Berkson, "Delay and Congestion in State Systems."

49. E. Keith Stott, "The Judicial Executive: Toward Greater Congruence in an Emerging Profession," *Justice System Journal* 7 (1982): 152–179.

50. Quoted in R. Dale Lefever, "Judge-Court Manager Relationships: The Integration of Two Cultures," *The Court Manager* 5 (Summer 1990): 8–11.

51. *Ibid.*, p. 10.

52. *Ibid.*

53. *Ibid.*, p. 9.

54. Mays and Taggart, "Court Clerks, Court Administrators, and Judges," p. 3.

55. Burton W. Butler, "Presiding Judges' Perceptions of Trial Court Administrators," *Justice System Journal* 3 (1977): 181.

56. Mort and Hall, "The Trial Court Administrator," p. 14.

57. See W. LeBar, "The Modernization of Court Functions: A Review of Court Management and Computer Technology," *Journal of Computers and Law* 5 (1975): 97–119; Burton W. Butler, "Presiding Judges' Perceptions of Trial Court Administrators"; J. M. Scheb, "Florida Conference Examines Education of Court Administrators," *Judicature* (1981): 465–468; David Saari, *American Court Management: Theories and Practice* (Westport, Conn.: Quorum Books, 1982).

58. Mays and Taggart, "Court Clerks, Court Administrators, and Judges," p. 4.

59. *Ibid.*

60. *Ibid.*, p. 5.

61. Saari, *American Court Management,* p. 62.

62. Mays and Taggart, "Court Clerks, Court Administrators, and Judges," p. 6.

63. *Ibid.*

64. For example, Mort and Hall, "The Trial Court Administrator."

65. Mays and Taggart, "Court Clerks, Court Administrators, and Judges," p. 7.

66. James Duke Cameron, Isaiah M. Zimmerman, and Mary Susan Downing, "The Chief Justice and the Court Administrator: The Evolving Relationship," 113 *Federal Rules Decisions* 443 (1987).

67. John M. Greacen, "Has Your Court Administrator Retired? Without Telling You?" National Association for Court Management, Conference Papers from the Second National Conference on Court Management, *Managing Courts in Changing Times* (Phoenix, Ariz.: September 9–14, 1990), pp. 5–20.

68. Adapted from Ron Zimmerman, "From Chaos to Excellence: Four Tough Years," *State Court Journal* 12 (Summer 1988): 13–18.

69. *Ibid.*

70. *Ibid.*, pp. 14–15.

71. *Ibid.*, p. 15.

72. *Ibid.*, pp. 15–16.

73. *Ibid.*, p. 16.

74. *Ibid.*, p. 18.

Chapter 9

Court Issues
and Practices

Justice is such a fine thing that we cannot pay too dearly for it.
—Alain Rene LeSage

✦ INTRODUCTION

Having looked at courts as organizations and explored the roles and functions of their personnel, next we examine the contemporary issues and practices related to them.

First we discuss the issue of case delay, a subject mentioned in earlier chapters; we look at the means to manage caseloads, the issue of case delays and the potentially exacerbating practical problems related to records and paperwork. We then address a matter that is becoming both more commonplace and difficult: the management of "notorious" cases involving celebrity defendants. Next we review the expanding role that the courts are forced to play in resolving society's delicate and controversial health-related issues, followed by the legal basis for, and recent increase in, using interpreters in the courtroom. We conclude the chapter with an examination of the problem of gender bias in the courts.

Three case studies concerning problems of court administration are provided at the end of the chapter.

✦ DRUG COURTS

The courts in the United States are becoming clogged with drug-related cases. Nationwide nearly 1.25 million arrests are made each year for drug offenses.[1] To cope with this massive problem, innovative drug courts are beginning to be used around the country. Perhaps the best known drug court—and the most widely observed and written about—is the one in the Miami, Florida, Diversion and Treatment program, established in the summer of 1989.

To qualify for the program, a defendant must be charged with possessing or purchasing drugs; may not have a history of violent crime, a drug-trafficking arrest, or more than two previous nondrug felony convictions; and the state attorney must agree to diversion. Program participants must have regular drug tests and return to court an average of once a month for a review of their progress. They must participate in and receive counseling, acupuncture, education courses, and vocational counseling, and their activities are monitored.[2]

The Miami drug court has only one judge but handles an average of 80 cases a day. The judge explains the program to defendants, making clear that it is difficult to complete. The judge also emphasizes that everyone involved in the program will assist and push the participants to complete it. Even with this large caseload, the judge talks with every defendant, offering a few words of encouragement for an improving offender or chiding one whose drug tests have been positive.

The year-long program consists of three phases: detoxification, stabilization, and aftercare; it is much more complex—and initially more costly—than prosecuting the offender. The program cost per client per year, however, is roughly the cost of jailing an offender for about nine days.

An evaluation of the program indicates a major benefit: whereas typical recidivism rates range up to 60 percent, only 11 percent of those who completed the program were rearrested in Dade County on any criminal charges in the year after graduation.[3]

Two research findings related to this drug court have found positive results of such courts. Several studies have shown that offenders referred to treatment by the courts have a powerful incentive to remain in treatment to avoid being jailed again; other research suggests that the longer an addict remains in treatment, the better his or her chances for long-term recovery.[4]

✦ THE DILEMMA OF DELAY

The principle "justice delayed is justice denied" says much about the long-standing goal of courts to process cases with due dispatch. Charles Dickens condemned the practice of slow litigation in 19th-century England, and Shakespeare mentioned "the law's delay" in *Hamlet*. The delay in processing cases remains one of the most visible problems of U.S. courts. The public often hears of cases that have languished on court dockets for years. More than half of all persons polled recently rated the efficiency of the courts as a "serious" or "very serious" societal problem.[5] The overload in our court system has been building for years. The most immediate source of pressure for the courts is the intensifying drug war; with increasing drug arrests, backlogs are becoming worse.

Case backlog and trial delay affect many of our country's courts. The magnitude of the backlog and the length of the delay vary greatly, however, depending on the court involved. Delay should be viewed as a symptom of a problem, not as a problem.[6] Generally, the term *delay* suggests abnormal or unacceptable time lapses in the processing of cases, yet some cases, by their nature, require lengthy preparation. *Unnecessary* delay is the concern, but no agreed upon definition of this term exists.

✧ CONSEQUENCES OF DELAY

The consequences of delay can be severe. Delay can jeopardize the values and guarantees inherent in our justice system. Delay deprives defendants of their Sixth Amendment rights to a speedy trial. Lengthy pretrial incarceration pressures can cause a defendant to plead guilty.[7] In contrast, delay can strengthen a defendant's bargaining position; prosecutors are more apt to accept such pleas to a lesser charge when dockets are crowded. Delays cause pretrial detainees to fill the jails, police officers to appear in court on numerous occasions, and attorneys to expend unproductive time appearing on the same case.[8]

One contributing factor to court delay is the little incentive that exists to process cases speedily. Although at least 10 states require cases to be dismissed and defendants to be released if they are denied a speedy trial,[9] the U.S. Supreme Court has refused to give the rather vague concept of "speedy trial" any precise time frame.[10] The problem with time frames is twofold: first, more complex cases legitimately take a long time to prepare; second, time limits may be waived because of congested court dockets. In sum, no legally binding mechanism to reduce the delay works.

✧ SUGGESTED SOLUTIONS TO THE DELAY PROBLEM

The best known legislation addressing the problem is the Speedy Trial Act enacted by Congress in 1974 and amended in 1979; it provides firm time limits: 30 days from the point of arrest to indictment and 70 days from indictment to trial. Thus, federal prosecutors have a total of 100 days between the time of arrest and trial.

While speedy trial statutes exist in all 50 states and 35 states provide for a speedy trial in their constitutions, the latter provisions apply only when the delay has been "extensive," another term that has no definition. Overall, speedy trial laws have had only a limited impact in speeding the flow of cases through the criminal courts.[11] As Neubauer noted, "State laws have failed to provide the courts with adequate and effective enforcement mechanisms."[12]

Over the years a number of proposals have been offered as solutions to alleviate the courts' logjam; they relate to juries and range from judicial jury selection and limits on criminal appeals to the use of only six-person juries. The latter was actually suggested more than two decades ago as a means to relieve the congestion of court calendars and reduce court costs pertaining to jurors.[13] Thirty-three states have specifically authorized juries of fewer than 12 members, but most allow these smaller juries only in misdemeanor cases. In federal courts, defendants are entitled to a 12-person jury unless the parties agree in writing to a smaller one.[14]

Some reform-minded persons concerned with delays suggest that requiring courts to be better managed and more efficient will address the delay issue. However the courts function, their purpose must be to serve justice. Where justice ends and expediency begins is difficult to determine and is open to interpretation.

✦ CASE SCHEDULING

A key part of court administration is the ability to set a certain date for trial. One study found that courts with low backlogs and little delay set a date for trial early in the history of a case.[15] Lawyers knew they had to be prepared by that date. If the judge sets an uncertain date and if lawyers know that court dates are fluid and easily continued, they do not prepare.

Scheduling people for trials is problematic because of forces outside the court administrator's control: slow or inaccurate mail delivery, resulting in notices to appear in court that arrive after the scheduled hearing; illegible addresses that prevent key witnesses or defendants from being contacted about a hearing or trial; and a jailer's inadvertent failure to include a defendant on a list for transportation. If only one key person fails to appear, the matter must be rescheduled. Another problem in schedules results from judges' limited authority to control the actions of personnel from law enforcement, probation, or court reporter's offices, all of which have their own scheduling problems.[16]

The two primary methods by which cases are scheduled by the courts are the individual calendar and master calendar systems.

✧ INDIVIDUAL CALENDAR SYSTEM

The simplest procedure for scheduling cases is the individual calendar. A case is assigned to a single judge, who must see it through all aspects: arraignment, pretrial motions, and trial. The primary advantage is continuity; all parties to the case know that a single judge is responsible for its conclusion. In addition, this system minimizes judge shopping and fixes administrative responsibility for each case. Identifying the judges who allow delays may be easier because one can easily compare judges' dockets.

This system, however, is often affected by major differences in "case stacking" or piling up, because some judges move cases quickly and others move them slowly. Also, when a judge is assigned a difficult or lengthy case, others assigned to that judge must wait. Because most cases will be pleaded, however, case stacking is not normally a major problem unless too many cases are scheduled for a given day. Conversely, scheduling too few cases for hearing or adjudication each day also results in delay. If all cases settle, the judge is free but with a large backlog and nothing scheduled for the day.

✦ MASTER CALENDAR SYSTEM

The master calendar is a more recent development than the individual system. In this approach, judges specialize (usually on a rotating basis) on specific stages of a case: preliminary hearings, arraignments, motions, bargaining, and trials. A judge is assigned a case from a central or master pool; once he or she has completed the assigned phase, the case is returned to the pool for assignment of a judge for the next phase. The primary advantage with this system is that judges who are good in one particular aspect of litigation (such as preliminary hearings) can be assigned to the job they do best. The disadvantage is that identifying the responsibility for delays is more difficult. Judges also have less incentive to keep their docket current because when they dispose of one case, another appears. The distribution of work can be quite uneven. If, for example, three judges are responsible for preliminary hearings and one's case proceeds more slowly than the others, the workload shifts unequally; in other words, the two judges whose cases move more quickly—for whatever reasons—must work on more cases.

✦ WHICH SYSTEM IS BEST?

Each of the calendaring systems described here has advantages and disadvantages, but a running debate has developed over which is best. This probably depends on the nature of the court. Some courts, such as U.S. district courts, use the individual calendar system more successfully. But due largely to their complex dockets, metropolitan and state courts almost uniformly use the master calendar system. There are indications that courts using the master calendar experience the greatest difficulty. Typical problems related to the master schedule include the refusal by some judges to take their fair share of cases; the often great administrative burden on the chief judge; and a significant backlog of cases that may develop as a result of these factors. Courts that discontinued the master calendar system in favor of the individual system realized major reductions in delay.[17]

✦ MANAGING NOTORIOUS CASES

✦ A Historical Phenomenon

The U.S. Supreme Court stated the following in 1966 in *Sheppard v. Maxwell*:

> Murder and mystery, society, sex and suspense were combined in this case in such a manner as to intrigue and captivate the public fancy to a degree perhaps unparalleled in recent annals. Throughout . . . the nine-week trial, circulation-conscious editors catered to the insatiable interest of the American public in the bizarre. In this atmosphere of a "Roman Holiday" for the news media, Sam Sheppard stood trial for his life.[18]

The existence of notorious cases has always been a part of courtrooms and caused problems in them. The trials of the Salem witches, of Aaron Burr, of Scopes, of the Lindbergh kidnapper, of Sacco and Vanzetti, of the Chicago 7, the Manson "family," and Alger Hiss are examples of notorious trials that have become classic notorious cases. More recently, the trials of O. J. Simpson, Susan Smith, Mike Tyson, William Kennedy Smith, Oliver North, Marion Barry, Bernhard Goetz, Imelda Marcos, John Gotti, Manuel Noriega, and the police officers tried for assaulting Rodney King have joined this notorious group. The media continued to focus on persons involved in these cases even after the actual trial ended.

Certainly, the work of the judge and the court administrator is greatly affected when such celebrated cases are on the docket. We examine administrative issues related to such cases in the next section.

✦ Administrative Issues

One issue in handling a notorious case is the selection of the judge; in these cases, having an experienced judge who has good legal skills, possesses a good reputation in the legal community, is temperate and in command in the courtroom, and is seen as fair and unbiased is particularly important. He or she also should be in good health and have the ability to deal with the media. These trial judges should be picked by presiding judges for this assignment.[19] They must take firm control, adhere to dates set for court processes, and avoid granting continuances unless absolutely necessary. He or she must insist on timely preparation by attorneys.

Court administrators and other court staff members must necessarily devote considerable thought and planning to these cases. They must anticipate all possible problems and concerns that might arise including media requests; courtroom and courthouse logistics for handling crowds, the media, and security; jury management; and management of the court's docket of other existing cases.

A notorious trial may require that an appropriate courtroom be used to accommodate an unusually large number of the press and the public, as well as the defendant(s) and attorneys. Planning is essential to provide adequate space for judge's chambers, jury rooms, witness rooms, clerk's office, security personnel, parking, and lunchroom facilities.[20] The care, comfort, and safety of the prospective and actual jurors must be provided. Jurors must be kept informed of all case details relating to their task and time frames relating to the proceedings.

If the judge decides to sequester the jury, the court administrator must consider security issues (protecting the jury from outside interference and providing for conjugal visits, room searches, transportation, and so on) and jurors' personal needs (meals, entertainment, medical supplies).[21]

A number of issues must be considered. Are identification and press passes needed? Are entry screening devices necessary? What seating arrangements are required? Should court observers be allowed to exit and reenter at will? Should purses, briefcases, and other such items be searched by hand? Should all mail and telephone calls coming to the courthouse be monitored? Is a special command center for coordination and communication desirable?[22]

Meanwhile, new cases will be filed, and other calendars will be in operation. Once a notorious case begins, the remaining trial and motion responsibilities of the trial judge in other pending cases should be transferred to another judge. The judge presiding over a notorious trial must avoid distractions and disruptions and take care not to overlook any of the several important matters that accompany such a trial.[23]

Perhaps the most important task in managing notorious cases and avoiding and resolving associated problems is communication with the media. Some judges have established an open-door policy in dealing with the media by which they set aside a certain time when they discuss the case with reporters. This method is quite effective in ensuring that the media receive accurate information rather than having to rely on rumor and other sources of questionable information.[24]

✦ THE IMPACT OF HEALTH-RELATED ISSUES ON THE COURTS

A very pervasive although not highly visible issue affecting the courts is related to the country's health care policy. The types of policy decisions judges must confront—many involving weighty medical ethics questions—are exemplified by actual events that occurred in a two-week period: a company that attempted to drastically cut its insurance coverage for employees with AIDS was sued; a woman convicted of child abuse was required by a court to accept implantation of a long-term birth control drug; a jury convicted a woman for child endangerment after passing an illegal drug to her infant through her breast milk, killing the child; a petition was filed to drop criminal charges because of the deteriorating health of the 85-year-old defendant.

Determining causality and damages in cases involving health problems stemming from silicone gel breast implants, whether to provide life-sustaining medical treatment, the rights and responsibilities related to new reproductive technologies (such as in vitro fertilization and surrogate parenthood), elder abuse and neglect, and even claims of brain cancer attributable to currents in cellular telephones is extremely difficult.[25] Such cases may create unique administrative problems and challenges for court processing. For example, they may be raised on an emergency basis and require an expedited decision. And because expert witnesses may not be available for these cases, the judge may have to spend a considerable amount of time obtaining necessary information.

The role of the courts in health-related issues is likely to expand as the onslaught of new litigation brings many additional health care–related issues before the courts.

✧ A RELATED PROBLEM: THE INCREASE IN SCIENTIFIC TESTIMONY

An exhibit in today's courtroom might be a brain scan from a neuroscientist's laboratory as well as a murder weapon. The complex testimony offered by experts who speak in technical, often scientific, language can cause problems for courts today. These experts often disagree with each other as to their findings. The demand for expert testimony has tripled in the past decade; scientists now make approximately 400,000 appearances per year to give depositions, attend briefings, and testify in court. Scientific evidence is used in nearly 30 percent of all court cases, and outcomes now often turn on the ability of judges and jurors with little or no scientific background to comprehend the complexities of such specialized subjects as physics, toxicology, and organic chemistry.[26]

Many persons now question whether courts and juries can properly digest this complex material and reach accurate decisions. Scientists shudder when a rapist is released by a jury despite a 99 percent probability that semen in evidence was the defendant's; they recoil when a judge fails to understand that animal studies can have strong implications for human beings and therefore does not admit such research into evidence. Attorneys and clients are befuddled and outraged when two cases with identical scientific evidence result in opposite verdicts. Growing concern over such inconsistencies has led scientific societies, legal scholars, and even the U.S. Department of Justice to call for changes to improve the quality of science-based verdicts.[27]

The most publicized dilemma for the courts is how to guarantee the quality and credibility of scientific testimony. Because lawyers seek the experts most likely to help them win a case, many scientists regard courtroom testimony as suspect and simply refuse to participate. One federal judge observed, however, that "an expert can be found to testify to the truth of almost any factual theory, no matter how frivolous."[28]

One solution to the problem is the use of court-appointed witnesses chosen by a judge to act as a neutral voice in the midst of scientific disputes. The American Association for the Advancement of Science has pledged to aid judges in their quest for court experts by screening scientists and providing lists of suitable candidates. A Federal Judicial Center study revealed that although 80 percent of judges think appointing neutral experts can be useful, only 20 percent have ever done so. Most judges express concern about affecting the outcome of a trial and worry that they lack the scientific expertise to choose an expert.[29]

The Department of Justice is considering offering seminars to help judges better understand scientific methods, but with 400 cases on the average federal judge's calendar, attending such seminars may be difficult if not impossible. An alternative plan is for other groups to prepare primers on subjects such as DNA evidence and statistical methodology to guide judges through the relevant issues and debates. Pretrial crash courses for jurors and juror notebooks are also possibilities.[30]

Notwithstanding these efforts, studies suggest that judges and jurors base their decisions on a wide range of human impulses—sympathy, dread, the desire for revenge—rather than on scientific rationality.[31] In the end, a verdict may not depend on their perception of scientific evidence but on their gut feelings of guilt and innocence.

✦ INTERPRETERS IN THE COURTROOM

✦ THE LEGAL BASIS

A recently added participant to the courtroom is an interpreter. Their presence is grounded in the Sixth Amendment, which allows criminal defendants to confront witnesses who testify against them, and the Fifth and Fourteenth Amendments that guarantee due process and afford "fundamental fairness" to defendants.

Since the late 1960s, the use of foreign-language interpreting in U.S. courtrooms has increased dramatically. The passage of Public Law 95-539, the federal Court Interpreters Act of 1978, was the legislation that affected this practice. It provides for court-appointed interpreter services:

> In any criminal or civil action initiated by the United States in a United States District Court . . . if the presiding judicial officer determines on such officer's own motion or on the motion of a party that such party . . . (1) speaks only or

primarily a language other than the English language; or (2) suffers from a hearing impairment . . . so as to inhibit such party's comprehension of the proceedings or communication with counsel or the presiding judicial officer, or . . . such witness' comprehension of questions and the presentation of such testimony. Note that the guarantee covers civil as well as criminal matters, and that the judge determines whether a given defendant or witness is in need of an interpreter's services.

Although specifically applicable to federal courts, this legislation has served to stimulate similar measures in state and municipal courts. Many states provide for courtroom interpreters by statute, and courts of lower jurisdiction are increasingly assigning foreign language interpreters to non-English-speaking or hearing-impaired defendants, witnesses, and litigants.[32]

The need for interpreters for a multitude of languages exists, ranging from the commonplace such as Spanish (96.6 percent of all interpreter appearances), Italian, and German, to the languages heard less frequently in the United States, such as those of Asia, Africa, and the Middle East. Court interpreters commonly participate in criminal trials for initial appearances, bail hearings, preliminary hearings, pretrial and in-trial motions, pleas and changes of plea, sentencing, trials, and probation department recommendations.[33] At trial, court interpreters must swear to interpret the proceeding at hand to the best of their ability and as accurately as possible.[34]

Interpreting is a highly complicated process. Interpretation has the potential to grossly distort what has been said. Appeals based on errors in interpreting or translating have increased dramatically in recent years.[35] Several appeals have been successful when interpreters were shown to be unqualified. For this reason, court interpreters at the federal level must be certified by the director of the Administrative Office of the U.S. Courts. Aspiring interpreters must pass a rigorous test certification; in 1986 only 4 percent of those taking the exam passed it in its entirety.[36]

✦ THE PROBLEM OF GENDER BIAS IN THE COURTS

The problem of gender bias exists in courtrooms as it does in many other segments of society. Although it might be difficult to imagine that such a problem exists, especially in the courts, as we enter the 21st century, several of the nation's legislatures and state supreme courts have deemed this issue to be of such concern that they are convening special task forces to investigate what can be done to address this problem. Certainly, researchers and court administrators can examine data, records, and other information and use them to highlight this problem, explore its existence, and seek ways to prevent it.

Gender bias has been described as "a problem with several aspects."[37] The term refers to society's perception of the relative worth of women and men, what is perceived as women's and men's work, and myths and misconceptions about the economic and social realities of women's and men's lives.[38]

More specifically, gender bias manifests itself in the courts in the following ways:

1. The American Bar Association has found that although the "crimes" that female juveniles are accused of are categorized as less serious and harmful to society than those males are charged with, the females are often held in detention for longer periods and are less likely to be placed in community programs than males are.[39]

2. Early studies noted the casual response of the legal profession and the judiciary to the plight of battered women. Some researchers interpreted this as evidence of faint echoes of the common law view of a wife as her husband's property that lingers in the minds of some judges and attorneys.[40]

3. Extensive literature created by the antirape movement suggests that judicial myths regarding the nature of male and female sexuality and attitudes toward the "proper" roles of women have caused courts to punish rape victims by defining rape and spousal abuse as "victim-precipitated" crimes.[41]

4. The looming problem in family law that most disturbs those interested in equal justice is the underclass of women and children being created as the result of inadequate child support and alimony awards. Social scientists studying the consequences of no-fault divorce in California uncovered the unwitting contribution that courts were making to the "feminization of poverty."[42]

In courtrooms across the country, females are still judged on the basis of factors that trial researchers and feminists consider antiquated and prejudicial. Bias and stereotypical images, they say, influence jury selection, the treatment of female witnesses, and attitudes toward female attorneys and judges. The New York Task Force on Women in the Courts has termed gender bias "pervasive" because of the tendency of some judges and attorneys to accord less credibility to the claims and testimony of females. These findings were nearly identical to those of a New Jersey study. These and other studies consistently identify stereotypes that female jurors are more likely than male jurors to acquit in criminal cases (except in cases involving a child or threat to family); female jurors are less likely to favor female defendants or plaintiffs; and in civil cases, female jurors are more likely than males to vote in favor of the plaintiff but vote for smaller awards than men do.[43] Such stereotypical beliefs have existed for decades.

The need to educate judges about the findings of researchers and the concerns of female lawyers was first articulated in 1969 by Sylvia Roberts, a pioneer Title VII litigator from Louisiana. Progress has been slow in coming, however; little has yet to be written on the topic, although courses and workshops are now included in numerous judicial education programs for state and federal court judges.[44]

Roberts said that women should adopt the Taoist philosophy of the Chinese ancients and "think of ourselves as water on stone."[45] Although the stone is hard and the water is merely splashing around it, the stone eventually wears away, leaving the landscape transformed. Women will continue to act as water on stone; perhaps through their consistent efforts, the stone will eventually give way.

Summary

This chapter discussed several challenges in the courts. It also identified several major problems and issues confronting the courts. The major problem today is that of case delay, for it impacts all of the courts' activities. We also examined several issues involving health, language interpretation, and gender bias that affect courts.

Questions for Review

1. Describe the two primary methods of case scheduling employed by the courts. Which of the two methods is used most frequently in the United States? What are its advantages and disadvantages?

2. What is a notorious court case? What are some of the administrative problems that accompany such cases? How have these cases resulted in changes in court operations?

3. What is the court administrator's role in dealing with non-English-speaking defendants? Why is this a potentially serious matter?

4. What are the philosophy, role, and methods of a drug court?

5. Do drug courts appear to have positive results?

6. In what ways may the courts be viewed as being guilty of gender bias? What can be done to address the problem?

Notes

1. U.S. Department of Justice, Federal Bureau of Investigation, *Crime in the United States, 1995* (Washington, D.C.: Author, 1996), p. 209.

2. U.S. Department of Justice, National Institute of Justice Program Focus, "Miami's Drug Court: A Different Approach," June 1993, p. 3.

3. *Ibid.,* p. 13.

4. Office of National Drug Control Policy, *Understanding Drug Treatment* (Washington, D.C.: The White House, 1990).

5. David W. Neubauer, *America's Courts and the Criminal Justice System* (5th ed.) (Belmont, Calif.: Wadsworth, 1996), p. 374.

6. David W. Neubauer, Maria Lipetz, Mary Luskin, and John Paul Ryan, *Managing the Pace of Justice: An Evaluation of LEAA's Court Delay Reduction Programs* (Washington, D.C.: U.S. Government Printing Office, 1981).

7. Neubauer, *America's Courts and the Criminal Justice System,* p. 376.

8. *Ibid.,* p. 377.

9. See *Barker v. Wingo,* 407 U.S. 514 (1972).

10. Neubauer, *America's Courts and the Criminal Justice System,* p. 438.

11. Raymond Nimmer, *The Nature of System Change: Reform Impact in the Criminal Courts* (Chicago: American Bar Foundation, 1978).

12. Neubauer, *America's Courts and the Criminal Justice System,* pp. 387–388.

13. National Advisory Commission on Criminal Justice Standards and Goals, *Courts* (Washington, D.C.: U.S. Government Prinitng Office, 1973).

14. Neubauer; *America's Courts and the Criminal Justice System,* p. 242.

15. *Ibid.,* p. 379.

16. Steven Flanders, *Case Management and Court Management in the United States District Courts* (Washington, D.C.: Federal Judicial Center, 1977).

17. Neubauer et al., *Managing the Pace of Justice.*

18. 86 S.Ct. 1507, 1519 (1966).

19. Timothy R. Murphy, Genevra Kay Loveland, and G. Thomas Munsterman, *A Manual for Managing Notorious Cases* (Washington, D.C.: National Center for State Courts, 1992), pp. 4–6.

20. *Ibid.,* p. 23.

21. *Ibid.,* pp. 53, 73.

22. *Ibid.,* pp. 89–94.

23. *Ibid.,* p. 22.

24. *Ibid.,* pp. 27–30.

25. U.S. Department of Justice, "Health and Criminal Justice: Strengthening the Relationship," National Institute of Justice Journal, *Research in Action,* November 1994, pp. 25–26.

26. Joannie M. Schrof, "Courtroom Conundrum," *U.S. News and World Report* (October 26, 1992): 67–69.

27. *Ibid.*

28. *Ibid.,* p. 68.

29. *Ibid.,* p. 69.

30. *Ibid.*

31. *Ibid.*

32. Susan Berk-Seligson, *The Bilingual Courtroom: Court Interpreters in the Judicial Process* (Chicago: University of Chicago Press, 1990), p. 1.

33. *Ibid.,* pp. 3–4, 8–9.

34. *Ibid.,* pp. 55, 57.

35. Berk-Seligson, *The Bilingual Courtroom,* pp. 199–200.

36. J. Leeth, *The Court Interpreter Examination* (Washington, D.C.: National Resource Center for Translation and Interpretation, Georgetown University, no date).

37. Lynn Hecht Shafran, "National Conference on Gender Bias in the Courts," in Marilyn Roberts (ed.), *State Court Journal* 13 (Summer 1989): 12.

38. *Ibid.*

39. American Bar Association, *Little Sisters and the Law* (Washington, D.C.: Author, 1977).

40. *Ibid.*

41. *Ibid.*

42. Norma J. Wikler, "Water to Stone: A Perspective on the Movement to Eliminate Gender Bias in the Courts," *State Court Journal* 13 (Summer 1989): 13–18.

43. Kathleen Mulvihill, "Female Stereotypes Persist in U.S. Courts, Recent Studies Show," *The Christian Science Monitor* (July 27, 1987): 7.

44. *Ibid.,* p. 14.

45. Marilyn Roberts, "National Conference on Gender Bias in the Courts," *State Court Journal* 13 (Summer 1989): 12.

CASE STUDIES

The Court Administrator and the Prudent Police Chief*

You are the court administrator in a court that has the following procedure for handling traffic matters:

1. All persons who receive traffic citations are required to appear in court at 9 A.M. on either Monday or Wednesday within two weeks of their arrest. They are given a specific date to appear.
2. At the initial appearance, the arresting agency is represented by a court officer who has previously filed copies of all the citations with the clerk of the court.
3. The clerk, prior to the return date on the citation, prepares a file for each citation.
4. The clerk calls each case, and those persons appearing are requested to enter a plea; if the plea is not guilty, the matter is set for trial at a future date.
5. One case is scheduled per hour. On the trial date, the prosecutor and arresting officer are required to appear, ready for trial.
6. Those persons who fail to appear either at the return date or at trial are not required to appear but have the option of forfeiting their bond, which they posted at their initial appearance.
7. Statistics show that 75 percent of those persons pleading not guilty in this jurisdiction fail to appear for trial.

The chief of police in the court's jurisdiction is very concerned about overtime for officers. He communicates with you, the court administrator, about this concern and explains that all police officers who appear in court for trial are entitled to the minimum two hours of overtime when they are not appearing during their regular shift. He views this as a tremendous and unnecessary expense to the city, because most of the officers are not needed because the defendants do not appear. He recognizes that defendants have a right to post bond under

---

*Contributed by Hon. Burton A. Scott, former Associate Dean of the National Judicial College, Reno, Nevada.

the law and simply forfeit it at the initial appearance or on the trial date. He is interested, however, in devising some system to save the city this cost for all the officers' overtime. He explains that other municipalities are faced with similar problems.

Questions for Discussion

1. What kind of a system would you propose to address the problem? How would you implement it? In creating a modified system, you must work within the existing law without changing statutes or ordinances.
2. After you have designed a system, explain how you would obtain the cooperation of the judges, prosecutors, clerk's office, and other law enforcement agencies as well as the defense lawyers. Discuss any proposed changes in the law you think might improve the system further.
3. How would you accomplish other *significant* changes to improve the procedures and operation of this system? Consider the creation of an ongoing mechanism or committee that would propose, discuss, adopt, and carry out changes for the benefit of the system as a whole.

Chief Judge Cortez's Embattled Court*

You have just been hired as the new court administrator for a medium-sized court with approximately 90 employees. Once on the job, you discover that you have been preceded by two heavy-handed court administrators who together lasted less than a year on the job because of their inability to handle employee conflicts and to achieve a minimal level of productivity. They were more or less forced to resign because of a lack of employee cooperation and increasing talk of unionization.

General turmoil and distrust exist throughout the organization. Employees do not trust each other and, as a group, they do not trust management. The courthouse runs on gossip and inertia. The organization has little official communication. Previous court administrators made no attempt to solicit employee opinions or ideas.

The judges are all aware of the problem, but they have formed no clear consensus as to how to respond to it. In fact, turmoil and conflict exist among the judges themselves. They engage in "turf protection" with operating funds and the court's cases and often take sides in office squabbles. As a result, they are unable to come to any clear consensus or to provide the court administrator with any guidance.

*Contributed by Dennis Metrick, management analyst, Court Services Department, Administrative Office of the Courts, Phoenix, Arizona.

The chief judge, Dolores Cortez, has served in that capacity for 10 years and is known to be exceedingly fair, compassionate, and competent; however, she will retire in six months and appears unwilling to take a firm stand on, or a strong interest in, intraoffice disputes and difficulties. In fact, she is not convinced that a problem exists. Furthermore, in past years she has been quite reluctant to intervene in arguments between individual judges.

Questions for Discussion

1. As the "new kid on the block," how would you respond to this organization problem? What is the first problem you would address, and how would you do it? What additional problems require your attention?

2. As court administrator, how would you respond to the judges' inability to develop a consensus? How could the decision-making process be improved?

3. What techniques could be employed to improve communication through the organization, lessen tension and strife, and generally create a more harmonious work environment?

4. What would be your general approach to Judge Cortez? To her successor?

An Unmanageable Case Management Quandary*

You are the court administrator for a court of 50 employees. This court, which once disposed of about 700 cases per month, now hears an average of 100 criminal and 400 civil cases per month. Case filings have doubled in the past seven years.

The present "hybrid" case management system has evolved over a long period of time through tradition and expediency. A growing caseload and increasing difficulties in avoiding a backlog has prompted the judges, however, to rethink the present system. Criminal cases that once reached final disposition in a month now require two to three months. The situation shows no signs of improving in the foreseeable future.

The court has a mixed calendar system. Two judges are assigned to hear criminal cases and motions for a one-month period while the remaining four judges hear all manner of civil matters on a random basis when a civil complaint is filed. The judges are responsible for managing these cases until final disposition.

At the end of the one-month period, the two judges hearing criminal cases return to the civil division and two other judges rotate onto the criminal bench; these two incoming criminal judges then hear any pending criminal cases or motions.

---

*Contributed by Dennis Metrick, management analyst, Court Services Department, Administrative Office of the Courts, Phoenix, Arizona.

One of the judges is assigned to juvenile-related matters in addition to any criminal and civil division cases. The court collects statistics on the number of court filings and motions filed in each division on a month-to-month basis.

Questions for Discussion

1. What are the merits and difficulties posed by this case management approach? In a general way, discuss them. Relate your response to the general advantages and disadvantages of both the individual and the master calendar systems.

2. What specific problems could arise in the criminal division? Why?

3. What specific problems could be created by the permanent assignment of a judge to the juvenile division? Advantages?

4. What comments would you make with regard to the court's statistical report? Are other data needed for management purposes? If so, what kind?

Part IV

CORRECTIONS

This part includes four chapters, each of which focuses on corrections administration. Chapter 10 examines the corrections organization and operation, including prisons and jails. Chapter 11 covers personnel roles and functions, and Chapter 12 discusses the administration of community corrections through probation and parole. Chapter 13 reviews corrections issues and practices. Specific chapter content is provided in the introductory section of each chapter. Case studies in corrections administration appear at the end of Chapter 13.

Chapter 10

Corrections Organization and Operation

Prisons are built with stones of Law.

—William Blake

The founders of a new colony . . . recognized it among their earliest practical necessities to allot a portion of the virgin soil as a cemetery, and another portion as the site of a prison.

—Nathaniel Hawthorne

✦ INTRODUCTION

The subculture of prisons and jails has been the subject of television and movie fare in the United States for several decades. Most of these dramas about prison and jail life portrayed prison administrators and their personnel and organizations as cruel, bigoted, corrupt, and morally base. Furthermore, prison literature such as Jack Henry Abbott's *In the Belly of the Beast,* Eldridge Cleaver's *Soul on Ice,* George Jackson's *Soledad Brother,* and Malcolm Braly's *On the Yard,* among others, have presented similar views. These television programs, movies, and books reflect the public's interest in and often contribute to its lack of knowledge about our correctional institutions. As this chapter discusses, corrections has become a boom industry and promises to continue being so well into the 21st century. Indeed, futurists believe corrections to be the most rapidly growing criminal justice career area for the future.[1]

This chapter first focuses generally on the organization, operation, and some unique aspects of correctional institutions. Then we consider the issue of the increasing amount of civil litigation filed by inmates. Next we examine the causes and effects of prison crowding. Some approaches and limitations to helping inmates who have serious emotional and behavioral problems, violent personalities, are addicted to narcotics or alcohol, or practice deviant sexual behaviors are reviewed.

We also look at local jails, including crowding, programs, and a relatively new jail design and philosophy. We conclude the chapter by considering recent research findings concerning the effects of incarceration, including solitary confinement and life on death row, and some issues for correctional administrators and society at large to consider.

✦ CORRECTIONAL ORGANIZATIONS

✧ GENERAL FEATURES

The correctional organization is a complex, hybrid organization that utilizes two distinct, yet related, management subsystems to achieve its goals: one is concerned primarily with managing correctional employees, and the other is concerned primarily with delivering correctional services to a designated offender population. The correctional organization, therefore, employs one group of people—correctional personnel—to work with and control another group—offenders.[2]

An interesting feature of the correctional organization is that every correctional employee who exercises legal authority over offenders *is a supervisor,* even if the person is the lowest-ranking member in the agency or institution. Therefore, two distinct, yet related, supervisory roles exist. One involves supervising employees, referred to as *first-level supervision;* the other involves supervising offenders, or *line* or *field supervision.* In most organizations, line supervisors normally provide labor that is used to convert materials into products or units of production. In correctional organization, line supervisors provide the type of correctional service being delivered to the correctional client, be the client an inmate, probationer, or parolee. The product or unit of production is the pattern of supervisory interaction between the line supervisor and the offender.[3]

Another feature of the correctional organization is that everything a correctional supervisor does may have civil or criminal ramifications, both for himself or herself and for the agency or institution. Therefore, the legal and ethical responsibility for the correctional supervisor is greater than it is for supervisors in other types of organizations.

Finally, two different philosophies exist as to what a correctional organization should be: (1) *custodial* organizations, which emphasize the caretaker functions of controlling and observing inmates, and (2) *treatment* organizations, which emphasize rehabilitation of inmates. These different philosophies contain potential conflict for correctional personnel.[4]

✧ OPEN SYSTEMS

Traditionally, many correctional organizations have been administered as a *closed system*. This limits the organization's responsibility only to the structural boundaries of the official organization.[5] These institutions experience a degree of difficulty in communicating with the outside world and are often loathe to provide information concerning their activities and methods.[6] Historically, this closed system has contributed to the problem of political alienation and fragmentation of correctional services.[7]

Today, however, most correctional administrators and policymakers recognize that their organizations are intricate components of government systems and of society itself. These *open systems* recognize that problems and solutions are generated by forces and resources outside the organization that must be managed. For example, the decision to close a state prison in a small community may result in significant political pressure not to close it because that community's economy depends on the prison. Local pressure can also prevent locating a pre-release center in an established residential area.[8]

In short, the contemporary correctional organization is an intricate part of the social, political, and economic setting in which the organization functions. Therefore, the organization must be administered as an open system.

✧ ADMINISTRATION AND MANAGEMENT
OF CORRECTIONAL INSTITUTIONS

According to Vernon Fox, correctional administration is "the organization and management of the delivery system that brings the basic necessities and treatment programs of the correctional institutions or agencies to the correctional client."[9]

Correctional administration and management are both concerned with internal organizational issues, such as personnel, budgets, and programs. Administration's major concerns are obtaining personnel, securing funds, and interfacing programs with other agencies. Management's concern is primarily using available personnel and resources to implement programs. Most of an administrator's time and energy are expended on activities outside the organization while most of management's time is spent on activities within the organization.[10]

Correctional administrators are responsible for developing policy; managers are responsible primarily for implementing it. Therefore, administrators are concerned with long-range planning that affects the entire organization, and managers are responsible for day-to-day planning. Finally, correctional administration is highly political, whereas management positions tend to be less so.[11]

Levels of Correctional Administration. Figure 10.1 represents the levels of correctional organizations, including top administration, executive management, middle management, supervisory management, and line correctional supervision. In the figure, top administration refers to the "person in charge" of an agency,

Figure 10.1 Levels of correctional organization.
(*Source:* William G. Archambeault and Betty J. Archambeault, *Correctional Supervisory Management: Principles of Organization, Policy, and Law.* Englewood Cliffs, N.J.: Prentice Hall, 1982, p. 53. Used with permission.)

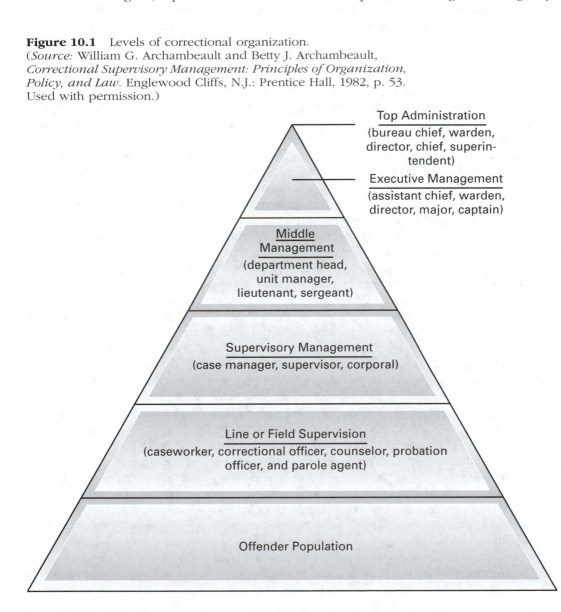

institution, or unit of government. They may be a bureau chief or commander, warden, executive director, or person with a similar title. Today, the head of each prison, generally appointed by the commissioner of corrections, is a warden, director, or superintendent, which is the more common title.[12] This person is responsible for the entire operation of the organization and is more often than not a political appointee.

The line between the levels of top administration and executive management is blurred in many organizations. Top administration usually makes major decisions, often merely approving recommendations made by executive management. Executive titles are often the same as those of top administration with the addition of *assistant, deputy,* or *vice* (e.g., deputy or assistant warden, assistant commander). Executive management is normally responsible for developing and reviewing long-range plans; evaluating key management personnel; developing policies, rules, regulations, and standards for the organization; and performing other functions designated by top administrators.[13]

Middle management in correctional administration may refer to a variety of positions and a number of levels within the organization structure. Middle management positions include *department head, captain, lieutenant, sergeant, team leader, manager, program head, coordinator,* and *shift commander.* Middle management is normally concerned with managing the delivery of one or more services, which may be organized into departments or divisions. Examples include custody, treatment, food services, maintenance, prison industries, personnel, research, and education. Each division is ultimately responsible to an executive manager (such as an assistant warden for custody or treatment). Major functions of middle managers are to develop plans, implement rules and regulations, maintain records, supervise subordinate supervisors, periodically evaluate personnel, account for unit resources (funds, property, equipment), and process grievances.[14]

The lowest level of correctional administration is that of the first-level supervision of employees, often using titles such as *unit manager, supervisor, corporal, team leader,* or *section leader.* These people are responsible for the day-to-day operations of specific areas within organizational units. They make first-level job assignments; maintain close contact with operational employees; make detailed and short-range operating plans; provide counseling, motivation, control, and training to employees; and implement agency policies, rules, and regulations at the employee level. In short, the first-level supervisor translates organizational policy, goals, and objectives into action.[15]

The line or field correctional supervision is not normally designated as part of administration and management; however, this area exercises legal supervisory authority over members of an offender population. Employees at this level must skillfully apply basic supervisory techniques to influence the offender. These people—be they correctional officers, counselors, or others—must carry out all of the administrators' plans by interpreting and applying institutional policy; planning, organizing, and supervising inmate activities and work functions; ensuring maintenance of the physical plant and equipment; avoiding circumstances that might lead to litigation; and engaging in decision making. These workers are the "point of delivery" for all correctional services within the organization; the organization's effectiveness is closely linked to its performance.[16]

✦ PRISONS AS ORGANIZATIONS

Until the beginning of the 20th century, prisons were administered by state boards of charities, boards composed of citizens or inspectors, state prison commissions, or individual prison keepers. Most prisons were individual provinces; wardens, who were given absolute control over their domain, were appointed by governors through a system of political patronage.

In the late 1990s, every state has some form of centralized department of corrections that is empowered to set and carry out policies for all correctional institutions within its jurisdiction. At the top of this department of corrections is the secretary or commissioner of corrections, who works directly with the governor to establish policy and institutional procedures and negotiates operating budgets for the various institutions and makes major personnel decisions.

In the past, individuals were attracted to the position of warden because it offered many fringe benefits such as lavish residences, unlimited inmate servants, food and supplies from institutional farms and warehouses, furnishings, and a personal automobile. Now most superintendents or wardens are civil service employees who are professionally trained and who have earned their position through seniority and merit.[17]

Because the traditional prison was autocratic, with the central purpose of maintaining custody of inmates, the organization was highly stratified and rigid, organized along military lines with authority and status related to rank. Decisions were made at the top. During the past few decades, many correctional institutions have been reorganized, adding another layer of hierarchy, commonly referred to as *noncustodial personnel*. These personnel are the *professional* staff of the prison, which includes psychiatrists, psychologists, medical personnel, chaplains, teachers, counselors, and dieticians.

Thus, the superintendent or warden may be assisted by one or more associate deputies: normally, one in charge of custody, including discipline, security, inmate movement, and control, and a second in charge of business matters, programs, records, library services, mail and visitation, recreation, and release procedures. A prison industries manager is in charge of prison industries, farms, production, and supplies. A medical supervisor is in charge of prison health services and sanitation.[18] This reorganization has produced a more vertical type of organization, forcing actual decision making downward within the organization, among deputies and their personnel. Organizing and managing a prison is obviously a major task, one that rivals such responsibilities in many large industries and businesses.

Figure 10.2 is an organization structure for a state maximum security prison serving a statewide population of about 2 million and an inmate population of about 5,000.

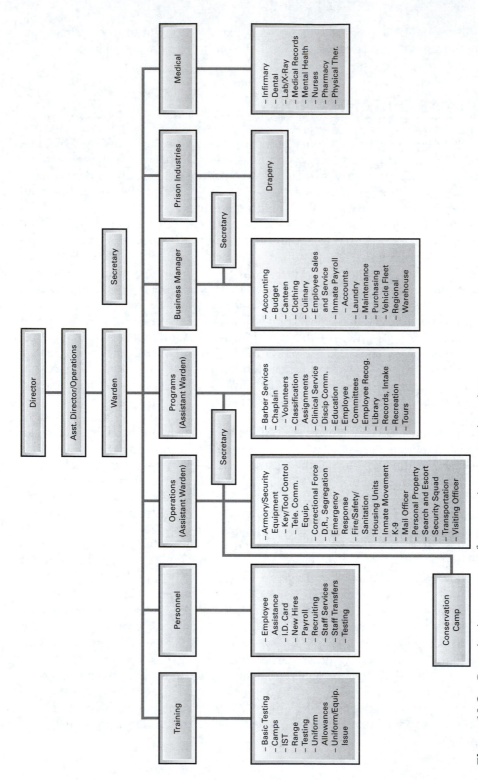

Figure 10.2 Organization structure for a maximum security prison.

DEVELOPMENT AND STATUS
OF INMATE CIVIL LITIGATION

RIGHTS OF PRISON INMATES

Although incarceration in jails and prisons entails stringent restrictions on freedom of movement and the loss of numerous privileges, inmates nonetheless enjoy several important constitutional rights. Legal circumstances of prison inmates have changed tremendously since 1871 when the Virginia Supreme Court told Woody Ruffin, a convicted murderer, that he was a "slave of the state" with no rights that need be recognized.[19]

The demise of the *hands-off doctrine,* by which courts deferred to the expertise of correctional administrators in the operation of their institutions, began in the mid-1960s; in *Cooper v. Pate,*[20] the Supreme Court held that state inmates could bring lawsuits against prison authorities under Title 42, Section 1983 of the Civil Rights Act. This decision began a new era for inmates and represented the beginning of what has been an explosion in inmate litigation. During the 1971–1972 Supreme Court term, following the deadly prison riot at Attica, New York, additional court decisions expanded prisoners' rights and remedies. One of the major decisions was *Wolff v. McDonnell,*[21] in which the Court stated that "there is no Iron Curtain drawn between the Constitution and the prisons of this country."

THE RESURGENCE OF THE HANDS-OFF DOCTRINE

The turning point in this expansion of inmates' rights was the well-known case of *Bell v. Wolfish,* 1979,[22] which considered, among other issues, double-bunking in the Metropolitan Correctional Center in New York City. The Court seemed to revert to the original hands-off doctrine, declaring in a 6-to-3 decision that jail management should be left to corrections personnel. In other words, the Court stated that deference should be extended to persons noted for their expertise in correctional matters, and administrative decisions should not be invalidated by the Court unless extreme circumstances required it.

PRISONER LITIGATION

The volume of inmate litigation has increased significantly since *Cooper v. Pate.* In 1966, 218 petitions were filed, and the number increased to 16,741 in 1981.[23] In 1980 inmates of state and federal correctional institutions filed 23,287 petitions alleging both civil and criminal violations and seeking compensatory damages, injunctions, and property claims.[24] By 1990 the number of such petitions had increased to nearly 43,000, and more than 64,000 petitions were filed in 1996.[25]

Prisoners sue primarily because they are either unwilling to accept their conviction or because they wish to hassle their keepers.[26] Prisoner litigants fall into two categories. First are those who file a single suit during their entire period of incarceration (usually requiring the assistance of others to do it); one study in the late 1980s found that 71 percent of all litigants filed only one action. These single petitions account for about half of all litigation.[27] The other group is composed of inmates who make law a prison career; they are the "jailhouse lawyers."[28]

There is an irony connected to this litigation explosion. Until the 1970s conditions in many prisons were almost insufferable for both staff members and inmates; the former often had to battle the same vermin and insects and eat the same food (some of which was poisoned with lead paint peeling from the kitchen walls), and for at least eight hours per day, generally had to endure the same conditions as the inmates. The irony here, of course, was that many administrators and staff had to hope to be sued by inmates for violating their Eighth Amendment rights and lose before working conditions could improve.

✦ THE DUE DEFERENCE DOCTRINE

As noted earlier, the Supreme Court decision in *Bell v. Wolfish* (1979), which is considered the "cornerstone of the future edifice of correctional law,"[29] reinstated the hands-off doctrine. From about that time to the present, federal courts have generally deferred to the expertise of prison administrators in cases involving prison administration. This is the emergence of the *due deference doctrine,* which refers to the courts' policy not to interfere in matters pertaining to prison administration. This doctrine has not been developed sufficiently, however, to determine when the courts should or should not intervene. Frequently, the result has been, as in *Bell,* that courts accept jurisdiction over prisoners' claims but fail to provide any remedies to them.[30]

Recent Supreme Court decisions have stated clearly that the federal doors to prison litigation have all but closed. Under due deference, the federal courts appear to distinguish substantive prisoner rights claims from frivolous complaints against prison administrators.[31] This "judicial retreat" or gradual return to the *Bell* decision troubles some observers, however, because it may reverse what has been termed "the most important development in the prisoner's environment,"[32] which substitutes the rule of law and rational/legal decision making for arbitrary prison administrative decision making. Although it is unlikely, given the current levels of education and attitudes of correctional administrators, some people fear that the implications for inmate participation are critical.[33]

✦ THE INCREASE IN THE PRISON POPULATION

A serious problem affecting prisons at the end of the 20th century is the increase in the prison population, which has resulted in overcrowding inmates in prisons. Many reasons are offered to explain the rapid increase in prison and jail populations in the United States. Some commonly cited factors include violence on television and in the movies and the general deterioration of morals and of the family. Indeed, a Pennsylvania State University study reported that the more television they watch, the more violent and disobedient schoolchildren become.[34] Nearly one-third of all state prison inmates abuse drugs, which is perhaps a symptom of fundamental social problems.[35]

✧ REHABILITATIVE VERSUS LOCK-'EM-UP PHILOSOPHIES

A philosophical shift toward criminals and the purpose of incarceration is contributing to prison overcrowding. In response to the apparent failure of *rehabilitative philosophy* and policies, the prevailing policy sees prisons as places to incarcerate and punish inmates in an effort to deter crime. This philosophy has resulted in get-tough sentence practices (including mandatory sentencing laws), which have contributed to the increase in prison populations. Legislators have essentially removed the word *rehabilitation* from the penal code while focusing on fixed sentences, which have had the effect of quadrupling the number of prisoners, and requiring $4.5 billion for new lockups in 1992.[36] This shift from rehabilitating inmates to giving them their "just desserts" is based on the fact that offenders make "free will" decisions to commit crime and therefore no longer deserve compassion and "correction." This philosophy has brought an "exclusionary" era of repressive social control, which attempts to banish, expel, and stigmatize the criminal.[37]

Americans are clearly becoming more punishment oriented. A 1995 survey indicated that about only 26 percent of all Americans believe that it is more important to try to rehabilitate prisoners who commit violent crimes than merely to punish them (58 percent), compared with 48 percent who favored rehabilitation and 38 percent who favored punishment in 1991.[38] These findings agree with the "conventional wisdom" concerning how to administer prison programs. Robert Martinson's well-publicized finding that "almost nothing works" in correctional treatment programs served to "ignite a firestorm of debate that has lasted" nearly two decades.[39] Martinson's assessment clearly had a major impact on corrections administrators, who became unwilling to fund treatment programs from dwindling budgets, and academics and policymakers, who claimed that the medical model of correctional treatment programs failed to accomplish their end. Paul Louis and Jerry Sparger noted that "perhaps the most lasting effect of the 'nothing works' philosophy is the spread of cynicism and hopelessness" among prison administrators and staff members.[40]

With the demise of the rehabilitative philosophy and the birth of the national call for "just desserts" in the 1970s, an even greater widening of the gap between the two perspectives occurred in the 1980s. Ted Palmer[41] identified these modified positions as the "skeptical" and the "sanguine" camps. The skeptical believed that relatively few prison programs work and that successful ones account for only negligible reductions in recidivism. Furthermore, they believed that rehabilitation programs have not been given an adequate chance in correctional settings because they were either poorly designed or implemented. The sanguine perspective is that although existing rehabilitation programs have not been very effective to date, evidence indicates that many programs provide positive treatment for selective portions of the offender population.

A recent reassessment of Martinson's "nothing works" statement by researchers such as Palmer has given new hope for rehabilitation. Palmer rejected Martinson's indictment of correctional treatment modalities and demonstrated that many of the programs that Martinson initially reviewed were actually quite successful.[42] Other research has supported Palmer's position.[43]

Although the rehabilitation philosophy has some support, the idea that "nothing works" is presently adhered to in the United States. That philosophy is not expected to be replaced in the foreseeable future. It is good to remember, however, the attempts made to rehabilitate criminals in earlier times; we may one day return to that approach. Palmer has made three points about rehabilitation: it (1) need not be married to a medical model, (2) need not be linked to indeterminate sentences, and (3) need not demean its participants or interfere with extant reform movements.[44]

Unfortunately, this just desserts or "lock-'em-up" philosophy and the addition of more prisons—and more prisoners (in 1996 nearly 1.6 million persons were incarcerated in the United States)[45]—have not caused a major decrease in crime. They have simply resulted in record numbers of inmates. As Malcolm Feely succinctly noted, "There is no evidence of imprisonment's deterrent effect."[46]

According to Ted Gest, the logic of the "lock-'em-up campaign" has been defeated by a combination of demography and justice system inefficiency. Each year, a new crop of youths in their upper teens represent the majority of those arrested for serious crimes. As these "seasoned" offenders are arrested and removed from the crime scene, a new crop replaces them. "The justice system is eating its young. It imprisons them, paroles them, and rearrests them with no rehabilitation in between," according to Dale Secrest.[47] Law enforcement seems to offer little deterrent to crime; even California, which uses an aggressive law enforcement approach to deal with criminals, reaches only a small fraction of those who commit approximately 1 million serious crimes annually in the state.[48]

Large-scale, long-term imprisonment unquestionably keeps truly serious offenders behind bars, preventing them from committing more crimes. The long-term incarceration of this class of criminals who would commit an average of 15 or more crimes per year if jailed for only short terms creates the greatest need for additional prison space.

✦ PROGRAMS TO ADDRESS INMATES' PROBLEMS

It is clear that

> offenders enter prison with a variety of deficits. Some are socially or morally inept; others are intellectually or vocationally handicapped; some have emotional hangups that stem from . . . psychological problems; still others have a mixture of varying proportions of some or even all of these.[49]

Having to deal with inmates suffering from such serious and varied problems obviously does not bode well for the correctional institutional treatment in general. Prison culture makes the environment inhospitable to programs designed to rehabilitate or reform, and, as noted, the failure of rehabilitative programs has shifted focus from them. High recidivism rates indicate that existing correctional strategies have not been successful and that these strategies cannot operate in a vacuum. As we will see later, the prison director's philosophy and practices with respect to inmate treatment and programs may in large measure impact the success rate of a particular institution.

According to statistics published in 1992, 36 percent of all male state prison inmates used illegal drugs daily in the month before their offense, and 31 percent were under the influence of drugs at the time they committed the offense responsible for their current incarceration.[50] Three types of treatment are available for drug-addicted offenders: punitive, medical, or communal approaches. The punitive modality, the most widely used model since the early 1920s, consists largely of subjecting the inmate to withdrawal; it is based on the premise that drug addiction is a crime, not a disease, that requires punishment. The treatment of drug addiction as a medical problem consists of providing detoxification, rebuilding physical health, counseling, and offering support from social services. The communal approach, using group encounters and seminars conducted by former addicts who serve as positive role models, has been used by various penal facilities.[51]

A survey of correctional administrators revealed that approximately 85,650 sexual offenders were in federal and state prisons. The 48 states participating in the survey, the Federal Bureau of Prisons, and the District of Columbia reported that they provided individual and/or group counseling for these offenders.[52] The treatment of sexual offenders is based on the premise that intervention should focus on the offender as a total person, not just on the deviant behavior.[53] The offender is encouraged to articulate fears, anxieties, wishes, fantasies, and ambitions to relieve mental and emotional distress. Rapists, voyeurs, and exhibitionists also may benefit through group therapy, which stresses touching and close physical contact. Child molesters, or pedophiles, also may be treated as whole personalities. Research has shown that the main concern, regardless of the sexual offender's specific problem, is to individualize treatment.[54] Treatment efforts in prison are unlikely to produce positive outcomes, however, because of the nature of the environment.[55]

No uniform, simple treatment modality exists for a wide range of violent offenders. The treatment for offenders diagnosed as having antisocial personality disorders by psychotherapeutic intervention is seldom successful.[56] A complicating factor is that alcoholism is prevalent among these offenders;[57] therefore, each case requires an individual treatment plan. Alcoholism is generally acknowledged as being a disease with medical, social, and psychological dimensions.[58] Psychological treatment to address this problem varies according to the offender's personality. The regimen used by Alcoholics Anonymous is frequently employed in the institutional setting.[59] Research has indicated that if the violent offender appears to possess the values of a subculture of violence, peer influences seem to work best in treatment; however, if deep-seated psychological factors appear to be present, a one-to-one relationship, in which the therapist is supportive, kind, and permissive but firm, may be utilized.[60]

✦ PRISON INDUSTRIES: VENTURES WITH THE PRIVATE SECTOR

Prison industries that used inmate labor to manufacture goods for private firms were thriving enterprises in the first quarter of this century. The sale of open market prisonmade products was banned in the 1930s and 1940s by Congress and the states, however, in response to protests from competing manufacturers and labor unions. In 1979 legislation was enacted to restore private sector involvement in prison industries to its former status. Within 15 years, the U.S. Department of Justice had certified 32 correctional agencies to operate private sector prison industries, employing more than 1,000 inmates (who earned more than $30 million) in joint ventures. In the mid-1990s, private companies employed inmates for data entry and information processing, electronic component assembly, garment manufacturing, contract packaging, metal fabricating, telemarketing, and handling travel reservations.[61]

Correctional administrators report that joint ventures provide meaningful, productive employment that helps to reduce inmate idleness. Other positive outcomes include the supply to companies of a readily available and dependable source of labor, with a cost-competitive, motivated workforce that can continue to work after release from prison; financial incentives, including low-cost industrial space and equipment purchase subsidy offered by corrections institutions; a safe work environment due to the presence of security personnel and metal detectors; and the partial return of inmate earnings to society in the form of state and federal taxes and to offset incarceration costs, contribute to the support of inmates' families, and compensate victims.

Different types of business relationships have developed to meet the needs of both correctional institutions and private companies. In one, the prisoners are employed by the state division of correctional industries, which in turn charges the companies a burden rate for their labor. For example, in South Carolina, companies that operate feeder plants inside correctional facilities supervise inmate workers with their own staff, but the inmates are employed by the state, which charges the companies for their labor.

In the *employer model,* in which the company employs the inmates, private companies own and operate their prison-based businesses, with prison officials providing the space in which to operate as well as a qualified labor pool from which the companies hire employees. An example is Trans World Airlines, which owns and operates several prison-based businesses and supervises and employs the inmate workforce.

A third partnering approach is the *customer model,* in which the company contracts with the prison to provide a finished product at an agreed-upon price. The correctional institution owns and operates the business that employs the inmate workforce. For example, a correctional facility in Minnesota provides a variety of light assembly, sorting, packaging, and warranty repair services for dozens of private firms in the area.

To be sure, these joint ventures provide challenges and problems. Absenteeism and rapid turnover of employees, limited opportunities for training, and logistical matters can be problems. Furthermore, the AFL-CIO remains concerned about these joint ventures and views them as a challenge to unionized and nonunionized civilian workforces. Also, a debate about the proper role of inmates in today's labor force is ongoing. Many entrepreneurs and prison administrators believe that these ventures are very valuable to inmates because of the benefits described. Because workers must have a good disciplinary record to participate in these programs, show up for their jobs on time, and work hard during their shifts, these ventures develop valuable work habits that are not reflected in financial statements. Indeed, many inmates have been hired by companies after their release.

Figure 10.3 Principal characteristics of three types of joint ventures.

Model	Workers employed by	Workers supervised by	Workers trained by	Benefits for company	Benefits for prison
Personnel	Prison	Company	Prison	Workforce Rent/utility Money for equipment Administrative support	Employment Overhead rate Wage deductions Payback on equipment
Employer	Company	Company	Company	Workforce Rent Utilities	Employment Wage deductions
Customer	Prison	Prison	Prison	Product or service	Payment for finished goods

✦ JAILS AS ORGANIZATIONS

Across the United States, an estimated 3,316 jails with approximately 542,000 inmates are locally administered.[62] As with prisons, no "typical" organization structure exists for jails; their organization and hierarchical levels are obviously determined by several factors: size, budget, level of crowding, local views toward punishment and treatment, and even the levels of training and education of the jail administrator. An organization structure for a jail serving a population of about 250,000 is suggested in Figure 10.4.

The administration of jails is frequently one of the major tasks of county sheriffs. Several writers have concluded that sheriffs and police personnel primarily see themselves as law enforcers first and view the responsibility of organizing and operating the jail as a millstone.[63] Therefore, their approach is often said to be at odds with advanced corrections philosophy and trends.

✧ THE "NEW GENERATION" JAIL

As noted previously, the federal courts in the mid-1960s began to abandon their traditional "hands-off" philosophy toward prison and jail administration. This change was largely in response to the deplorable conditions in jails and inappropriate treatment of inmates. The courts became more willing to hear inmate allegations of constitutional violations ranging from inadequate heating, lighting, and ventilation to the censorship of mail. One of every five cases filed in federal courts was on behalf of prisoners,[64] and 20 percent of all jails were parties in a pending lawsuit.[65]

In response to this deluge of lawsuits and to improve conditions, many local jurisdictions constructed new jail facilities. The court-ordered pressures to improve jail conditions afforded an opportunity for administrators to explore new ideas and designs. As described earlier, the term *new generation* was coined to characterize a style of architecture and inmate management totally new and unique to local detention facilities and a new generation in correctional thought.[66] The concept was endorsed by the American Correctional Association and the Advisory Board of the National Institute of Corrections. W. Walter Menninger, director of Law and Psychiatry at the Menninger Foundation in Topeka, Kansas, observed that

> Careful studies of these new generation facilities have found significant benefits for inmates, staff and society at large. There are fewer untoward incidents and assaults, (a) greater level of personal safety for both staff and inmates, greater staff satisfaction, more orderly and relaxed inmate housing areas, a better maintained physical plant. Finally, these facilities are cost effective to construct and to operate.[67]

According to Matt Leone, there are several reasons for the fact that the new generation jail concept is not expanding. First, new jails are not typically built until old jails either wear out or become too small. Second, there is often a public perception that such facilities are "soft on crime." Finally, these facilities, for many people, simply do not have the *appearance* of being a jail.[68] To the extent

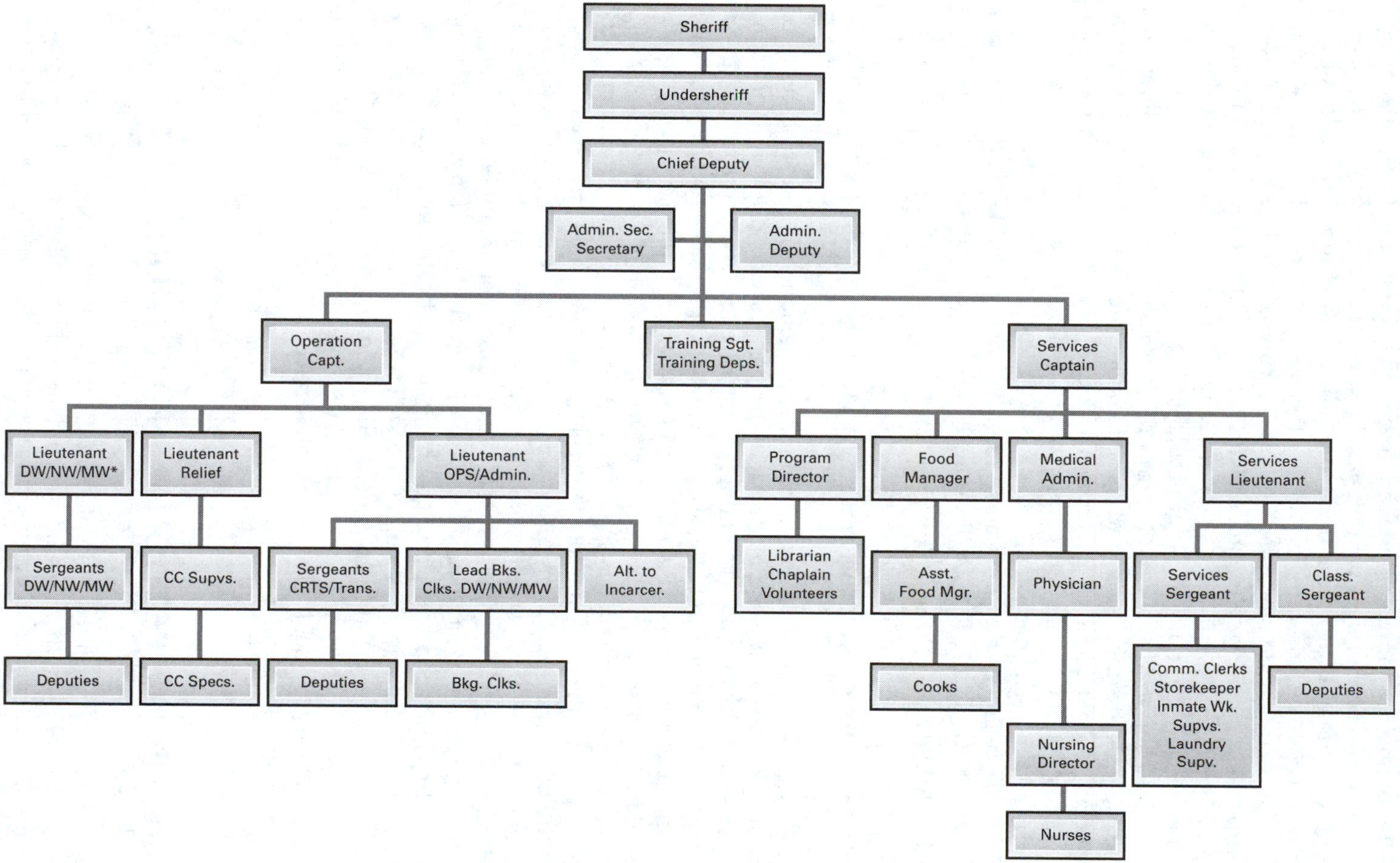

Figure 10.4 Organizational structure for a jail serving a county with a population of 250,000. (DW = day watch; NW = night watch; MW = mid-watch; CC = conservation camps)

possible, symbols of incarceration were to be removed in these new jails, which were to have no bars in the living units; windows were to be provided in every prisoner's room; and carpets, padded and movable furniture, and colorful wall coverings were to be used to reduce the facility's institutional atmosphere. Inmates were to be divided into small groups of approximately 40 to 50 for housing purposes. Officers were to interact with inmates rather than remain inside an office or behind a desk. Finally, interior features of the facility were to be designed to reduce the "trauma" of incarceration.[69]

The most important features of many of these facilities were one cell for each inmate, direct staff supervision, and "functional inmate living units," which were to locate all "sleeping, food, and hygiene facilities . . . in one self-contained, multilevel space."[70] A corrections officer was to be assigned to each unit to ensure direct and continuous supervision.

The first facility of the "new generation" jail opened in the 1970s in Contra Costa County, California. This facility quickly became a success, was deemed cost effective to build and safer for inmates and staff.

✦ MAKING JAILS PRODUCTIVE

The 1984 Justice Assistance Act removed some of the long-standing restrictions on interstate commerce of prisonermade goods. By 1987, private sector work programs were under way in 14 state correctional institutions and two county jails.[71] In the late 1990s, many inmates in U.S. jails are involved in productive work. Some simply work to acquire privileges, and others earn wages applied to their custodial costs and compensation to crime victims. Some hone new job skills, improving their chances for success following release. At one end of the continuum is the trusty who mows the grass in front of the jail and thereby earns privileges for doing so; at the other end are jail inmates working for private industry for real dollars.[72]

Some jails have undertaken training programs for their inmates, following the recommendations of the American Jail Association. For example, one state-of-the-art facility in the West trains inmates to operate a plastic sign-engraving machine and has plans to teach dog grooming at the local animal control center. The engraving equipment, as well as the facility's 24 computers for inmate use, cost taxpayers nothing; they were purchased through commissary funds. This jail's inmates also can earn a GED, and the facility is considering programs in auto detailing, food service, book mending, mail service, painting, printing, carpet installation, and upholstering.

✦ RESEARCH IN CORRECTIONAL INSTITUTIONS

Many writers have painted a horrible landscape of prisons, describing them as being devoid of even the most basic elements of humanity[73] and detrimental to the offender's humanity;[74] they generally issue a scathing indictment of prisons.[75]

The following research findings should establish whose assessment is more nearly correct. Although appearing similar on the outside, prisons have been proven via research to vary widely in terms of their security, programming, and living conditions.

✧ Prison and Jail Crowding

Many correctional administrators see crowding as *the* major barrier to the humane housing of offenders. As mentioned earlier, this problem has resulted in court intervention in 37 states. Researchers have viewed the problem as a complex phenomenon, with most agreeing that crowding is a psychological response to high population density, which is often viewed as stressful.[76] After reviewing the literature, Bonta and Gendreau found that the inmates' age played an important role, and that the relationship between misconduct and population density was more pronounced in institutions housing young offenders.[77] They also found evidence that prison variables other than overcrowding may influence aggressive behavior; for example, crowded prisons may be poorly managed.[78]

In summary, crowded prisons and jails may cause physiological and psychological stress among many inmates, although disruptive behavior depends on other factors such as age, institutional parameters (sudden shifts in the inmate membership), and the chronicity or extended length of overcrowding.[79] We discuss possible administrative approaches to crowding in Chapter 11.

✧ Spatial and Social Densities

The average number of square feet per inmate in a jail is referred to as *spatial density;* the average number of inmates per living unit is the *social density.* Organizing and managing jails becomes more difficult when a larger number of inmates are living in high-density situations. Maintaining high population densities can affect routine activities such as food service, visitation, recreation, medical care and sick call, inmate property management, and inmates' movements to and from court or consultations with attorneys. A high spatial density facility is identified as one in which more than 40 percent of the inmates have less than the standard of 60 square feet per person in housing where confined for 10 hours or more set by the American Correctional Association. A 1988 study found that 28.1 percent of jails were operating with a population in the highest spatial density category.[80]

The standard for the highest social density residence category is an average of five persons per housing unit. By that definition, 27.6 percent of all jails, which house 61.1 percent of all jail inmates nationwide, were high social density facilities. Higher population densities are more common in jails holding 500 to 999 inmates; of those, 43.8 percent had at least 40 percent of their inmates residing in less than 60 square feet for more than 10 hours per day.[81]

Inmate suicide rates are higher in small jails and highest in small jails with lower population densities.[82] Seventy percent of all jail suicides occurred in facilities with average daily populations of fewer than 250 inmates.[83] These facilities account for 37 percent of all jail inmates,[84] and 52 percent of all jail admissions nationwide.[85]

❖ HEALTH RISKS FROM INCARCERATION

Does incarceration threaten the health of the confined? A number of researchers have failed to find negative effects on inmate health as a result of incarceration.[86] In fact, two studies have even found a significantly lower incidence of hypertension among inmates than among the general population.[87]

Indeed, the evidence indicates that many prisons may actually be conducive to good health. In a number of cases, complaints either decrease during incarceration[88] or remain unchanged.[89] Interestingly, we may conclude that because most prisons afford regular and nutritious diets, access to recreational exercise, and opportunity to sleep, along with available medical care, the offender may receive a fortuitous benefit from being isolated from highly risky lifestyles in the community.[90]

In the United States, deaths due to homicide are actually less likely inside than outside prisons.[91] Regarding inmate suicide, the findings for a 20-year period indicate that they occurred at a rate of 17.5 per 100,000 inmates, compared with 11 per 100,000 people in the general population.[92] Self-mutilations, however, occur at an even higher rate.[93]

❖ EFFECTS OF LONG-TERM INCARCERATION

According to statistics published in 1992, more than 70,000 men and women are serving life sentences in state and federal prisons.[94] What happens to such people? Although few of them will actually spend an entire lifetime incarcerated, the advent of mandatory sentencing laws, increases in violent crimes, decreases in early paroles, and commission of new crimes by inmates, create the opportunity for long-term incarceration nonetheless.

Cognitive tests have been administered to long- and short-term inmates; their results indicated no differences in intellectual performance. Long-termers have demonstrated increased hostility and social introversion[95] and decreased self-evaluation and evaluation of work and father.[96] Other studies have found no evidence of psychological deterioration; in fact, these studies reported an improvement in verbal intelligence over time and a decrease in hostility.[97]

Timothy Flanagan compared misconduct rates of short- and long-term inmates, finding that even after controlling for age, the misconduct rate among the long-term inmates was approximately half that of the short-term offenders.[98] Additional studies assessing lifers found no deterioration in health, psychiatric symptoms, or intellect.[99] Even long-termers themselves have reported that the earlier portion of their sentences was more stressful and that with time they had learned to cope effectively.[100] Similar findings have occurred with respect to female offenders; in fact, long-term women inmates were more bothered by boredom and lack of activity than by anxiety.[101]

In summary, the evidence indicates little support for the notion that long-term imprisonment has detrimental effects on inmates' health. As a caution, however, Flanagan suggested that lifers may experience negative changes in areas that are as yet unmeasured,[102] such as family separation issues and vocational skill training needs.[103]

✦ Effects of Solitary Confinement

Solitary confinement, also referred to as *punitive segregation,* has been described as "the most individually destructive, psychologically crippling, and socially alienating experience that could conceivably exist within the borders of [Canada]."[104] The statement also applies in the United States. Is this scathing denouncement an accurate depiction? Is solitary confinement per se "cruel and unusual" punishment?

Studies using volunteers have found few detrimental effects for subjects placed in solitary confinement for periods of up to 10 days. Perceptual and motor abilities were not impaired, physiological levels of stress were lower than for control groups, and various attitudes toward the experience and the self did not worsen.[105] Studies using prison inmates have also found no detrimental effects. In general, inmates found the first 72 hours to be the most difficult but after that they adjusted quite well. Researchers concluded that there was "no support for the claim that solitary confinement . . . is overwhelmingly aversive, stressful, or damaging to the inmates."[106] Note, however, that two studies (that did not use control groups) found indications of pathology in inmates in solitary confinement for periods up to a year.[107]

✦ Effects of Living on Death Row

Statistics indicate that in 1994 nearly 3,000 prisoners were under sentence of death in 36 states.[108] Very little research concerning how inmates adjust to death row is available. The first such study, of 19 inmates awaiting execution in Sing Sing, was probably done in 1962. Expecting to find intense anxiety and depression among death row inmates, researchers found none.[109] Another study that investigated eight men awaiting execution found that five men showed no observable deterioration, but three displayed symptoms ranging from paranoia to insomnia.[110] A study of 34 death row inmates showed increased feelings of depression and hopelessness, but severe disturbances (psychoses) were not observed.[111]

Robert Johnson interviewed 35 men on death row and found them concerned over their powerlessness, fearful of their surroundings, and feeling emotionally drained. Younger inmates were more susceptible to these concerns.[112] Similar studies using unstructured interviews found that most inmates exhibited well-intact defenses regarding their alleged guilt[113] and that *all* slept well and felt relatively good about themselves.[114]

Although limited in number, these studies demonstrate a lack of evidence of severe psychological reactions to living on death row. In fact, there are indications that the family and friends of condemned inmates suffer more than the inmates themselves.[115]

✦ PRESSING AND IMPORTANT ISSUES RELATING TO CORRECTIONAL INSTITUTIONS

In view of numerous factors—the contemporary tough law-and-order stance toward offenders, the amount of violent crime, jail and prison overcrowding, recidivism rates, new prison and jail construction costs, and the paucity of programming for inmates—society must contemplate the message it is sending correctional administrators. If society's primary purpose of incarceration is *custody* and *incapacitation* for a set period, we have clearly succeeded. Recalling that 26 percent of all Americans support rehabilitative efforts, however, if society really wishes to *rehabilitate* them, it is failing to do so, according to research data.

We now know that the specter of imprisonment appears to do little to prevent crime. Most offenders today come from communities in which conditions fall below the living standards that most Americans would recognize.[116] We must wonder whether the threat of incarceration really holds any deterrent benefit for many members of our society.

John DiIulio complained that those who know the most about what prisons do have rarely taken part in the debates over their purpose. He noted that people who have actually spent their lives working with prisoners have ideas on the subject, but more attention is given to outside researchers whose focus is on the inmates rather than the correctional system.[117] Should correctional administrators crusade for greater latitude in punishing and treating their charges? Have the courts and society played too large a role in this traditionally "laissez-faire" area? Are correctional administrators in a position to make a difference in preventing, punishing, or rehabilitating criminals? Do administrators know what works better than those of us in the outside world? These are pressing and important issues to consider.

Summary

This chapter presented an overview of correctional organization, prison litigation, prison industries, crowding, and the treatment and custody operations. Increases in violent crime and the general finding that institutionalization can be more of a positive than negative experience have led us to conclude that serious offenders neither accept nor abide by society's norms. Again, we must question whether the threat of incarceration has any deterrent value whatsoever for many persons in our society.

Questions for Review

1. What is the typical organization of the modern prison?
2. In what ways are correctional organizations unique?
3. Why is it important that correctional organizations adhere to the open system of management?
4. What factors are presently contributing to the increase in the prison population in the United States?
5. What is the "new generation" jail, and how might it help reduce the effects of overcrowding and the quality of life in institutions?
6. What options for attempting to work with emotional or behavioral problems of inmates are available to administrators?
7. Is society interested in attempting to rehabilitate offenders? Why or why not?
8. Defend the recent trend for prisons to enter into joint ventures with private companies. What are some of the inherent problems that confront these ventures? What are the three types of ventures that now exist?
9. In what major ways do jails differ from prisons?
10. Discuss some major findings in corrections research regarding prison inmates and the effects of incarceration and death row on them. What are the implications for correctional administrators?

Notes

1. George F. Cole, personal communication, April 18, 1991.
2. William G. Archambeault and Betty J. Archambeault, *Correctional Supervisory Management: Principles of Organization, Policy, and Law* (Englewood Cliffs, N.J.: Prentice Hall, 1982), p. 5.
3. *Ibid.*
4. *Ibid.,* p. 6.
5. Jim L. Munro, "Towards a Theory of Criminal Justice Administration: A General Systems Perspective," *Public Administration Review* (November/December 1977): 621–631.
6. See Ken Peak, "Correctional Theory in Theory and Praxis," *Criminal Justice Review* 10 (1985).
7. Richter H. Moore, Jr., "The Criminal Justice Non-System," in R. Moore, T. Marks, and R. Barrow (eds.), *Readings in Criminal Justice* (Indianapolis, Ind.: Bobbs-Merrill, 1976), pp. 5–13.

8. Archambeault and Archambeault, *Correctional Supervisory Management,* pp. 44–45.

9. Vernon Fox, *Introduction to Corrections* (2d ed.) (Englewood Cliffs, N.J.: Prentice Hall, 1977), p. 406.

10. Archambeault and Archambeault, *Correctional Supervisory Management,* p. 48.

11. *Ibid.,* p. 49.

12. Harry E. Allen and Clifford E. Simonsen, *Corrections in America* (5th ed.) (New York: Macmillan, 1989), p. 469.

13. Archambeault and Archambeault, *Correctional Supervisory Management,* p. 54.

14. *Ibid.,* p. 55.

15. *Ibid.,* p. 56.

16. *Ibid.,* p. 59.

17. James A. Inciardi, *Criminal Justice* (3d ed.) (San Diego, Calif.: Harcourt Brace Jovanovich, 1990), p. 576.

18. *Ibid.*

19. *Ruffin v. Commonwealth,* 62 Va. 790, 796 (1871).

20. 378 U.S. 546 (1964).

21. 418 U.S. 539 (1974).

22. 441 U.S. 520 (1979).

23. A. E. D. Howard, "The States and the Supreme Court," 31 *Catholic University Law Review* 375 (1982), at 379.

24. Timothy J. Flanagan and Kathleen Maguire (eds.), *Sourcebook of Criminal Justice Statistics 1991.* U.S. Department of Justice, Bureau of Justice Statistics (Washington, D.C.: U.S. Government Printing Office, 1992), p. 555.

25. *Ibid.* Also see Kathleen Maguire and Ann L. Pastore (eds.), *Sourcebook of Criminal Justice Statistics 1995.* U.S. Department of Justice, Bureau of Justice Statistics (Washington, D.C.: U.S. Government Printing Office, 1996), p. 177.

26. Jim Thomas, Kathy Harris, and Devin Keeler, "Issues and Misconceptions in Prisoner Litigation," *Criminology* 24 (1987): 901–919.

27. Jim Thomas, "Repackaging the Data: The 'Reality' of Prisoner Litigation," *New England Journal of Criminal and Civil Confinement* 15 (1989).

28. *Ibid.,* p. 50.

29. Charles H. Jones, "Recent Trends in Corrections and Prisoners' Rights Law," in Clayton A. Hartjen and Edward E. Rhine (eds.), *Correctional Theory and Practice* (Chicago: Nelson-Hall, 1992), pp. 119–138.

30. *Ibid.,* p. 120.

31. *Ibid.,* pp. 121–122.

32. James Jacobs, *Stateville: The Penitentiary in Mass Society* (Chicago: University of Chicago Press, 1977).

33. Jones, "Recent Trends in Corrections and Prisoners' Rights Law," p. 122.

34. Marilyn Elias, "Study Links TV Violence, Behavior," *USA Today* (May 23, 1993).

35. U.S. Department of Justice, Bureau of Justice Statistics Bulletin, *Prisoners in 1991* (Washington, D.C.: Author, May 1993), p. 7.

36. Ted Gest, "The Prison Boom Bust," *Newsweek* (May 4, 1992): 28–31.

37. John P. Conrad, "The Redefinition of Probation: Drastic Proposals to Solve an Urgent Problem," in Patrick D. McAnany, Doug Thomson, and David Fogel (eds.), *Probation and Justice: Reconsideration of Mission* (Cambridge, Mass.: Oelgeschlager, Gunn, and Hain, 1984), p. 258.

38. Maguire and Pastore (eds.), *Sourcebook of Criminal Justice Statistics 1995,* p. 177. Also see Kathleen Maguire, Ann L. Pastore, and Timothy J. Flanagan (eds.), *Sourcebook of Crim-*

inal Justice Statistics 1992. U.S. Department of Justice, Bureau of Justice Statistics (Washington, D.C.: U.S. Government Printing Office, 1993), p. 210.

39. T. Paul Louis and Jerry R. Sparger, "Treatment Modalities within Prison," in John W. Murphy and Jack E. Dison (eds.), *Are Prisons Any Better? Twenty Years of Correctional Reform* (Newbury Park, Calif.: Sage Publications, 1990), pp. 147–162.

40. *Ibid.,* p. 149.

41. Ted Palmer, "The 'Effectiveness' Issue Today: An Overview," *Federal Probation* 42 (1983): 3–10.

42. Paul Gendreau and Robert R. Ross, "Correctional Treatment: Some Recommendations for Effective Intervention," *Juvenile and Family Court Journal* 34 (1984): 31–39.

43. See D. A. Andrews, "Program Structure and Effective Correctional Practices: A Summary of the CAVIC Research," in Robert R. Ross and Paul Gendreau (eds.), *Effective Correctional Treatment* (Toronto, Ontario, Canada: Butterworth, 1980); R. Peters, *Deviant Behavioral Contracting with Conduct Problem Youth* (Kingston, Ontario, Canada: Queen's University, 1981).

44. Louis and Sparger, "Treatment Modalities within Prison," p. 157.

45. U.S. Department of Justice, Bureau of Justice Statistics Bulletin, "Prison and Jail Inmates, 1995" (August 1996), p. 1.

46. Gest, "The Prison Boom Bust," p. 29.

47. *Ibid.*

48. *Ibid.*

49. Robert Levinson, "Try Softer," in Robert Johnson and Hans Toch (eds.), *The Pains of Imprisonment* (Beverly Hills, Calif.: Sage Publications, 1982), p. 246.

50. Maguire, Pastore, and Flanagan (eds.), *Sourcebook of Criminal Justice Statistics 1992,* p. 626.

51. Louis and Sparger, "Treatment Modalities within Prison," pp. 152–153.

52. CEGA Publishing, *Corrections Compendium* (Lincoln, Neb.: Author, July 1991), pp. 10–15.

53. Alexander B. Smith and Louis Berlin, *Treating the Criminal Offender* (New York: Plenum Press, 1988).

54. Murray L. Cohen, Theohans Seghorn, and Wilfred Calmas, "Sociometric Study of the Sex Offender," *Journal of Abnormal Psychology* 74 (1971): 249–255.

55. Louis and Sparger, "Treatment Modalities within Prison," p. 155.

56. Stanley L. Brodsky (ed.), *Psychologists in the Criminal Justice System* (Urbana, Ill.: University of Illinois Press, 1973); Fritz A. Henn, Marijan Herjanic, and Robert H. Vanderpearl, "Forensic Psychiatry: Profiles of Two Types of Sex Offenders," *American Journal of Psychiatry* 133 (1976): 654–696.

57. Samuel B. Guze, *Criminality and Psychiatric Disorders* (New York: Oxford University Press, 1976).

58. Louis and Sparger, "Treatment Modalities within Prison," p. 154.

59. See, for example, U.S. Department of Justice, Bureau of Justice Statistics, *Report to the Nation on Crime and Justice: The Data* (Rockville, Md.: National Criminal Justice Reference Service, 1983); C. R. Bartol and A. M. Bartol, *Criminal Behavior: A Psychosocial Approach* (Englewood Cliffs, N.J.: Prentice Hall, 1986); Marvin Wolfgang, *Patterns in Criminal Homicide* (Philadelphia: University of Pennsylvania Press, 1958).

60. Louis and Sparger, "Treatment Modalities within Prison," p. 157.

61. U.S. Department of Justice, National Institute of Justice, Program Focus, "Work in American Prisons: Joint Ventures with the Private Sector" (November 1995), pp. 2–3.

62. U.S. Department of Justice, Bureau of Justice Statistics Bulletin, *Prison and Jail Inmates, 1995* (Washington, D.C.: Author, 1996), p. 1.

63. For example, see James M. Moynahan and Earle K. Stewart, *The American Jail: Its Devel-*

opment and Growth (Chicago: Nelson-Hall, 1980), p. 100; Clemens Bartollas, Stuart J. Miller, and Paul B. Wice, *Participants in American Criminal Justice: The Promise and the Performance* (Englewood Cliffs, N.J.: Prentice Hall, 1983), p. 59.

64. J. Moore, "Prison Litigation and the States: A Case Law Review," *State Legislative Report* 8 (1981): 1.

65. National Sheriffs' Association, *The State of Our Nation's Jails, 1982* (Washington, D.C.: Author, 1982), p. 55.

66. Linda L. Zupan, *Jails: Reform and the New Generation Philosophy* (Cincinnati, Ohio: Anderson, 1991), p. 71.

67. Quoted in William R. Nelson and M. O'Toole, *New Generation Jails* (Boulder, Colo.: Library Information Specialists, Inc., 1983), pp. 35–36.

68. Matt Leone, personal communication, March 16, 1977.

69. Zupan, *Jails: Reform and the New Generation Philosophy,* p. 67.

70. R. Wener and R. Olson, *User Based Assessments of the Federal Metropolitan Correctional Centers: Final Report* (Washington, D.C.: U.S. Bureau of Prisons, 1978), p. 4.

71. U.S. Department of Justice, National Institute of Justice Research in Brief, *Making Jails Productive* (Washington, D.C.: Author, 1987), p. 1.

72. *Ibid.,* p. 16.

73. Cf. Gresham Sykes, *The Society of Captives: A Study of a Maximum Security Prison* (Princeton, N.J.: Princeton University Press, 1958).

74. Milton G. Rector, "Prisons and Crime," *Crime and Delinquency* 28 (1982): 505–507.

75. Jessica Mitford, *Kind and Unusual Punishment* (New York: Alfred A. Knopf, 1973).

76. Irwin Altman, "Crowding: Historical and Contemporary Trends in Crowding Research," in A. Baum and M. Y. M. Epstein (eds.), *Human Response to Crowding* (Hillsdale, N.J.: Lawrence Erlbaum, 1978), pp. 3–29.

77. James Bonta and Paul Gendreau, "Reexamining the Cruel and Unusual Punishment of Prison Life," *Law and Human Behavior* 14 (1990): 353.

78. See Gerald G. Gaes, "The Effects of Overcrowding in Prison," in Michael Tonry and Norval Morris (eds.), *Crime and Justice,* Vol. 6 (Chicago: University of Chicago Press, 1985), pp. 95–146.

79. Bonta and Gendreau, "Reexamining the Cruel and Unusual Punishment of Prison Life," p. 355.

80. U.S. Department of Justice, Bureau of Justice Statistics Special Report, *Population Density in Local Jails, 1988,* p. 4.

81. See *Manual of Standards for Adult Correctional Institutions* (College Park, Md.: American Correctional Association, 1977); and *Federal Standards for Correction* (Washington, D.C.: U.S. Department of Justice, 1980).

82. U.S. Department of Justice, Bureau of Justice Statistics Special Report, *Population Density in Local Jails: 1988,* pp. 2, 7.

83. *Ibid.,* p. 9.

84. *Ibid.*

85. *Ibid.*

86. See Seth B. Goldsmith, "Jailhouse Medicine: Travesty or Justice?" *Health Services Report* 87 (1972): 767–774; R. A. Derro, "Administrative Health Evaluation of Inmates of a City-County Workhouse," *Minnesota Medicine* 61 (1978): 333–337.

87. See L. Culpepper and J. Floom, "Incarceration and Blood Pressure," *Social Services and Medicine* 14 (1980): 571–574; Lloyd F. Novick, Richard Della-Penna, Melvin S. Schwartz, Elaine Remlinger, and Regina Lowenstein, "Health Status of the New York City Prison Population," *Medical Care* 15 (1977): 205–216.

88. Doris L. MacKenzie and Lynne Goodstein, "Long-Term Incarceration Impacts and Char-

acteristics of Long-Term Offenders: An Empirical Analysis," *Criminal Justice and Behavior* 13 (1985): 395–414.

89. J. S. Wormith, "The Effects of Incarceration: Myth-Busting in Criminal Justice," paper presented at the 94th Annual Conference of the American Psychological Association. Washington, D.C., August 1986.

90. Bonta and Gendreau, "Reexamining the Cruel and Unusual Punishment of Prison Life," p. 357.

91. R. Barry Ruback and Christopher A. Innes, "The Relevance and Irrelevance of Psychological Research: The Example of Prison Crowding," *American Psychologist* 43 (1988): 683–693.

92. W. T. Austin and Charles M. Unkovic, "Prison Suicide," *Criminal Justice Review* 2 (1977): 103–106.

93. Robert R. Ross and H. B. McKay, *Self Mutilation* (Lexington, Mass.: Lexington Books, 1979).

94. Maguire et al., *Sourcebook of Criminal Justice Statistics 1992*, p. 633.

95. K. J. Heskin, F. V. Smith, P. A. Banister, and N. Bolton, "Psychological Correlates of Long-Term Imprisonment: II. Personality Variables," *British Journal of Criminology* 13 (1973): 323–330.

96. K. J. Heskin, F. V. Smith, P. A. Banister, and N. Bolton, "Psychological Correlates of Long-Term Imprisonment: III. Attitudinal Variables," *British Journal of Criminology* 14 (1974): 150–157.

97. N. Bolton, F. V. Smith, K. J. Heskin, and P. A. Banister, "Psychological Correlates of Long-Term Imprisonment: IV. A Longitudinal Analysis," *British Journal of Criminology* 16 (1976): 36–47.

98. Timothy J. Flanagan, "Time Served and Institutional Misconduct: Patterns of Involvement in Disciplinary Infractions Among Long-Term and Short-Term Inmates," *Journal of Criminal Justice* 8 (1980): 357–367.

99. W. Rasch, "The Effects of Indeterminate Sentencing: A Study of Men Sentenced to Life Imprisonment," *International Journal of Law and Psychiatry* 4 (1981): 417–431.

100. MacKenzie and Goodstein, "Long-Term Incarceration Impacts and Characteristics of Long-Term Offenders: An Empirical Analysis," p. 414.

101. Doris L. MacKenzie, James W. Robinson, and C. S. Campbell, "Long-Term Incarceration of Female Offenders: Prison Adjustment and Coping," *Criminal Justice and Behavior* 16 (1989): 223–238.

102. Timothy J. Flanagan, "Lifers and Long-Termers: Doing Big Time," in Robert Johnson and Hans Toch (eds.), *The Pains of Imprisonment*, pp. 115–128.

103. Deborah G. Wilson and Gennaro F. Vito, "Long-Term Inmates: Special Needs and Management Considerations," *Federal Probation* 52 (1988): 21–26.

104. M. Jackson, *Prisons of Isolation: Solitary Confinement in Canada* (Toronto, Ontario, Canada: University of Toronto Press, 1983), p. 243.

105. Bonta and Gendreau, "Reexamining the Cruel and Unusual Punishment of Prison Life," p. 360.

106. P. Suedfield, C. Ramirez, J. Deaton, and G. Baker-Brown, "Reactions and Attributes of Prisoners in Solitary Confinement," *Criminal Justice and Behavior* 9 (1982): 303–340.

107. B. M. Cormier and P. J. Williams, "Excessive Deprivation of Liberty as a Form of Punishment," paper presented at the meeting of the Canadian Psychiatric Association, Edmonton, Alberta, Canada 1966; Stuart Grassian, "Psychopathological Effects of Solitary Confinement," *American Journal of Psychiatry* 140 (1983): 1450–1454.

108. U.S. Department of Justice, Bureau of Justice Statistics Bulletin, *Capital Punishment 1994* (Washington, D.C.: Author, 1996), p. 1.

109. Harvey Bluestone and Carl L. McGahee, "Reacting to Extreme Stress: Impending Death by Execution," *American Journal of Psychiatry* 119 (1962): 393–396.

110. Johnnie L. Gallemore and James H. Panton, "Inmate Responses to Lengthy Death Row Confinement," *American Journal of Psychiatry* 129 (1972): 81–86.

111. James H. Panton, "Personality Characteristics of Death Row Prison Inmates," *Journal of Clinical Psychology* 32 (1976): 306–309.

112. Robert Johnson, "Life under Sentence of Death," in Robert Johnson and Hans Toch (eds.), *The Pains of Imprisonment,* pp. 129–145.

113. Charles E. Smith and Richard Reid Felix, "Beyond Deterrence: A Study of Defenses on Death Row," *Federal Probation* 50 (1986): 55–59.

114. Julius Debro, Komanduri Murty, Julian Roebuck, and Claude McCann, "Death Row Inmates: A Comparison of Georgia and Florida Profiles," *Criminal Justice Review* 12 (1987): 41–46.

115. John O. Smykla, "The Human Impact of Capital Punishment: Interviews of Families of Persons on Death Row," *Journal of Criminal Justice* 15 (1987): 331–347.

116. Joan Petersilia, "When Probation Becomes More Dreaded Than Prison," *Federal Probation* 54 (March 1990): 23–27.

117. John J. DiIulio, Jr., *Governing Prisons: A Comparative Study of Correctional Management* (New York: Free Press, 1987), p. 165.

Chapter 11

Corrections Personnel Roles and Functions

The mood and temper of the public in regard to the treatment of crime and criminals is one of the most unfailing tests of the civilization of any country.

—Winston Churchill

The vilest weeds like poison-weeds/Bloom well in prison-air.

—Oscar Wilde

✦ INTRODUCTION

This chapter focuses on the administrative methods and problems of correctional organizations. First, we analyze several facets and challenges of prison administration (including how to administer prisons, carry out death sentences, deal with overcrowding, and use confidential information and inmate self-help groups). We then turn to the front-line personnel in prisons: the correctional officers, including a view of their stereotypical roles and functions as well as their professional orientation. Finally, we examine the "cousin" of prisons, the jails. In this section we highlight how jail staff, inmates, and facilities are in reality quite different from those of prisons.

Two basic principles constitute the philosophy of prison "keepers": first, whatever the reasons a person is sent to prison, he or she is not to suffer pains beyond the deprivation of liberty—confinement itself is the punishment. Second, regardless of the crime, the prisoner must be treated humanely and in accordance with his or her behavior; even the most heinous offender is to be treated with respect and dignity and given privileges if institutional behavior warrants it.[1] Our analysis of institutional management is predicated on those two principles.

✦ PRISON ADMINISTRATION FOR THE 21ST CENTURY

✧ SUPERINTENDENTS AND THE "NEW OLD PENOLOGY"

The key to the conditions and general climate of any prison is the superintendent (or warden). As we discussed in Chapter 10, the role of superintendent has changed over the past few decades, from one of a czar over a dominion to that of a well-trained manager of an organization. Like police administration, however, it is probably accurate to say that the "old ways" of many wardens—riding roughshod over staff and inmates alike—probably fostered the growth of unionism among correctional officers. As prison employees have gained power to confront superintendents through their unions, some superintendents have sought to rely more on inmates than employees to control the prison. For example, a superintendent at Walla Walla, Washington, sought to manipulate inmate clubs to control both inmates and disgruntled officers. This ploy did not work but resulted in increased inmate strikes and riots, along with upheaval among the guards.[2]

Another change brought by the "new penology" is women administrators and staff members in prisons. In 1995 women were employed at all levels in prisons. In fact, a recent survey found that 16.3 percent (4,431 of 27,145) of all supervisory officers in adult correctional institutions were women.[3] Until recently, however, women did not work in all-male institutions. Research into three areas of early concern about women working in prison—their fitness for correctional work, their disruptive influence on prisoners, and issues of inmate privacy—has shown that these are seldom problems for female employees and, when they are, they are easily overcome.[4]

✧ ADMINISTERING PRISONS

Throughout the 19th and the early part of the 20th centuries, studies of prisons generally focused on prison administrators rather than on the inmates. Beginning in the 1940s, however, an ideological shift from focus on prison administrators to the inmates occurred. The central reason for the shift seems to have been the recognition that these institutions were poorly managed or were what prison researcher John J. DiIulio, Jr. referred to as "ineffective prisons."[5] Many writers expressed grave doubts about the efficacy of correctional administrators and expressed the idea that prison managers could do nothing to improve conditions behind bars.

It is not surprising that when contemporary researchers attempt to relate prison management practices to the quality of life behind bars, the results are normally quite negative: Prisons that are managed in a tight, authoritarian fashion are plagued with disorder and inadequate programs, and those that are managed in a loose, participative fashion are equally troubled; those with a mixture of these two styles are not any better.[6]

In a three-year study of prison management in Texas, Michigan, and California, DiIulio found that levels of disorder (rates of individual and collective violence and other forms of misconduct), amenity (availability of clean cells, decent food), and service (availability of work opportunities, educational programs) did not vary with any of the following factors: a "better class" of inmates, higher per capita spending, lower levels of crowding, lower inmate-to-staff ratios, more extensive officer training, more modern plant and equipment, and more routine use of repressive measures. DiIulio concluded that "all roads, it seemed, led to the conclusion that the quality of prison life depended mainly on the quality of prison management."[7]

DiIulio also found that prisons managed by a stable team of like-minded executives, structured in a paramilitary, security-driven, bureaucratic fashion, had better order, amenity, and service than those managed in other ways, *even when* the former institutions were more crowded, spent less per capita, had higher inmate/staff ratios, and so on. *"The only finding of this study that, to me at least, seems indispensable, is that . . . prison management matters"* [emphasis in original].[8]

Studies analyzing the causes of major prison riots from 1971 and 1986 found that they were the result of a breakdown in security procedures—the daily routine of numbering, counting, frisking, locking, controlling contraband, and searching cells—that are the heart of administration in most prisons.[9] Problems in areas such as crowding, underfunding, festering inmate-staff relations, and racial animosities may make a riot more *likely,* but poor security management makes them *inevitable.*[10]

DiIulio offered six general principles of good prison leaders:

1. Successful leaders focus, and inspire their subordinates to focus, on results rather than process, on performance rather than procedures, on ends rather than means. In short, managers are judged on results, not on excuses.

2. Professional staff members—doctors, psychiatrists, accountants, nurses, and other nonuniformed staff—receive some basic prison training and come to think of themselves as correctional officers first. As an example, in a recent disturbance at a federal penitentiary, middle-aged secretaries in skirts toted guns on the perimeter.

3. Leaders of successful institutions follow the management by walking around (MBWA) principle. ("Walking George" Beto, discussed in Chapter 3, was a prime example of this approach to management.) These managers are not strangers to the cellblocks and are always on the scene when trouble erupts.

4. Successful leaders make close alliances with key politicians, judges, journalists, reformers, and other outsiders. (The need to practice openness is discussed later.)

5. Successful leaders rarely innovate, but the innovations they implement are far reaching and the reasons for them are explained to staff and inmates well in advance. Line staff are notoriously sensitive to what administrators do "for inmates" versus "what they do for us." Thus leaders must be careful not to upset the balance and erode staff loyalty.

6. Successful leaders are in office long enough to understand and, as necessary, modify the organization's internal operations and external relations. DiIulio used the terms "flies," "fatalists," "foot soldiers," and "founders" to describe prison managers. The flies come and go unnoticed and are inconsequential. Fatalists also serve brief terms, always complaining about the futility of incarceration and the hopelessness of correctional reform. The foot soldiers serve long terms, often inheriting their job from a fly or fatalist and make consequential improvements whenever they can. Founders either create an agency or reorganize it in a major and positive way.[11]

To summarize, to "old" penologists, prison administrators were admirable public servants, inmates were to be restricted, and any form of self-government was eschewed. To "new" penologists, prison administrators are loathsome and evil, inmates are responsible victims, and complete self-government is the ideal. DiIulio calls for a "new old penology," or a shift of attention from the society of captives to the government of keepers. He asserted that tight administrative control is more conducive to decent prison conditions than loose administrative control. This approach, he added, will "push administrators back to the bar of attention," treating them at least as well as their charges.[12]

✦ CONTEMPORARY CHALLENGES TO PRISON ADMINISTRATORS

Today's prison administrator is faced with a fascinating array of challenges, including locating correctional facilities; designing and building them (cheaper and quicker); containing health care costs; managing overcrowding; developing alternatives to incarceration; addressing issues of gangs, AIDS, and staff safety and training; continuing to satisfy old court orders and consent decrees (while avoiding new court oversight due to increasing institution populations); and enhancing security and programs (while facing a reduction in resources).[13]

In the 1970s and 1980s a solid correctional administrator focused on managing the institution but in the mid-1990s must spend large amounts of time in the public policymaking arena. The "tough on crime" stance adopted by the political process has required administrators to enter the political arena more than ever before.

Prisons experience the same problems that other sectors of the economy face: rising food, construction, and health care costs (the latter exacerbated by individuals who are living longer as well as those whose health has deteriorated as a result of alcoholism, drug use, and AIDS) in addition to personnel expectations with regard to salary and benefits (with greater union activism in those areas).

As discussed earlier, society's litigious nature has permeated the prison walls. Today's correctional administrators must spend time and money defending against inmate lawsuits. Inmates sue not only over alleged confinement abuses but also about tattoos, pornography, voting rights, accessibility to lottery tickets, too little dessert, clothing style, air quality, and so on. Death penalty cases are on appeal indefinitely, negligent supervision suits abound, and employees are increasingly seeking assistance from the courts to resolve their differences.[14]

The corrections field has been the subject of little research, which has provided few if any findings leading to new methodologies to control or change the behavior of the inmates. As a result of the lack of research, correctional administrators today develop or apply programs that are generally advertised as being inexpensive and that therefore inevitably hold political charm. Correctional administrators of the 1990s must deal with the Willie Horton legacy: On any given day an offender may reoffend, causing public and political opinion within a jurisdiction to change completely. Politicians, who have learned the lesson of Willie Horton well, perceive that the tough on crime stance is politically attractive.[15]

Many people working in correctional administration believe that the public image of the field is negative. A corrections consultant wrote that the low level of public esteem commences with the media:

> The public view of corrections in this country is, frankly, horrible. People are inundated with stories about explosions in offender populations, monopoly-money costs for new prison and jail construction, and vexatious prison and jail litigation. The big stories that reach the public about corrections are almost universally negative.[16]

Correctional administrators' "deafening silence" was criticized when prison furlough (the Willie Horton case) became an issue in the 1988 presidential campaign. Critics implied inflexible sentences were the only solution to prevent crime during furloughs. Correctional administrators have also been chastised for not being politically adept.

A "fortress corrections" mentality is said to have become a philosophy within the field; many staff, from the top to the bottom, do not understand the public's right to information, and paranoia about the media is rampant among corrections personnel. Most often, prison-media relations involve the institution announcing that a suicide occurred in the middle of the night or even avoiding the press in the hope that the newspapers and TV will not find out about it: "The myth persists that if one holds onto negative information tightly enough, one will be able to hide in plain sight."[17]

The corrections field has also been reproached by its own for the manner in which it communicates its research:

> There are no widely-read professional journals in the field. The lack of serious research efforts is criminal considering the magnitude of public policy questions arising from corrections. There is good research, but most of that is never published. Thus, we re-create each other's mistakes too often. That picture does not connote professionalism. We have a very poor self-image. We don't like ourselves a lot and we don't think well of ourselves. I defy [anyone] to identify an occupation in which such a high percentage of people acknowledge going into the field "by accident."[18]

✧ "DEATH WORK": CARRYING OUT EXECUTIONS

One of the major duties of prison administrators, at least in a majority of the states, is to carry out the wishes of the people and see that condemned persons are executed in a manner that is professional and does not shock the conscience. The discharge of the death penalty requires a number of people who are trained in individual tasks. Robert Johnson, who has referred to this entire undertaking as "death work,"[19] has studied and witnessed the process personally. Although no "typical" process of bringing executions to fruition exists, the following is a general description of the key events.

Preparation for execution gains momentum when a date draws near and the prisoner is moved to the death house, a short walk from the death chamber. The process culminates in the so-called "death watch," a 24-hour period that ends with the prisoner's execution. This final period is generally supervised by the execution team, which reports directly to the superintendent of the institution.

During the actual death watch, a member of the execution team is with the prisoner at all times. The officer keeps the inmate calm and attempts to meet his or her immediate needs. At this stage, the execution team views the prisoner as a person with a potentially explosive personality, so surveillance is constant and intense. During the last five or six hours, two officers are assigned to the prisoner. They attempt to maintain a conversation with the inmate, keeping tabs on his or her state of mind and trying to avoid subjects that might cause depression or anger. As the execution time approaches, the mood normally becomes more somber and subdued. A last meal is served, although prisoners normally eat little or nothing at all, and then the prisoner boxes all of his or her worldly goods, which are inventoried by staff, for delivery to family or friends.[20]

The prisoner then showers, dons a fresh set of clothes, and is placed in an empty tomblike death cell. At this point the prisoner normally exhibits a numb resignation and waits peacefully to be escorted to his or her death. The superintendent and the remainder of the execution team then come and the former reads the court order, or death warrant. Meanwhile, official witnesses are prepared for their role. Normally, from 6 to 12 disinterested citizens in good standing serve as witnesses to the execution.[21]

The steps that are taken from this point, with regard to the actual execution, depend, of course, on the actual method used. For example, 27 states employ lethal injection, 12 use electrocution, 7 gas, 4 hanging, and 1 a firing squad; 14 states authorize more than one method, generally at the election of the condemned prisoner.[22]

By law, the superintendent or a representative must preside over the execution. In many states a member of the death watch or execution team, acting under the superintendent's authority, actually performs the execution.[23]

Today most executions are carried out by a highly trained team. One prison administrator described the team thus:

> An execution is something that needs to be done and good people, dedicated people who believe in the American system, should do it. When they have to hang tough, they can do it and they can do it right. And it's just the right thing to do.[24]

"Do it right" in this context means that the execution should be accomplished professionally. Again, in the words of an administrator,

> We had to be sure that we did it properly, professionally, and that we gave as much dignity to the person as we possibly could in the process. . . . If you've gotta do it, it might just as well be done the way it's supposed to be done—without any sensation.[25]

Properly means that procedures are performed as intended; *professional* means without personal feelings that intrude on the procedures in any way.

Few personnel on the execution team actually support the death penalty without reservation. Nonetheless, they are committed to doing it right, "by the book." To minimize the possibility of error, the death watch team is carefully drilled in the mechanics of execution. The process has been broken down into distinct tasks and practiced repeatedly. Division of labor allows each team member to become a specialist, and practice allows him or her to become confident and, later, accurate under pressure.

✧ STAFF-INMATE RELATIONSHIPS

A common misconception held by the public is that prison administrators, through their correctional officers, have complete control over inmates. Historically, prisoners were expected to do as they were told. As discussed in Chapter 3, even the courts, stating that they did not have the expertise or the jurisdiction to determine how a prison should be managed,[26] deferred to the sometimes heavy-handed methods of superintendents.

At the end of the 20th century, inmates have power. Without their consent and cooperation, the modern correctional institution could not function. According to Victor Lofgreen, today's "mega-prison" has changed from a correctional facility with programs and activities to rehabilitate offenders to a racially segregated, gang-controlled warehouse for convicts to do their time. By depending on inmate labor and leadership in order to function, prisons give power to the inmate groups. In addition, correctional officers are under constant scrutiny by administrators and subject to litigation brought by inmates. In sum, "the modern prison has become a combat zone."[27]

Lofgreen described a model of the life cycle of the power relationship between the staff and inmates in an adult prison (Figure 11.1); the model demonstrates the change in the balance of power in the prison from staff to inmates over time, from total staff domination to total inmate domination. In Stage I, that of staff dominant–inmate submissive, administration and staff are in clear, visible, and total control of the institution, with inmates in a lockdown status, usually following a rebellion or major shakedown. A correctional facility cannot operate very long under these circumstances. The institution depends on inmate labor to function as cooks, laundry personnel, housekeepers, and so on. Therefore, to provide enough personnel for these tasks, the institution moves into Stage II, the staff dominant, inmate labor stage. As soon as possible following a disturbance, staff begin to classify inmates and identify those who can be trusted to work. Over time other inmates are released from lockdown and return to their work assignments. The institution regains its equilibrium and inmates are given increased autonomy, freedom of movement, and privileges. A balance of power

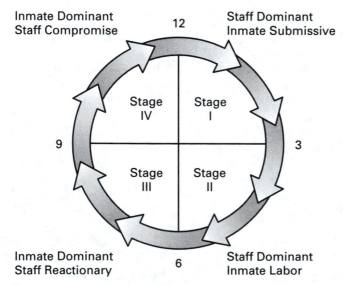

Figure 11.1
Model of the life cycle of the inmate–staff power relationship in an adult prison. (*Source:* Victor D. Lofgreen, "A Model of the Dynamic Power Relationship between Staff and Inmates in a Secure Correctional Facility," paper presented at the Annual Meeting of the Academy of Criminal Justice Sciences, 1991, Reno, Nevada. Used with permission.)

is created between the two groups, with each side cooperating with the other (although the inmates know they could take control of the prison whenever they wished).[28]

After reaching this state of equilibrium, however, a phenomenon occurs whereby each time the administration extends a privilege to the inmates, the inmates expect it to be a permanent offering. They meet any attempt by administration to withdraw privileges with extreme resistance. Eventually, if administration and staff continue to award new privileges to motivate inmates, the latter will have the most power. Inmates may expect to be catered to and even pressure officers to participate in activities that violate institutional rules or law. In this stage of development, known as the *inmate dominant–staff reactionary stage,* or Stage III, prison inmates are in a position of superiority over the administration and staff.[29]

Through this progression, the institution becomes more and more unstable. Certain inmates are protected; others are punished unfairly. At some point, the lack of consistent treatment and favoritism toward certain inmates causes a major loss of credibility in prison administration. Inmates and officers are confused, not knowing what to expect. This is Stage IV, inmate dominant–staff compromise. The tension and anxiety lead to a major disturbance. When the disturbance occurs, the institution is again thrown into an emergency lockdown status (Stage I). Order is restored and the process begins again. This cycle may take 2 or 20 years depending on how long it takes the inmate subculture to compromise administration and staff. The goal of the administrator is to develop an institutional culture that creates a balance between the power of the staff and the inmates.[30]

By managing change in a deliberate manner, the correctional administrator can keep the balance of power between Stages II and III for an extended period of time. Lofgreen recommended that administration occasionally "move inmates to a periodic scheduled lockdown to prevent the accumulation of contraband and maintain staff power over the inmates."[31]

✦ OVERCROWDING: POSSIBLE SOLUTIONS

As discussed in Chapter 10, overcrowding may well be the primary problem affecting prisons and jails today. According to some observers, however, a larger problem may be that corrections facilities have admitted defeat in the battle against overcrowding. The heart of the problem, it is argued, lies in the fact that density and crowding, although related, are not the same. "The major factors responsible for crowding effects lie within the dynamic properties of social interactions" rather than in density per se.[32]

In other words, the real pains of crowding come not from inmate density but from the fact that prisoners feel crowded and suffer ill effects as a result; crowding interferes with their preferred ways of living. Social interactions, marked by poor coping behavior, cause various difficulties. Therefore, improving the quality of prison life should be the first order of prison reform. Some reformers maintain that other changes, such as building new prisons and using alternative forms of punishment (see Chapter 12), are important but play a secondary role in reducing prison crowding. These strategies should be pursued *after* the crowding problem has been solved.[33]

Inmates feel crowded when they live under conditions of high density (many bodies), low resources (little to do), and limited control over their lives (few if any ways to escape unpleasant encounters). These conditions magnify the pressures of prison life. The key to avoiding problems of crowding, it is argued, is to provide more resources and expand the inmates' capacity to choose how resources are deployed. Prisoners will thus be treated as bona fide "consumers of correctional services."[34] Administrators could conduct consumer surveys to determine prisoners' perceptions of their needs and the means to meet them. Services that inmates do not want or use could be modified or discontinued; others could be retained for program development.[35] Prisoners themselves might even find sources of services through a variety of existing self-help organizations (described later).

Administration and inmates can work together to develop decent prisons. More areas of stable private space should be developed for prisoners in densely populated, close-custody institutions. Functional units offer a means for doing so. These subdivide large prisons into small "institutions" or "miniprisons." Cubicles can be used in dormitories, shops, and classrooms. "Small prisons with private spaces for inmates are very desirable for the physical and psychological welfare of the inmates as well as from a prison management perspective."[36] These functional units "rearrange the distribution of currently available resources with the likely result that if we are not doing more with less, at least we are doing it for the same costs."[37]

No new space is needed to house functional units; only existing space is needed. These, Johnson said, are eminently practical means to convert a crowded prison from an interpersonal wasteland to a civilized social environment.[38]

✧ PRISON RULE VIOLATORS

Institutional administrators must develop, implement, and enforce rules and procedures in their organizations. These rules regulate inmate conduct to ensure orderly operation of the institution and protection of all who live and work there; they help to manage confined populations that outnumber staff by a 3 to 1 ratio. Administrators respond to the more serious violations through administrative hearings in which they consider the merits of the charges and appropriate penalties.

Characteristics of Prison Rule Violators. A national survey of state prison inmates found that over half (53 percent) had been charged with violating prison rules at least once since entering prison on their current sentence.[39] This finding is consistent with that of a similar survey in 1979, which found that prison rule violators were likely to be young, unmarried, and incarcerated for a property offense or a robbery. They were also more likely than other inmates to be recidivists, to have been arrested for the first time at an early age, to have used drugs regularly, and to have completed less than 12 years of formal education. Furthermore, inmates housed in large or maximum-security prisons had higher percentages of rule violations than did prisoners in other types of facilities.[40]

A slightly higher percentage of male inmates (53 percent) than female inmates (47 percent) were charged with breaking rules. As noted, marital status seemed to influence violations: about 60 percent of inmates who had never married were charged with violating prison rules, compared with about 41 percent of married inmates. Age was the prisoner characteristic that related most directly to prison rule violation; the younger the age, the larger the percentage of inmates charged with rule violations. About 60 percent of the inmates age 18 to 24 were charged with infractions. White and black rule violators were responsible for nearly the same number of punishments for rule violations.[41]

✦ OBTAINING CONFIDENTIAL INFORMATION

Accurate information is necessary for the orderly and effective operation of every organization. Correctional institutions are certainly no exception. To have such information, prison and jail administrators and staff members observe conditions, listen to complaints, and monitor the results of their actions and regulations. The unique nature of these organizations, however, creates a need for information beyond that of normal businesses. Timely information is crucial for staff and administration to prevent riots, escape plots, or other threats to security. It is also essential that inmates involved in criminal activities that occur often in these institutions be identified and prosecuted successfully.[42]

Inmates themselves are obvious sources of this information. One of the strongest taboos in the inmate subculture, however, is to "snitch" on other inmates or cooperate with prison officials. That philosophy militates against obtaining needed information. Inmate informants can become targets of death threats, which are sometimes carried out. Protecting informants can become a serious problem for the administration.

Three types of inmate informants are employed: "snitches," the innocent witness or victim, and coconspirators. The idea of using snitches—trusted inmates who provide a regular flow of information—is attractive. This system often causes more problems than it solves, however. Inmates soon learn who the snitches are. Snitches can also become undependable; some clever informants take great delight in working as double agents.[43] The negative side of this system was ingloriously demonstrated during the 1980 New Mexico Penitentiary riot, when 33 inmates were murdered, some after being mutilated with blowtorches. Many inmates were also raped repeatedly. Among the first to be dragged from their cells and murdered were, of course, known snitches.

Instead of using designated snitches regularly, information can be sought from inmates when crimes and serious rule violations are investigated or in response to threats to the prison's safety and security. Although many inmates will report that they didn't see anything when crimes were committed, many serious crimes and incidents in prison have been solved as the result of cooperation from inmates. Coconspirators present special problems. Many serious crimes would never be solved without inside information from coconspirators wishing to save their own skins. Correctional administrators need to consider, however, that the coconspirator may actually be the principal offender, who is willing to sacrifice partners who played a minor role in order to obtain immunity. Unless conclusive evidence corroborates the information, determining whether inmates are innocent witnesses or coconspirators may be difficult.[44]

Legal problems arise when confidential information is to be presented to a disciplinary committee. Correctional administrators need a basic working knowledge of the law surrounding the use of confidential information as evidence to ensure that due process is allowed inmates and to avoid lawsuits as a result of inappropriate use. Information used as a basis for punishing an inmate must meet at least some minimal standard of reliability. The disciplinary committee must be shown that the informant had firsthand knowledge and must receive information to help it determine the informant's reliability. *Mendoza v. Miller*[45] explained three ways to establish an informant's reliability. First, the investigator can swear an oath that the investigative report is true and then appear before the disciplinary committee to answer questions. Second, the informant's information can be corroborated by other evidence (this is possible when there is more than one informant). Third, the committee can verify firsthand knowledge of the informant based on the past record.[46]

✧ ADMINISTRATIVE USE OF THE INMATE SELF-HELP MOVEMENT

The Seventh Step Program at Kansas State Prison in Lansing was a spinoff of Alcoholics Anonymous and was the original prisoner self-help organization. Like many self-help groups, it was based on the personal experiences of its founder, Bill Sands. Designed to help long-term, hard-core recidivists to return to the mainstream of life, Sands's program was simple:

> Such classes should be conducted by ex-convicts rather than correctional authorities. For two good reasons. One, because such a man knows what must be done, knows what it feels like to be out in the world, branded with a felony record; and two, because the men inside prisons refuse, for the most part, to take moral lessons from the so-called do-gooders.[47]

According to Mark Hamm, inmates have demonstrated a strong and sustained interest in self-help organizations during the past two decades. He asserted that this "movement" has captured the attention of correctional administrators concerned with the plight of special offender populations. From the familiar Alcoholics Anonymous to the little-known Schizophrenics Anonymous, Taking Pounds Off Sensibly, Women Who Love Too Much, Partners Without Partners, Mended-Hearts, Widow-to-Widow, Tough Love, and support groups for stutterers and diabetics to Hell's Angels seeking spiritual enlightenment and groups of transsexuals coping with their transitions, the self-help movement involves activities that reach into many areas of our social world. The American Veterans in Prison, Vietnam Veterans of America, and the Disabled American Veterans organizations also provide help for inmates.[48]

Historically, correctional treatment focused on past problems and errors and attempted to build a better tomorrow; however, several authors have observed that too often the immediate struggle for survival in prison distracts an inmate's attention from these "official" treatment programs.[49] As a result, inmates have increasingly turned to gangs, religious fellowships, and self-help organizations as alternatives to state-provided programs.[50]

The prisoner self-help groups provide certain opportunities for both administrators and inmates. First, they may relieve inmates' pains of imprisonment. These groups provide a support system that meets prisoners' social and/or cultural needs.[51] Some groups also provide leadership training, prisoner-administration politics, and organizational development and management. They also can relieve administration of some of the burden it carries for providing rehabilitative programs. These groups are of little threat to corrections administration.[52]

A number of ethnic self-help groups, including Black Awareness for Community Development, Chicanos Organizados Pinton Aztlan, Afro-American Coalition, Affirmative Action Latin Group, and the Native American Brotherhood also have been organized. These groups seek to develop strong ties between minority communities on the outside and inmates and try to elicit support for them from religious and university communities. Because group leaders have tended to provoke and challenge them, correctional administrators have often taken a dim view of ethnic self-help groups.[53]

Overall, however, Hamm suggested that inmate self-help groups can work in concert with administrators to improve confinement conditions. For the future, the challenge for administrators will be to understand the potential of these groups, how they may contribute to institutional stability, and the extent to which they might facilitate community integration. Hamm cautioned, however, that administrators will not tolerate threats from these groups, regardless of their noble intentions.[54]

✦ CORRECTIONAL OFFICERS: "THY BROTHER'S KEEPER"

Between the institutional director and the inmates is the correctional staff—members who, in the words of Gordon Hawkins, are "the other prisoners."[55] Their role and nature are particularly important, given that they provide the front line supervision and control of inmates and correctional administrators may be promoted from this level.

In close association with inmates, correctional officers know that brute force and the system of rewards and punishments (especially in light of recent court decisions) are inadequate as control mechanisms. The officers know that a day of reckoning when all IOUs come due, when they may become hostages of the inmates, may eventually come, and when the decision as to whether the officers live or die may turn on their treatment of, and their reputation, among the inmate population. Thus, to be successful, officers may feel compelled to engage in *quid pro quos*—*trades* or *deals*—overlooking small infractions by inmates in return for their general compliance with rules and orders. Gresham Sykes noted that "it is apparent, then, that the power of custodians is defective . . . the ruled are rebellious . . . the rulers are reluctant."[56] He also asserted that "it is a paradox that [the officers] can insure their dominance only by allowing it to be corrupted."[57]

❖ COMPARISON OF CORRECTIONS OFFICERS AND INMATES

One guard stated, "We're all doing time, some of us are just doin' it in eight-hour shifts."[58] Richard Hawkins and Geoffrey Alpert compared officers and inmates: both groups are likely to be drawn from lower- and working-class backgrounds; both are likely to be in their present roles because of lack of employment opportunities; both groups are largely invisible; both are closely watched and experience some depersonalization (e.g., they wear uniforms and are subject to psychological testing and probing into their past); both develop feelings of powerlessness; and both are fighting for their individual rights (conditions of incarceration and employment, respectively).[59]

Most applicants for positions as correctional officers probably had little knowledge of the job when they applied. A job description for the position might read something like this:

> [They] must prevent rape among two hundred convicts enraged by their powerlessness and sexual deprivation . . . prevent violence among the convicts . . . shake down all cells for contraband . . . know what is going on in the convicts' head and report it to their supervisors . . . account for all material entering or leaving each cellblock . . . maintain sanitation in each cell . . . give individual attention to all . . . convicts . . . [and] prevent the suicide or running amok of the raped, the depressed, and the terrified . . . and look out for their own physical and psychological survival.[60]

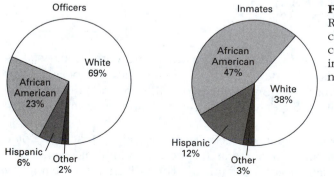

Figure 11.2
Racial/ethnic composition of correctional officers and inmates, adult systems nationwide.

In most assignments, correctional officers experience stimulus overload, are assailed with the sounds of "doors clanging, inmates talking or shouting, radios and televisions playing, and food trays banging . . . (and odors) representing an institutional blend of food, urine, paint, disinfectant, and sweat."[61]

Correctional officers are not allowed to provide informal counseling or to aid in the rehabilitative effort. Due process rights for prisoners have made corrections jobs even more difficult.[62] Therein lies what Hawkins and Alpert referred to as "the big bitch" of correctional officers: they are losing power and influence while inmates are gaining them as they are accorded more and more due process rights.[63] This frustration can be vented in physical ways. Although certainly not frequent today, beatings and even sexual attacks on inmates by some officers have been documented.[64]

✦ REQUIREMENTS OF CORRECTIONAL OFFICERS

The issue of what specific skills and level of education are needed to do the work of a correctional officer has rarely been raised. An issue of the Department of Labor's *Dictionary of Occupational Titles*[65] reported that the skill complexity level is the same for correctional officers and road construction flagpersons, school bus monitors, and morgue attendants!

Several federal commissions have strongly recommended higher educational standards among correctional officers, although none of them provided evidence that better educated persons necessarily make better officers.[66] The question of whether higher education is required for correctional officers is important. Education has a tendency to raise a person's aspirations and expectations. As one person put it, "Better educated people expect to do better."[67]

Considerable evidence suggests that higher education is not beneficial for correctional officers but may actually lower job satisfaction. One observer noted that "except for the somewhat disappointing finding that [correctional officers] with more education are less satisfied with their jobs, the overall picture shows that education is not related to any attitudinal variable examined thus far."[68] Other researchers have commented that "more highly educated officers were significantly less satisfied with their jobs"[69] than were less educated ones. Another study determined that as officers' educational levels increased, so did their desire to become administrators; the less likely they were to feel a sense of accomplishment working as correctional officers or to want to make a career of corrections; the more likely they were to express dissatisfaction with the pace of career advancement; and the more interest that they had in counseling.[70]

Two Canadian researchers studied the behavioral skills that effective correctional officers possessed; they compared the perceptions of correctional officers, supervisors, and inmates as to correctional officers' tasks.[71] Correctional officers and supervisors attributed more importance to the "responsibility/leadership" skills (including writing reports, enforcing rules and regulations, working independently without excessive supervision, working effectively with others, providing inmates with appropriate information on different aspects of their incarceration, and providing clear direction to inmates on how to improve un-acceptable behavior before applying negative consequences[72]) than the inmates did. Staff members perceived these job skills as the primary elements in their jobs, but inmates were obviously less concerned with them.

✧ RESULTS OF RESEARCH STUDIES CONCERNING CORRECTIONAL OFFICER CHARACTERISTICS

We now examine the professional orientation of correctional officers with respect to two broad aspects of their job: their individual views of the job and the performance of it and their philosophy and views as members of organizations.

Attitudes. Recent studies indicate a consensus that "many officers see correctional work as an intrinsically worthwhile endeavor."[73]

The attitudes of correctional officers toward race, gender, education, chronological age, and age of entry into correctional work have been examined. Studies have not found any significant relationship between race and punitive attitudes toward inmates.[74] One study found no differences in officers' professional orientation according to race or region (rural or urban).[75] Another researcher determined that nonwhite officers expressed an optimistic attitude toward inmates.[76] Finally, although one researcher found no significant differences regarding support for custody, black officers reported significantly greater support for rehabilitation.[77]

No studies have reported that officer gender was of significant concern to inmates.[78] One study did find a significant negative relationship between education and custody orientation, however.[79] Although chronological age was found not to be related to punitive attitude, a significant relationship between being older and support for a counseling orientation was discovered.[80] Similarly, older officers have been found significantly more optimistic regarding inmates.[81] Officers who entered corrections at a later age were significantly more likely to express support for rehabilitation.[82]

In summary, the results of studies into individual attitudes of corrections officers regarding the impact of race and age and the importance of gender and education are conflicting.[83]

A number of organizational conditions, such as institutional security, frequency of inmate contact, assigned shifts, seniority, role conflict, job stress, perceptions of danger, and supervisory support have been studied. One study detected a significantly greater punitiveness among officers in minimum security units,[84] but another found significantly more optimism toward rehabilitating inmates in minimum security units.[85] A study investigating whether frequency of inmate contact affected officers' attitudes did not uncover a significant relationship in the degree of optimism regarding inmates.[86]

Not surprisingly, officers assigned to the night or "graveyard" shift, when inmates are normally "locked down," have reported a significantly more custodial and less rehabilitative orientation.[87] Although seniority has not been significantly related to officers' attitudes toward inmates,[88] one study determined that seniority was significantly negatively related to their attitudes toward inmates' rehabilitation potential (as seniority increased, officers' expectation that rehabilitation was possible decreased).[89] Similarly, other studies found a significant positive relationship between seniority and custody orientation,[90] and that as seniority increased, optimism toward inmates' rehabilitation decreased.[91]

✦ JAILS

✧ PRISONERS

Most if not all of the research findings on prison administrators and staff members previously presented can be extended to workers in jails. Jails differ from prisons, however, in several ways. Although about one-half million people are incarcerated in the nation's 3,300 jails every day,[92] social scientists, like the general public, have shown little interest in them or the administration and operation of jails. In a legal sense, however, the jail is the point of entry into the criminal justice system. Jails hold persons booked for criminal activity and held for court appearances if they cannot arrange bail and those who are serving sentences of up to one year for misdemeanors.

John Irwin, a noted penal expert and author who served time in several jails and prisons, has some interesting views on jail inmates. They are detached because they are not well integrated into conventional society, have few ties to social networks, and carry unconventional values and beliefs. They are disreputable because they are perceived as irksome, offensive, threatening, and capable of arousal.[93]

Irwin referred to jail prisoners as "rabble," meaning "disorganized" and "disorderly"—the "lowest class of people." He also referred to jail administration as "managing rabble."[94] Certain significant physical characteristics and management processes, he wrote, reflect the fact that jails are intended to hold only the rabble. First, because not many of the rabble are expected to appear in court or even to stay in jail, security has been the fundamental concern in the construction of jails. The result has been massive buildings, complicated locking systems, and elaborate surveillance techniques. Second, Irwin maintained that because the rabble cannot be expected to behave themselves in jails, they must be controlled.[95] Hans Mattick agreed but noted that

> Some jail administrators go overboard when it comes to the smaller details of jail security. Instead of relying on good peripheral security and the rational internal deployment of staff, they deplete the time and energies of their limited staffs by harassing the inmates in the details of daily living by frequent head counts, strip

searches, cell "shakedowns," and the censorship of prisoner mail. In general, this is a wasteful use of scarce personnel. There is also a general tendency to treat *all* prisoners, except "trusties," as maximum security cases.[96]

Irwin believed that security-oriented measures caused jail inmates in general to experience more punishment per day than a convict in a state prison. Jailed persons, he said, suffered sudden interruption of their affairs, abrupt initiation to the jail, restriction of activities to a very small area, virtually no opportunities for recreation and expression, and a reduced health regimen that could lead to physical deterioration and occasionally to serious illness.[97] (*Note:* These characteristics do indeed indicate a harsher incarceration for those in jails as compared with those in prisons, especially with regard to health-related issues; see the discussion of research on prison inmates in Chapter 10.)

Although a large number of U.S. jails are undoubtedly similar to those described by Irwin and Mattick, a number of state-of-the-art facilities are progressive, treatment oriented to the extent possible, and generally "softer" than those described.

✧ CAREER PATHS FOR JAIL PERSONNEL

Because no single jail administrator is responsible for statewide jail management, detention officers (or "jailers") may manage their jails according to vastly different perceptions and philosophies concerning their staffing and operation. Most jails are supervised by a sheriff's office, where career advancement may be quite limited. When jails are separate units of local government with their own director, they tend to attract more qualified administrators with career commitments. A separate, jail-related career path for correctional workers in jail administration is currently needed.

In some facilities, however, detention officers may transfer to patrol on the basis of seniority. Many of them, after receiving their basic training, want to do "real police work" and go out on patrol; they eschew the confined, nonpolice duties of detention that many agencies first require of new personnel. Many good officers, unwilling to serve a period of several years working in jails, resign.

Police administrators should create two separate career paths, one in patrol and one in detention so that persons beginning one path can remain and be promoted in it and eventually retire from it.

✧ TRAINING OF JAIL PERSONNEL

Jail administrators need to be thoroughly trained in all aspects of their job. Jail workers have been criticized for being untrained and apathetic, although many are highly effective and dedicated. One observer wrote that

Personnel is still the number one problem of jails. Start paying decent salaries and developing decent training and you can start to attract bright young people to jobs in jails. If you don't do this, you'll continue to see the issue of personnel as the number one problem for the next 100 years.[98]

Training should be provided on the booking process, inmate management and security, general liability issues, policies related to AIDS, problems of inmates addicted to alcohol and other drugs, communication and security technology, and issues concerning inmate suicide, mental health problems, and medication.

✦ JAIL OVERCROWDING

Justice administrators across the country have identified overcrowding in correctional institutions as the most serious problem facing criminal justice today.[99] Nearly a third of the nation's jails are under court order to limit their populations or improve conditions, suggesting the seriousness of this problem. Overcrowding increases tensions for staff and inmates and wear and tear on facility and equipment, creates overtime budgetary problems, and exacerbates the problems related to meeting program and service standards. Judges, prosecutors, probation and parole officers, and other officials often find jail crowding a severe constraint when offenders need to be jailed but space is unavailable. Finally, court functions suffer overall when crowding affects the movement of inmates to and from scheduled appearances.[100]

Alleviating the Problem. Justice administrators and policymakers can affect jail crowding, however. As one judge said, they can use "a lot of little ways" to halt or reverse jail population increases without releasing serious offenders.[101] *Police administrators* can invoke policies concerning arrest practices—whether to arrest, transport to jail, book or detain for bail setting—which are critical determinants in jail populations. Stationhouse release before booking, field citations, and court-authorized bail schedules also can eliminate unnecessary confinement.

Jail administrators can reduce overcrowding by ensuring ready access for pretrial release screening and bail review. *Prosecutors* can engage in early case screening to reduce unnecessarily long confinements by eliminating or downgrading weak cases as soon as possible. Prosecutors also can use "vertical case screening," which assigns the same attorney or team of attorneys to a case from start to finish. "Horizontal case screening" (reassigning cases to one assistant prosecutor and then to another while the matter is before the court) may cause stagnation in case flow.

Judges make more decisions affecting jail population than anyone else; they can issue summonses instead of arrest warrants, provide guidelines authorizing direct release by police, jail, and pretrial staff; and provide for bail to be set after normal court hours. Courts may defer service of jail sentences when the jail is at capacity.

Defense attorneys can perform early screening for indigency, defender appointment, and defendant contact, which can decrease length of confinement and yield substantial savings of jail space.

Probation and parole agencies can provide nonjail alternatives for sentencing and enhance case-processing efficiency by streamlining presentence investigation procedures and expediting revocation decisions.[102]

Summary

Certainly, substantial pressures are now put on prison and jail administrators. They must maintain custody of and offer some degree of treatment to inmates while protecting inmates against themselves and others. At the same time, they must avoid decisions and behaviors that might lead to costly liability while attempting to prevent or remedy overcrowding.

Questions for Review

1. What is meant by the term *new old penology?*
2. What are some of the major elements of well-administered prisons? Enumerate the major principles of good prison administration.
3. Describe the life cycle of the inmate–staff power relationship. Why is it rare for a prison to pass through all phases of the cycle?
4. What can prison administrators do to alleviate overcrowding? How can they provide relief from overcrowding without adding new space?
5. What are some problems and methods of dealing with prison rule violators and snitches for correctional administrators?
6. What makes an effective correctional officer? Given research findings concerning their attitudes toward offenders, do these officers believe that rehabilitation of prisoners is likely?
8. How does jail administration differ from prison administration?

Notes

1. John J. DiIulio, Jr., *Governing Prisons: A Comparative Study of Correctional Management* (New York: Free Press, 1987), p. 167.
2. Charles Stastny and Gabrielle Tyrnauer, *Who Rules the Joint* (Lexington, Mass.: D. C. Heath, 1982).

3. Kathleen Maguire and Ann L. Pastore (eds.), *Sourcebook of Criminal Justice Statistics 1995.* U.S. Department of Justice, Bureau of Justice Statistics (Washington, D.C.: U.S. Government Printing Office, 1996), p. 90.

4. Richard Hawkins and Geoffrey P. Alpert, *American Prison Systems: Punishment and Justice* (Englewood Cliffs, N.J.: Prentice Hall, 1989), p. 359.

5. In George F. Cole (ed.), *Criminal Justice: Law and Politics* (Belmont, Calif.: Wadsworth, 1993), pp. 438–446.

6. *Ibid.,* p. 439.

7. DiIulio, *Governing Prisons,* p. 256.

8. *Ibid.*

9. Bert Useem, *States of Siege: U.S. Prison Riots, 1971–1986* (New York: Oxford University Press, 1988).

10. John J. DiIulio, Jr., "Well Governed Prisons Are Possible," in Cole, *Criminal Justice,* p. 440.

11. John J. DiIulio, Jr., *No Escape: The Future of American Corrections* (New York: Basic Books, 1991), chapter 1.

12. DiIulio, "Well Governed Prisons Are Possible," p. 445.

13. Chase Riveland, "Being a Director of Corrections in the 1990s," *Federal Probation* 55 (June 1991): 10–11.

14. *Ibid.,* p. 10.

15. *Ibid.,* p. 11.

16. Jeffrey A. Schwartz, "Fortress Corrections," *Corrections Today* 51 (August 1989): 216–223.

17. *Ibid.,* p. 222.

18. *Ibid.,* pp. 222–223.

19. See Robert Johnson, *Death Work: A Study of the Modern Execution Process* (Pacific Grove, Calif.: Brooks/Cole, 1990).

20. Robert Johnson, "This Man Has Expired," *Commonweal* (January 13, 1989): 9–15.

21. *Ibid.*

22. U.S. Department of Justice, Bureau of Justice Statistics Bulletin, *Capital Punishment 1994* (Washington, D.C.: Author, February 1996).

23. Johnson, "This Man Has Expired."

24. *Ibid.*

25. *Ibid.*

26. See *Banning v. Looney,* 213 F.2d 711 (10th. Cir., 1954).

27. Victor D. Lofgreen, "A Model of the Dynamic Power Relationship Between Staff and Inmates in a Secure Correctional Facility," paper presented at the Annual Meeting of the Western Social Science Association, Reno, Nev., 1991, p. 6.

28. *Ibid.,* pp. 8–10.

29. *Ibid.,* pp. 12–14.

30. *Ibid.,* pp. 14–16.

31. *Ibid.,* p. 18.

32. Verne C. Cox, Paul B. Paulus, and Garvin McCain, "Prison Crowding Research: The Relevance for Prison Housing Standards and a General Approach Regarding Crowding Phenomena," *American Psychologist* 39 (October 1984): 1148–1160.

33. Robert Johnson, "Crowding and the Quality of Prison Life: A Preliminary Reform Agenda," in Clayton A. Hartjen and Edward E. Rhine (eds.), *Correctional Theory and Practice* (Chicago: Nelson-Hall, 1992), pp. 139–145.

34. See Robert Johnson, *Hard Time: Understanding and Reforming the Prison* (Monterey, Calif.: Brooks/Cole, 1987).

35. Johnson, "Crowding and the Quality of Prison Life," p. 142.

36. Cox et al., "Prison Crowding Research," p. 1156.

37. Robert B. Levinson, "Try Softer," in Robert Johnson and Hans Toch (eds.), *The Pains of Imprisonment* (Prospect Heights, Ill.: Waveland Press, 1988), pp. 241–256.

38. Johnson, *Hard Time,* p. 170.

39. U.S. Department of Justice, Bureau of Justice Statistics Special Report, *Prison Rule Violators* (Washington, D.C.: Author, 1989), p. 1.

40. *Ibid.,* p. 2.

41. *Ibid.,* pp. 1–2.

42. Perry Johnson, "The Snitch System: How Informants Affect Prison Security," *Corrections Today* (July 1989): 26, 28, 72.

43. *Ibid.,* p. 28.

44. *Ibid.,* p. 72.

45. *Mendoza v. Miller* (7th Cir. 1985).

46. Van Vandivier, "Do You Want to Know a Secret? Guidelines for Using Confidential Information," *Corrections Today* (July 1989): 30, 32, 73.

47. Bill Sands, *My Shadow Runs Fast* (Englewood Cliffs, N.J.: Prentice Hall, 1964).

48. Mark S. Hamm, "Current Perspectives on the Prisoner Self-Help Movement," *Federal Probation* 52 (June 1988): 49–56.

49. John Irwin, "Adaptation to Being Corrected," in Daniel Glaser (ed.), *Handbook of Criminology* (Chicago: Rand McNally, 1974); Johnson, *Hard Time;* G. G. Kassebaum, D. A. Ward, and D. M. Wilner, *The Effectiveness of a Prison and Parole System* (Indianapolis, Ind.: Bobbs-Merrill, 1971).

50. E. M. Abdul-Mu'Min, "Prisoner Power and Survival," in Robert M. Carter, Leslie T. Wilkins, and Daniel Glaser (eds.), *Correctional Institutions* (New York: Harper & Row, 1985; John Irwin, *Prisons in Turmoil* (Boston: Little, Brown, 1980).

51. *Ibid.*

52. Hamm, "Current Perspectives on the Prisoner Self-Help Movement," p. 50.

53. Milton Burdman, "Ethnic Self-Help Groups in Prison and on Parole," *Crime and Delinquency* (April 1974); Patrick D. McAnany and Edward Tromanhauser, "Organizing the Convict: Self-Help for Prisoners and Ex-Cons," *Crime and Delinquency* (January 1977).

54. Hamm, "Current Perspectives on the Prisoner Self-Help Movement," p. 55.

55. Gordon Hawkins, *The Prison* (Chicago: University of Chicago Press, 1976).

56. Gresham Sykes, "The Defects of Total Power," in John R. Snortum and Ilana Hader (eds.), *Criminal Justice: Allies and Adversaries* (Pacific Palisades, Calif.: Palisades Publishers, 1978), p. 201.

57. *Ibid.*

58. Cited in Eric D. Poole and Robert M. Regoli, "Alienation in Prison: An Examination of the Work Relations of Prison Guards," *Criminology* 19 (1981): 251–270.

59. Hawkins and Alpert, *American Prison Systems: Punishment and Justice,* p. 338.

60. Adapted from Carl Weiss and David James Friar, *Terror in the Prisons* (Indianapolis, Ind.: Bobbs-Merrill, 1974), p. 209.

61. Ben M. Crouch, *The Keepers: Prison Guards and Contemporary Corrections* (Springfield, Ill.: Charles C. Thomas, 1980), p. 73.

62. Hawkins and Alpert, *American Prison Systems,* p. 340.

63. *Ibid.,* p. 345.

64. See Lee H. Bowker, *Prison Victimization* (New York: Elsevier, 1980), chapter 7.

65. United States Department of Labor, *Dictionary of Occupational Titles* (4th ed.) (Washington, D.C.: U.S. Government Printing Office, 1977).

66. Robert Rogers, "The Effects of Educational Level on Correctional Officer Job Satisfaction," *Journal of Criminal Justice* 19 (1991): 123–137.

67. Ivan Berg, *Education and Jobs: The Great Training Robbery* (New York: Praeger, 1970), p. 128.

68. Susan Philliber, "Thy Brother's Keeper: A Review of the Literature on Correctional Officers," *Justice Quarterly* 4 (1987): 9–37.

69. Nancy Jurik and Michael C. Musheno, "The Internal Crisis of Corrections: Professionalization and the Work Environment," *Justice Quarterly* 3 (1986): 457–481.

70. Rogers, "The Effects of Educational Level on Correctional Officer Job Satisfaction," p. 134.

71. Cindy Wahler and Paul Gendreau, "Perceived Characteristics of Effective Correctional Officers by Officers, Supervisors, and Inmates Across Three Different Types of Institutions," *Canadian Journal of Criminology* (April 1990): 265–277.

72. *Ibid.*, pp. 268–269.

73. Johnson, *Hard Time,* p. 138.

74. James B. Jacobs and Lawrence Kraft, "Integrating the Keepers: A Comparison of Black and White Prison Guards," *Social Problems* 25 (1978): 304–318; Ben M. Crouch and Geoffrey P. Alpert, "Sex and Occupational Socialization Among Prison Guards: A Longitudinal Study," *Criminal Justice and Behavior* 9 (June 1982): 159–176.

75. John Klofas, "Discretion Among Correctional Officers: The Influence of Urbanization, Age and Race," *International Journal of Offender Therapy and Comparative Criminology* 30 (1986): 111–124.

76. Nancy C. Jurik, "Individual and Organizational Determinants of Correctional Officer Attitudes Toward Inmates," *Criminology* 23 (August 1985): 523–539.

77. Francis T. Cullen, Faith E. Lutze, Bruce G. Link, and Nancy T. Wolfe, "The Correctional Orientation of Prison Guards: Do Officers Support Rehabilitation?" *Federal Probation* 53 (March 1989): 33–42.

78. Jurik, "Individual and Organizational Determinants of Correctional Officer Attitudes Toward Inmates"; Cullen et al., "The Correctional Orientation of Prison Guards."

79. Eric D. Poole and Robert M. Regoli, "Role Stress, Custody Orientation, and Disciplinary Actions: A Study of Prison Guards," *Criminology* 18 (August 1980): 215–226.

80. Hans Toch and John Klofas, "Alienation and Desire for Job Enrichment Among Correction Officers," *Federal Probation* 46 (1982): 35–44.

81. Jurik, "Individual and Organizational Determinants of Correctional Officer Attitudes Toward Inmates."

82. Cullen et al., "The Correctional Orientation of Prison Guards."

83. John T. Whitehead and Charles A. Lindquist, "Determinants of Correctional Officers' Professional Orientation," *Justice Quarterly* 6 (March 1989): 69–87.

84. Carol F. W. Smith and John R. Hepburn, "Alienation in Prison Organizations," *Criminology* (August 1979): 251–262.

85. Jurik, "Individual and Organizational Determinants of Correctional Officer Attitudes Toward Inmates."

86. *Ibid.*

87. Cullen et al., "The Correctional Orientation of Prison Guards."

88. Jacobs and Kraft, "Integrating the Keepers"; Cullen et al., "The Correctional Orientation of Prison Guards."

89. Boaz Shamir and Amos Drory, "Some Correlates of Prison Guards' Beliefs," *Criminal Justice and Behavior* 8 (June 1981): 233–249.

90. Poole and Regoli, "Role Stress, Custody Orientation, and Disciplinary Actions."

91. Jurik, "Individual and Organizational Determinants of Correctional Officer Attitudes Toward Inmates."

92. Maguire and Pastore, *Sourcebook of Criminal Justice Statistics 1995,* pp. 549–550.

93. John Irwin, *The Jail: Managing the Underclass in American Society* (Berkeley, Calif.: University of California Press, 1985), p. 2.

94. *Ibid.,* p. 8.

95. *Ibid.,* p. 43.

96. Hans Mattick, "The Contemporary Jails of the United States: An Unknown and Neglected Area of Justice," in Daniel Glaser (ed.), *Handbook of Criminology* (Chicago: Rand McNally, 1974).

97. Irwin, *The Jail: Managing the Underclass in American Society,* pp. 45–46.

98. Quoted in Advisory Commission on Intergovernmental Relations, *Jails: Intergovernmental Dimensions of a Local Problem* (Washington, D.C.: Author, 1984), p. 1.

99. U.S. Department of Justice, National Institute of Justice Research in Brief, *Systemwide Strategies to Alleviate Jail Crowding* (Washington, D.C.: Author, 1987), p. 1.

100. *Ibid.,* p. 2.

101. *Ibid.*

102. *Ibid.,* pp. 2–4.

Chapter 12

Community Corrections: Probation and Parole

Even I/Regained my freedom with a sigh.
—Lord Byron

✦ INTRODUCTION

Chapter 3 examined the development of the two primary forms of community corrections, probation and parole. We now view their contemporary role and functions from an administrative viewpoint. Community corrections, it has been stated, is "the last bastion of discretion in the criminal justice system."[1] Only a few decades ago, community-based corrections was enthusiastically viewed as a humane, logical, and effective approach for working with and changing criminal offenders.

The President's Task Force endorsed this approach in 1967, saying that it

includes building or rebuilding solid ties between the offender and the community, obtaining employment and education, securing in the large sense a place for the offender in the routine functioning of society. This requires . . . efforts directed towards changing the individual offender [and] mobilization and change of the community and its institutions.[2]

Changes in national ideological thought and other matters have combined to present difficulties in reaching these lofty ideals. These factors also have compelled us to increasingly use incarceration instead of community-based corrections.

We begin with what is perhaps the core of this chapter: the consideration of tough alternatives to imprisonment. Then we examine the problem of large caseloads. The types of administrative systems and issues that are related to probation administration are considered. Next we analyze the relatively new alternatives to incarceration and conventional probation and parole, known as *intermediate sanctions:* intensive supervision (of probation), electronic monitoring/house arrest, shock incarceration, and boot camp.

✦ ALTERNATIVES TO IMPRISONMENT

Sanctions or mechanisms of social control for enforcing society's standards are most likely to deter if they meet two conditions: injure "the social standing by the punishment," and make "the individual feel a danger of being excluded from the group."[3] The United States bases assumptions about what punishes on the norms and living standards of society at large. This view overlooks several very important facts: first, most serious offenders neither accept nor abide by those norms; and second, as noted previously, most people incarcerated today come from situations in which conditions fall far below the living standards that most Americans would accept.[4] The grim fact and national shame are that for many people who go to prison, the conditions inside are not all that different from, and might even be better than, the conditions outside.

Social isolation is the second presumably punitive aspect of imprisonment. When a person goes to prison, however, he or she seldom feels isolated but is likely to find friends, if not family, already there.[5]

Furthermore, it seems plausible that prison life is not perceived as being as difficult as it once was. Inmates' actions speak loudly in this respect: More than 50 percent of today's inmates have served a prior prison term. Knowing what prison is like, these inmates evidently still believe that the benefits of committing a new crime outweigh the costs of being in prison.[6] We must wonder how punitive the prison experience is for such offenders.

Finally, the stigma of having a prison record is not the same as in the past because many of the offenders' peers and family members also have done time. One survey found that 40 percent of youths in state training schools had parents who had been incarcerated.[7] Imprisonment also confers status in some neighborhoods. Gang members have repeatedly stated that incarceration was not a threat because they knew their sentence would be minimal. To many people, serving a prison term represents a badge of courage. It also is their source of food, clothing, and shelter.[8]

We have thus begun our discussion with these unfortunate statistics concerning the effectiveness of prisons to punish criminal behavior. This fact demands that society determine whether it is time to seriously consider alternatives to incarceration. Probation and parole administrators might question whether conventional probation and parole are effective alternatives to prison sentences in all cases or whether others—such as intensive supervision programs—should be implemented.

✦ THE BURDEN OF LARGE PROBATION AND PAROLE CASELOADS

Obviously, the quality of service that a probation or parole officer can provide to his or her clients is quite likely related to that officer's caseload. *Caseload* refers to the average number of cases supervised in a given period. Each case represents an offender on probation or parole who is supervised by an individual officer. As John Conrad observed,

> There is much that a good probation/parole officer can do for the people on his or her caseload. A parole officer who makes it clear that, "fellow, if you don't watch your step I'm gonna run your ass right back to the joint," is not in a position to be helpful as a counselor or facilitator. With the best intentions, a[n] officer struggling with the standard unwieldy caseload of 100 or more will deal with emergencies only, and sometimes will not be able to do that very well.[9]

Although ideal caseloads for some probation officers range from 25 to 50, many others actually have caseloads of 200 or more. Because the quality of their contact with probationers is affected directly by the officers' ability to have face-to-face contact with them regularly, probation is often judged unfairly as being ineffective as a deterrent to crime. Probation departments are often the last to be given additional funding to create new positions to handle the increasing number of offenders. Few agencies or courts consider the negative implications of giving understaffed and underfunded probation departments increasing numbers of persons to supervise.[10]

Regarding parole caseloads, the American Correctional Association determined that in the late 1980s approximately 11,000 parole officers nationwide supervised about 362,000 parolees.[11] This means that, on average, parole officer caseloads were about 31 offenders per officer. It is well known, however, that in some jurisdictions, the parolee/parole officer ratio is as high as 300 to 1.

Probation and parole administrators can probably do very little about excessively high caseloads. Being at the end of the justice system process, they have little control over the number of people whom police arrest, prosecutors formally charge, juries convict, or judges sentence to prison.

✦ PROBATION SYSTEMS

✧ TYPES OF SYSTEMS

Figure 12.1 depicts an organization structure for a regional probation and parole organization. Probation is the most frequently used sanction of all; it costs offenders their privacy and self-determination and usually includes some element of other punishments: jail time, fines, restitution, or community service.[12] Probation in the United States is administered by more than 2,000 different agencies.

Figure 12.1   Organization structure for a regional adult parole and probation agency.

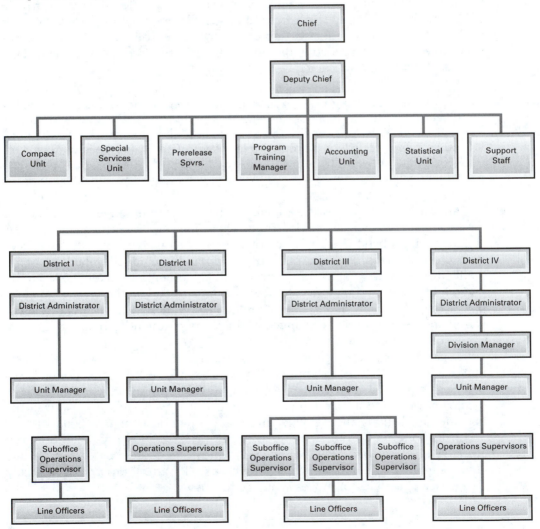

Its organization is a patchwork that defies simple explanation. Texas alone has more than 100 county adult probation departments, but in about three-fourths of the states, adult probation is part of the executive branch of state government. By contrast, more than half of the agencies providing juvenile probation services are administered on the local level.[13]

Furthermore, according to Howard Abadinsky, the administration of probation systems can be separated into six categories, one of which will be employed:

1. *Juvenile.* Separate probation services for juveniles are administered on a county or municipal level or on a statewide basis.
2. *Municipal.* Independent probation units are administered by the lower courts according to state laws and guidelines.
3. *County.* Under state laws and guidelines, a county operates its own probation agency.
4. *State.* One agency administers a central probation system, which provides services throughout the state.
5. *State combined.* Probation and parole services are administered on a statewide basis by one agency.
6. *Federal.* Probation is administered as an arm of federal courts.[14]

Regarding this patchwork nature of probation systems, two central organizational issues have been raised concerning the administration of probation services: Should probation be part of the judicial or the executive branch of government? Does the lack of uniformity in administering probation make justice less equitable statewide?[15] These important and lingering issues as to probation administration and organization have been considered for more than a quarter of a century by the President's Task Force on Corrections.[16]

Abadinsky argued that probation administered by the judiciary on a *county* level promotes *diversity:*

> Innovative programming can be implemented more easily in a county agency since it has a shorter line of bureaucratic control than would a statewide agency. A county agency can more easily adapt to change, and the successful programs of one agency can more easily be adopted by other probation departments . . . and unsuccessful programs avoided. Although the judiciary is nominally responsible for administering probation, the day-to-day operations are in the hands of a professional administrator—the chief probation officer.[17]

One problem with the county-level administration of probation services, however, is the increased dissimilarity in operations. The officer/client ratios may differ in large measure from one county to another, as would probably not be the case if probation were administered by a statewide agency whose personnel can easily be shifted from one county to another. Thus officer caseloads range widely from county to county.

This brings us to the second issue concerning whether this lack of uniformity in providing probation services makes justice less equitable statewide. This issue has led states with county-based probation systems to create statewide bodies for better coordination and uniformity of services.

✦ PROBATION DEPARTMENTS' NEED FOR AN ORGANIZATION PLAN

As early as 1924, a probation executive wrote that "without a consistent, orderly, and practical plan of organization, and without adequate, competent, and sensible methods of supervising the staff, a probation department cannot function properly."[18] Studies discussed later indicate that these are problems for probation departments at the end of the 20th century: "What are my resources? How can I use them to maximize our supervision and services?" These questions constantly challenge probation administrators but are seldom answered directly, according to Patricia L. Hardyman, who recently performed a major study of probation administration. The answers would enable the probation administrator to better control limited resources, select supervision strategies, and pursue attainable outcomes.[19]

Each year millions of dollars are invested in acquiring the capital to build office space for probation departments. This investment does not include the human resources invested by community volunteers and the families of probationers, yet little is known about how these resources are translated into activities or their outcomes and impacts.[20]

✦ SYSTEMS THEORY

As with the administration of a police, court, or prison organization, the probation department administrator's goals may affect the services provided to the probationer, which in turn may have an impact on the client's request for services. This systematic interaction between an organization's resources, structure, and community has been referred to as its *sociotechnical environment,*[21] meaning that the principles of the system are organized to execute the organization's basic outputs. Each probation administrator needs to recognize that the organization is a system of inputs, processes, and outputs. For probation, for example, inputs would be clients coming into the office for counseling and supervision (the processes); outputs would be the probationer's obtaining employment, acquiring a skill, observing a curfew, and so on. This understanding of probation, using systems theory, provides a means to learn how probation departments function and interact with their environment and to examine the resources, activities, and outcomes in a way that will identify the goals, describe the day-to-day activities, and link the department's activities to resources and outcomes.

According to systems theory, probation may be conceptualized as a network of interwoven resources, activities, and outcomes.[22] According to Hardyman, *resources* include the probation department's funding level, goals, policies and procedures, organization structure and caseloads; the probation staff's characteristics; the services available to probationers; and the rates of unemployment, poverty, and crime in the county. *Activities* are supervision techniques, rewards, leadership style, contacts, and direct/indirect services provided by the probation department. *Outcomes* according to systems theory are the number of probationers who were arrested, incarcerated, and/or received a technical violation during the follow-up period as well as the needs of probationers and the community that were considered.[23]

Hardyman's study of probation administrators focused on their management style—the fundamental determinant of the nature of the probation organization—and was instructive in terms of the impact of their style on the department's operation. Few departments, even those with hierarchical organizational structures, had a pure management style; most administrators vacillated among a variety of styles, including laissez-faire, democratic, and authoritarian. The degree to which administrators included the probation officers in the decision-making process and communicated with officers particularly varied. The *authoritarian* administrators created emotional and physical distance between themselves and the officers. Officers in such systems reported feeling that they had little control over their cases and that policies and procedures were developed and enforced by persons who were unconcerned with their plight.[24]

Surprisingly, the most common management style used by probation administrators was *laissez-faire*. Hardyman found that many probation administrators simply did not participate in the day-to-day activities and supervision strategies of the staff. They remained remote but made final decisions on critical policies and procedures.[25]

Hardyman found that few probation administrators across the country operated with the *democratic* style. Those who did, of course, were more likely to listen to the concerns and suggestions of the line supervisors and officers. The administrator still made final decisions, but information was generally sought from the line staff and their opinions were considered. Officers working under this style obviously had a better sense that their opinions mattered and that the administrator valued their input. An additional benefit of the democratic style was that the administrators had power both by virtue of their position and of their charisma, which inspired teamwork and task accomplishment.[26]

Hardyman also found several negative aspects of probation administration. Chaos was extremely high in urban, laissez-faire probation departments. She observed shouting matches between staff members, and officers reported conflicting departmental policies and standards of supervision. She noted a lack of communication between the administrator and the staff and an inability to create and finish projects. Changes were viewed as imposed from higher levels and were therefore resisted; officers were convinced that their administrators would not listen. Even in democratic probation departments with an open and friendly environment, projects to address current crises were abandoned, and line staff and administrators frequently disagreed. None of the probation departments studied was proactive.[27]

✦ PAROLE SYSTEMS

✧ MODELS FOR PROVIDING SERVICES

The administration of parole is much less complex than that of probation; consequently, less information is available concerning its needs, problems, and practices. (It should also be noted that in about 20 states, probation officers also serve as parole officers; thus, much of the information presented in the preceding section applies to parole officers as well.) One agency per state administers the parole function on a statewide basis, although with a slight deviation: in a number of states, persons paroled from a local jail come under the supervision of a *county* probation and parole department.[28]

A parole agency can provide three basic services: parole release, parole supervision, and executive clemency. In a number of states that have abolished parole release (such as California), parole officers continue to supervise offenders released, not by a parole board, but on *good time* (time automatically subtracted from a sentence).

The National Advisory Commission on Criminal Justice Standards and Goals delineated two basic models of parole systems:[29]

1. *The independent model.* A parole board is responsible for making release (parole) determinations as well as supervising persons released on parole (or good time). It is independent of any other state agency and reports directly to the governor.
2. *The consolidated model.* The parole board is a semiautonomous agency within a large department that also administers correctional institutions. Supervision of persons released on parole (or good time) is under the direction of the commissioner of corrections, not the parole board.

Both models sometimes combine probation services with parole services in a single statewide agency.

The President's Task Force on Corrections summarized the advantages of the independent model:[30]

1. The parole board is in the best position to promote the idea of parole and to generate public support for and acceptance of it. Because the board is accountable for parole failures, it should be responsible for supervising parolees.

2. The parole board that is in direct control of administering parole services can evaluate and adjust the system more effectively.

3. Supervision by the parole board and its officers properly divorces parole release and parolees from the correctional institution.

4. An independent parole board in charge of its own services is in the best position to present its own budget request to the legislature.

The advantages of including both parole services and institutions in a consolidated department of corrections were summarized by the Task Force as follows:[31]

1. The correctional process is a continuum; all staff, both institutional and parole, should be under a single administration rather than be divided, which avoids competition for public funds and friction in policies.

2. A consolidated correctional department has consistent administration, including staff selection and supervision.

3. Parole boards are ineffective in performing administrative functions; their major focus should be on case decision, not on day-to-day field operations.

4. Community-based programs that fall between institutions and parole, such as work release, can best be handled by a single centralized administration.

Critics of the independent model contend that it tends to be indifferent or insensitive to institutional programs and that the parole board places undue emphasis on variables outside the institution. Critics of the consolidated model contend that in it the parole board is pressured to emphasize institutional factors in making parole decisions.[32] Clearly, the trend in this country, beginning in the late 1960s, was in the direction of consolidation.

In the past, whether institution staff or independent parole boards should make the parole decision has been controversial. The arguments for staff deciding when to release inmates are based on the following: the staff knows the inmates better, independent agencies and parole boards are too far removed from institutions to know what goes on within them, and giving this responsibility to independent boards downgrades the professional competence of staff and is unnecessarily complicated. These arguments are countered by those contending that independent agencies granting paroles will eliminate irrational decision making by staff, that staff often lengthen stays for the violation of trivial and meaningless rules, and that staff may be secretive about the criteria for release and hold release over the heads of inmates.[33]

✦ THE DEMISE OF FEDERAL PAROLE

The U.S. Sentencing Commission established a new set of federal sentencing guidelines that were instituted on November 1, 1987. The guidelines also abolished parole for federal prisoners. Supervised release from prison was *not* discontinued entirely, however; in effect, something equivalent to parole is still in place, but the sentencing court is now the controlling authority over the inmate rather than a federal parole commission. The court has the authority to enforce penalties on released prisoners if they violate conditions of their release.

It is too soon to determine the impact of the demise of federal parole and the new federal sentencing guidelines. Many, if not most, prisoners sentenced under the new guidelines are still in prison (and have attempted a substantial amount of litigation attacking the new sentencing guidelines, most of which the courts have rejected). Prison superintendents have undoubtedly experienced a higher inmate population that is serving longer terms because of these changes and, as a result, must aggressively seek alternatives to incarceration.

✦ INTERMEDIATE SANCTIONS

As this and preceding chapters indicate, the health of corrections institutions is not good. The criminal justice community, including probation agencies, is said to be involved in guerrilla warfare, meaning that the highest-risk probationers are out of control and generally reside in "out-of-control communities."[34] As one author observed, offenders may be smiling because "revolving door justice" has become an all-too-frequent fact of prison and jail life.[35] Institutional and community systems are being utilized beyond capacity. The United States is not soft on crime, but because prisons are not in a position to effect great change,[36] the search for solutions must involve communities.

The demand for prison space has created a reaction throughout corrections. Many state systems have attempted to solve the problem by building more prisons or expanding existing ones; however, these reactive efforts have resulted in financial, legal, and administrative problems.[37] With the cost of prison construction now going as high as $150,000 per cell in maximum security institutions, cost-saving alternatives are becoming more attractive if not absolutely necessary. Opening the gates of jails and prisons and liberating inmates is, of course, one solution to the overcrowding problem. But it is not a serious alternative. A real alternative to incarceration must have three elements to be effective: it must incapacitate offenders enough so that it is possible to interfere with their lives and activities to make committing a new offense extremely difficult; it must be unpleasant enough to deter offenders from wanting to commit new crimes; and it must provide real and credible protection for the community.[38]

As mentioned in Chapter 10, in addition to overcrowding, two interrelated developments characterize the state of corrections today and reflect major correctional problems: ideological restatement and, as a result, intermediate initiatives. In response to the criticisms and failures of rehabilitative philosophy and policies, the prevailing ideology of incapacitation, punishment, and deterrence has resulted in get-tough sentencing practices that contribute to rising prison populations. This shift from rehabilitating inmates to giving them their just desserts focuses on the fact that offenders make free will decisions to commit crimes and therefore no longer deserve compassion and correction. This ideology has wrought an exclusionary era of repressive social control, which attempts to banish, expel, and stigmatize the criminal deviant.[39] This is a vicious cycle, however; we have seen that these actions do little to deter crime.

✧ ALTERNATIVES TO INCARCERATION

Probation and parole do not operate in a vacuum; their operations are affected in large measure by what occurs in the rest of the justice system and the actions of other justice administrators. As the number of crimes continues to increase, the availability of incarceration facilities decreases. The implication of this problem is not lost on offenders: if they commit more crimes, they cause more overcrowding, spend less time in an institution, and are quickly released to commit a new round of offenses.[40]

Much of the experimentation with community-based alternatives to imprisonment reflects the current crisis in our prisons. The tension between the get-tough philosophy and the realities of prison overcrowding has led to a "search for intermediate punishments . . . [in] an attempt to find mid-range solutions."[41] This in turn has brought about the emergence of a new generation of techniques, making community-based corrections, according to Barry Nidorf, a "strong, full partner in the fight against crime and a leader in confronting the crowding crisis. It is no longer considered a weak stepchild of the justice system."[42] Economic reality dictates that cost-effective measures be developed, and this is motivating the development of intermediate punishment.[43]

The growing interest in these techniques is not based solely on the need to develop less expensive alternatives to prisons, although the economic realities cannot be overlooked.[44] The probation and parole administrators of the late 1990s must have an arsenal of risk-control tools at their disposal. Community corrections agencies are using the following programs:

◊ *Intensive supervision*. This new form of community-based corrections might also be called *intrusive supervision*. It provides nearly constant surveillance of probationers and parolees. Intensive supervision is discussed more fully later.

◊ *Electronic monitoring*. Popularly known as *house arrest*, this is one of the most promising programs for toughening community corrections and, at the same time, relieving institutional crowding. This program is also discussed later in the chapter.

◊ *Probation/police cooperative action*. In this program, probation officers work closely with local police to share information about probationers being supervised in the community. This program may initially add to jail populations because those who violate their probation are rapidly returned to custody.

◊ *Probation/prosecution cooperative action*. Probation departments and local prosecutors work closely to remove dangerous repeat felons from the community and send them back to prison immediately if they recidivate. This eliminates long court hearings and trials.

◊ *Narcotics and drug deterrence programs.* Community-based corrections agencies have developed drug testing programs to detect and deter drug use among probationers and parolees, making it possible to effectively supervise thousands of drug-abusing offenders in the community instead of keeping them in prison or jail.[45]

Intensive Supervision. In the compelling and sobering article "When Probation Becomes More Dreaded Than Prison," Joan Petersilia, then director of the criminal justice program for the RAND Corporation, questioned whether community-based sanctions are punitive enough to convince the public that the punishment fits the crime. Petersilia considered that intensive supervision probation/parole programs (ISPs) offer some hope to relieve prison overcrowding without draining the public purse.[46]

Petersilia acknowledged that intensive supervision programs are still on trial. In several states, however, *given the option of serving prison terms or participating in ISPs, many offenders have chosen prison.*[47] Many offenders may prefer to serve a short prison term rather than spending five times as long in an ISP.

Consider the alternatives now facing offenders in one western state:

ISP. The offender serves two years under this alternative. During that time, a probation officer visits him or her two or three times per week and phones on the other days. The offender is subject to unannounced searches of his or her home for drugs and has his or her urine tested regularly for alcohol and drugs. The offender must strictly abide by other conditions the court sets—not carrying a weapon, not socializing with certain persons—and must perform community service and be employed or participate in a training or education program. In addition, the offender is strongly encouraged to obtain counseling and/or other treatment, particularly if he or she is a drug offender.

or

PRISON. The alternative is a sentence of two to four years of which the offender will actually serve only about three to six months. During this term, the offender is not required to work or to participate in any training or treatment but may do so voluntarily. Once released, the offender is placed on a two-year routine parole supervision and must visit his or her parole officer about once a month.[48]

Note that the ISP does not represent freedom. In fact, it may isolate repeat offenders more than imprisonment does.

When choosing punishment of offenders, policymakers must consider the attitudes of this country's serious offenders. Obviously, imprisonment no longer represents a horrible punishment and therefore has lost much of its deterrent power. If fear of prison does not prevent criminal behavior, other methods should be tried. This country must get over its preoccupation with imprisonment as the only suitable punishment for serious offenses.[49]

No common standard exists for deciding how many contacts with probationers are necessary in an intensive supervision. A review of ISP programs in 37 states identified a wide range from two contacts per month by probation officers with probationers in Texas to as many as 32 contacts per month in Idaho.[50] To clarify, ISP has the following characteristics:

◊ Small client-officer caseloads, no more than a 10-to-1 ratio.

◊ A weekly face-to-face contact between officer and clients.

◊ Regular field visits at a probationer's workplace, perhaps monthly or bi-monthly.

◊ The inclusion of preventive conditions such as regular drug and alcohol testing.

◊ Swift and certain administrative review and revocation procedures for violating one or more probation conditions.[51]

The effects of ISP have been the subject of a great deal of interest and research.[52] Its value in reducing recidivism has been questioned since the late 1980s.[53]

An evaluation of ISPs in the mid-1990s by Joan Petersilia and Susan Turner[54] expressed similar misgivings. Petersilia and Turner noted that a growing number of jurisdictions had come to believe that the use of ISPs with serious offenders within the community could both relieve prison overcrowding and lessen the risks to public safety that such offenders pose—and all at a cost savings. Some of this enthusiasm was generated by early reports from programs such as that of the Georgia Department of Corrections, which seemed to indicate a number of benefits of the program.

(*Note:* Georgia's program is what many believe to be a model ISP. Georgia, known by some as the chain gang capital of the world, has historically had one of the highest imprisonment rates in the country. It launched an ISP program in the mid-1980s. The program could accommodate about 1,400 offenders annually; its cost, with 33 trained two-person surveillance teams, was about one-fifth as much as caring for and feeding a prisoner and was paid entirely by the state's probationers. The state cited a 78 percent success rate.[55])

The RAND study noted the claim by many ISPs to have saved at least $10,000 each year for each offender who otherwise would have been sentenced to prison.[56] In many places where ISPs were adopted, however, the results were mixed. Some states (such as Illinois and New Jersey) reported cost savings, but others (Massachusetts and Wisconsin) did not. Some (such as Iowa) reported reducing recidivism; others (Ohio and Wisconsin) did not. The ambiguous results of these programs indicate that assumptions about the ability of ISPs to relieve prison overcrowding, lower costs, and control crime may not have been well founded. Petersilia and Turner stated that "It appears not that the ISPs themselves have failed, but that the objectives set for them may have been overly ambitious, raising expectations they have been unable to meet."[57]

✦ ELECTRONIC MONITORING/HOUSE ARREST

Like ISP, the use of electronic monitoring began in the mid-1980s. In the early 1980s, Jack Love, a judge in New Mexico, saw a Spiderman comic in which evil-doers placed an electronic monitor on Spiderman to track his whereabouts. Love persuaded a friend to develop the idea and the technology; the rest is history.[58] Electronic monitoring has become another form of intermediate punishment; it is applied to offenders whose crimes are less serious than those whose offenses require long-term incarceration but are more serious than those committed by persons serving standard probation. At the beginning of 1990, nearly 7,000 pro-bationers were under electronic monitoring, about 13 percent of all those under intensive supervision. Furthermore, of the parolees who were under intensive supervision, about 1,300 were under electronic monitoring.[59]

Two basic types of electronic monitoring devices are available. Continuously signaling devices attached to the offender constantly monitor his or her presence at a particular location. A receiver-dialer apparatus is attached to the offender's telephone and detects signals from the transmitter. A central computer accepts reports from the receiver-dialer over telephone lines, compares them with the offender's curfew schedule, and alerts corrections officials to unauthorized absences.[60]

The second type involves the use of programmed contact devices that contact the offender periodically to verify his or her presence. Various manufacturing companies use a different method to ensure that the offender is the person responding to the call and is in fact at the monitored location as required. One system uses voice verification technology. Another requires a wristlet, a black plastic module strapped to the offender's arm. When the computer calls, the wrist-let is inserted into a verifier box connected to the telephone to verify that the monitored offender answers the telephone. Use of the telephone requires corrections officials to verify that certain technologies are not in use on the offender's telephone. For example, call forwarding and a portable telephone would make it easy for the offender to respond to calls while away from home, but call waiting might interfere with the equipment's efforts to call the central computer.[61]

As with ISP, the use of electronic monitoring has generated controversy. Some believe that monitoring is improper. Its use has led to some debate concerning the purpose of correctional supervision in the community. Indeed, a conference of the American Probation and Parole Association stated the conflict in its title, "Supervision in the 1990s: Surveillance vs. Treatment."[62] The American Civil Liberties Union (ACLU) agrees with probation administrators that the system is an effective, inexpensive method to supervise probationers but is concerned that the state can use these devices to monitor its citizens in the last bastion of privacy, the home. Unlike old-fashioned probation, electronic monitoring empowers the government to control a population with more oversight and authority, which is an increase in police power. The ACLU argues that the prospects for deeper incursions into privacy are ominous. For example, videocameras have already been used to monitor drunk drivers in Maryland; cameras are installed in offenders' homes, and a jailer calls the offender once or twice a day and asks him or her to step in front of the camera, take a self-administered breath alcohol test, and to display the results in front of the camera.[63]

The ACLU also believes that the devices that turn homes into jails are not the answer to prison overcrowding because the nation's penal institutions are overcrowded by the thousands, not by the hundreds. The ACLU concurs with federal judge Henry Bramwell, who wrote in the *Howard Law Journal* that

> the poor and the minority defendant is usually one who has committed a violent crime, is without means, and has little or no recognition in his community. As a result, the middle-class defendant gets alternative sentencing or part-time imprisonment, usually without incarceration, and the poor and minority defendant gets a heavy jail term. This certainly is not justice. Alternative sentencing and part-time imprisonment have strong class overtones.[64]

In contrast, Rolando Del Carmen maintains that electronic monitoring provides a more structured environment and better supervision and accomplishes a curfew situation for the probationer. He contended that judges can be prevented from "widening the net," a term for punishing (in this case, putting someone on electronic monitoring) people who would normally not have been punished (or, in this situation, would have been placed on regular probation): "You identify certain offenses where defendants are currently sent to jail, such as burglary, or where the penal code provides mandatorily that the defendant would have gone to prison. You want to hit that middle cohort instead of dipping down."[65]

✦ SHOCK INCARCERATION

Originally adopted in 1964, shock incarceration (or shock probation) grants the sentencing judge the discretionary authority to release an offender from prison early and then place that offender on probation.[66] It uniquely combines the elements of probation and parole while attempting to impress offenders with the reality of prison life, provide protection to society, and make offenders appreciate the seriousness of their crimes without employing a long and possibly debilitating prison experience.[67] Shock incarceration is now used in 35 states (the earliest being initiated in Idaho in 1975) and by the Federal Bureau of Prisons, with a total of about 9,100 inmates participating. Several other states have authorized programs that have not been funded or are reviewing them. The average sentence is 3 to 10 months, with most (14) states having programs of about 3 months' duration.[68]

Shock incarceration also encompasses the basic theories of deterrence and reintegration. The judge, using a presentence investigation, has a number of options available. The offender can be placed on probation, sentenced to a stay in a community-based correctional facility, or sentenced to jail or prison. When the offender is sentenced to prison, a motion for release on shock incarceration may be initiated by the offender or the trial lawyer or by the court's unilateral action. The decision to grant shock incarceration lies with the judge; state and local probation departments cannot release offenders on shock incarceration through their own initiative.[69]

Several studies of shock incarceration have attempted to compare its effectiveness with regular probation. One study in Ohio[70] discovered that regular probation resulted in a 42 percent lower probability of reincarceration than did shock incarceration. Another study reported that those serving shock incarceration had a higher rearrest rate than did those on regular probation.[71] Still another study examined the effects of using intensive supervision on shock probationers; no significantly lower recidivism rates were found.[72]

On the basis of such studies, it has been concluded that (1) shock probationers generally have a higher recidivism rate than regular probationers, (2) no evidence of a deterrent effect for shock probation has been documented, and (3) given the financial and human costs associated with incarceration, the diversionary aspects of keeping offenders out of institutions should be emphasized in the future.[73] Put simply, shock probation should not be used with offenders who could be considered as candidates for regular probation.

✦ BOOT CAMPS

The use of boot camp programs, a variation on shock incarceration, has also become popular. These programs place offenders in a quasi-military program similar to a basic training program to instill discipline, routine, and unquestioning obedience to orders. Offenders serve a short institutional sentence and then are put through a rigorous regimen of drills, strenuous workouts, marching, and hard physical labor.

Proponents of the boot camp concept argue that many young offenders become involved in crime because they lack self-respect and are unable to structure their lives; consequently, the boot camp model targets young first offenders who seem to be embarking on a path to continued criminality.[74] Proponents also maintain that these youths can benefit from this militarylike atmosphere as well as exposure to relevant educational opportunities, vocational training, drug treatment, and general counseling.

These offenders may experience improvements in self-esteem, educational achievement, and physical fitness. Research to date has found, however, that this regimen and its harsh atmosphere do little to overcome the problems that cause inner-city youths to get in trouble with the law in the first place. In fact, follow-up of boot camp graduates show that they do no better after release from the program than other offenders without this experience.[75] Only boot camps that are carefully designed, target the right offenders, and provide them rehabilitative services and aftercare are likely to save the state money and reduce recidivism.[76]

Too many boot camps overemphasize the value of discipline; in fact, in one California county, a special parole caseload had to be established for boot camp graduates because their failure rates were so high after leaving the program.

Summary

This chapter has focused on probation and parole. It is clear that probation and parole agencies continue to bear the brunt of the combined effects of increased crime, tough mandatory sentencing laws leading to increased incarceration of offenders, a get-tough public and justice system attitude toward crime that permeates the country, and tremendously overcrowded prisons. Given this situation, it is probably a credit to probation and parole administrators that they have managed to cope under such circumstances and have even implemented several alternative methods, known as *intermediate sanctions,* to address these problems.

Questions for Review

1. What are the various types of probation systems being used in the United States? Describe each.
2. Should probation services be placed within the judicial or executive branch of government? Defend your answer.
3. What are some of the major needs, problems, and concerns of probation administrators?
4. What are the two basic models of parole administration?
5. Why are intermediate sanctions being used so widely in probation and parole?
6. What do *intensive supervision* and *electronic monitoring/house arrest* mean?
7. How can shock incarceration further the goals of corrections? Boot camps? What successes and problems have been found with these practices?

Notes

1. Todd R. Clear, "Punishment and Control in Community Supervision," in Clayton A. Hartjen and Edward E. Rhine (eds.), *Correctional Theory and Practice* (Chicago: Nelson-Hall, 1992), pp. 31–42.
2. See the President's Commission on Law Enforcement and Administration of Justice, *Task Force Report: Corrections* (Washington, D.C.: U.S. Government Printing Office, 1967), p. 7.

3. Franklin E. Zimring and Gordon J. Hawkins, *Deterrence: The Legal Threat in Crime Control* (Chicago: University of Chicago Press, 1973).

4. Joan Petersilia, "When Probation Becomes More Dreaded Than Prison," *Federal Probation* 54 (March 1990): 23.

5. *Ibid.*

6. *Ibid.,* p. 25.

7. Allen Beck, Susan Kline, and Lawrence Greenfield, *Survey of Youth in Custody: 1987* (Washington, D.C.: U.S. Department of Justice, Bureau of Justice Statistics, 1988).

8. Petersilia, "When Probation Becomes More Dreaded Than Prison," p. 24.

9. John Conrad, "The Pessimistic Reflections of a Chronic Optimist," *Federal Probation* 55 (June 1991): 4–9.

10. Dean J. Champion, *Corrections in the United States: A Contemporary Perspective* (Englewood Cliffs, N.J.: Prentice Hall, 1990), p. 37.

11. American Correctional Association, *Directory* (College Park, Md.: Author, 1988).

12. Barry J. Nidorf, "Community Corrections: Turning the Crowding Crisis into Opportunities," *Corrections Today* (October 1989): 82–88.

13. Howard Abadinsky, *Probation and Parole: Theory and Practice* (5th ed.) (Englewood Cliffs, N.J.: Prentice Hall, 1994), p. 32.

14. *Ibid.*

15. *Ibid.,* pp. 32–36.

16. See the *Task Force Report: Corrections,* pp. 35–37.

17. Abadinsky, *Probation and Parole,* p. 35.

18. E. P. Volz, "Staff Supervision and Organization," in *Proceedings of the National Probation Association—1924* (New York: National Probation Association, 1924), pp. 103–105.

19. Patricia L. Hardyman, "Management Styles in Probation: Policy Implications Derived from Systems Theory," in Hartjen and Rhine (eds.), *Correctional Theory and Practice,* pp. 61–81.

20. David Duffee, "The Community Context of Probation," in Patrick McAnany, Doug Thompson, and David Fogel (eds.), *Probation and Justice: Reconsideration of Mission* (Cambridge, Mass.: Oelgeschlager, Gunn, and Hain, 1984).

21. Eric Trist, "On Socio-Technical Systems," in Kenneth Benne and Robert Chin (eds.), *The Planning of Change* (2d ed.) (New York: Holt, Rinehart and Winston, 1969), pp. 269–281.

22. Daniel Katz and Robert I. Kahn, *The Social Psychology of Organizations* (New York: John Wiley, 1966).

23. Hardyman, "Management Styles in Probation," p. 68.

24. *Ibid.,* p. 70.

25. *Ibid.*

26. *Ibid.,* p. 71.

27. *Ibid.,* pp. 74–75.

28. Abadinsky, *Probation and Parole,* p. 32.

29. National Advisory Commission on Criminal Justice Standards and Goals, *Corrections* (Washington, D.C.: U.S. Government Printing Office, 1973), pp. 396–397.

30. *Task Force Report: Corrections,* p. 71.

31. *Ibid.*

32. National Advisory Commission, *Corrections,* pp. 396–397.

33. *Task Force Report: Corrections,* p. 65.

34. Donald Cochran, "Corrections' Catch 22," *Corrections Today* (October 1989): 16–18.

35. Nidorf, "Community Corrections," p. 82.

36. John P. Conrad, "The Redefinition of Probation: Drastic Proposals to Solve an Urgent Problem," in McAnany et al., *Probation and Justice,* p. 258.

37. Peter J. Benekos, "Beyond Reintegration: Community Corrections in a Retributive Era," *Federal Probation* 54 (March 1990): 53.

38. *Ibid.*

39. *Ibid.,* p. 53.

40. Nidorf, "Community Corrections," p. 84.

41. Belinda R. McCarthy, *Intermediate Punishments: Intensive Supervision, Home Confinement, and Electronic Surveillance* (Monsey, N.J.: Criminal Justice Press, 1987), p. 3.

42. Nidorf, "Community Corrections," p. 85.

43. Benekos, "Beyond Reintegration," p. 54.

44. McCarthy, *Intermediate Punishments,* p. 3.

45. *Ibid.,* pp. 85–86.

46. Petersilia, "When Probation Becomes More Dreaded Than Prison," pp. 23–27.

47. *Ibid.,* p. 23.

48. This information was compiled from ISP brochures and information from the Oregon Department of Correction by Joan Petersilia.

49. Petersilia, "When Probation Becomes More Dreaded Than Prison," p. 27.

50. James M. Byrne, "The Control Controversy: A Preliminary Examination of Intensive Probation Supervision Programs in the United States," *Federal Probation* 50 (1986): 4–16.

51. Adapted from Vincent O'Leary and Todd R. Clear, *Directions for Community Corrections in the 1990s* (Washington, D.C.: National Institute of Corrections, 1984).

52. See, for example, Don Gottfredson and Marc Neithercutt, *Caseload Size Variation and Difference in Probation/Parole Performance* (Pittsburgh, Pa.: National Center for Juvenile Justice, 1974); J. Banks, A. L. Porter, R. L. Rardin, T. R. Silen, and V. E. Unger, *Issue Paper: Phase I Evaluation of Intensive Special Probation Project* (Atlanta, Ga.: School of Industrial and System Engineering, Georgia Institute of Technology, 1976); and D. Fallen, C. Apperson, J. Holt-Milligan, and J. Roe, *Intensive Parole Supervision* (Olympia, Wash.: Dept. of Social and Health Services, Analysis and Information Service Division, Office of Research, 1981).

53. R. Adams and H. J. Vetter, "Effectiveness of Probation Caseload Sizes: A Review of the Empirical Literature," *Criminology* 9 (1971): 333–343; Edward Latessa and Gennaro F. Vito, "The Effects of Intensive Supervision on Shock Probationers," *Journal of Criminal Justice* 16 (1988): 319–330.

54. U.S. Department of Justice, National Institute of Justice Research in Brief, "Evaluating Intensive Supervision Probation/Parole: Results of a Nationwide Experiment," May 1993.

55. Kathy Sawyer, "The Alternative to Prison," *The Washington Post National Weekly Edition* (September 2, 1985): 6–7.

56. James Byrne, Arthur J. Lurigio, and Christopher Baird, "The Effectiveness of the New Intensive Supervision Programs," *Research in Corrections* 2 (1989).

57. U.S. Department of Justice, National Institute of Justice Research in Brief, "Evaluating Intensive Supervision Probation/Parole: Results of a Nationwide Experiment," May 1993, p. 2.

58. Keenen Peck, "High-Tech House Arrest," *The Progressive* (July 1988): 26–28.

59. U.S. Department of Justice, Bureau of Justice Statistics Bulletin, *Probation and Parole: 1990,* p. 4.

60. Annesley K. Schmidt, "Electronic Monitors: Realistically, What Can Be Expected?" *Federal Probation* 59 (June 1991): 47–53.

61. *Ibid.,* p. 47.

62. *Ibid.,* p. 48.

63. Peck, "High-Tech House Arrest," p. 27.

64. Quoted in *ibid.*

65. *Ibid.*

66. Latessa and Vito, "The Effects of Intensive Supervision on Shock Probationers," p. 320.

67. Gennaro F. Vito, "Developments in Shock Probation: A Review of Research Findings and Policy Implications," *Federal Probation* 48 (June 1984): 22–27.

68. Kathleen Maguire and Ann L. Pastore (eds.), *Sourcebook of Criminal Justice Statistics— 1995* (Washington, D.C.: U.S. Department of Justice, Bureau of Justice Statistics, 1996), p. 95.

69. Timothy Flanagan and Kathleen Maguire (eds.), *Sourcebook of Criminal Justice Statistics— 1991* (Washington, D.C.: U.S. Department of Justice, Bureau of Justice Statistics, 1992), pp. 22–23.

70. Gennaro F. Vito and Harry E. Allen, "Shock Probation in Ohio: A Comparison of Outcomes," *International Journal of Offender Therapy* 25 (1981): 70–76.

71. Gennaro F. Vito, Ronald M. Holmes, and Deborah G. Wilson, "The Effect of Shock and Regular Probation Upon Recidivism: A Comparative Analysis," *American Journal of Criminal Justice* 9 (1984): 152–162.

72. Latessa and Vito, "The Effects of Intensive Supervision on Shock Probationers," p. 327.

73. Vito, "Developments in Shock Probation," p. 27.

74. Todd R. Clear and George F. Cole, *American Corrections* (4th ed.) (Belmont, Calif.: Wadsworth, 1997).

75. Doris L. MacKenzie, "Boot Camp Prisons and Recidivism in Eight States," *Criminology* 33(3) (1995): 327–358.

76. Doris Layton MacKenzie and Alex Piquero, "The Impact of Shock Incarceration Programs on Prison Crowding," *Crime and Delinquency* 40(2) (1994): 222–249.

Chapter 13

Corrections Issues and Practices

I never saw a man who looked/With such a wistful eye/
Upon that little tent of blue/Which prisoners call the sky.

—Oscar Wilde

✦ INTRODUCTION

In the preceding two chapters we addressed several issues related to prisons, jails, and probation/parole agencies. In this chapter we discuss additional challenges for contemporary correctional administrators. We briefly focus on coed prisons and smoke-free facilities. Next we examine several of the pressing issues concerning sex offenses, violence (both by and on staff and inmates), and drug use, interdiction, and treatment. Next we discuss inmate gangs, and then we examine prison riots and inmate classification. We then consider how the costs of corrections can be hidden or completely ignored. The chapter concludes with an overview of two relatively new correctional issues: the privatization and accreditation of prisons.

Case studies concerning problems of corrections administration are provided at the end of the chapter.

✦ RECENT INNOVATIONS IN CORRECTIONAL FACILITIES

✧ COED PRISONS

Segregation of prisoners according to their gender dates back several centuries to the Walnut Street Jail in Pennsylvania and the Auburn Penitentiary in New York. Reasons for this policy included the improvement of inmate morality, the reduction in inmate promiscuity, and the increased privacy for inmates of both sexes. In recent years, however, prisoners of both sexes have expressed interest in co-correctional, or coed, prisons.[1] In some of these institutions, men and women prisoners are housed in the same prison supervised by male and female staff and can participate in all activities together. Unlike the practice in Denmark and other countries, U.S. prisons do not allow inmates in coed prisons to share the same quarters or have sexual encounters.

The ratio of male to female inmates is recommended to be 50-50.[2] When women are in the minority, they feel conspicuous and tend to be treated as a minority group by their male counterparts.[3] Jealousies among the dominant sex may arise because of increased competition for social encounters and more intimate relationships with the opposite sex.

A major public misconception about co-correctional prisons is that they allow unchecked promiscuity and male and female inmates to share quarters, resulting in numerous illegitimate births.[4]

Coed prisons have experienced several positive results. Staff enthusiasm has increased, and their parolees have found employment more easily. One institution realized a 40 percent reduction in the number of violent discipline charges, a 73 percent reduction in the number of general discipline charges, and a 42 percent reduction in the number of grievances filed by inmates.[5]

These institutions also experience negative outcomes. A superintendent of a women's prison in a western state offered several caveats to co-correctional institutions. The look-but-don't-touch policy of these institutions can aggravate sexual frustrations of both sexes and may actually encourage homosexual relationships. Husbands and wives of the residents of a co-correctional institution may become jealous. Finally, the stresses and strains caused by sexual frustrations may well be detrimental to the programmatic planning designed for a given inmate. If an inmate is strongly attracted to a member of the opposite sex but can make no advances, treatment may be more difficult.[6]

✧ SMOKE-FREE CORRECTIONAL FACILITIES

Cigarette smoking has been recognized at the end of the 20th century as the single most preventable cause of death in our society; the American Cancer

Society estimates that more than 419,000 Americans die each year as a result of cigarette smoking and that 3,000 others die from secondhand smoke.[7] The Surgeon General has suggested that the simple separation of smokers and non-smokers within the same airspace may significantly reduce this latter statistic.[8]

Largely as a result of these findings, smoking is becoming less socially acceptable, and Americans are fighting over where, when, and whether a person may smoke. This is an issue for correctional institutions as well. The American Correctional Association conducted a survey in 1987 on implementing smoking restrictions in correctional institutions. The survey results indicated that most correctional institution administrators had very serious reservations about the effect of such policies; most believed that it would make their jobs more difficult and worsen the overall environment of their facilities.[9]

This issue has resulted in a number of lawsuits. Hearing of studies concerning secondhand smoke, inmates have not been reluctant to file lawsuits over their right to a smoke-free environment. Furthermore, a number of court decisions in the past few years have held that inmates have no constitutional right to smoke while incarcerated. Once a few facilities made the decision to become smoke free, others have followed.

Thus, an increasing number of correctional administrators have outlawed smoking in their facilities. When the decision is first announced, there is normally an outcry from all sectors about worker and prisoner rights and threats of rebellion. Administrators have had to hold their ground and refuse to capitulate on any point or relinquish any small area of their facilities for smokers. They have typically followed a certain protocol in implementing the plan: (1) requesting a legal opinion from the appropriate counsel's office concerning the constitutionality of the proposal and its chance for prevailing in the face of inmate challenges (it is more likely that a nonsmoking inmate's suit would prevail on the grounds that he or she is forced to share a cell with a smoking companion); (2) discussing the plan openly with employees to assuage their concerns and explain, among other things, that institutions that have initiated smoke-free programs have experienced no extraordinary inmate behavior; (3) announcing the decision well in advance of its implementation to allow time for people to adjust to the idea, smoke their cigarettes, and, perhaps most important, attend counseling and smoking cessation programs provided by the county health department.[10]

It has been found that following a few months of minor irritation and complaints, the policy has met with little resistance. Inmates eventually appreciate the benefits of the policy: improvement in their breathing and general health, cleaner walls and ceilings, and an overall healthier environment. The administration spends less on repainting walls and replacing cigarette-burned carpets and air filters.[11] Perhaps the greatest advantage of all is the elimination of a potential fire hazard.

✦ SEX AND VIOLENCE
IN CORRECTIONAL INSTITUTIONS

✧ SEXUAL VICTIMIZATION

People serving terms in correctional institutions do not leave their sexuality at the front gate. Paul Tappan maintained that homosexuality is a universal concomitant of sex-segregated living, a perennial problem in camps, boarding schools, one-sex colleges, training schools, and, of course, correctional facilities. From a biological point of view, he argued, homosexuality is normal behavior in the latter institutions.[12]

Persons entering prisons and jails express their sexuality in many forms, some of which are innocuous and others very violent. If placed on a continuum, solitary or mutual masturbation or the use of a sexual object (rolled-up magazines, towels, and so on, sometimes referred to in prison jargon as a *Fifi bag*) would be at one end, consensual homosexual behavior in the middle, and gang rapes at the other end. The most frequent form of sexual release is solitary masturbation: "Nobody—inmate, staff, or visitor—is in a prison very long before seeing an inmate masturbating in a toilet, shower, or cell."[13] Estimates are that between 30 percent and 45 percent of inmates have experienced homosexual behavior, depending upon the degree of custodial surveillance, the nature of the inmate population, and the average length of confinement in a given prison.[14]

As in the outside world, people in prison are often extremely dominant or submissive, and the latter can easily be exploited. As in the outside world, heterosexual rape does not result from sexual *need* but from hate and a desire to dominate, control, and conquer. This problem exists in women's institutions as well as in those for men. Women rarely sexually assault other women prisoners; however, when such attacks do occur, they can be quite brutal and involve the use of such objects as broom handles.[15]

Violent sexual incidents among male inmates fall into two categories. In the first, the aggressor violently coerces his target; the type of force is decided upon in advance. The primary cause of this violence is the need to uphold men's "rights" to use force to gain sexual access. The second category of incidents involves targets who react violently to propositions they perceive as threatening. This act often resembles victim-precipitated homicide in the outside world because words or gestures perceived as offensive provoke retaliatory insults, threats, or violence.[16]

The actual extent of sexual aggression in prisons is difficult to assess. A few authors have contended that homosexual rape is *the* major problem inside correctional institutions; others (including many administrators) maintain that sexual violence is practically no problem at all. Indeed, although early studies of prisons[17] suggested a high rate of homosexual rapes, later studies[18] suggested that the actual incidence of homosexual rape is far lower. The latter researchers, however, do report widespread fear of sexual victimization among inmates. Norman Smith and Mary Ellen Batiuk argued that because the social setting of prisons is hostile, the fear of being sexually victimized permeates every social act (e.g., inmates are extremely conscious of the need to act macho, hide their emotions, and be careful of what they wear; they try to do nothing that can be interpreted as a weakness or "signal" of homosexual propensities).[19]

It is clear that today's violent gang- and clique-dominated prison society fosters increased fears of rape and other unwanted sexual activity. The fear is greatest—and most justified—among young white prisoners, 83 percent of whom are targets of rape and other aggressive sex, in contrast to about 15 percent of blacks and 2 percent of Hispanics. Most aggressors are black (80 percent), some are Hispanic (14 percent), but only a few are white (6 percent).[20]

> Rape is a way for the black man to get back at the white man. It's one way he can assert his manhood. Anything white, even a defenseless punk, is part of what the black man hates. It's part of what he's had to fight all his life just to survive, just to have a hole to sleep in and some garbage to eat. . . . It's a new ego thing. He can show he's a man by making a white guy into a girl.[21]

In his study of prison victimization Lee Bowker commented that "like heterosexual rape on the streets, prison homosexual rape has effects that go beyond the immediate victims. Homosexual rape impacts all prisoners and fundamentally alters the social climate of correctional institutions."[22]

Inmate fear of sexual victimization is justified. In fact, many believe that homosexual attacks are quite common, even reaching epidemic proportions in some institutions:

> Sexual assaults are epidemic in some prison systems. Virtually every slightly built young man committed by the courts is sexually approached within a day or two after his admission to prison. Many of these young men are overwhelmed and repeatedly "raped" by gangs of inmate aggressors.[23]

It is probably surprising that sexual aggression in correctional institutions is not more widespread. Even in men's prisons, estimates of the incidence of sexual assault among the general population run as low as 1 percent.[24] Still, it remains a serious problem for the weak and unprotected.

Is there anything correctional administrators can do to reduce or eliminate the problem of homosexual rapes, given the violent tendencies of many inmates? Programs that may reduce prison sexual violence are aimed at targets as well as aggressors. Such a program faces difficulties, however. Aggressors with histories of violence ruthlessly exploit others, and targets often use force to protect themselves and to promote masculine images. Furthermore, threatened men are often reluctant to report such problems to the staff because existing official remedies can cause more problems than they solve.

Daniel Lockwood suggested that administrators consider offering human relations training, with the goals of increasing interpersonal skills, relieving interpersonal or intergroup tension, and developing individual and group problem-solving skills to address the problem of homosexual rape.[25]

✦ INSTITUTIONAL VIOLENCE

Violence by Inmates. Personal safety for prisoners and staff members is at best uncertain; some risk of injury or material loss at the hands of aggressive or unbalanced fellow prisoners and prison gangs always exists.[26] Violent actions by inmates include homicides and very serious assaults inflicted with a variety of ingeniously homemade weapons.

As with incidents of homosexual rape, the extent of violence by inmates against other inmates in prisons is not known precisely nor do we know whether institutional assaults occur with more or less frequency than they do in the community at large.[27] Prisons are unquestionably violent settings, however, particularly those penal institutions that house large proportions of young inmates, who account disproportionately for disruptive behavior.[28] The probabilities that violence will occur increase when large numbers of "state-raised" youths, prisoners who have extensive experience in juvenile institutions, are housed in an institution.[29] In addition to inmate age, the amount of violence in an institution is normally influenced by its population density and factors tied to prisonization, such as deprivation and continuation of violent, aggressive, and unacceptable *previous* behavior patterns in the institutional setting.

Conventional prison violence is confined almost exclusively to male prisons, although violence (often angry outbursts in reaction to stressful situations) does occur in women's institutions. Former inmates have noted that although men may engage in fights to prove their manhood and achieve a reputation but cause little permanent harm to victims, women inmates' fights often leave permanent scars from earrings torn from pierced ears or facial scratches from fingernails.[30]

Prisoner violence frequently follows court efforts to improve prison conditions; this reaction has been referred to as the *paradox of reform*. Studies show that prisoners are often safer *before* reforms and that high rates of violence and fear become a normal element of postreform prison life.[31]

Inmates assault correctional officers with some frequency. Examining assaults against correctional officers, Peter Kratcoski determined that four factors were significantly related to these assaults: location (more than 70 percent of the assaults occurred in detention/high-security areas; shift (the majority of all such assaults occurred during the day); work experience (inexperienced trainees received a disproportionate number of assaults); and age of the assaultant (most assaults against staff members were committed by inmates age 25 and younger). He also examined the type of situation. Only 3 percent of federal correctional officers were assaulted while attempting to break up inmate fights, but 32 percent of state correctional officers were assaulted during such situations. Policy dictates that an officer who is required to break up a fight request backup assistance. An inexperienced officer may try to handle such a situation alone and be assaulted. The sex of correctional officers was not found to have a relationship to assaults.[32]

Violence Against Inmates. When they perceive a loss of control over prisoners, guards sometimes employ violent tactics.[33] In these situations, guards become more custodial and punitive toward prisoners; in addition to using more insults and obscenities, they may perform violent actions. Guards' attempts to maintain control may create relatively unstable conditions and may even produce rebellious prisoners and an unsafe working environment for themselves.[34]

✧ ADMINISTRATIVE APPROACHES TO VIOLENCE

Each of the four groups who are part of the prison community has a reason to prevent violence. (1) The administration wants to prevent violence; (2) inmates want to live without fear; (3) the correctional officers desire a safe work environment and control over inmates; and (4) noncustodial staff want information about and the ability to control inmates. Indeed, two major administrative problems that can occur within an institution are (1) a lack of control over staff and inmates, and (2) polarization between custodial and noncustodial staff.[35]

One approach used to curb violence is the unit management concept, which has been described as one of a number of small, self-contained "institutions" operating in semiautonomous fashion within the confines of a large facility.[36] This approach involves housing 50 to 100 inmates together in one physical area and keeping them together for as long as possible. These inmate groups (units) are supervised by a multidisciplinary management team normally composed of at least a unit manager, a caseworker, a secretary, a correctional counselor, a correctional officer, an educator, and a psychologist or other mental health worker. These teams have disciplinary authority and are guided by a set of specific policies and procedures.[37]

✦ DRUG INTERDICTION AND TREATMENT IN PRISONS

As discussed previously, a major problem in prisons is drug abuse, which was a major problem for many inmates prior to their incarceration. Thirty-five percent of all male inmates were under the influence of drugs at the time of their current offense.

A related problem for correctional administrators is the availability of illegal drugs in prison and their use by inmates *after* incarceration. This is not an insignificant matter, according to a study of 957 state confinement facilities for adults. About seven of every eight U.S. prisons performed drug tests for one or more illegal drugs on about 565,500 inmates. Of those tests, 1.4 percent were positive for cocaine, 1 percent for heroin, 2.3 percent for methamphetamines, and 5.8 percent for marijuana.[38]

Drug interdiction methods include making physical checks, questioning inmates, having inmates exchange clothing, searching body cavities, and using patdowns. All persons entering prisons, random groups, and those suspected of carrying drugs were checked in these ways. About three-fourths (76 percent) of all federal and state confinement institutions tested inmates for drugs when use was suspected. The most intrusive technique was body cavity searches; facilities testing with body cavity search showed lower rates of drug use among inmates than did facilities using other methods.

Questioning visitors to both state and federal facilities and searching their belongings were also widely used. More than 80 percent of federal facilities patted down all inmates and required them to exchange clothing. Almost 78 percent of state confinement facilities frisked all inmates, and 57 percent substituted prison clothes.[39]

Inmates may acquire illegal drugs from visitors and staff members. Because of this potential security breach, about half of all state confinement administrators had policies to question or pat down staff when they report to work. About one-fourth of state facilities randomly frisked staff members. Most interdiction activities involving staff were conducted when someone was suspected of smuggling drugs.[40]

Correctional administrators have responded to the growing number of drug-involved offenders by increasing the number of available prison programs. Still, the number of drug-using inmates far exceeds the number enrolled in such programs. In addition to providing treatment benefits, these programs help provide good security, improve working conditions for staff, reduce staff conflict, and provide a resource for conflict resolution and the potential for positive publicity.[41]

✦ PRISON GANGS

It has been argued that because of the weakened authority of correctional administration over inmates as a result of court decisions that recognize prisoners' rights and redress of remedies, inmate gangs have formed to share and eventually dominate, through violent means, the power base once occupied by the "keepers."[42] For whatever reason, it is clear that gangs have gained a substantial foothold in the day-to-day activities and operation of prisons and even jails.

The formation of prison gangs began in 1950, at Washington Penitentiary in Walla Walla, when a group of prisoners organized themselves and became known as the *Gypsy Jokers*.[43] Then, in 1967, a tightly knit Chicano clique of youths from Los Angeles and a number of prisons began to take over San Quentin. Known as the *Mexican Mafia*, they quickly gained a reputation for toughness, which was enhanced by the rumor that to become a member, one had to kill another prisoner.[44] Soon a rival Chicano group, La Nuestra Familia, formed; the rivalry between these two gangs became so deadly that the state segregated them; the Mexican Mafia went to San Quentin, and La Nuestra Familia went to Soledad.[45]

To protect themselves from violent crimes committed by these two groups, black and white inmates began to form gangs. Whites formed the Aryan Brotherhood, and blacks organized the Black Guerilla Family. Amid escalating racial tension, the Aryan Brotherhood formed an alliance with the Mexican Mafia, and the Black Guerillas allied with La Nuestra Familia.[46]

Statistics show that prison gangs exist in the federal prison system as well as in 32 state prisons. In 29 of those 32 prisons, administrators have identified 114 gangs by name; they have an estimated membership of about 12,600 inmates. Overall, gang members comprise about 3 percent of the total federal and state prison populations.[47]

With the emergence of prison gangs, two serious problems have developed: the increased difficulty prison officials have in maintaining order and discipline[48] and the rapid increase in inmate violence, often related to increases in drug trafficking, extortion, prostitution, protection, gambling, and contract inmate murders.[49] One study of prison gangs reported that they account for half or more of all prison problems.[50]

Gang members have a belligerent attitude toward all institutions and authority when they enter prison; members are preoccupied with status and gang rivalry. They plan boycotts, strikes, and even riots. Despite administrative attempts to accommodate gangs in some prisons, they continue to seek to obtain "loot, sex, respect, revenge, [and] will attack any outsider."[51] The close confinement and limited space in prisons make ignoring gang threats impossible. Prisoners who want to circulate beyond their own cells often must join a clique or gang for protection.

Superintendents and wardens have been brought into gang-ridden prison systems specifically to do something about the gang problem; by transferring gang leaders and using other methods to segregate and isolate members, some have managed to greatly diminish gangs' power. The crowding problem; the court decisions, court orders, and consent decrees; and other contemporary administrative limitations, however, have curtailed the power of correctional administrators to use such tactics.

✦ PRISON RIOTS

Prison riots have occurred throughout history; they can be expected to continue in the future and to pose serious challenges to corrections administrators. In an effort to provide guidance to these administrators prior to, during, and after such incidents, a recent in-depth study sponsored by the National Institute of Justice and the Federal Bureau of Prisons examined eight disturbances across the country. The following is an overview of the major findings gleaned from that study.[52]

✦ Before the Riot

Planning is an important aspect of riot preparation. A riot plan to describe the special responsibilities to be met, the resources to be used, and the contribution of each individual or group involved should be developed.

Who should take command during the incident must be decided according to factors such as knowledge of the facility, effects of the assignment on the chain of command, and breadth of experience and communication. The administrative framework is also a consideration. Some of these factors favor assigning command to the superintendent, who is likely to have greater knowledge of the facility; this would maintain the chain of command. If the superintendent is new or inexperienced, however, someone else, such as a state department of corrections administrator or the commissioner of corrections, may assume command instead. Another factor to be considered is who knows how to use resolution strategies, understands existing policies, and is familiar with agencies outside the prisons (such as those providing medical care, added security, investigation, and so on).

A critical element of such planning is the development of a use-of-force policy. Which staff members will be authorized to order the use of force? What responses are appropriate in various situations? What weapons and less-than-lethal munitions (such as tear gas) are appropriate?

Training is also very important because readiness can best be achieved through field practice and instruction. Demanding, unannounced onsite riot exercises are also beneficial; they integrate the activities of command, hostage negotiation teams, and tactical teams. A small group of administrators should receive extensive training in hostage negotiations and problem solving; they should be chosen on the basis of intelligence, levelheadedness, verbal skills, and the ability to think quickly.

Planning cannot prevent all prison riots, but it can help administrators to avoid some disturbances, take action to prevent the small-scale disturbance from expanding, and terminate a riot should one occur in the least costly way.

✦ During the Riot

During the riot, prison administrators have three main options to attempt to bring about resolution: forcibly retake the prison, negotiate an end, or wait and let the riot die of its own accord. Many times, however, the boundaries between these strategies are indistinguishable. For example, negotiations can be used to collect information for a tactical assault or to tire and demoralize the inmates; a waiting policy can be used to strengthen the administration's tactical capabilities or to force inmates to bargain seriously.

In general, a riot can be terminated at any time by using overwhelming force. Nevertheless, such a deployment of force can be costly (a lesson learned from the 1971 riot in the Attica, New York, prison in which 39 people died). Therefore, commanders must develop strategies to minimize the risks to hostages, assault forces, and inmates. Force may be used, however, as a first response to a disturbance. Armed personnel may rush in to prevent inmates from becoming organized, fashioning weapons, fortifying positions, and recruiting additional participants. The greatest challenge in the early use of force is assembling the necessary personnel and equipment with sufficient speed; a riot control squad that is deployed too quickly runs the risk of being unsuccessful and even taken hostage.

A planned tactical strike maximizes the element of surprise in order to rescue hostages or retake the facility before inmates can react. Key elements in a tactical strike are intelligence information (concerning riot leadership, location of hostages, and so on), drills and rehearsals (simulating the planned mission), timing (determining a maximum opportunity for success), weaponry (including stun grenades), speed, and surprise. The disadvantages of using a tactical strike are they may be unnecessary because negotiations may resolve the incident and they may be too risky.

Negotiations involve a dialogue between inmates and authorities, with inmates hoping to use any hostages as bargaining chips with the negotiators to obtain publicity, amnesty, improved conditions, or other benefits. Administrators may be pitted against a single, unified group of inmates or individual inmates with no organization whatsoever. For negotiations to progress, an inmate or group of inmates with whom officials can talk with a measure of continuity must be identified. Those persons with command authority should refrain from talking directly with inmates. In some instances, bringing in an outside person (such as a popular inmate, legislator, lawyer, reporter) may prove useful in negotiations.

✦ AFTER THE RIOT

A riot's aftermath consists of short-term, medium-term, and long-term problems. Short-term problems include securing the prison (including searching for contraband and moving inmates to secure units), assessing damage, providing necessary medical care, and collecting evidence for prosecutions. Medium-term problems relate to providing continued support to employees in coping with their experience, repairing damage to the facility, normalizing institutional operations, and undertaking the administrative follow-up associated with a disturbance. Long-term problems are solved by assessing what caused the riot and developing new policy reflecting that assessment. The unique characteristics of each institution, its administration, its staff, and its inmate population as well as other variables will shape the aftermath of a riot.

✦ INMATE CLASSIFICATION

One of the most important and potentially far-reaching responsibilities for today's correctional administrators is inmate classification.

Relating human and environmental variables can improve prisoner adjustment and prison management.[53] As rehabilitation fell into disfavor and prison populations began to rise, traditional diagnostic classification techniques were no longer appropriate or practical, and a shift in the function and structure of classification occurred.

Classification systems are intended to help administrators manage the prison population, treat inmates, and understand and predict their behavior.[54] More broadly, these four primary functions of classification are used to assign each inmate to the appropriate security level, to place him or her in specific living quarters, to designate the required custody level for each, and to select appropriate program activities for each. Classification forms the basis for assigning inmates to settings to minimize problems cost-effectively and to make policy decisions regarding their proper care and supervision.[55]

The search for accurate and precise classification models has become a legal issue for correctional administrators. Courts have repeatedly found that traditional classification procedures and criteria were based on unsupported assumptions regarding inmate behavior and that criteria were not applied uniformly to all inmates.[56] In several cases,[57] courts have also held that classification methods cannot be "capricious, irrational, or discriminatory." For a classification model to be "coherent" and thus judicially acceptable, "placement and assignment must be clearly understandable, consistently applied and conceptually complete."[58]

The search for classification systems that meet these criteria has gone in several directions. Three of the most commonly used systems today are *Megargee's MMPI typology,* which uses a psychological inventory to classify inmates into groups with particular characteristics related to their criminality and projected behavior in and adjustment to prison; *Toch's Prison Preference Inventory,* which measures inmates' concerns about eight environmental attributes to determine individual needs; and *risk assessment,* currently the most common form of classification, which uses demographic, criminal, and behavioral characteristics to distinguish inmates according to the likelihood that they will be involved in institutional misconduct.[59]

These three systems serve different purposes, use different variables to classify inmates into groups, and are operationalized in quite different ways. Each predicts some adjustment outcomes but not others. According to an analysis of the three methods by Kevin Wright, no system emerges as clearly superior. Risk assessment appears to predict aggressive behavior, whereas neither of the other two was useful in this regard. Risk assessment did not predict the probabilities of self-reported internal and physical problems, but the other two systems did. All three successfully predicted self-reports of external problems. Of the three, Toch's system predicted outcomes least successfully.[60]

✧ IMPLICATIONS FOR INSTITUTIONAL MANAGEMENT

If for no other reason, classification is justified on the grounds that it provides a security strategy. With offenders receiving longer prison sentences than ever before and a national recidivism rate of more than 30 percent, the task of protecting the public must involve more than architectural design. Indeed, with the enactment of the 1987 federal sentencing guidelines and life-without-parole statutes in many states, classification of inmates has in effect become a continuous, lifelong process. Institutional administrators must realize that the classification of offenders for security purposes is essential to the operation of an orderly and safe prison.

Classification eases the burden of a major consent decree regarding crowding and conditions of confinement; provides consistency and equity in placing and treating inmates; and allows funds and human resources to be planned and managed in a cost-efficient manner. Classification processes can prevent escapes and reduce the need for protective custody; furthermore, they can limit violent incidents to certain units of the institution.[61]

✦ CALCULATING CORRECTIONAL COSTS

Correctional administrators and several organizations, including the U.S. Census Bureau and the American Correctional Association, report annual costs associated with housing prison inmates. At the end of the 1980s, the cost to house an inmate in prison for a year was estimated to be in the $16,000 to $20,000 range; however, the actual cost was probably much higher. For jails, estimated costs appear not to be reliable.[62]

The problem is that expenditures that should be counted as costs of providing a particular service to a correctional institution are overlooked. The total cost of a particular correctional service should include both *direct* costs, that is, expenditures made by a government agency to provide the service in question, and *indirect* costs, which are those borne by government or nongovernmental parties to support a particular correctional activity. Although the latter costs are real, their calculation is often difficult, speculative, and controversial.[63] Figure 13.1 shows the general kinds of costs that are associated with corrections.

The direct costs that other agencies incur in serving a correctional agency's mission must also be counted as direct correctional costs. For example, teachers in prisons and jails are sometimes paid by a school district, not by the correctional agency; the same holds true for doctors and other medical workers paid by local or state departments. In-hospital care is often charged to a public hospital, utility bills in correctional facilities are sometimes paid by departments of public works, and departments of transportation often provide vehicles to move prisoners. The failure to count these and other services provided by outside agencies and levels of government result in significantly underestimating the total direct cost of a correctional service.[64]

How much higher are the real costs of corrections likely to be? Studies indicate that the actual cost of operating public correctional programs is about 33 percent to 66 percent higher than is usually reported.[65]

Obviously, correctional administrators need good data and cost figures for planning and projecting, and account to the general public. To the extent possible, the shortcomings in determining the total direct cost of a correctional service noted must be addressed.

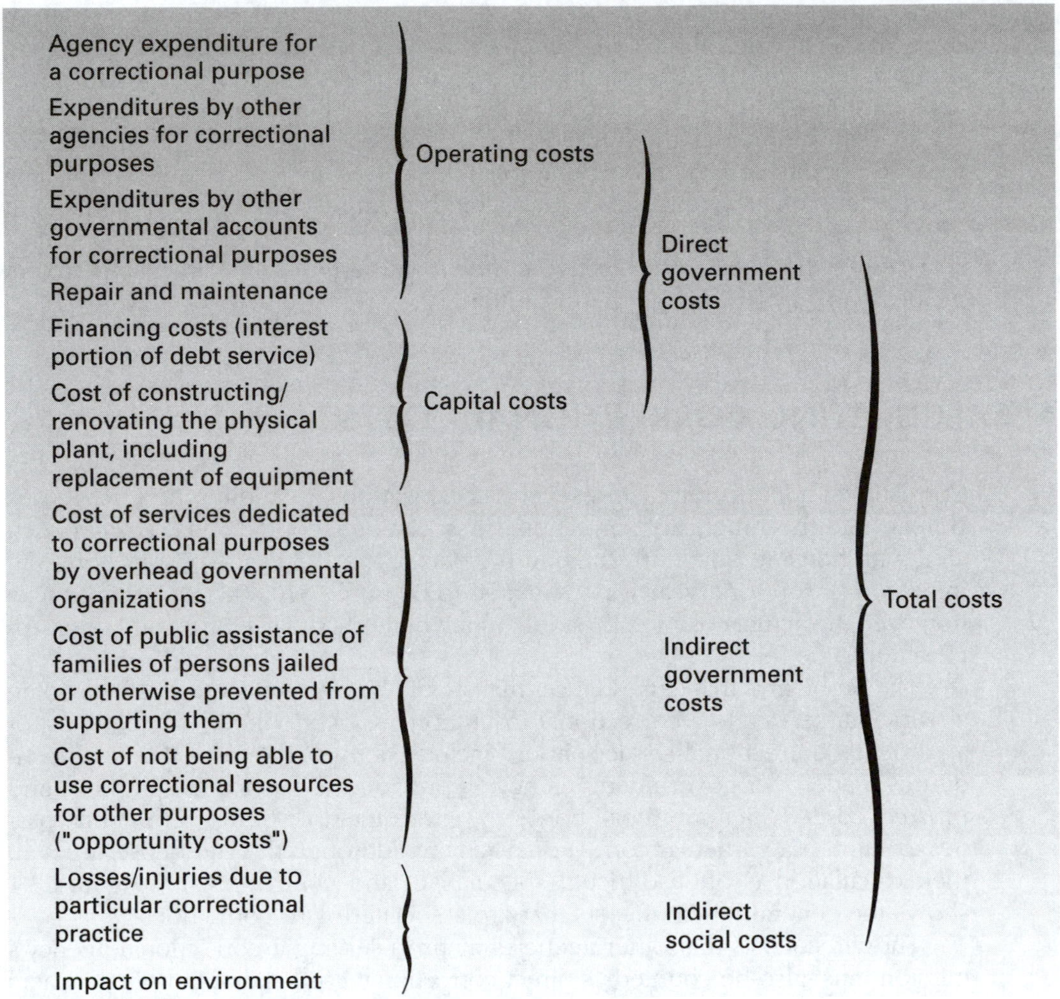

Figure 13.1 Components of corrections costs. (*Source:* Douglas C. McDonald, "The Cost of Corrections: In Search of the Bottom Line," in *Research in Corrections,* U.S. Department of Corrections, National Institute of Corrections, February 1989, p. 7.)

✦ THE MOVE TOWARD PRIVATIZATION

✧ EMERGENCE OF THE CONCEPT

"Punishment for Profit," "The Corporate Warden," and "Incarceration Unlimited"— these headlines in business journals have proclaimed a new opportunity for venture capital: criminal punishment.[66] Attracted by the huge sums of money devoted each year to holding adult criminals behind bars, entrepreneurs have been trying to turn prisons into profit-making corporations. One commentator remarked, "There's a whole new industry developing, from the likely meeting of pinstripes and prison stripes."[67] These entrepreneurs are often cheered on by prison administrators, who believe that the government can stand the competition.[68]

Private vendors already supply health care services, educational and vocational training, and an array of other services to public institutions.[69] The largest and most prominent of the corporations attempting to operate correctional institutions privately is Corrections Corporation of America (CCA), formed in 1983.[70]

Corporations pursue contracts to construct and/or manage prisons and detention facilities. Most of the private contracts awarded since 1984 have been for small, low-security facilities for the Immigration and Naturalization Service, the Federal Bureau of Prisons, or county jails.[71] "The private jail market is ripe," says one source, "and it's the brokers, architects, builders and banks—not the taxpayers—who will make out like bandits."[72]

✦ ADVANTAGES AND DISADVANTAGES

Proponents for privatization of prisons and jails believe that it will be able to offer a greater diversity of programs and facilities and increase the ability to handle special inmate populations or offer special rehabilitative or training programs.[73] The strongest argument, however, is the belief that private industry can respond more quickly than government bureaucracies and in a cost-effective manner to the current pressure for more prison space because they are not bound by state civil service rules or by employee unions. Proponents maintain that a private prison will charge the state less per day to hold each inmate than the publicly operated facility will by reducing building and labor costs and using economies of scale. They also argue that the profit motive creates an inherent efficiency.[74]

Critics of the privatization of prisons suggest that the profit motive may restrict or eliminate services to underprivileged groups or those with special needs.[75] They are also concerned that reduced costs will come at the expense of reduced salaries and training for staff members. Indeed, one contracted site provided its staff less than 50 hours of training, compared to the 320-hour program mandated for public employees.[76] Critics also question the hidden costs of privately operated prisons, such as the administration of contracts. They argue that the largest hidden cost would involve the necessary creation of a regulatory bureaucracy to oversee the private corporation's operations.[77]

Alexis Durham suggests that adequate effort has not been committed to evaluating these private corporations:

Only through exacting monitoring and evaluation can a reasoned assessment of achievements of privatization be made. Furthermore, only with the information produced by such evaluations can sensible correctional policy be developed. Thus it is crucial that adequate effort be committed to evaluating the initiatives of the private sector.[78]

Finally, opponents believe that for the state to abdicate its power of punishment to the lowest bidder will seal off prisons more completely from constitutional and societal controls.[79]

✦ CORRECTIONS ACCREDITATION

The effort to accredit correctional facilities became more organized and effective as a result of the efforts by the U.N. Commission on the Prevention of Crime and the Treatment of Offenders.[80] The commission formulated an agreed upon set of standards and by the spring of 1980 had accredited 47 different correctional facilities or agencies in the United States and Canada, and nearly 400 more were in various stages of the process of qualifying.[81]

The development of corrections standards and the accreditation process in the United States began in 1974, when the Law Enforcement Assistance Administration (LEAA) funded a new organization, the Commission on Accreditation for Corrections (CAC). The CAC was directed by a board of 19 persons from various aspects of the field. The American Correctional Association (ACA) was chosen to be the sponsor of the new commission.[82]

Although the commission exists today, the ACA has assumed the responsibility for day-to-day accreditation operations through its Division of Standards and Accreditation. The ACA does not actually grant accreditation, however; that function is still performed by the CAC.

Any agency wishing to be accredited applies to the CAC and pays a fee for the services involved in the process. The agency then conducts a self-evaluation. For those items not in compliance, the commission reviews the self-evaluation reports and audits the agency's evaluation through on-site visits by staff and a visiting committee of consultants. The agency must submit a plan for correcting any deficiency identified during these visits or by the self-evaluation. The process is rigorous.

This system of voluntary accreditation is believed to possess several benefits; in short, it provides the best means to ensure quality correctional services, to mobilize and capitalize professional talent, and to infuse research findings into correctional practices. It also provides support for elected and appointed state and federal officials committed to improving corrections, correctional administrators with a sound rationale when appropriations for correctional services are requested, interested citizens with factual measurements of the correctional services in their communities or states, and overall professionalization of correctional services.[83]

Summary

This chapter has examined the major issues confronting today's corrections administrators: sexual violence, drug interdiction and treatment, gangs, riots, inmate classification, and calculating and containing corrections costs. These issues do not lend themselves to our society's frequent demand for a "quick fix" and will continue to challenge these administrators for many years to come.

Questions for Review

1. What new and successful programs are offered in correctional institutions?
2. What can be done to reduce sexual victimization and violence in correctional facilities?
3. To what extent is drug abuse a problem in correctional institutions? How may administrators interdict and treat this problem?
4. What can correctional administrators do to control gangs in prisons?
5. Why is inmate classification an important responsibility for correctional administrators?
6. What are some advantages and disadvantages of privatization?
7. What are some problems inherent in calculating the cost of correctional services? What actual costs tend to be ignored or undercounted? How might this problem be rectified?

Notes

1. Clarice Feinman, *Women in the Criminal Justice System* (2d ed.) (New York: Praeger, 1986), pp. 64–65.
2. Sue Mahan, "Co-corrections: Doing Time Together," *Corrections Today* 48 (1986): 134–165.
3. *Ibid.,* p. 134.
4. Sally Chandler Halford, "Kansas Co-Correctional Concept," *Corrections Today* 46 (1984): 44–54.
5. *Ibid.,* p. 54.
6. Jacqueline K. Crawford, "Two Losers Don't Make a Winner: The Case Against the Co-Correctional Institution," in John Ortiz Smykla (ed.), *Coed Prison* (New York: Human Sciences Press, 1980), pp. 262–268.
7. *U.S. News and World Report,* "Database" (November 12, 1996): 24.
8. U.S. Department of Health and Human Services, *The Health Consequences of Involuntary Smoking: A Report of the Surgeon General* (Rockville, Md.: Author, 1986).
9. American Correctional Association, *Corrections Today* 49 (August 1987): 14.

10. Brad L. Neiger, "Development of a Smoke-Free Jail Policy: A Case Study in Davis County, Utah," *American Jails* (Summer 1988): 23.

11. *Ibid.*

12. Paul W. Tappan, *Crime, Justice, and Correction* (New York: McGraw-Hill, 1960), pp. 678–679.

13. Gene Kassebaum, "Sex in Prison," *Psychology Today* (January 1972): 39.

14. Joseph Fishman, *Sex in Prison* (New York: National Library Press, 1934); Donald Clemmer, *The Prison Community* (New York: Rinehart, 1958), pp. 249–273; Gresham Sykes, *The Society of Captives: A Study of a Maximum Security Prison* (Princeton, N.J.: Princeton University Press, 1958); Peter C. Buffum, *Homosexuality in Prisons* (Washington, D.C.: U.S. Government Printing Office, 1972).

15. See Rose Giallombardo, *Society of Women: A Study of a Women's Prison* (New York: Wiley, 1966); David Ward and Gene Kassebaum, *Women's Prisons* (Chicago: Aldine, 1965), pp. 80–101; John H. Gagnon and William Simon, "The Social Meaning of Prison Homosexuality," *Federal Probation* 32 (March 1968): 23–29.

16. Daniel Lockwood, "Reducing Prison Sexual Violence," in Robert Johnson and Hans Toch (eds.), *The Pains of Imprisonment* (Prospect Heights, Ill.: Waveland Press, Inc., 1982), pp. 257–265.

17. Clemmer, *The Prison Community;* Sykes, *The Society of Captives;* Alan J. Davis, "Sexual Assaults in the Philadelphia Prison System and Sheriff's Vans," *Trans-Action* 6 (1968): 8–16.

18. Clemens Bartollas, Stuart J. Miller, and Simon Dimitz, *Juvenile Victimization: The Institutional Paradox* (New York: Halsted, 1976); Lee Bowker, *Prison Victimization* (New York: Elsevier, 1980); Daniel Lockwood, *Prison Sexual Violence* (New York: Elsevier, 1980); Ulla Bondeson, *Prisoners in Prison Societies* (New Brunswick, N.J.: Transaction Publishers, 1989).

19. Norman E. Smith and Mary Ellen Batiuk, "Sexual Victimization and Inmate Social Interaction," *The Prison Journal* 69 (Fall/Winter 1989): 29–38.

20. "Sexual Assaults in Prison," from *Report on Sexual Assaults in a Prison System and Sheriff's Vans* (1968), cited in Leon Radzinowicz and Marvin E. Wolfgang (eds.), *Crime and Justice: The Criminal under Restraint* (New York: Basic Books, 1977).

21. Leo Carroll, "Humanitarian Reform and Biracial Sexual Assault in a Maximum Security Prison," *Urban Life* 5 (January 1977): 422.

22. Bowker, *Prison Victimization,* p. 1.

23. Lockwood, *Prison Sexual Violence,* p. 29.

24. *Ibid.,* p. 30.

25. Lockwood, "Reducing Prison Sexual Violence," pp. 261–262.

26. Lee H. Bowker, "Victimizers and Victims in American Correctional Institutions," in Robert Johnson and Hans Toch (eds.), *The Pains of Imprisonment,* pp. 63–76.

27. D. Jones, *The Health Risks of Imprisonment* (Lexington, Mass.: D. C. Heath, 1976); Sawyer F. Sylvester, John H. Reed, and David O. Nelson, *Prison Homicide* (New York: Spectrum, 1977); and Bowker, *Prison Victimization.*

28. Timothy J. Flanagan, "Correlates of Institutional Misconduct Among State Prisoners," *Criminology* 21 (1983): 29–39.

29. John Irwin, *The Felon* (Englewood Cliffs, N.J.: Prentice Hall, 1970); Bartollas et al., *Juvenile Victimization.*

30. Tom Howard, personal communication.

31. Ben M. Crouch and James W. Marquart, "Resolving the Paradox of Reform: Litigation, Prisoner Violence, and Perceptions of Risk," *Justice Quarterly* 7 (March 1990): 103–123.

32. Peter C. Kratcoski, "The Implications of Research Explaining Prison Violence and Disruption," *Federal Probation* 52 (March 1988): 27–32.

33. Lucien X. Lombardo, "Stress, Change and Collective Violence in Prison," in Johnson and Toch (eds.), *The Pains of Imprisonment,* pp. 77–93.

34. John R. Hepburn, "Prison Guards as Agents of Social Control," in Lynne Goodstein and Doris Layton MacKenzie (eds.), *The American Prison: Issues in Research and Policy* (New York: Plenum Press, 1989), pp. 191–206.

35. J. Forbes Farmer, "A Case Study in Regaining Control of a Violent State Prison," *Federal Probation* 52 (March 1988): 41–47.

36. Robert B. Levinson and Roy E. Gerard, "Functional Units: A Different Correctional Approach," *Federal Probation* 37 (December 1973): 8–16.

37. Farmer, "A Case Study in Regaining Control of a Violent State Prison," p. 46.

38. U.S. Department of Justice, Bureau of Justice Statistics Special Report, *Drug Enforcement and Treatment in Prison: 1990* (Washington, D.C.: Author, 1992), p. 1.

39. *Ibid.,* pp. 1–2.

40. *Ibid.,* p. 2.

41. U.S. Department of Justice, Office of Justice Programs, National Institute of Justice, *Prison Programs for Drug-Involved Offenders* (Washington, D.C.: Author, 1989), pp. 1, 4.

42. Jacobs, *Stateville: The Penitentiary in Mass Society.*

43. George M. Camp and Camille G. Camp, *Prison Gangs: Their Extent, Nature, and Impact on Prisons,* Grant 84-NI-AX-0001, U.S. Department of Justice, Office of Legal Policy (Washington, D.C.: U.S. Government Printing Office, 1985).

44. John Irwin, *Prisons in Turmoil* (Boston: Little, Brown, 1980), pp. 189–190.

45. *Ibid.,* p. 190.

46. Joel Samaha, *Criminal Justice* (St. Paul, Minn.: West, 1988), p. 558.

47. *Ibid.*

48. Jacobs, *Stateville: The Penitentiary in Mass Society.*

49. Irwin, *Prisons in Turmoil.*

50. George M. Camp and Camille G. Camp, *The Correctional Year Book* (South Salem, N.Y.: Criminal Justice Institute, 1987).

51. Irwin, *Prisons in Turmoil,* p. 192.

52. U.S. Department of Justice, National Institute of Justice, Research in Brief "Resolution of Prison Riots," October 1995.

53. K. N. Wright, J. M. Harris, and Nancy Woika, *Improving Correctional Classification through a Study of the Placement of Inmates in Environmental Settings,* Final Report, NIJ Grant 83-IJ-CX-0011 (Washington, D.C.: U.S. Government Printing Office, 1985).

54. Doris Layton MacKenzie, C. Dale Posey, and Karen R. Rapaport, "A Theoretical Revolution in Corrections: Varied Purposes for Classification," *Criminal Justice and Behavior* 15 (March 1988): 125–136.

55. Kevin N. Wright, "The Relationship of Risk, Needs, and Personality Classification Systems and Prison Adjustment," *Criminal Justice and Behavior* 15 (December 1988): 454–471.

56. James Austin, "Assessing the New Generation of Prison Classification Models," *Crime and Delinquency* 29 (1983): 561–576.

57. See *Holt v. Sarver,* 1971; *Morris v. Travisono,* 1970; *Pugh v. Locke,* 1976; *Laman v. Helgemoe,* 1977; *Palmigiano v. Garrahy,* 1977; *Ramos v. Lamm,* 1979.

58. Austin, "Assessing the New Generation of Prison Classification Models," pp. 562–563.

59. *Ibid.,* p. 455.

60. Wright, "The Relationship of Risk, Needs, and Personality Classification Systems and Prison Adjustment," p. 468.

61. Parker Evatt, Sammie Brown, and Lorraine T. Fowler, "Offender Classification: Don't Overlook This Important Security Strategy," *Corrections Today* (July 1989): 34–37.

62. National Institute of Corrections, *Research in Corrections* 2 (February 1989): 4.

63. Douglas C. McDonald, "The Cost of Corrections: In Search of the Bottom Line," in National Institute of Corrections, *Research in Corrections* 2 (February 1989): 6.

64. *Ibid.,* p. 8.

65. *Ibid.,* p. 11.

66. Craig Becker and Mary Dru Stanley, "The Downside of Private Prisons," *The Nation* (June 15, 1985): 728–730.

67. Quoted in Becker and Stanley, "The Downside of Private Prisons," p. 728.

68. Kerry Elizabeth Knobelsdorff, "The Move to Hand Prisons Over to Private Businesses Draws Flak," *The Christian Science Monitor* (July 27, 1987): 17–18.

69. Camille Camp and George Camp, "Correctional Privatization in Perspective," *The Prison Journal* 65 (1985): 14–31.

70. Becker and Stanley, "The Downside of Private Prisons," p. 729.

71. Charles W. Thomas and Suzanna L. Foard, *Private Correctional Facilities Census* (Gainesville, Fla.: University of Florida, Center for Studies in Criminology and Law, 1991).

72. Quoted in Becker and Stanley, "The Downside of Private Prisons," p. 728.

73. Robert B. Levinson, "Okeechobee: An Evaluation of Privatization in Corrections," *The Prison Journal* 65 (1985): 75–94; J. Mullen, "Corrections and the Private Sector," *The Prison Journal* 65 (1985): 1–13.

74. Ted Gest, "Prisons for Profit: A Growing Business," *U.S. News and World Report* (July 2, 1984): 45–46.

75. Christine Bowditch and Ronald S. Everett, "Private Prisons: Problems Within the Solution," *Justice Quarterly* 4 (September 1987): 441–453.

76. *Ibid.,* p. 447.

77. *Ibid.,* p. 448.

78. Alexis M. Durham III, "Evaluating Privatized Correctional Institutions: Obstacles to Effective Assessment," *Federal Probation* 52 (June 1988): 65–71.

79. Becker and Stanley, "The Downside of Private Prisons," p. 730.

80. Paul Keve, *Corrections* (New York: Wiley, 1981), p. 478.

81. *Ibid.,* p. 480.

82. *Ibid.,* p. 481.

83. Adapted from E. Preston Sharp, "Why Accreditation?" *Proceedings of the 104th Annual Congress of Correction, Houston, Texas, August 18–22, 1974* (College Park, Md.: American Correctional Association, 1975), pp. 31–32.

CASE STUDIES

Prisons, Politics, Poverty, and the Rebellious Rurals*

It is time to prepare the annual budget for the Department of Prisons for the legislature. The entire country is suffering a recession, and your state is no different. Tax revenues are down. All state agencies, including the Department of Corrections, suffered a blanket 10 percent budget cut during the current fiscal year. For the prison system, this meant closing a prison and firing more than 100 staff members. Your state is overwhelmingly urban in distribution of population and political power.

The director of the prison system has just returned from the governor's cabinet meeting, where he has been told that the governor will recommend to the legislature an even lower budget amount for prisons next year. This is very troubling, given that the legislature will be considering a budget that will not even begin for another 18 months and that the inmate population is sure to grow during that time.

Meetings among prison officials result in a three-part proposal to operate with the smaller budget:

1. Closing all minimum custody work camps in the rural areas of the state.
2. Operating the remaining institutions and facilities at the absolute limit of their capacity.
3. Proposing the enactment of an emergency release bill that would parole inmates who are closest to discharge 60 days early to keep from exceeding prison capacity.

The governor approves the early release proposal, and it is presented to the legislature.

At present, the state's prison system houses 12,000 inmates. Population projections estimate that 800 inmates would be eligible for release under this program; two-thirds from the minimum custody institutions, one-fourth from camps, and the remainder from medium or maximum custody facilities.

Upon learning of this plan, the rural areas of the state protested loudly over the closure of their work camps and, consequently, the ensuing lay-off of many workers and the negative impact on their local economy. Furthermore, some legislators (exhibiting their traditional tough-on-crime posture) complain to the

---

*Contributed by Ron Angelone, director, Virginia Department of Corrections, and Glen Whorton, chief of classification and planning, Nevada Department of Prisons.

governor and prison director about the early release program. A sticky political situation has developed because the rurals carry clout when they band together on an issue.

Legislative hearings on this issue are imminent, and the media have begun to clamor for responses to the concerns of rural interest groups and tough-on-crime advocates, who include the camp staff members who are at risk of being laid off. The attacks on the program generally relate to one or more of the following categories:

1. "Why doesn't the department close prisons instead of camps, so that rural communities can continue to benefit from the economic influence of salaries, purchases, and the public works performed by the inmates?"
2. "Releasing inmates early into the community will place our citizens at risk."
3. "How does the Department justify the practice of not operating institutions at their emergency capacities at all times, during good economies as well as bad?"

As the department's budget analyst, you have been instructed by the director to prepare a response to these questions as well as a general position paper on the three-point plan.

Questions for Discussion

1. What is the rationale for the closure of the camps? Is it basically sound?
2. What would be the effect of closing prisons instead of camps as the rural people desire?
3. What is the risk to the community? Is the public's concern legitimate?
4. How can the department defend its practice of not operating prisons at their emergency capacity levels?
5. What, if any, action(s) should the director take against staff members in rural areas who appear to be engaging in political mutiny?
6. To what extent, if any, should the prison director play the political game and begin contacting state legislators to solicit their support of this proposal?

The Prison Director Versus the Irate Inmate*

The director of the state Department of Prisons has received a grievance from an inmate who indicates that the classification staff at the maximum prison has classified him incorrectly. Specifically, the inmate argues that he is serving a sen-

---

*Contributed by Ron Angelone, director, Virginia Department of Corrections, and Glen Whorton, chief of classification and planning, Nevada Department of Prisons.

tence for forgery but he is classified as if it were murder. He also maintains that the staff has begun to retaliate against him because of his grievances regarding his classification. The inmate states that if he does not receive satisfaction in regard to the classification, he is going to file suits based on the conditions of confinement at the prison. This is troubling to the director, given the prison's overcrowding, its physical deficiencies, and the type and extent of programs it offers.

A review of the inmate's file indicates that he is incarcerated for three life sentences as a habitual offender. He has been incarcerated only 18 months on the first life sentence. The root offenses for the habitual offender findings were indeed forgery. He has four prior felonies for similar offenses in other states. The inmate is 56 years old and in poor health.

The inmate's file is replete with complaints about other inmates and staff. He sued the central records staff on one previous occasion, claiming that staff misconduct resulted in the mishandling of a request for a speedy trial on a detainer that had been lodged against him. This suit was dismissed when it was discovered that the inmate had lied about having requested the trial. The file also notes numerous disciplinary violations related to refusing to work and possession of unauthorized property. The record includes no reports of violence or evidence of serious misconduct.

The file also discloses that the inmate is embroiled in a dispute with the chief of the prison medical division over his treatment for cancer. The inmate recently claimed that staff physicians have completely ignored his medical condition and have refused to treat the cancer. The computerized inmate information system indicates that about four months ago, he was taken to a local hospital and remained there for approximately one week. A call to the institution doctor reveals that the inmate's cancer was surgically removed during that visit.

A review of classification documents reveals that the staff has correctly scored the inmate's offense on the objective classification instrument. The score for Murder II and Habitual Offender are the same. The instrument's computed score on the classification documents indicates, however, that he is a medium custody inmate. He was assigned to a higher level of custody because of the extremely long sentence that he is serving. This custody assignment and the original transfer to the maximum prison were approved by the central classification staff who review classification recommendations for the director.

You are the director's administrative aide and enjoy the director's trust. She has asked that you prepare a position statement on this matter, presenting all relevant viewpoints and possible pitfalls and developing recommendations. You are told that "the bottom line is to do what's right for the inmate."

Questions for Discussion

1. What is the primary inmate-related issue that the director must deal with: classification or transfer? Was the classification staff technically correct in sending the inmate to a maximum security institution in the first place?
2. Can the inmate be safely transferred to a lower-level institution? If so, to a

medium or minimum security one? (Remember that although the inmate is infirm and relatively old, he is serving a lengthy sentence.)

3. If the inmate is transferred, have the director and staff lost any real power in the eyes of other inmates?

4. How does the director deal with these issues without giving an obviously litigious inmate more ammunition with which to harass staff or sue the department? Should the director ask the classification team to reconsider the case?

5. With what staff-related issues must the director deal? What are the options in dealing with them?

6. Are any broader policy issues presented in this situation? If so, what action do they suggest?

"Out of Town Brown" and the Besieged Probation Supervisor*

Joan Casey is a career probation officer. She majored in criminal justice as an undergraduate and plans to get her master's degree in criminology within the next few years. She holds memberships in several national correctional organizations, attends training conferences, and does a significant amount of reading on her own time to stay current in the field.

Joan began working for the Collier County Probation Department soon after she graduated from college and was promoted to a supervisory position within five years, a remarkable accomplishment considering her relative lack of seniority in the organization. She supervises an adult probation unit consisting of eight experienced probation officers, all of whom have been in the work force longer than she has. The unit is responsible for investigating approximately 80 offenders a month and preparing presentence investigation reports on them.

Collier County Probation Department has made the front page of the local newspapers twice in the past year. Both times it was a nightmare for the chief probation officer, Jack Brown, and the entire agency. "Collier County Soft on Crime!" screamed the first headline and then, just a month later, "Northside Stalker Gets Probation!"

Brown called a management team meeting. It was short and to the point: "No more lousy publicity," he said, "or heads are gonna roll! Has everybody got it?" Everybody got it. No written policy concerning media relations exists, however, nor is any particular person authorized to release agency information.

---

*Contributed by Catherine Lowe, director, California Center for Judicial Education and Research, Emeryville, California.

This week Brown is on annual leave, the assistant chief is out of state at an American Correctional Association meeting, and Joan Casey is the designated officer in charge. One of Joan's probation officers has recommended community-based treatment for a 16-year-old mentally retarded boy who was prosecuted as an adult. The youth murdered his stepfather with an axe after submitting to many years of physical and mental abuse. He had been an incest victim since he was 5 years old.

Joan is aware of the probation officer's recommendation and agrees with it. After all, she reasons, the boy is a low risk for recidivism, and he is as much a victim of this offense as was his stepfather.

It is 4:45 P.M. on Thursday. Joan's phone rings; her secretary has put through a call from a reporter at a local newspaper. The reporter is a strong crusader in the local war against crime. He has his own weekly column at the paper. He knows that the "kiddie-killer" will be sentenced tomorrow.

Questions for Discussion

1. What should Joan's response to the reporter be other than hanging up or telling him to call back?
2. If she elects to discuss her officer's recommendation, what should she say to justify it?
3. What should the chief probation officer do upon his return to work?
4. Was the probation officer's recommendation correct based on these facts?
5. Should a policy be immediately drafted for this situation? Should any personnel actions be taken?

"Cheerless Chuck" and the Parole Officer's Orientation Day*

"So, you're the new parole officer with a criminal justice degree from the university? Well, I hope you last longer than the last recruit I had. She meant well, but I guess her idealism about the job of parole officer couldn't handle the realities of the work.

"In a way, I understand what she went through. Same thing happened to me 12 years ago when I started this job. There I was, fresh out of college with a brand new diploma with 'Social Work' written on it. I figured that piece of paper made me a social worker, and I better get right to work fixing society. It didn't take me long to realize that the real world was different from what I had learned

---

*Contributed by Matthew Leone, assistant professor of criminal justice, University of Nevada, Reno.

in college. It was like I had been trained as a sailor, and I was about to set out on a voyage, but I couldn't take the time to steer the ship because I was so busy bailing water. The crises we deal with here make it darned difficult to do the work we all see needs to be done.

"Years ago, when I first started with the parole department, things were a lot better than they are now. Caseloads were lower, fewer people who didn't deserve it were getting parole, and the rest of the criminal justice system was in a lot better shape, which made our jobs a lot easier to do. Think about it. We vote in politicians who promise the public that they are going to 'get tough' on crime and the first thing they do is allot more money for law enforcement stuff: beat cops, car computers, helicopters, and so on. These things are great, but all they do is add more people into a system that is already overloaded. No one gets elected by promising to build more courts or add jail and prison space or probation and parole officers. Eventually these added police officers arrest more people than the system can handle.

"The courts back up, which in turn messes up the prisons and the jails. The inmates stuck in these crowded places get tired of living like sardines, so they sue the prisons and jails. Remember, the Constitution prohibits cruel and unusual punishment. A lot of times inmates' complaints are legitimate, and they win. The judge orders the prison to lower its population to a reasonable level, which forces the parole board to consider more inmates for early release. They come knocking on our doors, hoping we can get them out of the mess that politics and budgets have created. Nobody mentions giving the parole department more officers, or a bigger budget for added administrative help. No, the bucks go to the flashy, visible things like cops and cars. Meanwhile, in the past 10 years our average caseload for a parole officer has increased 75 percent. We have more people who need supervision, and we are doing it on a budget that has not kept pace with the remainder of the criminal justice system.

"This wouldn't be so bad if the system was at least adding things to other areas, like the jail or the courts. The problem here is that we depend on the jail to hold our parolees who have violated their conditions. We catch some of them using booze or drugs, and we are *supposed* to bring them in to the county jail to wait for a hearing to decide if they are going back to prison, or back on the street. But the jail has its own set of problems. A couple of years ago the U.S. District Court slapped a population cap on our jail. If it goes over that population, the jail will not accept our violators. So we send them home. If they get into more serious trouble, we call it a new crime, the police arrest them, and the jail has to take them. Then they have to sit and wait for the court to catch up, since the courts are not in much better shape than the jail.

"I guess the job would be easier if the prisons were doing their jobs, too. I can't really blame them, since the prisons are funded in much the same way that parole is. We are not 'glamorous' places to send your tax dollars, but if the prisons were getting more money, they might be able to improve the quality of inmate they send to us. Maybe a little more vocational training and substance abuse counseling, so they could stay off the booze and drugs. Maybe then fewer of these parolees would wind up back behind bars a few years later.

"The worst part about the job is the caseload. We presently have so many on parole that I am lucky if I can get a phone call to each of them once a week, and maybe a home visit once a month. You can't tell me that a phone call and a home visit are really keeping these guys from committing crimes. The sad part about it is that with the proper budget and staff, we could really make a difference. We spend so much time bailing water out of the boat, we don't realize that there is no one steering, and we are just drifting in circles.

"By the way, my name is Charlie Matthews, but everyone calls me Chuck. I'm a supervisor here as well as the designated new-employee orientation specialist and all-round public relations person. I hope I've not depressed you too much on your first day, but now is a good time to drop your idealism and get to work 'bailing.' What're *your* views and ideas?"

Questions for Discussion

1. How would changes in politics affect the parole system directly and indirectly?
2. How does an old criminal justice planning adage that "you can't rock one end of the boat" seem to be applicable to what Chuck says about law enforcement getting so much new political funding?
3. What could you tell Chuck about existing means of dealing with bloated caseloads?
4. What kinds of administrative problems and practices might be responsible for this agency's situation?
5. Why do crowded jails and prisons make the job of parole officers more difficult?
6. How could practices of the jails and prisons change the success of the parole system?
7. Based on Chuck's assessment of the local situation, where do you believe the greatest misconceptions about courts and corrections exist?
8. Should Chuck be retained as orientation coordinator? Why or why not?

The Wright Way*

Randall Wright has been a shift supervisor at the Granite County Jail Facility for the past 10 years and has worked at the jail for a total of 18 years. Wright enjoys taking visitors on tours of the facility and takes pride in the fact that he knows every aspect of the jail's operation.

---

*Contributed by Ted Heim, professor, Department of Criminal Justice, Washburn University, Topeka, Kansas.

This summer, Wright is providing some of the supervision for an intern the facility has accepted from the local university's criminal justice program. The intern, Tom Sharpe, finds Wright to be an interesting and outspoken person. In their conversations about work in the jail, Tom asks Wright how he deals emotionally with his job; he has read about stress in his textbooks.

"I'm glad you asked that, young fella," the veteran responds. "I have some good advice for you if you are going into any kind of correctional work." He continues, "First, I never take this job home with me. My wife and kids used to ask about what I do at work, but I have made it a strict policy never to discuss what happens here. My family wouldn't understand what goes on here. They might be concerned about what I do, so I decided long ago that it was best to dummy up about it all.

"Second, I find that you have to be realistic about your chances for having any positive influence on these birds who come through here. Oh, I have seen lots of guys who thought they could change the world come in here, and they are the ones who will come down hard. Me? Well, I'm a realist. Let's face it. We get the people everyone else has given up on, so what can we be expected to do? I tell visitors that 'we get the cream of the crap here,' and I mean it. Don't set your expectations very high, and you won't be disappointed.

"The job tends to get you down if you let it. I have found that you have to find a relief from all the frustrations you experience and the problems created by some of the SOBs who come through here. About once a week, the gang and I hold choir practice. Kelsey's Place down the street is where we go. After about five or six beers, this place and the world look a helluva lot better. People who don't work corrections don't understand the need to let off a little steam, but I can tell you that 'choir practice' keeps me going.

"One more bit of advice for you, Sharpe: Don't lose your sense of humor. I have always prided myself on my ability to laugh at almost any situation. Hell, the top brass around here and the politicians over at the courthouse are easy to laugh at. All you need to do when you're down is look at some of the orders these clowns put out and some of the things our glorious leaders tell the public about rehabilitation, efficiency, blah, blah, blah. I usually tell my staff to disregard new memos and such. Sometimes it's hard to stop laughing. It has all worked for me. Why, in just 9 years, 3 months, and 20 days I will be able to retire and walk away from this place."

Questions for Discussion

1. Assume that you are Wright's supervisor and, while standing in the hallway, you overhear this conversation. What would be your *immediate* reaction to his speech about on-the-job actions? What *long-term* actions—disciplinary or otherwise—would you take with Wright?

2. If you were Wright's supervisor, would you feel compelled to look into, leave alone, or halt the "choir practices"?

3. Assume that you are the student intern who just listened to this delivery. Of all the points Wright made, which do you agree with? Disagree with? Would

you now feel more or less compelled to enter the field? Do you value such a person's candor?

4. In your estimation, is Wright the sort of employee who should be supervising others? Greeting interns? Will an employee of this nature last until retirement?

5. Do you believe such cynicism is common in corrections? In criminal justice, generally? In most other occupations? Is it healthy or debilitating?

Part V

SPANNING THE SYSTEM: ISSUES CHALLENGING THE JUSTICE SYSTEM

This part consists of four chapters, all of which focus on administrative problems spanning the entire justice system. In Chapter 14, we examine the rights and liabilities of criminal justice employees, Chapter 15 discusses financial administration, Chapter 16 reviews the latest technological hardware and software now in use in criminal justice agencies, and Chapter 17 contemplates what the future holds for justice administration.

Rights and Legal Responsibilities of Criminal Justice Employees

We have all enough strength to bear other people's troubles.
—Duc de la Rochefoucauld

Good orders make evil men good and bad orders make good men evil.
—James Harrington

Uneasy lies the head that wears the crown.

—William Shakespeare

✦ INTRODUCTION

In the past few decades, the rights and obligations of criminal justice employees, like those of workers in the private sector, have changed dramatically. The contemporary criminal justice employee must be far more sophisticated about employee rights than in the past.[1] Contemporary criminal justice managers must be aware of the law surrounding employee rights. Several contemporary issues, such as drug testing, privacy, and sexual harassment, as well as major limitations on the hiring, disciplining, and firing of criminal justice personnel, present great challenges for the justice administrator.[2] This chapter examines these challenges.

This chapter also examines a companion issue: the responsibilities of criminal justice administrators and their employees. No group of workers (with the exception of physicians) is more susceptible to litigation related to their work than police and corrections personnel. Frequently cast into confrontational situations and given the complex nature of their work and the training necessary to prepare them for their work, police and corrections personnel from time to time may act in a manner that evokes public scrutiny and complaints.

✦ AN OVERVIEW OF LEGISLATION

Criminal justice employees are affected by the provisions of federal and state constitutions, statutes, administrative regulations, and judicial interpretations and rulings, as well as employee handbooks (sometimes poorly written) or long-standing agency customs or practices. Improper or illegal hiring, training, discipline, or discharge can lead not only to poor agency performance and morale but also to substantial legal and economic liability. The following overview and the court decisions discussed later should illustrate that understanding and adhering to these regulations and utilizing good common sense as well as a sense of fairness go a long way to prevent legal problems in the employment relationship.[3]

It should also be noted that the Civil Rights Act of 1991 may result in significant changes in public- and private-sector employment; however, it will be several years before significant court decisions will indicate how the Supreme Court interprets the provisions of this act.

As an introduction to this chapter's examination of administrative rights and duties, the following list presents an overview of pertinent legislation that will provide the basis for this discussion.

◊ *The Fair Labor Standards Act* (at 29 U.S.C. 203 et seq.) provides minimum pay and overtime provisions covering both public- and private-sector employees. Part 7(a) contains special provisions for firefighters and police officers. We discuss this act more fully later.

◊ *Title VII of the Civil Rights Act of 1964 and its Amendments* (42 U.S.C. 2000e) is a broadly based act that established a federal policy requiring fair employment practices in both the public and private sectors. It prohibited employment discrimination based on race, color, religion, sex, and national origin in areas such as the hiring, discharge, and discipline processes; working conditions; and the provision of benefits. Its provisions extend to "hostile work environment" claims based on sexual, racial, or religious harassment.

◊ *The Equal Pay Act* [29 U.S.C. 206(d)] provided an alternative remedy to Title VII for sex-based discrimination in wages and benefits for similar work. It applies the simpler Fair Labor Standards Act procedures to claims. Note that the Equal Pay Act does not provide for "comparable worth," a concept that attempts to determine wages by requiring equal pay for employees whose work is of comparable worth even if the job content is totally different.

◊ *The Pregnancy Discrimination Act of 1978* [42 U.S.C. Section 2000e(k)] is an amendment to the scope of sexual discrimination under Title VII. It prohibits unequal treatment of women because of pregnancy or related medical conditions (e.g., nausea). The act requires that employers treat pregnant women as they would other temporarily disabled employees. The U.S. Supreme Court decided a major case in 1991 that limited employers' ability to exclude women who are pregnant or of childbearing years from certain jobs through a fetal protection policy.[4]

◊ *The Age Discrimination in Employment Act* (29 U.S.C. 623) generally prohibits the unequal treatment of applicants or employees based on their age, if they are age 40 or over, in regard to hiring, firing, receiving benefits, and other conditions of employment.

◊ *Americans with Disabilities Act of 1990* (42 U.S.C. 12112) has as its goal to remove barriers that might prevent otherwise qualified individuals with disabilities from enjoying the same employment opportunities available to persons without disabilities. Although this act has only recently been implemented, the Rehabilitation Act of 1973 (see 29 U.S.C. 701) and its amendments have long prevented similar disability discrimination among public agencies receiving federal funds.

◊ *42 U.S.C. 1983* is a major piece of legislation that allows an employee to sue an employer for civil rights violations based on the deprivation of constitutional rights. It is the most versatile civil rights action and is also the most often used against criminal justice agencies.

In addition to these legislative acts and statutes that prohibit various acts of discrimination in employment, additional remedies are available to public-sector employees. They may bring civil tort claims against employers for a wide variety of claims, ranging from assault and battery to defamation. Contractual claims may result from collective bargaining agreements; such agreements may include procedures for assignment, seniority, due process (such as in the "Police Officers' Bill of Rights"), and grievance procedures. Often the source of the right defines the remedy and the procedure to obtain it. For example, statutes or legal precedents often provide back pay, compensatory damages, injunctive relief, or punitive damages for employees whose rights were violated.

✦ THE EMPLOYMENT RELATIONSHIP

✧ RECRUITMENT AND HIRING

Numerous selection methods for hiring police officers have been tried over the years. Issues in recruitment, selection, and hiring often involve internal promotions and assignments to special units, such as an "alert team" in a prison. Requirements concerning age (e.g., the FBI will hire no one older than 37 years of age), height, weight, vision, education, and possession of a valid driver's license have all been used over the years in criminal justice systems. In addition, they commonly use tests to determine intelligence, emotional suitability and stability (with psychological examinations and oral interviews), physical agility, and character (with polygraph examinations and extensive background checks).[5] More recently, drug tests also have become frequently used. They will be discussed more fully later.

The critical question concerning these tests is whether they validly test the types of skills needed for the job. A companion concern is whether the tests are used for discriminatory purposes or have unequal impact on protected groups. In order to obtain job relatedness, a number of private companies have developed so-called canned examinations that provide reliable test instruments for use in the public sector.

✧ DISPARATE TREATMENT

Note that nothing in the law states that an employer must hire or retain incompetent personnel. In effect, the law does not prohibit discrimination on justifiable, legal grounds. Thus, it is not unlawful to refuse to hire people who have records of driving while intoxicated for positions that require driving. What *is* illegal is to treat people differently because of their age, gender, sex, or other protected status; that is *disparate treatment*. It is also illegal to deny equal employment opportunities to such persons; that is *disparate impact*.[6] Federal equal opportunity law prohibits the use of selection procedures for hiring or promotion that have a discriminatory impact on the employment opportunities according to gender, race, or other protected classes. An example of overt discriminatory hiring is a situation that occurred in 1987 in a sparsely populated county in Virginia. Four women sued because they had been denied positions as courtroom security officer, deputy, or civil process server because of their gender. Sheriffs had refused to hire the women, justifying their decision by contending that being male was a *bona fide occupational qualifier* (BFOQ) for the positions and because the positions were within the personal staff of the sheriff, thus exempting such positions from Title VII protection. In overturning a lower court decision, the Fourth Circuit Court found that the sheriff did not establish that gender was a BFOQ for the positions and that the positions were not part of the sheriff's personal staff (the positions were not high level, policymaking, or advisory in nature). Thus, the refusal to hire the women violated Title VII provisions.[7]

A "business justification" for a hiring policy may be allowed even though it has a disparate impact. For example, in one case an employer required airline attendants to cease flying immediately upon discovering they were pregnant. The court upheld the policy on the ground that pregnancy could affect one's ability to perform routine duties in an aircraft, thereby jeopardizing the safety of passengers.[8]

A classic example of an apparent neutral employment requirement that actually had a disparate impact on gender, race, and ethnicity, is the height requirement used by most public safety agencies. Minimum height requirements of 5 feet, 10 inches or above were often advertised and effectively used to exclude most women and many Asians and Hispanics from employment.[9] Such a requirement has gradually been superseded by a height in proportion to weight requirement. Many existing physical agility tests serve to discriminate against the lesser upper-body strength of women and smaller men. One is forced to wonder how performing pushups and negotiating 6-foot walls or ditches and attics relate to a police officer's work. (Occasionally, the situation of testing preemployment physical abilities becomes ludicrous. For example, the author once allowed a recruiter from a major western city to recruit students in an upper-level criminal justice course. The recruiter said the city's physical test included climbing over a 6-foot wall; however, he quickly pointed out that testing staff would boost all female applicants over it.)

Litigation has caused agencies to reevaluate these tests. For example, a woman in a western city challenged the police department's physical abilities test as being discriminatory and not job related, prompting the agency to hire a Canadian consultant to develop a job-related preemployment agility test (currently used by the Royal Canadian Mounted Police and other agencies across Canada), based on data provided by officers. These data were later computer analyzed for incorporation into the test. In other words, recruits are now tested on the physical demands placed on police officers in that specific community (no pushups or 6-foot walls are included).[10]

Discrimination may also exist in promotions and job assignments in criminal justice systems. As an example of the former, a Nebraska female correctional center worker brought suit alleging that her employer violated her Title VII and equal protection rights by denying her a promotion. She also alleged that her employer treated women inequitably and unprofessionally, that assertiveness in women was viewed negatively, and that women were assigned clerical duties not assigned to men. The woman was qualified for the position she sought. The court found that she was indeed denied a promotion because of her sex, in violation of Title VII and the equal protection clause of the Fourteenth Amendment; she was awarded back pay ($7,500), front pay ($122 biweekly, until a comparable position became available), general damages, and court costs.[11]

With respect to litigation in the area of job assignments, four women matron/dispatchers who were refused assignments to correctional officer positions in Florida, even though they had been trained and certified as jail officers, were awarded damages. The court ruled that a state regulation prohibiting females in male areas of the jail was discriminatory without proof that gender was a BFOQ.[12] A particular assignment may validly exclude one sex, however. For example, an assignment to work as a decoy prostitute could validly demonstrate a "business necessity" for women.[13]

✦ How Old Is "Too Old" in Criminal Justice?

State and public agencies with arbitrary age restrictions are subject to age discrimination suits. In Florida, a state highway patrol lieutenant with 29 years of service was forced by statute to retire at age 62. The Equal Employment Opportunity Commission (EEOC) brought suit, alleging that Florida's statute violated the Age Discrimination in Employment Act (ADEA). The court held that age should not be a BFOQ because youthfulness is not a guarantee of public safety but that a physical fitness standard would better ensure that the person is able to perform the tasks of the position.[14]

Indeed, the U.S. Supreme Court has rejected mandatory retirement plans for municipal firefighters and police officers.[15] Until 1985 the City of Baltimore had relied on a *federal* police officer and firefighter statute (5 U.S.C. 8335b), an exemption to the ADEA, to establish age limits for appointing and retiring its fire and police officers. The Supreme Court said that although Congress had exempted federal employees from application of the ADEA, another agency cannot just "adopt" the same standards without showing an agency-specific need. Age is not a BFOQ for nonfederal firefighters (or, by extension, police officers). The Court also established a "reasonable federal standard" in its 1984 decision in *EEOC v. Wyoming*,[16] when it overturned a state statute providing for the mandatory retirement of state game wardens at age 55. It held that the ADEA did not require employers to retain unfit employees but to make individualized determinations as to fitness.

✦ Criminal Justice and Affirmative Action

Probably no single employment practice has caused as much controversy as affirmative action. The very words bring to mind visions of quotas and unqualified people being given preferential hiring treatment.[17] Indeed, quotas have been at the center of legal, social, scientific, and political controversy for more than two decades.[18] The reality of affirmative action is substantially different from the myth, however; as a general rule, affirmative action plans give preferred treatment only to affected groups when all other criteria (e.g., education, skills) are equal.[19]

The legal (and, for many persons, moral) issue that arises from affirmative action is: when does preferential hiring become *reverse* discrimination? The leading case here is *Bakke v. Regents of the University of California*.[20] Allan Bakke was passed over for medical school admission at the University of California, Davis, partly because the school set aside a number of its 100 medical school admissions slots annually for "disadvantaged" applicants. The Supreme Court held, among other things, that race could be used as a criterion in selection decisions, but it could not be the only criterion.

In a series of cases beginning in 1986,[21] the Supreme Court considered the development and application of affirmative action plans and established a two-step inquiry that must be satisfied before an affirmative action plan can be put in place. A plan must have (1) a remedial purpose to correct past inequities, and (2) its implementation must correct a manifest imbalance or significant disparity. (The Court emphasized, however, that such plans cannot completely foreclose employment opportunities to nonminority or male candidates.)

Generally, however, the validity of such plans is determined on a case-by-case basis. For example, 21 past and present detectives of the District of Columbia's Metropolitan Police Department who were passed over for promotion challenged the department's voluntary affirmative action plan designed to place "special emphasis" on the hiring and advancement of females and minorities in those employment areas where an "obvious imbalance" existed in their numbers.[22] The plaintiffs believed that their failure to be promoted was attributable to illegal preferential treatment of blacks and women—reverse discrimination—violating their rights under Title VII and the due process clause of the Fifth Amendment. The District of Columbia Circuit Court held in 1987 that an affirmative action plan covering the promotion of blacks to management positions in the police department was justified, because only 174 of the 807 positions (22 percent) above the rank of sergeant were filled by blacks in a city in which 60 percent of the labor market was black.[23]

The court held that the nonminority and male employees of the department failed to prove that the plan was invalid; there was a considerable body of evidence that racial and sexual imbalance had existed when the plan was adopted, and the plan did not unnecessarily trammel any legitimate interests of the nonminority or male employees because it did not call for displacement or layoff and did not totally exclude them from promotion opportunities.[24]

In summary, then, a criminal justice employer who wishes to implement and maintain job requirements must make sure that they are job related. Furthermore, when a job requirement discriminates against a protected class, it should have a strong legitimate purpose and be the least restrictive alternative. Finally, attempts to remedy past hiring inequities by such means as affirmative action programs need substantial justification to avoid becoming reverse discrimination.[25]

✧ PROPERTY RIGHTS IN EMPLOYMENT

The Fourteenth Amendment to the U.S. Constitution provides in part that

> no state shall make or enforce any law which shall abridge the privileges or immunities of citizens of the United States; nor shall any state deprive any person

of life, liberty, or property without due process of law; nor deny to any person within its jurisdiction the equal protection of the law.

Furthermore, the Supreme Court has set forth four elements of a due process claim under Section 1983 that must be met: a (1) person acting under color of state law (2) deprived an individual (3) of constitutionally protected property (4) without due process of law.[26]

A long line of court cases has established the legal view that public employees have a property interest in their employment. This flies in the face of the old view that employees served "at will" or until their employer, for whatever reason, no longer needed their services. The Supreme Court has provided some general guidance on how the question of a constitutionally protected "property interest" is to be resolved:

> To have a property interest in a benefit, a person clearly must have more than an abstract need or desire for it. He must have more than a unilateral expectation of it. He must, instead, have a *legitimate claim of entitlement to it.* It is a purpose of the ancient institution of property to protect those claims *upon which people rely in their daily lives, reliance that must not be arbitrarily undermined"* [emphasis added].[27]

The Court has also held that employees are entitled to both a pretermination and posttermination notice[28] and an opportunity to respond and that state legislators are free to choose not to confer a property interest in public employment.

The development of a property interest in employment has an important ramification: it means that "due process" must be exercised by a public entity before terminating or interfering with an employee's property right. What has been established, however, is that a probationary employee has little or no property interest in employment. For example, in one case the Ninth Circuit Court held that a probationary civil service employee ordinarily has no property interest and can be discharged without a hearing or even "good cause." In that same decision, however, the court held that a woman who had passed her six-month probationary period and had then been promoted to a new position for which there was a probationary period had the legitimate expectation of continued employment.[29]

An Indiana police captain was deemed to have a property interest in his position even though a state statute allowed the city manager to demote without notice. In this case, a captain of detectives, a Democrat, was demoted by a newly elected Republican mayor. The court determined that the dismissal of even a "policymaking" public employee for politically motivated reasons is forbidden unless the employee's position is "policymaking" in the sense that the position inherently encompasses tasks that render political affiliation an appropriate prerequisite for effective performance.[30]

Normally, however, policymaking employees (often called *exempt appointments*) have an automatic exception to the contemporary property interest view. Generally, these personnel, often elected agency heads, are free to hire and fire those employees who are involved in making important decisions and policy. This area includes new sheriffs who appoint undersheriffs and wardens who in turn appoint deputy wardens. These deputy employees currently have no property interest in their positions and may be asked at any time to leave the agency or revert to a previously held rank.

This property interest in employment is, of course, generally implied. In a Utah case, a property interest was found to exist based on an implied contract founded on an employment manual. Due process standards were therefore violated when the police department fired an officer without showing good cause or giving him a chance to respond to the charges against him.[31] In a Pennsylvania case involving a patrol officer who was suspended for 30 days without pay for alleged violations of personnel policies and was not given an opportunity to file a written response to the charges, the court held that the officer's suspension resulted in a deprivation of property.[32]

The property right in one's employment does not have to involve discipline or discharge to afford an employee protection. For example, a parole officer's claim that he was harassed, humiliated, and interfered with in a deliberate attempt to remove him from his position established a civil rights action for deprivation of property.[33] This decision against the Illinois Department of Corrections resulted from allegations that the department engaged in "a deliberate and calculated effort to remove the plaintiff from his position by forcing him to resign, thereby making the protections of the personnel code unavailable to him." As a result, the plaintiff suffered anxiety and stress and eventually went on disability status at substantially reduced pay.[34]

The key questions, then, once a property right is established, are these: What constitutes adequate grounds for interference with that right? What is adequate process to sustain that interference?[35]

✦ DISCIPLINE AND DISCHARGE

Well-established, minimum due process requirements for discharge of public employees exist. Employees have the following rights:

1. To be afforded a public hearing.
2. To be present during the presentation of evidence against them and to have an opportunity to cross-examine their superiors.
3. To have an opportunity to present their own witnesses and other evidence concerning their side of the case.
4. To be represented by counsel.
5. To have an impartial referee or hearing officer preside over the hearing.
6. To have an eventual decision based on the weight of the evidence introduced during the hearing.

Such protections apply to any disciplinary action that can significantly affect a criminal justice employee's reputation and/or future chances for special assignment or promotion. A disciplinary hearing that might result, for example, in only a reprimand or short suspension may involve fewer procedural protections than one that could result in more severe sanctions.[36]

When a particular disciplinary action does not seek termination or suspension, however, it may still be subject to due process considerations. An example involves the case of a Chicago police officer who was transferred from the Neighborhood Relations Division to less desirable working conditions in the patrol division, but with no loss in pay or benefits. The court found that the officer's First Amendment free speech rights had been violated because his de facto demotion was in retaliation for his political activities (for inviting political opponents of the mayor to a civic function and for a speech given there criticizing the police department) and that he was thus entitled to civil damages. The court stated that "certainly a demotion can be as detrimental to an employee as denial of a promotion."[37]

On the other hand, no due process protection may be required when the property interest (one's job) was fraudulently obtained. Thus, a deputy sheriff was not deprived of due process when he was summarily discharged for lying on his application about a juvenile felony charge, which would have barred him from employment in the first place.[38]

In sum, agency rules and policies should state what due process procedures will be utilized under certain disciplinary situations. The key issues regarding due process are whether the employer followed established agency guidelines and, if not, whether the employer had a compelling reason not to do so.

Adequate grounds for discipline or discharge can vary widely from agency to agency. Certainly, an agency's formal policies and procedures should specify and control what constitutes proper and improper behavior. Normally, agency practice and custom enter into these policies. Sometimes, however, administrators wink at the formal policies and procedures, overlooking or only occasionally enforcing certain provisions contained in them. But the failure of the agency to enforce a rule or policy for a long period of time may provide "implied consent" by the employer that such behavior, although officially prohibited, is permissible. (In other words, don't allow an employee to violate a smoking policy for three months in your dynamite factory and then decide one day to fire him or her summarily for this violation.) Attempts to fire employees for behavior that has been ignored or enforced only infrequently at best may give the employee a reason to sue.

Hiring minority employees to meet state hiring goals and then attempting to terminate them as quickly as possible violates an employee's Title VII rights. Such a situation was decided in a 1988 Indiana case that alleged that black prison correctional officers were hired to fulfill an affirmative action program only to be fired for disciplinary reasons for which white officers were not discharged.[39] The court held that the prison guard-plaintiff was entitled to present statistics to support his claims concerning the employee disciplinary procedures at the prison.

Generally, violations of an employee's rights occur in discharge and discipline when such actions are taken (1) in violation of a protected interest, (2) in retaliation for the exercise of protected conduct, (3) with a discriminatory motive, or (4) with malice.[40]

✧ Pay and Benefits

The Fair Labor Standards Act (FLSA), briefly described earlier, has had a major impact on criminal justice agencies. One observer referred to the FLSA as the criminal justice administrator's "worst nightmare come true."[41] Initiated in 1938 to establish minimum wages and to require overtime compensation in the private sector, amendments added in 1974 extended its coverage to state and local government employees and special work period provisions for police and firefighters. In 1976, however, the U.S. Supreme Court ruled that the extension of the act into the area of traditional local and state government functions was unconstitutional.[42] In 1985 the Court reversed itself, bringing local police employees under FLSA coverage. In this major (and very costly) decision, *Garcia v. San Antonio Transit Authority,*[43] the Court held, 5 to 4, that Congress had intended the requirements of the FLSA to apply to state and local governments.

Criminal justice operations can require 24-hour per day, 7-days per week service and often require overtime and participation in off-duty activities such as court appearances and training sessions. FLSA provisions require these employees to be paid for overtime. It provides that an employer must generally pay employees time and a half for all hours worked beyond 40 per week. Overtime also must be paid to personnel for all work in excess of 43 hours in a 7-day cycle or 171 hours in a 28-day period. Public safety employees may accrue a maximum of 480 hours of compensatory time, which, if not used as leave time, must be paid to the employee upon his or her separation from employment at his or her final rate of pay or at the average pay over the last three years, whichever is higher.[44] Furthermore, employers usually cannot require employees to take compensatory time in lieu of cash. The primary issue with FLSA is the rigidity of the definition of compensable work. The act prohibits an agency from taking compensatory time from employees.

According to FLSA requirements, an officer who works the night shift must receive pay for attending training or testifying in court during the day. Officers who are ordered to remain at home in anticipation of emergency actions must be compensated for their time. The FLSA's overtime provisions do not apply, however, to persons employed in a bona fide executive, administrative, or professional capacity. In criminal justice, FLSA has generally been held to apply to detectives and sergeants but not to those holding the rank of lieutenant and above.

(*Note:* As this book was going to press, the U.S. House of Representatives passed a bill, similar to one in the Senate, that would allow employers to offer workers compensatory time off as a substitute for overtime pay. This bill, "The Working Families Flexibility Act," was opposed by unions as being too management oriented and because of the fear that workers would be coerced out of their overtime pay. Conversely, business interests wanted control in the hands of employers. The issue became polarized, with no middle ground being apparent in this labor-management dispute.)

A companion issue with respect to criminal justice pay and benefits is that of equal pay for equal work. Claims of disparate treatment in pay and benefits can be litigated under Title VII or statutes such as the Equal Pay Act or the equal protection clause. An Ohio case involved matron/dispatchers who performed essentially the same job as jailers but were paid less. This was found to be in violation of the Equal Pay Act and, because discriminatory intent was found, of Title VII.[45]

In a related case, a court ruled that a Section 1983 claim by 133 southern Virginia state troopers could be filed because the plaintiffs did not receive a salary differential as did troopers in the northern part of the state. The plaintiffs argued that the salary differential was arbitrary, without any rational relationship to legitimate state interests, and as such was an unconstitutional denial of their rights to due process and equal protection under the Fourteenth Amendment. Conversely, the State of Virginia argued that based on the results of a statewide study, the need for higher salaries to attract qualified applicants in the north, and to prevent in-service troopers from leaving to take positions in private security, the differential was necessary.[46]

Other criminal justice employee benefits are addressed in Title VII, the ADEA, and the Pregnancy Discrimination Act (PDA). For example, it is illegal for an employer to provide less insurance coverage for a female employee who is more likely to use maternity leave or one who is older and more liable to use more coverage. An older person or a woman cannot be forced to make higher pension contributions because they likely would be paying in for a shorter period of time or would be expected to live longer.

Regarding pregnancy, the PDA does not require an employer to discriminate in favor of a pregnancy-related condition. It demands only that the employer not treat pregnancy differently from any other temporary medical condition. For example, if an agency has a six-month leave policy for officers who are injured or ill from circumstances not related to their work (on-duty circumstances would probably be covered by worker's compensation), that agency would have to provide a six-month leave (if needed) for a pregnancy-related condition.[47]

✦ CRIMINAL JUSTICE AND A SAFE WORKPLACE

It is presently unclear the extent to which public employers owe their employees a safe workplace. Federal, state, and local governments are exempted from the coverage of the Occupational Safety and Health Act, in 29 U.S.C. 652. Nonetheless, criminal justice work is often dangerous, involving the use of force and occurring in locations outside governmental control. Therefore, criminal justice workplace safety issues are more likely to revolve around adequacy of training and supervision than physical plants.[48]

The Supreme Court has noted the unique nature and danger of public service employment. In one case, the Court specifically stated that an employee could not bring a Section 1983 civil rights action alleging a workplace so unsafe that it violated the Fourteenth Amendment's due process clause. In this matter, a sewer worker was asphyxiated while clearing a sewer line. The widow alleged that the city knew the sewer was dangerous but had failed to train or supervise the deceased properly.[49]

Other federal courts, especially the federal circuits, have ruled inconsistently on the safe workplace issue. One federal circuit held that a constitutional violation could be found if it was proven that the city actively engaged in conduct that was "deliberately indifferent" to the employee's constitutional rights.[50]

Another circuit court held differently in a Louisiana case, based on an agency's failure to comply with a court order to have three officers on duty at all times in a prison disciplinary unit.[51] In this case, a prison correctional officer in Baton Rouge was the only guard on a dangerous cellblock. While attempting to transfer a handcuffed inmate, the guard got into a scuffle with the inmate and was injured, although not severely. He claimed, however, that he received insufficient medical attention and that, as a result, he became permanently disabled and that the prison "consciously" and with wanton disregard for his personal safety conspired to have him work alone on the cellblock. He cited 42 U.S.C. 1983 in his case, claiming that the prison acted in an indifferent, malicious, and reckless manner toward him and that he suffered "class-based discrimination." The court held that the guard had no cause of action (no federal or constitutional grounds for litigation).

Liability for an employee's injury, disability, or death is a critical concern for criminal justice agencies. In particular, police and correctional officers often work under circumstances in which violent actions occur. Although state worker's compensation coverage, disability pensions, life insurance, and survivor pensions are designed to meet such tragedies, this coverage is typically limited and intended only to be remedial. On the other hand, civil tort actions in these cases can have a devastating impact on governmental budgets. Clearly, these issues are difficult and costly to resolve; they pose moral dilemmas as well as legal problems. Consider, for example, the case of a prison intelligence unit that has knowledge of an impending disturbance but fails to alert its officers (who are subsequently injured). Might a police department with knowledge that its new police vehicles have defective brakes fail to take immediate action for fear that its officers will refuse to drive them and thus reduce its effective personnel?[52] These moral and legal dilemmas in the criminal justice realm are not easily resolved.

✦ CONSTITUTIONAL RIGHTS OF CRIMINAL JUSTICE EMPLOYEES

✧ FREE SPEECH

Most, if not all, criminal justice employees—especially police officers, judges, and probation or parole officers—know much about other citizens; they observe people in their most embarrassing and vulnerable moments. Therefore, because of their position in our society, information that criminal justice practitioners pass on in formal or informal conversations assumes a tremendous air of importance and gravity. A former midwestern police commissioner described the situation well, commenting that "I'm sorry to say that many police, without realizing they carry such authority, do pass on rumors. The average police officer does not stop to weigh what he or she says." That statement could probably be made about many other types of criminal justice employees. Given the delicate nature of their work, they must all guard against being indiscreet with the information they possess.

The 24-hour shift configuration found in criminal justice work exacerbates the "grapevine." While on routine patrol, police officers witness many illegal or immoral acts for which citizens would gladly pay the officers for silence. Thus, police officers are often involved in issues that relate to speech-related activities. Criminal justice personnel can also become chronic complainers. Normally, passive grumbling is not unhealthy, but it can take a serious turn when a grapevine is running rampant, incomplete or inaccurate information is being disseminated, or when personnel go public to air their views.

Many criminal justice executives have attempted to harness what their employees say to the public; executives develop and rely on policies and procedures designed to govern employee speech. On occasion those restrictions are challenged; a number of court decisions have attempted to define the limits of criminal justice employees' exercise of free speech.

Although the right of freedom of speech is one of the most fundamental of all rights of Americans, the Supreme Court has indicated that "the State has interests as an employer in regulating the speech of its employees that differ significantly from those it possesses in connection with regulation of the speech of the citizenry in general."[53] Thus, the state may impose restrictions on its employees that it could not impose on the citizenry at large. These restrictions must be reasonable, however.[54]

A police regulation may be found to be an unreasonable infringement on the free speech interests of officers in two basic situations.[55] The first occurs when the action is overly broad. A Chicago Police Department rule prohibiting "any activity, conversation, deliberation, or discussion which is derogatory to the Department" is a good example; it obviously prohibits all criticism of the agency by its officers, even in private conversation.[56] The New Orleans Police Department had a regulation that prohibited statements by a police officer that "unjustly criticize or ridicule, or express hatred or contempt toward, or . . . which may be detrimental to, or cast suspicion on the reputation of, or otherwise defame, any person."[57] The regulation was revised and later ruled constitutional.[58]

The second situation in which free speech limitations may be found to be unreasonable is in the way in which the governmental action is applied. Specifically, a police department may be unable to demonstrate that the statements by an officer being disciplined actually adversely affected the department's operation. For example, a Baltimore regulation prohibiting public criticism of police department action was held to have been unconstitutionally applied to a police officer who was president of the police union and had stated in a televised interview that the police commissioner was not leading the department effectively[59] and that "the bottom is going to fall out of this city."[60]

Government agencies may restrict the political behavior of their employees. The rationale is that without such restrictions, employees could be pressured under threat of loss of employment or other adverse action by their superiors to support certain political candidates or engage in political activities. At the federal level, various types of political activity by federal employees are controlled by the Hatch Act; its constitutionality has been upheld by the U.S. Supreme Court.[61] Many states have similar statutes, often referred to as *little Hatch Acts*.

Although it may appear that Supreme Court decisions have laid to rest all controversy as to the political behavior of government employees, that has not been the case. In two cases lower courts opted to limit the authority of the state to restrict political activities of their employees. In Pawtucket, Rhode Island, two firefighters ran for public office (mayor and city council member) despite a city charter provision prohibiting all political activity by employees (except voting and privately expressing their opinions). The Rhode Island Supreme Court issued an injunction against enforcing the charter provision on the ground that it applied only to *partisan* political activities.[62] In a similar case in Boston, however, the Massachusetts Supreme Court upheld the police department rule on the basis that whether the partisan-nonpartisan distinction was crucial was a matter for legislative or administrative determination.[63]

A Michigan court declared unconstitutional as being too broad two city charter provisions that prohibited contributions to or solicitations for any political purpose by city employees.[64] Clearly, although the Supreme Court seems to support governmental attempts to limit the political activities of their employees, lower courts seem just as intent to limit the Supreme Court decisions to the facts of those cases.

May a police officer be disciplined, even discharged, because of his or her political affiliations? The Supreme Court ruled on that question in a case involving the Sheriff's Department in Cook County, Illinois.[65] The newly elected sheriff, a Democrat, fired the chief deputy of the process division and a bailiff of the juvenile court, both of whom were nonmerit employees, because they were Republican. The Court ruled that these employees' discharge from nonpolicymaking positions solely on the basis of their political party affiliation was a violation of their First Amendment rights.[66]

Nonpolitical associations are also protected by the First Amendment; however, it is common for police departments to prohibit officers from associating with known felons or others of bad reputation on the ground that "such associations may expose an officer to irresistible temptations to yield in his obligation to impartially enforce the law, and . . . may give the appearance that the police are not themselves honest and impartial enforcers of the law."[67]

Rules against association, as with other First Amendment rights, must not be too broad. A Detroit Police Department regulation prohibiting knowing and associating with known criminals or persons charged with crimes, except in connection with regular duties, was declared unconstitutional; the court held that it prohibited some associations that had no bearing on the officers' integrity or public confidence in the officer (e.g., an association with a fellow church member who had been arrested on one occasion years before and the befriending of a recently convicted person who wanted to become a productive citizen).[68]

Criminal justice employees cannot be disciplined for improper association if it cannot be demonstrated that the association had a detrimental affect on the employee or the agency. For example, a Maryland court held that a fully qualified police officer who was a practicing nudist could not be fired simply on that basis.[69] On the other hand, the Arizona Supreme Court upheld the discharge of an officer who had had sexual intercourse at a party with a woman he knew to be a nude model at a local "adult theater of known disrepute."[70]

Although the First Amendment's protection includes means of expression other than verbal utterances, regulations may restrict this freedom. For example, the Supreme Court upheld the constitutionality of a regulation of the Suffolk County, New York, Police Department that established several grooming standards (regarding hair, sideburn, and moustache length) for its male officers.[71] In *Kelley v. Johnson,* the court found that to make officers readily recognizable to the public and to maintain the esprit de corps within the department, the agency justified the regulations and did not violate any right guaranteed by the Fourteenth Amendment.

✧ SEARCHES AND SEIZURES

The Fourth Amendment to the U.S. Constitution protects "the right of the people to be secure in their persons, houses, papers, and effects, against unreasonable searches and seizures." In an important case in 1967, the Supreme Court held that the amendment also protected individuals' reasonable expectations of privacy in addition to property interests.[72]

The Fourth Amendment usually applies equally to police officers at home or off duty in the same manner as it applies to all citizens. Because of the nature of their work, however, police officers can be compelled to cooperate with investigations of their behavior when ordinary citizens would not. Regarding the equipment and lockers provided them by the department, officers have no expectation of privacy.[73] Lower courts have established limitations on searches of employees themselves, however. The issue of the rights of prison authorities to search their employees was decided in a 1985 Iowa case in which employees were forced to sign a search consent form as a condition of hire; the court disagreed with such a broad policy, ruling that the consent form did not constitute a blanket waiver of all Fourth Amendment rights.[74]

A police officer may be forced to appear in a lineup, a clear "seizure" of his or her person. Normally this requires probable cause, but a federal appeals court upheld a police commissioner's order that 62 officers appear in a lineup during an investigation of police brutality, holding that "the governmental interest in the particular intrusion [should be weighed] against the offense to personal dignity and integrity." The court cited the nature of the work, noting that police officers do "not have the full privacy and liberty from police officials that [they] would otherwise enjoy."[75]

✦ SELF-INCRIMINATION

The Supreme Court has addressed questions concerning the Fifth Amendment as it applies to police officers who are under investigation. *Garrity v. New Jersey*[76] involved a police officer who was ordered by the attorney general to answer questions or be discharged. The officer testified that information obtained as a result of his answers were later used to convict him of criminal charges. The Supreme Court held that the information obtained from the officer could not be used against him at his criminal trial because the Fifth Amendment forbids the use of coerced confessions.

Gardner v. Broderick[77] involved a police officer who had refused to answer questions asked by a grand jury investigating police misconduct because he believed that his answers might tend to incriminate him. The officer was terminated from his position as a result. The Supreme Court ruled that the officer could not be fired for his refusal to waive his constitutional right to remain silent. The Court added, however, that the grand jury could have forced the officer to answer or be terminated for his refusal provided that the officer was informed that his answers would not be used against him later in a criminal case.

Although some difference of opinion exists among lower courts on the question of whether an officer may be compelled to submit to a polygraph examination, the majority of courts that have considered the question have held that an officer can be required to take the examination.[78]

✦ RELIGIOUS PRACTICES

Criminal justice work often requires personnel to be available and on duty 24 hours per day, 7 days a week. Although it is not always convenient or pleasant, such shift configurations require that many criminal justice employees work weekends, nights, and holidays. The nature of such work also generally requires the employee to abide by other conditions (i.e., police officers carry a weapon).

On occasion, one's religious beliefs are in direct conflict with the requirements of the job. For example, one's work assignments may conflict with his or her ability to attend religious services or practice religious beliefs. In these situations, employees may be forced to choose between their work and their religion. (The author is acquainted with a midwestern state trooper who experienced a job-religion conflict; his religion banned the carrying or use of firearms. He chose to give up his weapon and, thus, his job.) A number of people have chosen to bring suit concerning the work-religion conflict rather than cave in to agency work demands.

Title VII of the Civil Rights Act of 1964, discussed earlier, prohibits religious discrimination in employment. It defines religion as including "all aspects of religious . . . practice, as well as belief, unless an employer . . . is unable to reasonably accommodate an employee's . . . religious . . . practice without undue hardship on the conduct of the employer's business."[79] Thus, Title VII requires reasonable accommodation of religious beliefs but not to the extent that the employee has complete freedom of religious expression.[80] For example, an Albuquerque firefighter was a Seventh Day Adventist and refused to work Friday or Saturday nights because he honored the Sabbath. He refused to trade shifts or take leave with or without pay, even though existing policy permitted him to do so, saying the *department* should make such arrangements to cover his shifts or simply excuse him from them. The department refused to do either and discharged him. In upholding the firing, the court ruled that the department's accommodations were reasonable and that no further accommodation could be made without causing it an undue hardship. The court emphasized, however, that future decisions would depend on the facts of the individual case.[81]

A court also has held that the termination of a Mormon police officer for practicing polygamy (plural marriage) in violation of state law was not a violation of his right to freely exercise his religious beliefs.[82]

✦ SEXUAL MISCONDUCT

To be blunt, criminal justice employees have ample opportunity to become engaged in sexual affairs, incidents, trysts, dalliances, or other behavior. History (and news accounts) have shown that wearing a uniform, occupying a high or extremely sensitive position, or being sworn to maintain an unblemished and unsullied lifestyle does not mean that all people will do so all of the time. Some people are not bashful about their intentions. Several officers have told the author they aspired to police work because they assumed that wearing a uniform made them sexually irresistible. A number of police "groupies" do in fact chase police officers and others in uniform.

Instances of sexual impropriety in criminal justice work can range from casual flirting while on the job to becoming romantically involved with a foreign agent whose principal aim is to learn delicate matters of national security. All manner of incidents have occurred between those extremes, including female police officers who posed nude for magazines.

Clearly, sexual behavior is a delicate area in which discipline can be and has been meted out as police managers attempt to maintain high standards of officer conduct. It has also resulted in litigation; some officers believe that such discipline violates their right to privacy.

Instances for which police officers may be disciplined for impropriety involving sexual conduct are generally cases involving adultery and homosexuality. Most court decisions of the 1960s and 1970s agreed that adultery, even when involving an off-duty police officer in private, could result in disciplinary action[83]

Copyright © United Features Syndicate, Inc. Reprinted by permission.

because such behavior brought debilitating criticism on the agency and under-mined public confidence in the police. The views of the courts in this area seem, however, to be moderating with the times. A case involving an Internal Revenue Service agent successfully argued that to uphold disciplinary action for adultery, the government would have to prove that the employing agency was actually discredited.[84] The U.S. Supreme Court appeared to be divided on the issue of ex-tramarital sexual activity by those in public service, however. In 1984 the Sixth Circuit held that a Michigan police officer could not be fired simply because he was living with a woman to whom he was not married (a felony under Michi-gan law).[85]

The issue of homosexual activity as grounds for termination of public em-ployees was decided in an Oklahoma case in which a state law permitted school-teachers to be discharged for engaging in "public homosexual activity."[86] A lower court held the law to be unconstitutionally restrictive, and the Supreme Court agreed.[87] Another federal court held that the firing of a bisexual guidance coun-selor did not deprive the counselor of her First or Fourteenth Amendment rights. The counselor's discussion of her sexual preferences with teachers was not pro-tected by the First Amendment.[88]

✦ RESIDENCY REQUIREMENTS

Many government agencies specify that all or certain members in their employ must live within the geographical limits of their jurisdiction. In other words, em-ployees must reside within the county or city in which they are employed. Such residency requirements have been justified by employing agencies, particularly in criminal justice, on the grounds that employees should become familiar with and visible in the jurisdiction of employment and that they should reside where they are paid by the taxpayers. Perhaps the strongest rationale given by employing agencies is that criminal justice employees must live within a certain proximity of their work in order to respond quickly in the event of an emergency.

Before 1976 numerous challenges were made to residency requirements, even after the Michigan Supreme Court ruled that Detroit's residency requirement for police officers was not irrational.[89] In 1976, when the U.S. Supreme Court held that Philadelphia's requirement that firefighters live in the city did not violate the Constitution, the challenges subsided. Cases now seem to revolve around the question of what constitutes residency. Generally, a police officer must demonstrate that he or she spends a substantial amount of time at a residence in the employing jurisdiction.[90] Strong arguments have been made, however, that in areas where housing is unavailable or is exceptionally expensive, a residency requirement is unreasonable.[91]

✦ MOONLIGHTING

Courts have traditionally supported criminal justice agencies' limitations on the amount and types of outside jobs their employees can take.[92] For example, police department restrictions on moonlighting range from a complete ban on outside employment to permission to engage in certain forms of work, such as investments, private security, and teaching police science courses. The rationale for agency limitations is that "outside employment seriously interferes with keeping the [police and fire] departments fit and ready for action at all times."[93]

In a Louisiana case, however, firefighters successfully provided evidence that moonlighting had been a common practice for 16 years before the city banned it, had never caused firefighters to need sick leave as a result of injuries sustained while moonlighting, had never resulted in a problem with locating off-duty firefighters to respond to an emergency, and had never caused a level of fatigue that was serious enough to impair a firefighter's work. With this evidence, the court invalidated the city ordinance prohibiting moonlighting.[94]

✦ MISUSE OF FIREARMS

Because of the need to defend themselves or others and be prepared for any exigency, police officers are empowered to use firearms when justified. Although officers are restricted in their use of force as a result of the Supreme Court's 1985 decision in *Tennessee v. Garner*[95] (deeming the killing of unarmed, nondangerous suspects as unconstitutional), the possession of and familiarity with firearms remain central requirements in the performance of their duties. Some officers take this responsibility to the extreme, however, and become overly reliant on and consumed with their firepower.

Thus, police agencies typically attempt to restrain the use of firearms through written policies and frequent "Shoot/Don't Shoot" programs. Still, a broad range of potential and actual problems remain with respect to the use and possible misuse of firearms.

As mentioned, in response to the extremely serious potential and actual problems involving misuse of firearms and the omnipresent specter of liability suits, police agencies' policies generally regulate their officers' use of handguns and other firearms, both on and off duty. The courts have held that such regulations need only be reasonable and that the burden rests with the disciplined police officer to show that the regulation was arbitrary and unreasonable.[96] The courts also grant considerable latitude to administrators in determining when their firearms regulations have been violated.[97] Police firearms regulations tend to address three basic issues: (1) requirements for the safeguarding of the weapon, (2) guidelines for carrying the weapon while off duty, and (3) limitations on when the weapon may be fired.[98]

Courts and juries are increasingly becoming more harsh in dealing with police officers who misuse their firearms. The current tendency is to investigate police shootings to determine whether the officer acted negligently or the employing agency negligently trained and supervised him or her. In one case, a federal appeals court awarded a $500,000 judgment against the District of Columbia when a police officer who was not in adequate physical shape shot a man in the course of an arrest. The court noted that the officer had received no fitness training in four years and was physically incapable of subduing the victim; the court found that had the officer been physically fit and adequately trained in disarmament techniques, the use of the gun would not have been necessary. In his condition, however, the officer posed a "foreseeable risk of harm to others."[99]

Courts have found against police officers and/or their employers for other acts involving misuse of firearms, such as when an off-duty officer shot a person while intoxicated in a bar;[100] as noted earlier, an officer accidentally killed an arrestee with a shotgun while handcuffing him;[101] an unstable officer shot his wife five times and then committed suicide with an off-duty weapon the department required him to carry;[102] and, as previously mentioned, an officer accidentally shot and killed an innocent bystander while pursuing another man at nighttime (the officer had had no instruction on shooting at a moving target, night shooting, or shooting in residential areas).[103]

✦ ALCOHOL AND DRUGS IN THE WORKPLACE

Alcoholism and drug abuse problems have taken on a life of their own in contemporary criminal justice; employees must be increasingly wary of becoming involved with alcohol and drugs, and administrative personnel must be able to recognize symptoms of their abuse and attempt to counsel and treat them.

Indeed, in the aftermath of the November 1992 beating death of Malice Green by a group of Detroit police officers, it was reported that the Detroit Police Department had "high alcoholism rates and pervasive psychological problems connected with the stress of policing a city mired in poverty, drugs, and crime."[104] It was also revealed that although the Detroit Police Department had paid $850,000 to two drug-testing facilities, it did not provide counseling programs that many other cities offered their officers. A psychologist asserted that "there are many, many potential time bombs in that department."[105]

Obviously, given the nature of their work, criminal justice employees must not be walking time bombs but must be able to perform their work with clear heads, unbefuddled by alcohol or drugs.[106] Police departments and prisons often specify in their manuals of policy and procedures that no alcoholic beverages can be consumed within a specified period prior to reporting for duty.

Such regulations have been upheld uniformly as rational because of the hazards of the work. A Louisiana court went further, upholding a regulation that prohibited police officers from consuming alcoholic beverages on or off duty to the extent that it caused the officer's behavior to become obnoxious, disruptive, or disorderly.[107] Enforcing such regulations occasionally results in criminal justice employees to be ordered to submit to drug or alcohol tests.

Drug Testing. The courts have had several occasions to review criminal justice agency policies requiring employees to submit to urinalysis to determine the presence of drugs or alcohol in their system. The courts held as early as 1969 that a firefighter could be ordered to submit to a blood test when the agency had reasonable grounds to believe he was intoxicated and that it was appropriate for the firefighter to be terminated from employment if he refused to submit to the test.[108]

In March 1989, the U.S. Supreme Court issued two major decisions on drug testing of public employees. *Skinner v. Railway Labor Executives Association*[109] and *National Treasury Employees Union v. Von Raab*[110] dealt with drug testing plans for railroad and U.S. Customs workers, respectively. Under the Fourth Amendment, government workers are protected from unreasonable search and seizure, including how drug testing can be conducted. The Fifth Amendment protects federal, state, and local workers from illegal governmental conduct.

In 1983, the Federal Railway Administration promulgated regulations that required railroads to conduct urine and blood tests on their workers following major train accidents or incidents. The regulations were challenged, one theory arguing that because railroads were privately owned, the Fourth Amendment protection could not legally be applied. The Supreme Court disagreed in *Skinner,* ruling that railroads must be viewed as an instrument or agent of the government.

Three of the most controversial drug testing issues have been whether testing should be permitted when no drug problem has been indicated in the workplace, whether the testing methods are reliable, and whether a positive test proves on-the-job impairment.[111] The *Von Raab* case addressed all three issues. The U.S. Customs Service had implemented a drug screening program that required urinalysis for employees who desired a transfer or promotion to positions that were directly involved in drug interdiction, were required to carry a firearm, and handled classified material. Only five of 3,600 employees tested positive. The Treasury Employees Union argued that such an insignificant number of positives created a "suspicionless search" argument; in other words, drug testing was unnecessary and unwarranted. The Supreme Court disagreed, ruling that although only a few employees tested positive, drug use is such a serious problem that the program could continue.

In addition, the Court found nothing wrong with the testing protocol, which used an independent contractor; succinctly, the worker, after discarding outer garments, produced a urine specimen while being observed by a member of the same sex; the sample was signed by the employee, labeled, placed in a plastic bag, sealed, and delivered to a lab for testing. The Court found there was no grave potential for arbitrary and oppressive interference with the privacy and personal security of the individuals in this method.

Proving the connection between drug testing and on-the-job impairment has been an ongoing issue. Urinalysis, for example, cannot prove when a person who tests positive actually used the drug. Therefore, tests may punish and stigmatize a person for extracurricular drug usage that may have no effect on his or her on-the-job performance.[112] In *Von Raab,* the Court indicated that this dilemma is still no impediment to testing. It stated that the Customs Service had a compelling interest in having a "physically fit" employee with "unimpeachable integrity and judgment."

Together, these two decisions may set a new standard for determining the reasonableness of drug testing in the criminal justice workplace. They may allow agencies to require testing that might have been considered a risky policy. *Von Raab* presented three compelling governmental interests that could be weighed against the employee's privacy expectations: the integrity of the work force, the need for public safety, and the protection of sensitive information. *Skinner* stated that railroad workers had diminished expectations of privacy because they are in an industry that is widely regulated to ensure safety.[113]

◆ THE AMERICANS
WITH DISABILITIES ACT (ADA)

Many monographs and brochures are available concerning the powerful Americans With Disabilities Act (ADA), which was signed into law in 1990. Therefore, we will cover the law only briefly here; however, persons in an administrative capacity are strongly urged to become familiar with the literature to avoid conflicts with ADA mandates; the law has implications for background checks, psychological and medical exams, and agility, drug, and polygraph tests.

Although certain agencies in the federal government, such as the Federal Bureau of Investigation, are exempt from ADA provisions, state and local governments and their agencies are subject to them. Developing written policies and procedures consistent with the ADA and implementing them before a problem arises are critical for administrators.[114]

Title I of the ADA makes it illegal to discriminate against persons with disabilities. The law defines *disability* as a mental or physical impairment that substantially limits a major life activity, such as walking, talking, breathing, sitting, standing, or learning.[115] Therefore, criminal justice agencies may not discriminate against qualified individuals with disabilities. This mandate applies to the agency's recruitment, hiring, and promotion practices. ADA is not an affirmative action law, so persons with disabilities are not entitled to preference in hiring. But the law will cause police agencies throughout the United States to adjust and perhaps even completely overhaul their recruitment and selection procedures.

Employers are to provide reasonable accommodation to disabled persons. Reasonable accommodations—80 percent of which have been found to cost less than $100 to effect[116]—can include modifying existing facilities to make them accessible, restructuring jobs, offering part-time or modified work schedules, acquiring or modifying equipment, and changing policies. Hiring decisions must be made on whether an applicant meets the established prerequisites of the position (for example, experience or education) and is able to perform the essential functions of the job. Under the law, blanket exclusions of individuals with a particular disability (such as diabetes) are, in most cases, prohibited.

The ADA also covers corrections agencies—jails, prisons, and detention facilities; programs offered to inmates must be accessible. For example, if a hearing-impaired inmate wishes to attend Alcoholics Anonymous meetings, the corrections facility must make reasonable accommodation to allow him or her to do so by such means as providing a sign language interpreter or taking notes as needed.[117]

✦ CIVIL LIABILITY IN JUSTICE ADMINISTRATION

Criminal justice work often is performed in a fishbowl; it has become even more so following the Rodney King and similar incidents in Los Angeles in 1991. Compounding this problem is the fact that some police and corrections officers are overzealous in their work; they may, intentionally or not, violate the rights of the citizens whom they are sworn to protect or whom they are to detain. We briefly examine the types of malicious or negligent behaviors and activities that can lead to civil liability and even incarceration for those who work in the justice system; we begin by discussing the major legislative tool that is used by the public to redress such activities: Title 42, United States Code Section 1983.

✧ DEVELOPMENT OF SECTION 1983 LEGISLATION

Following the Civil War, Congress, in reaction to the activities of the Ku Klux Klan, enacted the Ku Klux Klan Act of 1871, later codified as Title 42, United States Code Section 1983. It states that "every person who, under color of any statute, ordinance, regulation, custom, or usage of any State or Territory, subjects, or causes to be subjected, any citizen of the United States or any other person within the jurisdiction thereof to the deprivation of any rights, privileges, or immunities secured by the Constitution and laws, shall be liable to the party injured in an action at law, suit in equity, or other proper proceeding for redress. . . ." This legislation provides civil rights protection to all "persons" protected under the act when a defendant acted "under color of law" (misused power of office) as well as an avenue to the federal courts for relief of alleged civil rights violations.

✧ LIABILITY OF POLICE SUPERVISORS

Section 1983 also allows for a finding of personal liability on the part of police supervisory personnel when it can be proved that they provided officers inadequate or improper training or that they knew, or should have known, of their officers' misconduct but failed to take corrective action.

A case in point was *McClelland v. Facteau*.[118] McClelland was stopped by Officer Facteau for speeding and taken to the city jail; there Facteau did not allow him to make any phone calls, questioned him, but did not advise him of his rights, and beat and injured him in the presence of two city police officers who were from different jurisdictions. McClelland sued, claiming that the two police chiefs were directly responsible for his treatment and injuries due to their failure to train and supervise their subordinates properly. Evidence of prior misbehavior by Facteau was produced. The court ruled that the chiefs could be held liable if they knew of prior misbehavior but did nothing about it.

A related case was *Brandon v. Allen,*[119] in which two teenagers parked in a lovers' lane were approached by off-duty police officer Allen, who showed his police identification and demanded that the male exit from the car. Allen struck the male with his fist, stabbed him with a knife, and then attempted to break into the car where the female was seated. The young male was able to reenter the car and escape. As the two teenagers sped off, Allen fired a shot at them with his revolver, shattering the windshield and injuring the youths to the point that they required plastic surgery. Allen was convicted of criminal charges, and his police chief was also sued under Section 1983. The plaintiffs charged that the chief and others knew of Allen's reputation as a mental case; none of the other police officers wished to ride in a patrol car with him. At least two formal charges of misconduct had been filed previously, yet the chief failed to take any remedial action and to review the disciplinary records of officers when he became chief. The court called this behavior "unjustified inaction," held the police department liable, and allowed the plaintiffs damages. The U.S. Supreme Court upheld this judgment.[120]

Police supervisors also have been found liable for injuries resulting from an official policy or custom of their department. Injuries caused by excessive force used by officers resulting from a chief's verbal or written support of heavy-handed behavior have resulted in such liability.[121]

✦ LIABILITY OF CORRECTIONS PERSONNEL WHEN SUICIDES OCCUR

Corrections workers are often found liable when they do not provide due care for persons in their custody. This responsibility primarily concerns police officers and civilians responsible for inmates in local jails.

When an inmate commits suicide while in custody, police agencies are frequently—and often successfully—sued in state courts for negligence and wrongful death. The standard used by the courts is whether the agency's act or failure to act created an unusual risk to an inmate. Police officers are expected to provide a special duty of care to protect inmates who suffer mental disorders and who are impaired by drugs or alcohol. *Foreseeability,* the reasonable anticipation that injury or damage may occur, occurs when inmates make statements of intent to commit suicide, have a history of mental illness, are in a poor emotional state, or appear to be in a high level of intoxication or drug dependence.[122]

Suicides are not uncommon among jail inmates; each year, between 150 and 300 of them take their own lives.[123] As noted previously, inmate suicide rates are higher in small jails and highest in small jails with low population densities.[124] State courts generally recognize that police officials have a duty of care to persons in their custody.[125] Thus, jail administrators are ultimately responsible for taking reasonable precautions to ensure the health and safety of persons in their custody; they must protect inmates from harm, render medical assistance when necessary, and treat inmates humanely.[126]

Emotionally disturbed arrestees can also create a greater duty for jail personnel. In an Alaskan case, a woman arrested for intoxication had trouble talking, standing, and walking; her blood-alcohol content was 0.26 percent. Two and a half hours after her incarceration, officers found her hanging by her sweater from mesh wiring in the cell. The Alaska Supreme Court said the officers knew she was depressed and that in the past few months one of her sons had been burned to death, another son was stabbed to death, and her mother had died. Thus, the court found that the officers should have anticipated her suicide.[127]

In New Mexico, a 17-year-old boy was arrested for armed robbery; later he told his mother he would kill himself before he would go to prison. He subsequently tried to cut his wrists with an aluminum can top. The assistant chief ordered the officers to keep watch over him, but he was found dead by hanging the following morning. The New Mexico Supreme Court held that the knowledge the officers possessed was an important factor in determining liability and negligence in such cases.[128] A New Jersey case involved the arrest of a young man for intoxication; he was put in a holding cell, but officers failed to remove his leather belt, which he used to take his own life. The court found that the officers' conduct could have been a "substantial" factor in his death.[129]

The behavior of jail personnel *after* a suicide or attempted suicide also may indicate a breach of duty. Officers are expected to give all possible aid to an inmate who is injured or has attempted suicide. Thus, in a case involving officers who found a young inmate slumped in a chair with his belt around his neck and left him in that position instead of trying to revive him or call for medical assistance, the court ruled that this behavior was a causal factor in the boy's death.[130]

✧ OTHER LIABILITIES

Several court decisions have helped to establish the duties and guidelines of jail administrators for their employees concerning the care of their charges. An intoxicated inmate in possession of cigarettes and matches started a fire that resulted in his death; the court stated that "the prisoner may have been voluntarily drunk, but he was not in the cell voluntarily . . . [he] was helpless and the officer knew there was a means of harm on his person." The court concluded the police administration owed a greater duty of care to such an arrestee.[131]

Courts have also found that the design of detention facilities can be a source of negligence. A Detroit holding cell did not permit officers to observe inmates' movements unless they were standing directly in front of the door or electronic monitoring devices were used. A suicide in this cell led the court to hold that these conditions, and the absence of a detoxification cell, were proximate causes and constituted a building defect.[132] In another incident, an intoxicated college student was placed in a holding cell at the university's public safety building. Forty minutes after being placed in the cell, officers found him hanging from an overhead heating device by a noose fashioned from his socks and belt. The court found the university liable for operating a defective building and awarded the plaintiff $650,000.[133]

It is clear that correctional administrators must ensure that their employees understand their legal responsibilities concerning the custodial role of their detainees.

Summary

After providing an overview of related legislation, this chapter examined several areas of criminal justice employee rights including the issues of drug testing, privacy, sexual harassment, hiring and firing, and disciplining. Criminal justice employers' responsibilities and liabilities were also discussed.

Working in the field of justice administration has never been easy. However, the issues facing today's practitioners have probably never been more difficult.

This chapter demonstrated quite clearly that these are litigious times for the justice system; one act of negligence can mean financial disaster for an individual or a supervisor.

Questions for Review

1. What are criminal justice employees' rights in the workplace according to federal statutes?

2. What is the general employee-employer relationship in criminal justice regarding recruitment and hiring and affirmative action?

3. It has been stated that criminal justice employees have a "property interest" in their jobs as well as a right to a safe workplace. What does this mean?

4. What constitutional rights are implicated for criminal justice employees on the job? (In your response, address their rights regarding freedom of speech, searches and seizures, self-incrimination, and religion.)

5. In what regard is a greater standard of proper conduct expected of criminal justice employees? (In your response, include discussions of sexual behavior, residency, moonlighting, use of firearms, and alcohol/drug abuse.)

6. What is the potential for civil liability for criminal justice employees, especially for police and corrections personnel, in the areas of training and in their custodial function?

Notes

1. Robert H. Chaires and Susan A. Lentz, "Criminal Justice Employee Rights: An Overview," *American Journal of Criminal Justice* 13 (April): 259.
2. *Ibid.*
3. *Ibid.*
4. See *United Autoworkers v. Johnson Controls,* 111 S.Ct. 1196 (1991).
5. See Kenneth J. Peak, *Policing America: Methods, Issues, Challenges* (2d ed.) (Upper Saddle River, N.J.: Prentice Hall, 1997), pp. 70–78.
6. Chaires and Lentz, "Criminal Justice Employee Rights: An Overview," p. 260.
7. *U.S. v. Gregory,* 818 F.2d 114 (4th Cir. 1987).
8. *Harris v. Pan American,* 649 F.2d 670 (9th Cir. 1988).
9. Chaires and Lentz, "Criminal Justice Employee Rights: An Overview," p. 267.
10. See Ken Peak, Douglas W. Farenholtz, and George Coxey, "Physical Abilities Testing for Police Officers: A Flexible, Job-Related Approach," *The Police Chief* 59 (January 1992): 52–56.

11. *Shaw v. Nebraska Department of Corrections,* 666 F.Supp. 1330 (N.D. Neb. 1987).

12. *Garrett v. Oskaloosa County,* 734 F.2d 621 (11th Cir. 1984).

13. Chaires and Lentz, "Criminal Justice Employee Rights: An Overview," p. 268.

14. *EEOC v. State Department of Highway Safety,* 660 F.Supp. 1104 (N.D. Fla. 1986).

15. *Johnson v. Mayor and City Council of Baltimore,* 105 S.Ct. 2717 (1985).

16. 460 U.S. 226, 103 S.Ct. 1054, 75 L.Ed.2d 18 (1983).

17. Chaires and Lentz, "Criminal Justice Employee Rights: An Overview," p. 269.

18. Paul J. Spiegelman, "Court-Ordered Hiring Quotas After *Stotts:* A Narrative on the Role of the Moralities of the Web and the Ladder in Employment Discrimination Doctrine," 20 *Harvard Civil Rights Review* 339 (1985).

19. Chaires and Lentz, "Criminal Justice Employee Rights: An Overview," p. 269.

20. *Regents of the University of California v. Bakke,* 98 S.Ct. 2733, 438 U.S. 265, 57 L.Ed.2d (1978).

21. See *Wygant v. Jackson Board of Education,* 106 S.Ct. 1842 (1986).

22. *Ledoux v. District of Columbia,* 820 F.2d 1293 (D.C. Cir. 1987), at 1294.

23. Chaires and Lentz, "Criminal Justice Employee Rights: An Overview," p. 269.

24. *Ibid.*

25. Chaires and Lentz, "Criminal Justice Employee Rights: An Overview," p. 270.

26. See *Parratt v. Taylor,* 451 U.S. 527, 536–37, 101 S.Ct. 1908, 1913–14, 68 L.Ed.2d 420 (1981).

27. *Board of Regents v. Roth,* 408 U.S. at 577, 92 S.Ct. at 2709 (1971).

28. *Cleveland Board of Education v. Loudermill,* 470 U.S. 532, 541 (1985).

29. *McGraw v. City of Huntington Beach,* 882 F.2d 384 (9th Cir. 1989).

30. *Lohorn v. Michael,* 913 F.2d 327 (7th Cir. 1990).

31. *Palmer v. City of Monticello,* 731 F.Supp. 1503 (D. Utah 1990).

32. *Young v. Municipality of Bethel Park,* 646 F. Supp. 539 (W.D.Penn. 1986).

33. *McAdoo v. Lane,* 564 F.Supp. 1215 (D.C.Ill. 1983).

34. *Ibid.,* at 1217.

35. Chaires and Lentz, "Criminal Justice Employee Rights: An Overview," p. 273.

36. *Ibid.*

37. *McNamara v. City of Chicago,* 700 F.Supp. 917 (N.D. Ill. 1988), at 919.

38. *White v. Thomas,* 660 F.2d 680 (5th Cir. 1981).

39. *Yarber v. Indiana State Prison,* 713 F. Supp. 271 (N.D. Ind. 1988).

40. Chaires and Lentz, "Criminal Justice Employee Rights: An Overview," pp. 273–274.

41. Lynn Lund, "The 'Ten Commandments' of Risk Management for Jail Administrators," *Detention Reporter* 4 (June 1991): 4.

42. *National League of Cities v. Usery,* 426 U.S. 833 (1976).

43. 105 S.Ct. 1005 (1985).

44. Charles R. Swanson, Leonard Territo, and Robert W. Taylor, *Police Administration* (3d ed.) (New York: Macmillan, 1993), p. 439.

45. *Jurich v. Mahoning County,* 31 Fair Emp. Prac. 1275 (BNA) (N.D. Ohio 1983).

46. *Eldridge v. Boulchard,* 620 F.Supp. 678 (D.C. Va.).

47. Chaires and Lentz, "Criminal Justice Employee Rights: An Overview," p. 280.

48. *Ibid.*

49. *Collins v. City of Harker Heights,* 112 S.Ct. 1061 (1992).

50. See *Ruge v. City of Bellevue,* 892 F.2d 738 (1989).

51. *Galloway v. State of Louisiana,* 817 F.2d 1154 (5th Cir. 1987).

52. Chaires and Lentz, "Criminal Justice Employee Rights: An Overview," pp. 280–283.

53. *Pickering v. Board of Education,* 391 U.S. 563 (1968), p. 568.

54. *Keyishian v. Board of Regents,* 385 U.S. 589 (1967).

55. Swanson et al., *Police Administration,* p. 419.

56. *Muller v. Conlisk,* 429 F.2d 901 (7th Cir. 1970).

57. *Flynn v. Giarusso,* 321 F.Supp. 1295 (E.D. La. 1971), at p. 1299.

58. *Magri v. Giarusso,* 379 F.Supp. 353 (E.D. La. 1974).

59. Swanson et al., *Police Administration,* p. 419.

60. *Brukiewa v. Police Commissioner of Baltimore,* 263 A.2d 210 (Md. 1970).

61. *United Public Workers v. Mitchell,* 330 U.S. 75 (1947); *U.S. Civil Service Commission v. National Association of Letter Carriers,* 413 U.S. 548 (1973).

62. *Magill v. Lynch,* 400 F.Supp. 84 (R.I. 1975).

63. *Boston Police Patrolmen's Association, Inc. v. City of Boston,* 326 N.E.2d 314 (Mass. 1975).

64. *Phillips v. City of Flint,* 225 N.W.2d 780 (Mich. 1975).

65. *Elrod v. Burns,* 427 U.S. 347 (1976); see also *Ramey v. Harber,* 431 F.Supp 657 (W.D. Va. 1977); and *Branti v. Finkel,* 445 U.S. 507 (1980).

66. *Connick v. Myers,* 461 U.S. 138 (1983); *Jones v. Dodson,* 727 F.2d 1329 (4th Cir. 1984).

67. Swanson et al., *Police Administration,* p. 421.

68. *Sponick v. City of Detroit Police Department,* 211 N.W.2d 674 (Mich. 1973), p. 681; but see also *Wilson v. Taylor,* 733 F.2d 1539 (11th Cir. 1984).

69. *Bruns v. Pomerleau,* 319 F.Supp. 58 (D. Md. 1970); see also *McMullen v. Carson,* 754 F.2d 936 (11th Cir. 1985), in which the court held that a Ku Klux klansman could not be fired from his position as a records clerk in the sheriff's department simply because he was a klansman. But the circuit court upheld the dismissal, however, because his active KKK participation threatened to negatively affect the agency's ability to perform its public duties.

70. *Civil Service Commission of Tucson v. Livingston,* 525 P.2d 949 (Ariz. 1974).

71. 425 U.S. 238 (1976).

72. *Katz v. United States,* 389 U.S. 347 (1967).

73. See *People v. Tidwell,* 266 N.E.2d 787 (Ill. 1971).

74. *McDonell v. Hunter,* 611 F.Supp. 1122 (S.D. Iowa 1985), affd. as mod., 809 F.2d 1302 (8th Cir. 1987).

75. *Biehunik v. Felicetta,* 441 F.2d 228 (1971), p. 230.

76. 385 U.S. 483 (1967).

77. 392 U.S. 273 (1968).

78. See *Gabrilowitz v. Newman,* 582 F.2d 100 (1st Cir. 1978). Cases upholding the department's authority to order a polygraph examination for police officers include *Eshelman v. Blubaum,* 560 P.2d 1283 (Ariz. 1977); *Dolan v. Kelly,* 348 N.Y.S.2d 478 (1973); *Richardson v. City of Pasadena,* 500 S.W.2d 175 (Tex. 1973); *Seattle Police Officer's Guild v. City of Seattle,* 494 P.2d 485 (Wash. 1972); *Roux v. New Orleans Police Department,* 223 So.2d 905 (La. 1969); and *Farmer v. City of Fort Lauderdale,* 427 So.2d 187 (Fla. 1983), *cert. den.,* 104 S.Ct. 74 (1984).

79. 42 U.S.C. 200e(j).

80. *United States v. City of Albuquerque,* 12 EPD 11, 244 (10th Cir. 1976); see also *Trans World Airlines v. Hardison,* 97 S.Ct. 2264 (1977).

81. *United States v. Albuquerque,* 545 F.2d 110 (10th Cir. 1977).

82. *Potter v. Murray City,* 760 F.2d 1065 (10th Cir. 1985).

83. *Faust v. Police Civil Service Commission,* 347 A.2d 765 (Pa. 1975); *Stewart v. Leary,* 293 N.Y.S.2d 573 (1968); *Brewer v. City of Ashland,* 86 S.W.2d 669 (Ky. 1935); *Fabio v. Civil Service Commission of Philadelphia,* 373 A.2d 751 (Pa. 1977).

84. *Major v. Hampton,* 413 F.Supp. 66 (1976).

85. *Briggs v. City of North Muskegon Police Department,* 563 F.Supp. 585 (6th Cir. 1984).

86. *National Gay Task Force v. Board of Education of Oklahoma City,* 729 F.2d 1270 (10th Cir. 1984).

87. *Board of Education v. National Gay Task Force,* 53 U.S.L.W. 4408, No. 83-2030 (1985).

88. *Rowland v. Mad River Sch. Dist.,* 730 F.2d 444 (6th Cir. 1984).

89. *Detroit Police Officers Association v. City of Detroit,* 190 N.W.2d 97 (1971), appeal denied, 405 U.S. 950 (1972).

90. *Miller v. Police Board of City of Chicago,* 349 N.E.2d 544 (Ill. 1976); *Williamson v. Village of Baskin,* 339 So.2d 474 (La. 1976); *Nigro v. Board of Trustees of Alden,* 395 N.Y.S.2d 544 (1977).

91. *State, County, and Municipal Employees Local 339 v. City of Highland Park,* 108 N.W.2d 898 (1961).

92. See, for example, *Cox v. McNamara,* 493 P.2d 54 (Ore. 1972); *Brenckle v. Township of Shaler,* 281 A.2d 920 (Pa. 1972); *Hopwood v. City of Paducah,* 424 S.W.2d 134 (Ky. 1968); *Flood v. Kennedy,* 239 N.Y.S.2d 665 (1963).

93. Richard N. Williams, *Legal Aspects of Discipline by Police Administrators,* Traffic Institute Publication 2705 (Evanston, Ill.: Northwestern University, 1975), p. 4.

94. *City of Crowley Firemen v. City of Crowley,* 264 So.2d 368 (La. 1972).

95. 471 U.S. 1, 105 S.Ct. 1694, 85 L.Ed.2d 1 (1985).

96. See *Lally v. Department of Police,* 306 So.2d 65 (La. 1974).

97. See, for example, *Peters v. Civil Service Commission of Tucson,* 539 P.2d 698 (Ariz. 1977); *Abeyta v. Town of Taos,* 499 F.2d 323 (10th Cir. 1974); *Baumgartner v. Leary,* 311 N.Y.S.2d 468 (1970); *City of Vancouver v. Jarvis,* 455 P.2d 591 (Wash. 1969).

98. Swanson et al., *Police Administration,* p. 433.

99. *Parker v. District of Columbia,* 850 F2d 708 (1988), at 713, 714.

100. *Marusa v. District of Columbia,* 484 F.2d 828 (1973).

101. *Sager v. City of Woodlawn Park,* 543 F.Supp. 282 (D.Colo. 1982).

102. *Bonsignore v. City of New York,* 521 F.Supp. 394 (1981).

103. *Popow v. City of Margate,* 476 F.Supp. 1237 (1979).

104. Eloise Salholz and Frank Washington, "Detroit's Brutal Lessons," *Newsweek* (November 30, 1992): 45.

105. *Ibid.*

106. See *Krolick v. Lowery,* 302 N.Y.S.2d 109 (1969), p. 115; *Hester v. Milledgeville,* 598 F.Supp. 1456, 1457 (M.D.Ga. 1984).

107. *McCracken v. Department of Police,* 337 So.2d 595 (La. 1976).

108. *Krolick v. Lowery,* op. cit.

109. 489 U.S. 602 (1989).

110. 489 U.S. 656 (1989).

111. Robert J. Aalberts and Harvey W. Rubin, "Court's Rulings on Testing Crack Down on Drug Abuse," *Risk Management* 38 (March 1991): 36–41.

112. *Ibid.,* p. 38.

113. *Ibid.,* p. 40.

114. Paula N. Rubin and Susan W. McCampbell, "The Americans With Disabilities Act and Criminal Justice: Providing Inmate Services," U.S. Department of Justice, National Institute of Justice Research in Action (July 1994): 2.

115. Paula N. Rubin, "The Americans With Disabilities Act and Criminal Justice: An Overview," U.S. Department of Justice, National Institute of Justice Research in Action (September 1993): 1.

116. U.S. Department of Justice, *National Institute of Justice Journal,* Research in Action, "Health and Criminal Justice: Strengthening the Relationship" (November 1994): 40.

117. *Ibid.,* p. 41.

118. 610 F.2d 693 (10th Cir., 1979).

119. 516 F.Supp. 1355 (W.D. Tenn., 1981).

120. *Brandon v. Holt,* 469 U.S. 464, 105 S.Ct. 873 (1985).

121. See, for example, *Black v. Stephens,* 662 F.2d 181 (1991).

122. U.S. Department of Justice, Bureau of Justice Statistics Bulletin, *Jail Inmates, 1990* (Washington, D.C.: U.S. Government Printing Office, 1991), p. 4.

123. U.S. Department of Justice, Bureau of Justice Statistics Special Report, *Population Density in Local Jails, 1988* (Washington, D.C.: U.S. Government Printing Office, 1991), p. 9.

124. *Thomas v. Williams,* 124 S.E.2d 409 (Ga. App. 1962).

125. Victor E. Kappeler and Rolando V. delCarmen, "Avoiding Police Liability for Negligent Failure to Prevent Suicide," *The Police Chief* (August 1991): 53–59.

126. *Ibid.,* p. 53.

127. *Kanayurak v. North Slope Borough,* 677 P.2d 892 (Alaska 1984).

128. *City of Belen v. Harrell,* 603 P.2d 711 (N.M. 1979).

129. *Hake v. Manchester Township,* 486 A.2d 836 (N.J. 1985).

130. *Hake v. Manchester Township.*

131. *Thomas v. Williams.*

132. *Davis v. City of Detroit,* 386 N.W.2d 169 (Mich. App. 1986).

133. *Hickey v. Zezulka,* 443 N.W.2d 180 (Mich. App. 1989).

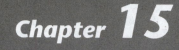

Chapter 15

Financial Administration

How pleasant it is to have money, heigh ho! How pleasant it is to have money.

—Arthur Hugh Clough

Money is like muck, not good except it be spread.

—Francis Bacon

✦ INTRODUCTION

The importance of financial administration to organizations for this country is unquestionable. Budgets are the key to financial administration; their development involves planning, organizing, directing, and other administrative functions. If unlimited funds were available, planning would not be needed. As Frederick Mosher observed, "Not least among the qualifications of an administrator is [one's] ability as a tactician and gladiator in the budget process."[1]

Just as individuals need to be responsible with their personal finances to avoid legal and personal difficulties, so must governmental administrators be responsible stewards of the public's funds. This is an indispensable part of administration.

This chapter presents some of the fundamental elements of the control of fiscal resources through budgeting. It is not intended to prepare the reader to be an expert on fiscal management, but it provides an overview of some of the basic methods and issues surrounding financial administration.

Of the four components of financial administration—budgeting, auditing, accounting, and purchasing—budgeting is our primary focus. Specifically included are discussions of budget definitions and uses; the influence of politics and fiscal realities in budgeting, which often lead to constricted financial conditions for the organization; the several elements of the budget, including formulation, approval, execution, and audit; budget formats; and some strategies for augmenting criminal justice budgets in tight fiscal times.

✦ THE BUDGET

✧ A WORKING DEFINITION

The word *budget* is derived from the old French *bougette,* meaning a small leather bag or wallet. Initially, it referred to the leather bag in which the chancellor of the exchequer carried the documents stating the government's needs and resources to the English Parliament.[2] Later, it came to mean the documents themselves. More recently, *budget* has been defined as a plan stated in financial terms, an estimate of future expenditures, an asking price, a policy statement, the translation of financial resources into human purposes, and a contract between those who appropriate the funds and those who spend them.[3] To some extent, all of these definitions are accurate.

In addition, the budget is a management tool, a process, and a political instrument. It is a "comprehensive plan, expressed in financial terms, by which a program is operated for a given period." It includes (1) the services, activities, and projects composing the program; (2) the resultant expenditure requirements; and (3) the resources usable for their support.[4] It is "a plan or schedule adjusting expenses during a certain period to the estimated income for that period."[5] Lester Bittel added that

> a budget is, literally, a financial standard for a particular operation, activity, program, or department. Its data is presented in numerical form, mainly in dollars . . . to be spent for a particular purpose—over a specified period of time. Budgets are derived from planning goals and forecasts.[6]

Although these descriptions are certainly apt, one writer warns that budgets contain an inherently irrational process: "Budgets are based on little more than the past and some guesses."[7]

Financial management of governmental agencies is clearly political. Anything the government does entails the expenditure of public funds.[8] Thus, the single most important political statement that any government unit makes in a given year is its budget. Essentially, the budget causes administrators to follow the gambler's adage and "put your money where your mouth is."[9] When demands on government increase while funds are stable or decline, the competition for funds is keener than usual, forcing justice agencies to make a strong case for their budgets. The heads of all departments, if they are doing their jobs well, are also vying for appropriations. Special interest groups, the media, politicians, and the public, with their own views and priorities, often engage in arm twisting for funds during the budgeting process.

✦ ELEMENTS OF A BUDGET

✧ THE BUDGET CYCLE

Administrators must think in terms of a budget cycle, which in government (and, therefore, all public criminal justice agencies) is typically on a fiscal year basis. Some states have a biennial budget cycle; their legislatures, such as those in Kentucky and Nevada, budget for a two-year period. Normally, however, the fiscal year is a 12-month period that may coincide with a calendar year or, more commonly, runs from July 1 through June 30 of the following year. The federal government's fiscal year, however, is October 1 through September 30. Obviously, the budget cycle is important because it drives the development of the budget and determines when new monies become available.

The budget cycle consists of four sequential stages, repeated every year at about the same point in time: (1) budget formulation, (2) budget approval, (3) budget execution, and (4) budget audit.

Budget Formulation. Depending on the size and complexity of an organization and the financial condition of its jurisdiction, budget formulation can be a relatively simple or an exceedingly difficult task; it is by far the most complicated stage of the budgeting process. The administrator must anticipate all types of costs—overtime, gasoline, postage, and maintenance contracts—and predict expenses related to major incidents or events that might occur. Certain assumptions based on the previous year's budget are made while formulating the budget. Those assumptions are not necessarily accurate, however. One observer noted that "every expense you budget should be fully supported with the proper and most logical assumptions you can develop. Avoid simply estimating, which is the least supportable form of budgeting."[10] Another criminal justice administrator, discussing budget formulation, added that

> the most important ingredient for any budgeting process is planning. [Administrators] should approach the budget process from the planning standpoint of "How can I best reconcile the [criminal justice] needs of the community with the ability of my jurisdiction to finance them, and then relate those plans in a convincing manner to my governing body for proper financing and execution of

programs?" After all, as budget review occurs, the document is taken apart and scrutinized piece by piece or line by line. This fragmentation approach contributes significantly to our inability to defend interrelated programs in an overall budget package.[11]

To illustrate, let us assume that a police department budget is being prepared in a city having a manager form of government. Long before a criminal justice agency (or any other unit of local government) begins to prepare its annual budget, the city manager and/or the staff of the city has made revenue forecasts, considered how much (if any) of the current operating budget will be carried over into the next fiscal year, analyzed how the population of the jurisdiction will increase or shift (affecting demands for public services), and examined other priorities for the coming year. The city manager also may appear before the governing board to obtain information about its fiscal priorities, spending levels, pay raises, new positions, programs, and so on. The city manager may then send all department heads a memorandum outlining the general fiscal guidelines to be followed in preparing their budgets.

Upon receipt of the city's guidelines for preparing its budget, the heads of functional areas, such as the chief of police, have a planning and research unit (assuming a city large enough to have this level of specialization) prepare an internal budget calendar and an internal fiscal policy memorandum. Table 15.1 shows an internal budget calendar for a large municipal police department. This memo may include input from unions and lower supervisory personnel. Each bureau is then given the responsibility for preparing its individual budget request.

In small police departments with little or no functional specialization, the chief may prepare the budget alone or with input from other officers or the city finance officer. In some small agencies, chiefs and sheriffs may not even see their budget or assist in its preparation. Because of tradition, politics, or even laziness, some administrators have abdicated control over the budget. This puts the agency in a precarious position indeed; it will have difficulty engaging in long-term planning and spending money productively for personnel and programs when the executive must obtain approval from the governing body to buy items such as office supplies.

The planning and research unit then reviews the bureau's budget requests for compliance with the budgeting instructions and the chief's and city manager's priorities. Eventually, a consolidated budget is developed for the entire police department and submitted to the chief, who may meet with the planning and research unit and bureau commanders to discuss it. Personalities, politics, priorities, personal agendas, and other issues may need to be addressed; the chief may have to mediate disagreements concerning these matters while sometimes rewarding the loyal and reducing allotments to the disloyal.[12] Requests for programs, equipment, travel expenses, personnel, or anything else in the draft budget may be deleted, reduced, or enhanced.

The budget is then presented to the city manager. At this point, the chief executive's reputation as a budget framer becomes a factor. If the chief is known to pad the budget heavily, the city manager is more likely to cut the police

TABLE 15.1   BUDGET PREPARATION CALENDAR FOR A LARGE POLICE DEPARTMENT

What Should Be Done	By Whom	On These Dates
Issue budget instructions and applicable forms	City administrator	November 1
Prepare and issue budget message, with instructions and applicable forms, to unit commanders	Chief of police	November 15
Develop unit budgets with appropriate justification and forward recommended budgets to planning and research unit	Unit commanders	February 1
Review unit budget	Planning and research staff with unit commanders	March 1
Consolidate unit budgets for presentation to chief of police	Planning and research unit	March 15
Review consolidated recommended budget	Chief of police, planning and research staff, and unit commanders	March 30
Obtain department approval of budget	Chief of police	April 15
Forward recommended budget to city administrator	Chief of police	April 20
Review recommended budget by administration	City administrator and chief of police	April 30
Approve revised budget	City administrator	May 5
Forward budget document to city council	City administrator	May 10
Review budget	Budget officer of city council	May 20
Present to council	City administrator and chief of police	June 1
Report back to city administrator	City council	June 5
Review and resubmit to city council	City administrator and chief of police	June 10
Take final action on police budget	City council	June 20

(*Source:* National Advisory Commission on Criminal Justice Standards and Goals, *Police.* Washington, D.C.: U.S. Government Printing Office, 1973, p. 137.)

Steps in Budget Development

Hal Rubin described how the $550 million budget for the California Highway Patrol (CHP) is typically developed. According to the budget section, "It's an all-year and year-on-year process" that begins at the level of the 99 area commands, where budget requests originate. The requests are dealt with in one of three ways: (1) funded within the department's base budget, (2) disapproved, or (3) carried forward for review by CHP personnel.

At the division level, managers review the area requests, make needed adjustments, and submit a consolidated request to the budget section at headquarters. This section passes input from the field to individual section management staff (e.g., planning and analysis, personnel, training, communications) for review. Budget section staff meet with individual section management staff. Within two or three months, the budget section identifies proposals for new funding that have departmentwide impact and passes them on to the executive level.

The commissioner and aides review the figures along with those from other state departments and agree on a budget to submit to the governor. The governor submits this budget to the legislature, which acts on it and returns it to the governor for signature.

Source: Hal Rubin, "Working Out a Budget," *Law and Order* (May 1989): 27–28.

---

department request than if the chief is known to be reasonable in the budget request, engage in innovative planning, and have a flexible approach to budget negotiations.

The city manager consolidates the police budget request with those from other municipal department heads and then meets with them individually to discuss their requests further. The city manager directs the city finance officer to make any necessary additions or cuts and then prepare a budget proposal to present to the governing body.

The courts have a similar budgetary process. For a large court, the process may involve five major procedures: (1) developing an internal budgetary policy, (2) reviewing budget submissions, (3) developing a financial strategy, (4) making a budget presentation, and (5) monitoring the budget. Figure 15.1 illustrates the relationships of the steps in the process.

Budget Approval. With the city manager's proposed budget requests in hand, the governing board begins its deliberations on the citywide budget. The city manager may appear before the board to answer questions concerning the budget; individual department heads also may be asked to appear. Suggestions for getting monies approved and appropriated include the following:

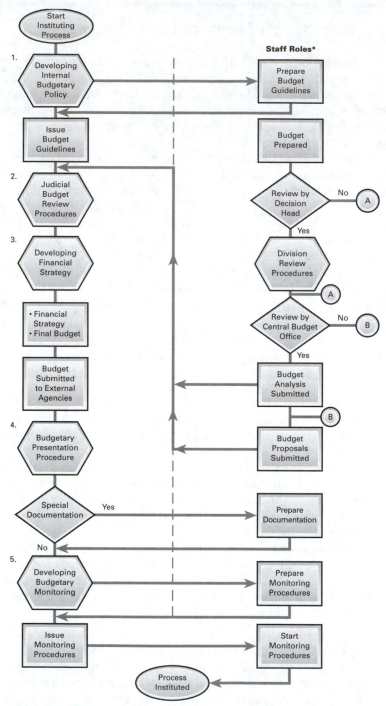

Figure 15.1   Steps in a judicial budgetary process.

* Particularly applicable in a large court, much less so in a small court.

1. Have a carefully justified budget.
2. Anticipate the environment of the budget hearing by reading news reports and understanding the priorities of the council members. Know what types of questions elected officials are likely to ask.
3. Determine which "public" will be at the budget hearing and prepare accordingly. Public issues change from time to time; citizens who were outraged over one issue one year may be incensed by another the next.
4. Make good use of graphics in the form of pie charts and histograms but be selective and do not go overboard. Short case studies of police successes are normal and include graphics.
5. Rehearse and critique the presentation many times.
6. Be a political realist.[13]

After everyone scheduled has spoken, the city council gives directions to the city manager such as to make more cuts in the budget, or to reinstate certain funds or programs cut earlier, and so on. The budget is then approved. It is fair to say that at this stage, budgeting is largely a legislative function that requires some legal action, as a special ordinance or resolution approving the budget is passed each year by the governing board.

The column headings in Table 15.2 indicate (1) the budget amount requested by the chief of police, (2) the amount recommended by the city manager, and (3) the amount finally approved by the city council.

Budget Execution. The third stage of the budget process, execution, has several objectives: (1) to carry out the police department's budgeted objectives for the fiscal year in an orderly manner, (2) to ensure that the department undertakes no financial obligations or commitments other than those funded by the city council, and (3) to provide a periodic accounting of the administrator's stewardship over the department's funds.[14]

Supervision of the budget execution phase is an executive function that requires some type of fiscal control system, usually directed by the city or county manager. Periodic reports on accounts are an important element of budget control; they are designed to reduce the likelihood of overspending by identifying areas in which deficits might occur due to such things as gasoline price increases, extensive overtime, natural disasters, and unplanned emergencies (such as riots). A periodic budget status report informs the administrator of the percentage of the total budget that has been expended to date (see Table 15.3).

Prudent administrators normally attempt to manage the budget conservatively for the first eight or nine months of the budget year, holding the line on spending until most fiscal crises have been averted. Because unplanned incidents and natural disasters can wreak havoc with any budget, this conservatism is normally the best course. Then the administrator can plan how best to allocate funds if emergency funds have not been spent.

TABLE 15.2 POLICE OPERATING BUDGET IN A COMMUNITY OF 150,000 POPULATION

Description	FY1995–96 Expenses	FY1996–97 Expenses	FY1997–98 Dept. Req.	City Manager	City Council
Salaries/wages					
Reg. salaries	$14,315,764	$14,392,639	$16,221,148	$16,221,148	$16,221,148
Overtime	988,165	782,421	951,875	951,875	711,875
Severance pay	36,194	226,465	82,000	–0–	–0–
Holiday pay	395,952	591,158	698,958	698,958	698,958
Call back pay	45,499	49,833	49,555	49,555	49,555
Subtotals	15,781,574	16,042,516	18,003,536	17,921,536	17,681,536
Employee benefits					
Retirement	3,345,566	3,485,888	4,069,521	4,069,521	4,069,521
Group ins.	1,256,663	1,467,406	1,752,718	1,752,718	1,752,718
Life ins.	43,797	53,164	117,590	117,396	117,396
Disability ins.	726,885	794,686	1,346,909	1,346,038	1,024,398
Uniform allowance	188,079	193,827	196,750	196,750	196,750
Medicare	77,730	80,868	100,058	99,739	99,739
Long-Term dis.	11,583	21,974	48,517	48,517	48,517
Subtotals	5,650,303	6,097,813	7,583,546	7,630,679	7,309,039
Services and supplies					
Office supp.	62,357	49,292	51,485	51,485	51,485
Operating supp.	227,563	148,569	270,661	270,661	270,661
Repair/Maint.	248,922	195,941	233,118	233,118	233,118
Small tools	49,508	788	12,175	12,175	12,175
Prof. serv.	337,263	290,359	334,765	334,765	334,765
Communication	287,757	223,200	392,906	392,906	392,906

TABLE 15.2 (continued)

Description	FY1995–96 Expenses	FY1996–97 Expenses	FY1997–98 Dept. Req.	City Manager	City Council
Services and supplies					
Public utility	111,935	116,773	121,008	121,008	121,008
Rentals	81,840	96,294	113,071	113,071	113,071
Vehicle rental	834,416	1,193,926	1,363,278	1,363,278	1,169,278
Extradition	20,955	22,411	20,000	20,000	20,000
Other travel	4,649	5,123	23,500	23,500	23,500
Advertising	2,662	2,570	4,100	4,100	4,100
Insurance	328,360	595,257	942,921	942,921	942,921
Books/manuals	16,285	12,813	12,404	12,404	12,404
Employee training	47,029	30,851	–0–	–0–	–0–
Aircraft exp.	–0–	–0–	15,000	15,000	15,000
Special inv.	11,527	13,465	15,000	15,000	15,000
Other serv. & supplies	1,386,201	1,039,651	1,386,201	1,386,201	1,386,201
Subtotals	4,059,229	4,037,283	5,311,593	5,311,593	5,117,593
Capital outlay					
Machinery and equipment	572,301	102,964	–0–	–0–	–0–
Totals	$26,063,407	$26,280,576	$30,898,675	$30,863,808	$30,108,168

353

TABLE 15.3 A POLICE DEPARTMENT'S BUDGET STATUS REPORT

Line Item	Amount Budgeted	Expenses to Date	Amount Encumbered	Balance to Date	Percentage Used
Salaries	$16,221,148	$8,427,062.00	–0–	$7,794,086.00	52.0
Professional services	334,765	187,219.61	$8,014.22	139,531.17	58.3
Office supplies	51,485	16,942.22	3,476.19	31,066.59	39.7
Repair/maintenance	49,317	20,962.53	1,111.13	27,243.34	44.8
Communication	392,906	212,099.11	1,560.03	179,246.86	54.4
Utilities	121,008	50,006.15	10,952.42	60,049.43	51.4
Vehicle rental	1,169,278	492,616.22	103,066.19	573,595.59	51.9
Travel	23,500	6,119.22	2,044.63	15,336.15	34.7
Extraditions	20,000	12,042.19	262.22	7,695.59	61.5
Printing/Binding	36,765	15,114.14	2,662.67	18,988.19	48.4
Books/Manuals	12,404	5,444.11	614.11	6,345.78	48.8
Training/Education	35,695	19,661.54	119.14	15,914.32	55.4
Aircraft expense	15,000	8,112.15	579.22	6,308.63	57.9
Special investigation	15,000	6,115.75	960.50	7,922.75	47.2
Machinery	1,000	275.27	27.50	697.23	30.3
Advertising	4,100	1,119.17	142.50	2,838.33	30.8

The Audit. The word *audit* means to verify something independently.[15] The basic rationale for the audit has been described by the Comptroller General of the United States as follows:

> Governments and agencies entrusted with public resources and the authority for applying them have a responsibility to render a full accounting of their activities. This accountability is inherent in the governmental process and is not always specifically identified by legislative provision. This governmental accountability should identify not only the object for which the public resources have been devoted but also the manner and effect of their application.[16]

After the close of each budget year, the year's expenditures are audited to ensure that the agency spent its funds properly. Audits are designed to investigate three broad areas of accountability: *financial* (focusing on proper fiscal operations and reports of the justice agency), *management* (determining whether funds were utilized efficiently and economically), and *program* (determining whether the budget agency's goals and objectives were accomplished).[17]

Financial audits determine whether funds were spent legally, the budgeted amount was exceeded, and the financial processes proceeded in a legal manner. For example, auditors investigate whether funds transferred between accounts were authorized, grant funds were used properly, computations were made accurately, disbursements were documented, financial transactions followed established procedures, and established competitive bidding procedures were employed.[18]

Justice administrators should welcome auditors' help to identify any weaknesses and deficiencies and correct them.

✦ BUDGET FORMATS

One type of budget is the operating budget, which usually covers one year. It is for items that have a short life expectancy, are consumed in the normal course of operations, or are reincurred each year. Included in operating budgets are such items as paper, duplicating and telephone expenses, salaries, and fringe benefits.[19] The three types of budgets used primarily are the line-item (or object-of-expenditure) budget, the performance budget, and the program (or results or outcomes) budget. Two additional types, the planning-programming-budgeting system (PPBS) and the zero-based budget (ZBB), are discussed in the literature but are used to a lesser extent.

✧ THE LINE-ITEM BUDGET

The line-item or object budget is the most commonly used budget format. It is the basic system on which all other systems rely because it affords control. It is so named because it breaks the budget into the major categories commonly used in government (e.g., personnel, equipment, contractual services, commodities, and capital outlay items); every amount of money requested, recommended, appropriated, and expended is associated with a particular item or class of items.[20] In addition, large budget categories are broken down into smaller line-item budgets (in a police department, for example, the patrol, investigation, communications, or jail functions). The line-item format fosters budgetary control because no item escapes scrutiny.[21] We show line-items for actual budgets for police (see Table 15.2), court (Table 15.4), probation and parole (Table 15.5), and state prison organizations (Table 15.6), respectively. Each demonstrates the range of the agency's activities and funding needs. Note in Tables 15.2, 15.5, and 15.6 how the recent recession has affected budgets and requests from year to year in a number of categories, resulting in severe cuts and even total elimination of items previously funded. Also note some of the ways in which administrators are attempting to save money (e.g., the police budget indicates that leasing its patrol vehicles rather than buying them is more economical).

The line-item budget has several strengths and weaknesses. Its strengths include ease of control, development, comprehension (especially by elected and other executive branch officials), and administration. Weaknesses are its neglect of long-range planning and its limited ability to evaluate performance. Furthermore, the line-item budget tends to maintain the status quo; ongoing programs are seldom challenged. Line-item budgets are based on history: this year's allocation is based on last year's history. Although that allows an inexperienced manager to prepare a budget more easily, it often precludes the reform chief's careful deliberation and planning for the future.

The line-item budget provides ease of control because it clearly indicates the amount budgeted for each item, the amount expended as of a specific date, and the amount still available at that date. See, for example, Table 15.3.

Virtually all criminal justice agencies are automated to some extent, whether the financial officer prepares the budget using a computerized spreadsheet or a clerk enters information onto a database that will be uploaded to the state's mainframe computer. Some justice agencies use an automated budgeting system (ABS) that can store budget figures, make all necessary calculations for generating a budget request, monitor expenditures from budgets (similar to that shown in Table 15.3), and even generate some reports.

✧ THE PERFORMANCE BUDGET

The key characteristic of a performance budget is that it relates the types of volume of work to be done to the amount of money spent.[22] It is input-output oriented, and it increases the responsibility and accountability of the manager for output as opposed to input.[23] This format specifies an organization's activities, using a format similar to that of the line-item budget. It normally measures activities that are easily quantified, such as issuing traffic citations, solving crimes, recovering property, hearing cases in the courtroom, and monitoring caseloads

TABLE 15.4   OPERATING BUDGET FOR A DISTRICT COURT IN A COUNTY OF 300,000 POPULATION

Categories		Amounts
Salaries and wages		
Regular salaries		$2,180,792
Part-time temporary		9,749
Incentive/Longevity		50,850
	Subtotal:	$2,241,391
Employee benefits		
Group insurance		170,100
Worker comp.		8,470
Unemployment comp.		3,220
Retirement		412,211
Social security		605
Medicare		13,503
	Subtotal:	$608,109
Services and supplies		
Computers and office equipment		22,865
Service contracts		2,000
Minor furniture/Equipment		1,000
Computer supplies		10,000
Continuous forms		4,000
Office supplies		36,066
Advertising		50
Copy machine expense		40,000
Dues and registration		4,000
Printing		24,000
Telephone		16,000
Training		2,000
Court reporter/Transcript		235,000
Court reporter per diem		265,000
Law books/Supplements		9,000
Jury trials		75,000
Medical examinations		80,000
Computerized legal research		20,000
Travel		1,500
	Subtotal:	$847,481

(table continues)

TABLE 15.4 *(continued)*

Categories	Amounts
Child support	
Attorneys and other personnel	$66,480
Court-appointed attorneys	656,000
Grand juries	18,600
Family court services	762,841
TOTAL	$5,200,902

of probation officers. These activities are then compared to these of the unit that performs the most. This ranking according to activity attempts to allocate funds fairly. Using a police department as an example, the commander of the traffic accident investigation unit requests an additional three investigators, which the chief approves. Later the chief might compare the unit's output and costs to these before the three investigators were added to determine how this change affected productivity.[24] An example of the police performance budget is provided in Table 15.7.

The performance budget format could be used in justice system components in addition to the police. For example, the courts could use performance measures such as filing cases, writing opinions, disposing of cases, and investigating presentence motions.

Advantages of the performance budget include a consideration of outputs, the establishment of the costs of various justice agency efforts, improved evaluation of programs and managers, an emphasis on efficiency, increased availability of information for decision making, and the enhancement of budget justification and explanation.[25] The performance budget works best for an assembly line or other organization in which work is easily quantifiable, such as paving streets. Its disadvantages include its expense to develop, implement, and operate because of the extensive use of cost accounting techniques and the need for additional staff (Figure 15.2 [see p. 366] illustrates the elements used to determine the cost of providing a criminal justice service); the controversy surrounding attempts to determine appropriate workload and unit cost measures (in criminal justice, although many functions are quantifiable, such reduction of duties to numbers often translates to quotas, which is anathema to many people); its emphasis on efficiency rather than effectiveness; and the failure to lend itself to long-range planning.[26]

Determining which functions in criminal justice are more important (and should therefore receive more financial support) is difficult. Therefore, in terms of criminal justice agency budgets, the selection of meaningful work units is very difficult and irrational. How can a justice agency measure its successes? How can it count what does not happen?

TABLE 15.5 PROBATION AND PAROLE BUDGET FOR A STATE SERVING
3,000,000 POPULATION

Description	FY1996–97 Actual	FY1997–98 Agency Req.	FY1997–98 Gov. Recomm.	Legis. Approval
Personnel	$13,741,104	$14,290,523	$13,620,991	$13,540,222
Travel	412,588	412,588	412,588	401,689
Operating expenses	1,307,020	1,395,484	1,307,020	1,256,787
Equipment	10,569	4,379	4,379	4,379
Loans to parolees	4,500	4,500	4,500	4,500
Training	9,073	9,073	9,073	9,073
Extraditions	200,000	200,000	200,000	185,000
Client drug tests	112,962	112,962	112,962	112,962
Home arrest fees	114,005	114,005	114,005	114,005
Community programs	50,000	50,000	50,000	47,500
Residential confinement	496,709	500,709	496,709	487,663
Utilities (paid by building lessors)				
Totals	$16,458,530	$17,094,223	$16,332,227	$16,163,780

TABLE 15.6 OPERATING BUDGET FOR A STATE MEDIUM-SECURITY PRISON
WITH 1,000 INMATES

Description	FY1996–97 Actual	FY1997–98 Agency Req.	FY1997–98 Gov. Recomm.	Legislature Approved
Personnel				
Salaries	$5,051,095	$5,370,979	$5,186,421	$5,105,533
Worker's comp.	184,362	143,462	201,198	198,016
Retirement	1,142,010	1,174,968	1,215,674	1,196,028
Recruit tests	49,447	51,528	45,692	44,972
Insurance	474,330	488,250	513,000	500,175
Retirement ins.	30,963	31,872	35,917	35,349
Unemployment comp.	6,003	6,383	6,162	6,065
Overtime	165,856	–0–	–0–	–0–
Holiday pay	150,519	158,500	154,643	151,936
Medicare	39,965	45,140	42,225	40,948
Shift differential	95,925	101,011	98,553	96,828
Standby pay	6,465	6,807	6,641	6,526
Longevity pay	18,095	18,095	18,095	18,095
Subtotals	$7,415,035	$7,596,995	$7,524,221	$7,400,471
Services and supplies				
Operating supplies	$180,672	$277,495	$180,647	$214,859
Communications/freight	4,877	5,314	5,023	5,023
Printing/copying	20,900	47,222	19,016	21,527
Equipment repair	14,385	13,542	14,817	14,817
Vehicle operation	20,405	21,601	21,016	21,016
Uniforms—custody	118,122	105,976	103,237	113,856

Table 15.6 (continued)

Description	FY1996–97 Actual	FY1997–98 Agency Req.	FY1997–98 Gov. Recomm.	Legislature Approved
Inmate clothing	72,436	184,790	72,430	86,167
Equipment issued	20,403	13,236	15,451	17,086
Inmate wages	36,645	52,815	35,572	42,309
Food	895,897	1,299,838	895,759	1,065,403
Postage	7,738	8,793	7,036	7,738
Telephone	24,808	23,802	22,130	24,808
Subscriptions	382	401	725	401
Hand tools	110	286	113	113
Subtotals	$1,417,780	$2,055,111	$1,392,972	$1,635,123
Special equipment	$116,863	$34,088	$12,557	$13,661
Grounds maint.	150,098	209,003	138,560	185,843
Inmate law library	18,564	20,115	16,419	21,836
Special projects	53,237	8,887	8,887	8,887
Gas and power	554,478	586,604	505,823	604,335
Water	60,390	69,377	52,266	67,171
Garbage	80,035	101,240	82,436	82,436
Canine unit	13,936	2,521	4,260	2,543
Grand total	$9,880,416	$10,683,941	$9,738,401	$10,022,306

✧ The Program Budget

The best known budget for monitoring the activities of the organization is the *program budget* developed by the Rand Corporation for the U.S. Department of Defense. This format examines cost units as units of activity rather than as units and subunits within the organization. This budget becomes a planning tool; it demands justification for expenditures for new programs and for deleting current ones that have not met their objectives.

A police agency probably has more opportunities for creating new community-based programs than do the courts or corrections agencies. Some of these include crime prevention and investigation, drug abuse education, home security, selective enforcement (e.g., drunk driving) programs, and career development programs for personnel. Each of these endeavors requires instructional materials or special equipment, all of which must be budgeted. For example, traffic accident investigation (TAI) may be a cost area. The program budget emphasizes output measures; outputs for TAI, for example, include the number of accidents worked and the enforcement measures taken (such as citations issued, arrests for driving under the influence and other offenses, public safety speeches given, and so on). If the budget for these programs were divided by the units of output, the administrator could determine the relative cost for each unit of output or productivity. The cost of TAI, however, entails more than just the TAI unit; patrol and other support units also engage in this program.

Thus, the program budget is an extremely difficult form to execute and administer because it requires tracking time of all personnel by activity as well as figuring in the cost of all support services and supplies. For this reason, criminal justice agencies rarely use the program budget.[27] Examples of police and court program budgets are presented in Tables 15.8 and 15.9. Other disadvantages include its cost in terms of time and money to develop, implement, and administer; developing objectives and performance measures are difficult, data collection may be costly, and agency managers may not have or want to develop the skills necessary to direct large-scale, complex programs.[28]

Some advantages of the program budget include emphasis on the social utility of programs conducted by the agency, its clear relationship between policy objectives and expenditures, its ability to justify and explain the budget, its establishment of a high degree of accountability, and its format and wide involvement in formulating objectives, which lead employees at all levels of the organization to understand more thoroughly the importance of their roles and actions.

✧ PPBS and Zero-Based Budgeting Formats

General Motors used the planning-programming-budgeting system (PPBS) as early as 1924,[29] and the Rand Corporation contributed to its development in a series of studies dating from 1949.[30] By the mid-1950s, several states were using it, and Secretary Robert McNamara introduced PPBS to the Defense Department in the

TABLE 15.7   EXAMPLE OF A POLICE PERFORMANCE BUDGET

Total Budget		$
Units/Activities		
Administration (chief)	Subtotal	$
Strategic planning		$
Normative planning		$
Policies and procedures formulation		$
Etc.		
Patrol	Subtotal	$
Calls for service		$
Citizen contacts		$
Special details		$
Etc.		
Criminal investigation	Subtotal	$
Suspect apprehension		$
Recovery of stolen property		$
Transportation of fugitives		$
Etc.		
Traffic services	Subtotal	$
Accident investigation		$
Issuance of citations		$
Public safety speeches		$
Etc.		
Juvenile services	Subtotal	$
Locate runaways/missing juveniles		$
Arrest of offenders		$
Referrals and liaison		$
Etc.		
Research and development	Subtotal	$
Perform crime analysis		$
Prepare annual budget		$
Prepare annual reports		$
Etc.		

TABLE 15.8 EXAMPLE OF A POLICE PROGRAM BUDGET

Total Budget	$
Program Area	
Crime prevention	
Salaries and benefits	$
Operating expenses	$
Capital outlay	$
Miscellaneous	$
Subtotal	$
Traffic accident investigation	
Salaries and benefits	$
Operating expenses	$
Capital outlay	$
Miscellaneous	$
Subtotal	$
Traffic accident prevention	
Salaries and benefits	$
Operating expenses	$
Capital outlay	$
Miscellaneous	$
Subtotal	$
Criminal investigation	
Salaries and benefits	$
Subtotal	$

TABLE 15.8 *(continued)*

Total Budget	
Operating expenses	$
Capital outlay	$
Miscellaneous	$
Juvenile delinquency prevention	Subtotal $
Salaries and benefits	$
Operating expenses	$
Capital outlay	$
Miscellaneous	$
Special investigations	Subtotal $
Salaries and benefits	$
Operating expenses	$
Capital outlay	$
Miscellaneous	$
Etc.	

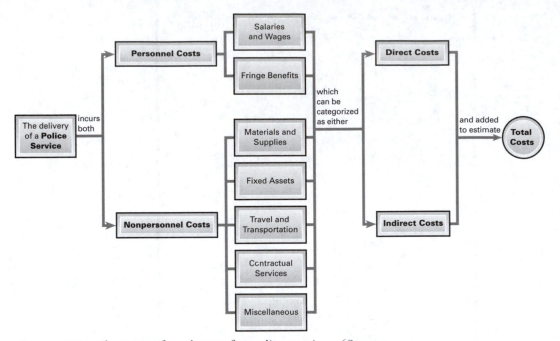

Figure 15.2   Elements of total costs for police services. (*Source:* U.S. Department of Justice, National Institute of Justice, *Measuring the Costs of Police Services.* Washington, D.C.: Author, 1982, p. 20.)

mid-1960s.[31] By 1971, a survey revealed, however, that only 28 percent of the cities and 21 percent of the counties contacted had implemented PPBS or significant elements of it;[32] and in 1971 the federal government announced that it was discontinuing its use.

PPBS treated the three basic budget processes—planning, management, and control—as compatible; they were treated as co-equals. It was predicated on the primacy of planning.[33] This future orientation transformed budgeting from an annual ritual into "formulation of future goals and policies."[34] The PPBS budget featured a program structure, zero-based budgeting, the use of cost-budget analysis to distinguish among alternatives, and a budgetary horizon, often five years.[35]

Associated with PPBS, the zero-based planning and budgeting process requires managers to justify their entire budget request in detail rather than simply to refer to budget amounts established in previous years.[36] That is, each year all budgets begin at zero and must justify any funding. Following Peter Phyrr's use of zero-based budgeting (ZBB) at Texas Instruments, Governor Jimmy Carter adopted it in Georgia in the early 1970s and then as president implemented it in the federal government for fiscal year 1979. An analysis of this experience at the Department of Agriculture indicated that although its use saved $200,000 in the department's budget, it cost at least 180,000 labor-hours to develop it.[37]

TABLE 15.9   EXAMPLE OF A COURT'S PROGRAM BUDGET

Total Budget	$	
Program Area		
Adjudicate criminal cases	Subtotal	$
Adjudicate felony cases	Total	$
Adjudicate misdemeanor appeals	Total	$
Adjudicate civil cases	Subtotal	$
Adjudicate major civil cases	Total	$
Adjudicate minor civil cases	Total	$
Adjudicate domestic relations cases	Total	$
Adjudicate juvenile cases	Subtotal	$
Adjudicate delinquency and dependent and neglect cases	Total	$
Adjudicate crimes against juveniles	Total	$
Provide alternatives to adjudication	Subtotal	$
Divert adult offenders	Total	$
Divert juvenile offenders	Total	$
Provide security	Subtotal	$
Handle prisoner transport	Total	$
Provide courtroom security	Total	$
Etc.		

(*Source:* U.S. Department of Justice, National Institute of Law Enforcement and Criminal Justice, *Financial Management*. Washington, D.C.: The American University, 1979, p. 41.1.)

It is important to note that few organizations have budgets that are purely one format or another; therefore, it is not "bad" or unusual to find that because of time, tradition, and personal preferences, a combination of several is generally used.

✦ POTENTIAL PITFALLS IN BUDGETING

✧ THE NEED FOR BUDGETING FLEXIBILITY

Ancient Greek mythology tells of a highwayman named Procrustes who had an iron bedstead. He measured all who fell into his hands on the bed. If they were too long, their legs were lopped off to fit it. If they were too short, they were stretched to fit the bed. Few criminal justice administrators have not seen their monies and programs laid out on the Procrustesean bed of a state or municipal budget officer and lopped off.

It therefore becomes imperative to build as much flexibility into the planned program and budget as possible. One technique utilized is to make up three budgets: an optimistic one, reflecting the ideal level of service to the jurisdiction and organization; an expected one, giving the most likely level of service that will be funded; and finally, a pessimistic budget plan that will provide a minimum level of service.[38]

To maximize the benefits of using budgets, managers must be able to avoid major pitfalls, which, according to Samuel Certo,[39] include the following:

1. *Placing too much emphasis on relatively insignificant organizational expenses.* In preparing and implementing a budget, managers should allocate more time to deal with significant organizational expenses and less time for relatively insignificant organizational expenses. For example, the amount of time spent on developing and implementing a budget for labor costs typically should be more than the amount of time managers spend on developing and implementing a budget for office supplies.

2. *Increasing budgeted expenses year after year without adequate information.* Perhaps the best-known method developed to overcome this potential pitfall was zero-based budgeting, just discussed.[40]

3. *Ignoring the fact that budgets must be changed periodically.* Administrators must recognize that such factors as costs of materials, newly developed technology, and demand for services are constantly changing and that budgets should reflect that fact by being reviewed and modified periodically in response to those changes. A special type of budget, the performance budget (discussed earlier), is designed to assist in determining how many resources should be allocated for each organizational activity.

✧ COMMON COST AND WASTE PROBLEMS

To manage costs, managers must be able to identify areas where waste and costs might be controlled. Louise Tagliaferri[41] identified 14 common cost factors that can be found in most organizations. Note that some costs are simply uncontrollable, but others are within the scope of the manager to reduce or at least maintain within a reasonable scope:

Absenteeism and turnover	Paperwork
Accident loss	Planning and scheduling
Direct and indirect labor	Productivity
Energy	Product quality
Maintenance	Tools and equipment

Materials and supplies	Transportation
Overtime	Waste

Tagliaferri also noted that "literally billions of dollars are lost to industry [and criminal justice!] each year through carelessness, inattention, waste, inefficiency and other cost problems."[42]

✦ A DIVERSION: EXIGENCY AND POLITICS

✧ SLASHING BUDGETS TO THE BONE

During the 1970s, financial assistance from the federal government increased the budgets of state and local units immensely. Federal agencies pumped billions of dollars into the criminal justice projects across the country; much of the time the local matching funds amounted to a mere 5 percent of the total cost of a project. To obtain these funds, justice administrators were required merely to complete an application for them.

This largesse was discontinued, however, in the 1980s, with the economic downturn and the realization that all of these monies had done little to reverse increases in crime. With the cessation of federal assistance, state and local governments had to make very tough choices, some of which involved job layoffs and reduced governmental services. Even greater financial havoc with government revenues occurred across the country in 1991 and 1992. Because of the deep national recession, actual and threatened layoffs of criminal justice personnel, including police officers, increased more than at any time in recent memory. Adding to the problem were unplanned, unbudgeted events, such as the Los Angeles riots in the aftermath of the Rodney King verdict, which resulted in overtime costs of nearly $138 million. The following are budget-related issues reported in the news during the nation's deep recession:

◊ The mayor of New York City announced that he anticipated laying off 3,600 police officers in an attempt to close an expected budget gap of $2.6 billion over an 18-month period.[43] Massachusetts imposed a hiring freeze on new state troopers, and existing troopers had to forgo pay raises.[44] Detroit planned to lay off 300 police officers,[45] and the Teterboro, New Jersey, city manager proposed eliminating the eight-member police department and its $500,000 budget completely.[46]

◊ District of Columbia Metropolitan police reached an impasse in contract talks; district officials cited a $400 million budget deficit as the main obstacle to reaching an agreement.[47]

◊ The Alabama corrections commissioner stated that the corrections agency would lay off 468 employees and close two detention facilities unless legislators provided $13 million in funds. Lawyers seeking an injunction against

the layoffs argued that the staff reductions could result in increased prison violence. This attempted layoff followed the furloughs of 300 correctional employees and the closing of a prison in 1991.[48]

◊ New Orleans, Louisiana, police officials said that unless $4 million was added to the Police Department's budget, 24 recruits would not be sworn in and the agency could lose up to 75 officers through attrition.[49]

◊ The thousands of officers who worked 12-hour shifts for two weeks during the Los Angeles riots were paid with $16.7 million in federal funds. Los Angeles received an additional $4.7 million to be divided among the fire, water and power, and general services departments.[50]

◊ Arkansas officials reported that the prison system's new regional unit was near completion but there was not enough money to open it because $2.7 million to pay for guards and operating costs had been cut from the budget.[51]

◊ Township trustees voted to disband the St. Clair Police Department in Ohio after residents refused to approve a 3-mill, five-year levy. Only a part-time police chief remained after the vote. The defeated levy would have provided $168,000 in revenues each year and provided around-the-clock coverage for the 20-square-mile township.[52]

◊ The governor of New Jersey vetoed a bill that would have barred him from laying off state police troopers and corrections officers to deal with budget cuts proposed by legislators.[53]

◊ The mayor of Baltimore said a court order forcing the city to pay $3.3 million to police officers and teachers furloughed for two days in early 1992 could force layoffs. A judge ruled that budget constraints did not allow the city to break the terms of union contracts.[54]

In addition, unforeseen events such as civil judgments against a government agency for negligence, excessive force, or sexual harassment and embezzlement by administrators (as occurred in the Detroit Police Department) may have negative impacts on budgets.

✧ LAW ENFORCEMENT: CUTTING SERVICES, ALTERING PRIORITIES

Because of their relatively high cost and overall proportion of total justice system funding, police agencies have probably suffered the largest budget cuts but they also have done much to address these problems. Police executives have reassessed many services that agencies have traditionally provided free of charge, have restricted some nonemergency services, and charged the public for others. For example, because the vast majority of calls from burglar alarms are false (set off by weather conditions or, often, an embarrassed property owner), many police agencies no longer respond quickly to the scene. In addition, they charge for answering false alarms. For example, in the affluent Meridian Township outside Lansing, Michigan, responding to false alarms costs residents or business owners $25 the first time, $50 the second, and up to $100 per call the rest of the year. With only 33 officers in a community of 38,000, township officials recognized that more than 1,000 false alarm responses by police per year threatened to stretch the police budget dangerously thin.[55]

Another chronic problem that results in calls to the police involves people who lock themselves out of their cars. In Detroit, the police send a patrol car only if one is available; in nearby Lansing, the police limit their assistance to providing names of available locksmiths. Calls for police assistance from gas stations whose patrons drive away without paying have become a problem, according to a Newport News, Virginia, study. Even when the police caught the absconders, station managers often refused to press charges, and the police became bill collectors. Consequently, the department adopted a policy to dispatch a patrol car to the scene only if the caller first agrees to press charges. In Aurora, Colorado, the police now refuse to handle obscene telephone call complaints unless the telephone company has identified a suspect. The rationale is that private corporations can more easily pass along the costs to the consumer than can the police.[56]

✧ CHARGING USER FEES IN THE COURTS

With court dockets full and waiting time extended in our litigious society, some people advocate rethinking courts' funding mechanisms. They recognize that users of the courts pay only nominal fees and costs (but pay tremendous sums for the services of private attorneys) and believe that the long-standing view that society is obligated to provide public resources for the court system should be reconsidered. They also maintain that because the courts now cost users so little, people tend to overuse their service; thus no natural incentives for reducing costs within the system exist. Charging user fees, it is asserted, would both provide adequate funds for running an efficient court and reduce unnecessary litigation.[57]

Under the users-pay-what-they-cost-the-courts proposal, user fees would be determined by such factors as the amount of court time used, the cost of processing papers, the salaries of clerks, and time spent on the case by all court personnel, including judges. Criminal cases would be more difficult than civil cases to cost, but it has been recognized that crime has an important economic dimension (especially for white-collar criminals). Criminal defendants with financial means would pay costs, but those who are unable to pay would be excused from this responsibility.[58]

The problem is that this proposed system of court users' fees seems to many people to ration justice and represents what a democratic system of justice is *not* intended to do: compel suspected criminals to bear the costs of defending their actions. These people often quote the words of highly respected Judge Learned Hand: "If we are to keep our democracy, there must be one commandment: Thou shalt not ration justice."[59] This system, they add, would lead to justice on the basis of ability to pay.

✦ STRATEGIES FOR AUGMENTING CRIMINAL JUSTICE BUDGETS

In difficult fiscal times, agencies of criminal justice welcome any means by which they can increase their operating budgets. Unfortunately, opportunities for doing so are limited, especially for courts and corrections agencies; however, the police have recently fared better in this regard, albeit some measures have been controversial. Prisons and jails have some income-producing inmate-labor programs (see Chapter 10), and the police can presently draw supplemental funds from several sources.

Federal and general foundation grants are available to police agencies. Police have used them for a variety of purposes, such as vehicle and riot equipment, communications centers, regional crime laboratories, and programs for alcohol safety-accident prevention, rape victims, and the elderly. Potential grantors are located through publications such as the *Federal Directory of Domestic Aid Programs*.

Criminal justice agencies also receive private contributions. For example, the Erie County, New York, sheriff's office received $5,000 from a local bank to renovate an old van for use in a crime prevention program. On a larger scale, the New York City Police Foundation has raised money since 1971 for endeavors such as scholarships, a police stress program, and a bomb squad. In one recent year the foundation raised $1.3 million. The Chicago Police Department raised $1.5 million recently to purchase bulletproof vests for officers.[60]

Huge supplemental revenues for police agencies come from confiscated cash and property involved with narcotics and contraband goods trafficking, racketeering, gambling, and other offenses. States' forfeiture laws allow the police to initiate forfeiture proceedings on seized goods such as airplanes, cash, cars, boats, and guns. Between 1980 and 1983, the Fort Lauderdale, Florida, Police Department accumulated forfeitures totaling $5,500,000.[61]

Extra income also comes from user fees, which some police departments have initiated. These fees for services formerly provided free, such as unlocking vehicles and responding to false burglar alarms, are controversial. Less controversial have been fees for permitting burglar alarms to be hooked up to the police alarm board or computer-assisted dispatch system. In one year, Miami, Florida, collected $270,000 in alarm permit and false alarm fees.[62]

Finally, Internal Revenue Service rewards have been paid to police agencies that capture racketeers who have not properly reported their income taxes. The program began in Atlanta, Georgia; the police department approached the IRS about collecting the 10 percent informer's fee on unpaid taxes. Through a special city ordinance, the police department was awarded the informer's fee on behalf of the city. By 1988, the department had filed 31 such claims.[63]

Summary

This chapter has focused on a singularly important area of financial administration, budgeting, and included its elements, formats, and potential pitfalls. Emphasis was placed on the need for administrators to develop skill in budget formulation and execution.

This chapter has discussed the budget process and the different types of budgets. No single budgeting format is best; through tradition and personal preference, a hybrid format normally evolves in an organization. Nor should an administrator, under any normal circumstances, surrender control of the organization's budget to another individual or body; the budget is too integral to planning, organizing, and directing programs and operations. In these fiscally tight times, the justice administrator should attempt to become knowledgeable about opportunities for enhancing the budget through grants, donations, user fees, forfeitures, rewards, and other such means of "fattening" the budget. Uncommon times call for uncommon methods.

Questions for Review

1. What is a budget? How is it used?
2. What is the rationale for the increasing practice of charging the public for criminal justice services that have traditionally been provided free of charge? What is the rationale for keeping them free?
3. What is a budget cycle? What is its importance in budgeting?
4. What is involved in formulating a budget? Its approval and execution?

5. List four types of budget formats. Which type is used most frequently? What are its major advantages and component parts?

6. How are criminal justice agencies augmenting their budgets? Can additional means be used in this regard? Provide some examples.

Notes

1. Charles R. Swanson, Leonard Territo, and Robert W. Taylor, *Police Administration* (3d ed.) (New York: Macmillan, 1993), p. 561.

2. See James C. Snyder, "Financial Management and Planning in Local Government," *Atlanta Economic Review* (November/December 1973): 43–47.

3. Aaron Wildavsky, *The Politics of the Budgetary Process* (2d ed.) (Boston: Little, Brown, 1974), pp. 1–4.

4. Orin K. Cope, "Operation Analysis—The Basis for Performance Budgeting," in *Performance Budgeting and Unit Cost Accounting for Governmental Units* (Chicago: Municipal Finance Officers Association, 1954), p. 8.

5. Lester R. Bittel, *The McGraw-Hill 36-Hour Management Course* (New York: McGraw-Hill, 1989).

6. *Ibid.,* p. 187.

7. Robert Townsend, *Further Up the Organization: How to Stop Management from Stifling People and Strangling Productivity* (New York: Alfred A. Knopf, 1984), p. 2.

8. Roland N. McKean, *Public Spending* (New York: McGraw-Hill, 1968), p. 1.

9. S. Kenneth Howard, *Changing State Budgeting* (Lexington, Ky.: Council of State Governments, 1973), p. 13.

10. Michael C. Thomsett, *The Little Black Book of Budgets and Forecasts* (New York: AMACOM, a division of the American Management Association, 1988), p. 38.

11. Quoted in V. A. Leonard and Harry W. More, *Police Organization and Management* (7th ed.) (Mineola, N.Y.: Foundation Press, 1987), p. 212.

12. Swanson et al., *Police Administration,* p. 573.

13. Adapted from Wildavsky, *The Politics of the Budgetary Process,* pp. 63–123.

14. Lennox L. Moak and Kathryn W. Killian, *A Manual of Techniques for the Preparation, Consideration, Adoption, and Administration of Operating Budgets* (Chicago: Municipal Finance Officers Association, 1973), p. 5, with changes.

15. Lennis M. Knighton, "Four Keys to Audit Effectiveness," *Governmental Finance* 8 (September 1979): 3.

16. The Comptroller General of the United States, *Standards for Audit of Governmental Organizations, Programs, Activities, and Functions* (Washington, D.C.: General Accounting Office, 1972), p. 1.

17. *Ibid.*

18. Peter F. Rousmaniere (ed.), *Local Government Auditing* (New York: Council on Municipal Performance, 1979), Tables 1 and 2, pp. 10, 14.

19. Swanson et al., *Police Administration,* p. 568.

20. *Ibid.,* p. 586.

21. Allen Schick, *Budget Innovation in the States* (Washington, D.C.: Brookings Institution, 1971), pp. 14–15. Schick offered 10 ways in which the line-item budget fosters control.

22. Malchus L. Watlington and Susan G. Dankel, "New Approaches to Budgeting: Are They Worth the Cost?" *Popular Government* 43 (Spring 1978): 1.

23. Jesse Burkhead, *Government Budgeting* (New York: Wiley, 1956), p. 11.

24. Larry K. Gaines, Mittie D. Southerland, and John E. Angell, *Police Administration* (New York: McGraw-Hill, 1991), p. 398.

25. Swanson et al., *Police Administration,* p. 591.

26. *Ibid.*

27. Gaines et al., *Police Administration,* pp. 396, 398.

28. *Ibid.,* p. 600.

29. David Novick (ed.), *Program Budgeting* (New York: Holt, Rinehart, and Winston, 1969), p. xxvi.

30. *Ibid.,* p. xxiv.

31. See Council of State Governments, *State Reports on Five-Five-Five* (Chicago: Council of State Governments, 1968).

32. International City Management Association, *Local Government Budgeting, Program Planning and Evaluation* (Washington, D.C.: Urban Data Service Report, 1972), p. 7.

33. Allen Schick, "The Road to PPBS: The Stages of Budget Reform," *Public Administration Review* 26 (December 1966): 244.

34. *Ibid.*

35. Swanson et al., *Police Administration,* p. 593.

36. Peter A. Phyrr, "Zero-Base Budgeting," *Harvard Business Review* (November/December 1970): 111–121; see also E. A. Kurbis, "The Case for Zero-Base Budgeting," *CA Magazine* (April 1986): 104–105.

37. Joseph S. Wholey, *Zero-Base Budgeting and Program Evaluation* (Lexington, Mass.: Lexington Books, 1978), p. 8.

38. Donald F. Facteau and Joseph E. Gillespie, *Modern Police Administration* (Englewood Cliffs, N.J.: Prentice Hall, 1978), p. 204.

39. Samuel C. Certo, *Principles of Modern Management: Functions and Systems* (4th ed.) (Boston: Allyn and Bacon, 1989), pp. 484–485.

40. George S. Minmier, "Zero-Base Budgeting: A New Budgeting Technique for Discretionary Costs," *Mid-South Quarterly Business Review* 14 (October 1976): 2–8.

41. Louise E. Tagliaferri, *Creative Cost Improvement for Managers* (New York: Wiley, 1981), p. 7.

42. *Ibid.,* p. 8.

43. Josh Barbanel, "Dinkins Is Expected to Lay Off 16,000 to Close Budget Gap," *The New York Times* (January 16, 1991): B14.

44. "Mass. SP Transfers Personnel to Offset Manpower Drain," *Law Enforcement News* 16 (1991): 322.

45. Angel Cannon, "DPOA Sues to Bar 300 Police Layoffs," *Detroit Free Press* (March 29, 1991).

46. Robert Hanley, "Tax Haven in Jersey in Bind, Plans to Drop Police," *The New York Times* (February 12, 1991): A13.

47. *Law Enforcement News,* John Jay College of Criminal Justice (November 15, 1992): 2.

48. *Ibid.* (September 15, 1992): 2.

49. *Ibid.* (November 15, 1992): 2.

50. *Ibid.* (June 30, 1992): 2.

51. *Ibid.* (September 15, 1992): 2.

52. *Ibid.,* p. 4.

53. *Ibid.* (September 30, 1992): 2.

54. *Ibid.* (October 15, 1992): 2.

55. Robert Trojanowicz and Bonnie Bucqueroux, "Restructuring Police Priorities: Police Chiefs Must Take the Lead in Enlisting Support," *Footprints: The Community Policing Newsletter* (Michigan State University) 3 (Summer 1990): 1–2.

56. *Ibid.,* p. 2.

57. David Bresnick, "User Fees for the Courts: An Old Approach to a New Problem," in Charles R. Swanson and Susette M. Talarico (eds.), *Court Administration: Issues and Responses* (Athens, Ga.: University of Georgia, 1987), pp. 43–66.

58. *Ibid.,* pp. 45–46.

59. Learned Hand, "Address Before the Legal Aid Society," 9 *NLADA Briefcase* 5 (February 16, 1951).

60. Swanson et al., *Police Administration*, p. 605.

61. *Ibid.,* pp. 605–606.

62. *Ibid.,* p. 606.

63. *Ibid.,* pp. 613–614.

Chapter 16

Technology Review

God hath made man upright; but they have sought out many inventions.
—Ecclesiastes 7:29

Progress . . . is not an accident, but a necessity. It is a part of nature.
—Herbert Spencer

✦ INTRODUCTION

Criminal justice involves a wide range of professional participants. For decades, even centuries, participants primarily have worked independently, sharing information by the printed page. As the world enters the fast lane of the Information Age, criminal justice has fallen behind dramatically. As Judges George Nicholson and Jeffrey Hogge pointed out,

> It is not enough to shovel faster. Criminal justice must enter the Information Age by incorporating technology as a tool to make the system run efficiently and effectively. It doesn't take a brilliant futurist to know criminal justice will eventually be paperless. All documents will be created, filed, stored, and retrieved electronically, [at] lower costs, time savings, and improvements in storage, retrieval, portability, and access.[1]

The paperless Information Age will probably not come soon, however; as Nicholson and Hogge noted, most of today's more experienced criminal justice participants learned to perform their basic functions the old way. Furthermore, these participants are reluctant to try new methods when past attempts have been disappointing and embarrassing because of partial or complete failure of the system to live up to its advance billing.[2] Still, one thing that is clear is that, for the justice system to improve and become more coordinated, it must incorporate technology.

This chapter discusses the technological advances that are now used; few involve getting the three justice system components working together, as Nicholson and Hogge advocate. The technologies described in this chapter demonstrate what each component is doing to help itself.

◆ TECHNOLOGY IN POLICING

We begin with a discussion of several exciting developments involving computer technology in police work. It is not surprising that most of the technological developments today involve the police, given the nature of their work, tools, and crime problems. In this section we discuss a wide variety of technologies involving patrol officers, dispatchers, forensic scientists, crime analysts, and records personnel.

✧ USE OF WIRELESS TECHNOLOGY

The first digital data were transmitted from police headquarters to a police car in the mid-1980s. Until recently, this capability was available only to those police agencies that could afford the private radio networks and mobile data terminals (MDTs). Today, however, even a small agency can afford a laptop computer and a modem to send encrypted data to officers in the field.[3]

A growing number of U.S. police departments, including small agencies, are using laptop computers with wireless connections to crime and motor vehicle databases. These systems are believed to pay for themselves in increased fines and officer safety. Officers can access court documents, in-house police department records, and a CAD system, as well as entering license numbers into their laptop computers. Through a national network of motor vehicle and criminal history databases, the police can locate drivers with outstanding warrants, expired or suspended licenses, and criminal backgrounds. Furthermore, rather than using open radio communications, police officers use their computers to communicate with each other via e-mail.[4]

At the end of the 20th century, police officers require computing tools with flexibility, a quality that MDTs lack. Advances in technology have pushed well beyond the ability to send and receive short bursts of alphanumeric data. Police administrators need to become more innovative. As one consultant put it,

> We see over and over the RFP (Request for Proposal) that says the agency wants to purchase the latest, greatest high-tech widget, but it has to be proven, have five previous installations, and have been in existence for four years. There's a phenomenal contradiction there.[5]

✧ TECHNOLOGY AIDS COMMUNITY POLICING

In Chapter 4 we discussed community policing and problem solving (COPPS). This strategy entails identifying—through scanning and analysis—"hot spots" of neighborhood disorder that are in need of police attention. Certainly, technology can assist in these endeavors.

Some cities now employ a sophisticated system that uses an integrated computer-aided design (CAD) system, MDTs, and message switching and routing tools to collect, store, monitor, and retrieve information needed by COPPS officers. Officers can quickly perform license plate checks, produce slips if they tow a vehicle, check on stolen property, and perform online incident and booking reports. The system also automatically captures shift activities to produce the daily shift-ending reports and helps officers sort data so they can present information to citizens in an easy-to-understand format at neighborhood meetings.[6]

Some cities are developing a Geographic Information System (GIS), which enables officers to plot criminal activity on an electronic map. Layers of information can then be added to the map to create a picture of crime trends. One unique way officers can use community policing strategies is to develop a database of problems and solutions. When an officer answers a call for service or encounters a problem, he or she can enter it into the database, as well as all information about the problem, the action taken, and a list of resources that were applied to the problem. The next time officers confront a similar problem, they can search the database and get a report on everything that has been done about that problem in the past.[7]

✦ ELECTRONICS IN TRAFFIC INVESTIGATIONS AND ENFORCEMENT

A multicar accident can turn a street or highway into a parking lot for many hours, sometimes days. The police must collect evidence relating to the accident, take measurements and make sketches of the scene and vehicle and body positions, skid marks, street or highway elevations, intersections, and curves. These tasks typically involve a measuring wheel, steel tape, pad, and pencil. The cost of traffic delays—especially for commercial truck operators—for every hour traffic is stalled is substantial.

Some police agencies have begun using a version of a surveyor's total station that electronically measures and records distances, angles, elevations, and the names and features of objects. Data from the station can be downloaded onto a computer for display or printed on a plotter. In vehicular homicide cases requiring reconstruction of the crime scene, some courts now prefer the precision, scope, and professional appearance of court exhibits collected and generated by this electronic system.

With this system, officers can spend an hour or so getting measurements at major traffic accidents, push a button, and have the system draw lines pertinent to the accident to scale; this process enables officers to get 40 percent more measurements in only about 40 percent of the time, thus allowing the traffic flow to resume much more quickly. This system is also being used at major crime scenes. Its only drawback is that it cannot be used in heavy rain or snow.[8]

Technological development has raised traffic enforcement to a higher level with the advent of traffic cameras, nicknamed *the photocop,* and electro-optical traffic enforcement devices that include both radar and cameras. Traffic cameras, either mounted on a mobile tripod or permanently fixed on a pole, emit a narrow radar beam that triggers a flash camera when a targeted vehicle exceeds the speed limit by a certain amount, usually 10 miles per hour. The ticket is then mailed to the vehicle's registered owner. If the owner has a question about or defense to the citation (such as having loaned the vehicle to another person on the day of the violation), he or she may contact the police department or take the matter to court.

Several companies now manufacture and provide traffic cameras to the police. The devices cost nothing in taxes; the manufacturer receives approximately $25 per paid ticket, so violators actually finance the program.

Some schemes to fool photocop are already being developed. For example, a license plate cover advertised in auto magazines allows the license plate numbers to be read from straight ahead; however, from the angle of the traffic camera, the license numbers are obliterated.

✦ EXPEDITING DUI ARRESTS

During a DUI stop, officers might spend a lengthy period of time questioning a driver and conducting a barrage of screening tests. Then, if an arrest is made, the officer necessarily devotes a good deal of time transporting and processing the arrestee at the jail, including making a urine or blood test. This delay in formal testing can skew test results because it can allow the alcohol to metabolize.

Recently, the California Department of Justice and the California Highway Patrol began looking at a way to help automate the drunk-driving process. One tool used routinely during a drunk-driving stop is a small, portable machine that resembles a video game cartridge for breath screening. The DUI suspect blows into it, and the officer takes the reading of the amount of alcohol in the suspect's system. Law enforcement officials hope that this device can be adapted so that the test can be used in court. If it can be, it could save time in transporting DUI suspects, testing them, and finding that their blood level was below the legal limit.

The revamped instrument would be attached to a notebook or laptop computer that an officer would use by running a California mag-stripe driver's license through a reader on the computer to bring up pertinent information about the driver. The computer would then prompt the officer to start the test and would provide a readout of the results on the screen. The officer would transfer the test results over telecommunications lines to a central location to be recorded.

Other potential uses of the system include allowing the police to share data, specifically a database of blood alcohol arrests and results,[9] with the division of motor vehicles and the courts.

✧ IMAGE ENHANCEMENT TECHNOLOGY

Another technological weapon in the war against crime is image processing, which can turn the most blurred video images into clear visions. Until recently, image processing usually meant enhancement by enlarging photographs, but they can be enlarged only to a certain extent before clarity is completely lost. The new image processing is based on technology created by NASA to clear up the blurred photos taken by the Hubble space telescope. The technique relies on linear mathematical equations that can manipulate a photo's shades of gray.[10]

The U.S. Secret Service uses image enhancement technology to attempt to spot individuals under surveillance in large crowd photos.

✧ IMAGED FINGERPRINTS AND MUGSHOTS

The Boston Police Department, like most departments in the country, was devoting tremendous resources in identifying prisoners with mugshots and fingerprints. Then the department, with what is the first system of its kind in North America, replaced all filmed mugshots and ink fingerprinting with a citywide, integrated electronic imaging identification system. Its system also was the first to receive the FBI's certification for electronic fingerprint submission.

Instead of transporting prisoners to a central booking facility in downtown Boston—a task that took 40,000 hours of officers' time per year—officers at the

11 district police stations can electronically scan a prisoner's fingerprints, take digital photographs, and then route the images to a central server for easy storage and access. This network gives investigators timely access to information and mugshot lineups and is saving the police department a million dollars in labor and transportation costs while freeing officers for duties other than transporting prisoners.[11]

✧ COMPUTERIZED MAPPING FOR CRIME CONTROL

Police department crime analysts have long used paper pin maps to indicate criminal activity in a given area. The use of computers and mapping software has greatly extended these maps and offers far greater flexibility and analytical capabilities. Although computers have been used to display and manipulate maps since the 1960s, widespread use of mapping software is a relatively new phenomenon resulting, in large part, from the availability of inexpensive yet sophisticated PC-based mapping software packages.[12] Computerized mapping is an effective tool to help police departments track criminal activity in neighborhoods known in community policing, as previously mentioned, as *hot spots*. Combined with a technique known as *geocoding* (which verifies addresses and links other geographic information with them), computer mapping software can combine data sets to provide a multidimensional view of crime and its potential contributing factors.[13]

Many large police agencies are using this technology, and some are doing so in conjunction with their CPPS initiative. Computerized mapping is particularly useful for police departments with computer-aided dispatch and records management systems, which store and maintain calls for service and incident, arrest, and other data that are potentially mappable. Geographic information useful in planning includes the locations of crimes committed during the past month; the locations of abandoned houses, stripped cars, and other conditions indicating neighborhood decay; and the locations where persons who could benefit from crime prevention actually live. Perhaps the most important feature of mapping software is its ability to join or overlay disparate data sets. For example, one "layer" of a map display could represent a descriptive variable such as the locations of crimes in the past month, and another layer could represent a possible explanatory variable, such as the unemployment rates of persons living on each city block, the locations of abandoned houses, or citizen reports of drug activity.[14]

Crime analysts use mapping software to prepare crime alert bulletins and other reports that police commanders use in planning operations and patrol officers use in obtaining quick visual overviews of current crime conditions in their patrol areas.

Figure 16.1 shows a crime map of street gang homicide, other violence, and drug crime.

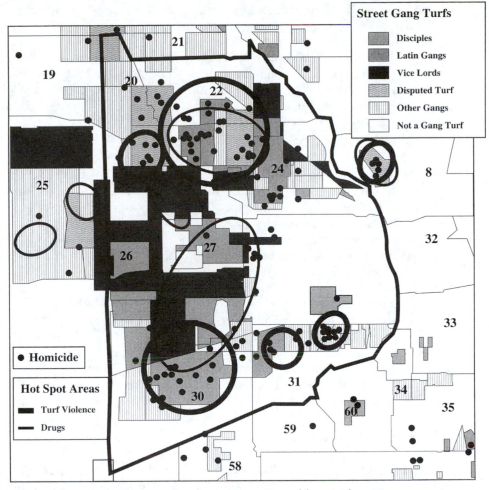

Figure 16.1 Sample map of street gang-motivated homicide, other violence, and drug crime. (*Source:* Adapted from U.S. Department of Justice, National Institute of Justice, "The Use of Computerized Mapping in Crime Control and Prevention Programs," July 1995, p. 4.)

✧ THREE-DIMENSIONAL CRIME SCENE DRAFTING

For years, police have used tape and, when necessary, pieces of string to measure crime scenes and then used these measurements to painstakingly draw the scene to scale for later use in court. Today, three-dimensional computer-aided drafting (3-D CAD) software can be purchased for a few hundred dollars. By working in 3-D, CAD users can create scenes that can be viewed from any angle.

Suddenly, very technical evidence can be visualized by nontechnical people. Juries can "view" crime scenes and see the location of evidence; they can view just what the witness says he or she saw.

Police program the exact dimensions into the CAD system and receive a scaled drawing. What is also needed, however, is training to teach officers or detectives how to create such drawings. A five-day, 40-hour course is available for police investigators, traffic accident reconstructionists, and evidence technicians.[15]

✦ GUNSHOT LOCATOR SYSTEM

In some cities, random gunshots have become such a problem that citizens are storming into city council meetings to demand action. During holidays such as New Year's Eve and the Fourth of July, people shooting guns in celebration create a potentially lethal problem.

A primary obstacle for the police in addressing this problem is to determine the location of such gunshots. Technology that is similar to that used to determine the strength and epicenter of earthquakes is now being tested to determine such locations. Known as a *Gunshot Locator System,* it uses microphonelike sensors placed on rooftops and telephone poles to record and transmit the sound of gunshots by radio waves or telephone lines. A software program then alerts a dispatcher and pinpoints the origin of gunshots via a flashing icon on a computerized map. At minimum, the system, which bases location on how long it takes the sound to reach the sensors, has the potential to greatly reduce police response time to crime scenes, which can decrease the time needed to obtain aid for victims and can increase the likelihood of arrests.[16]

✦ FIREARMS TRAINING

Recruits and in-service officers alike use the Firearms Training System (FATS), which ranges in cost from $32,000 to a military model selling for $5 million and is said to be "as close to real life as you can get"[17] in firearms training. Users can be shown on a movie screen a wide variety of computer-generated scenarios led by an instructor at a console. Using laser-firing replicas of their actual weapons, users learn marksmanship as well as judgment—when to shoot and not to shoot. The system, which consists of a container about the size of a large baby buggy with a computer, a laser disk player, a projector, and a hit detect camera, can be transported to various sites. At some sites, such as Miami-Dade County, Florida, FATS is combined with a driving simulator; recruits drive to the scene of a bank robbery and then bail out of their car into a FATS scenario.

✦ GANG INTELLIGENCE SYSTEMS

The escalating problem of street gangs prompted the Keller, Texas, Police Department to search for a tool that could help them deal with the problem. An officer with a background in electronics and computers eventually developed a system that could be used to collect information in a database and then facilitate the exchange of that information among officers and agencies. The system makes it easier for officers in Texas to work with other states in tracking down wanted gang members.[18]

The system works by allowing officers to enter information and access key pieces of data such as gang names, vehicles, weapons, suspect associates, and incident dates. Even if an officer has a very small piece of information to work with, such as a partial license plate number of a suspect's car, the system's cross-referencing function connects that information to more information in the database about gang members, their activities, addresses, descriptions, and photos. Officers can even access the database in their patrol cars utilizing laptops. The system also allows photographs to be stored on the system and linked with other information about a suspect.

✦ ENHANCED DISPATCH SYSTEMS SAVE LIVES

Recently, when a call came in to the Edmonton, Alberta, dispatch center, its enhanced system displayed an icon indicating six prior calls to that address, four for family violence and two for a missing juvenile. The dispatcher called up the incident address in Canada's firearms registry and discovered that weapons were registered to the occupant; in addition, a male occupant had threatened responding officers. This information was relayed to the two responding officers both verbally and via MDT in their patrol car. With this information, the officers acted with caution and did not stand in front of the occupants' front door. This information proved crucial, because he shot through the door with a rifle, commencing a 16-hour standoff that ended with his suicide. Officers in Edmonton believe that dispatchers provide information that is as valuable as a bullet-proof vest.[19]

Many police departments have a similar system, but most are tied to only one database. The Edmonton police can access information from the national crime information center (on wants, warrants, and stolen vehicles); the Operational Support Communications and Records System, an incident database linked to other national, provincial, and municipal databases; and the Computer Aided Dispatch system (CAD), which handles call history. Officers also have direct links to databases of city utilities and the local telephone company.

✦ DRUGFIRE NETWORK CONNECTS GUNS TO CRIMES

Drugfire is a federal networked system begun in 1992; it holds images of spent cartridges that can help link weapons to shootings. It is essentially an imaging system with networked search capabilities. A dedicated microscope is attached to a computer, and an image of the cartridge case primer (the area where the firing pin hits the cartridge) is loaded into the system. The image is stored and accessible later by other crime laboratories checking for connections with evidence they hold. Forensic scientists compare fired bullets and used casings to determine whether a firearm in custody was used in other shootings. Since its inception in 1992, more than 1,000 matches have been made by labs around the country using Drugfire, and 68 firearms labs in 19 states and the District of Columbia were linked to Drugfire or were in the planning stages in late 1996.[20]

✧ NCIC 2000

The Federal Bureau of Investigation (FBI) began operating the National Crime Information Center (NCIC) in 1967; this system has since been accessed hundreds of millions of times and is responsible for the recovery of billions of dollars of property, the capture of tens of thousands of criminals, and the location of thousands of missing persons.[21] NCIC holds more than 24 million records that are accessible by over 60,000 criminal justice agencies in all 50 states.[22]

NCIC, developed in first and second generation computer languages, has grown old, however, and badly needs replacing. Therefore, in 1986 the FBI began a $46 million project to replace it with NCIC 2000. System enhancements will include new hardware and software; image capabilities for pictures of subjects, stolen property, and fingerprint matching; a choice of communications protocols; electronic validation of records submitted by state and local police agencies; electronic access to federal prison records as well as Canadian criminal justice records; improved response times; the ability to multi thread queries, which are currently processed one at a time; improved system security; and live scan fingerprint capability.[23]

The transition to NCIC 2000 began in 1996 and will take three years; during that period, state and local police agencies will be able to continue using current communications protocols. To take advantage of NCIC 2000's enhancements, state and local police agencies will need to upgrade their hardware and software. At a minimum, they must decide whether to replace their terminals with personal computer workstations and laptop computers in patrol vehicles. Experts believe that the cost of these upgrades would be no greater than amounts that the police agencies would normally spend during this period of time.[24]

✧ DATABASES FOR BRADY ACT BACKGROUND CHECKS

The 1993 Brady Act mandated instant background checks on persons seeking to purchase a handgun to prevent convicted felons, among others, from buying a handgun on the open market. State and local police agencies worked hard to prepare to meet the 1998 deadline for compliance with the National Instant Criminal Background Check System. The federal government distributed about $88 million to states in 1995 to assist this process; each state received at least some money. This system will use the Interstate Identification Index (III) as the basis for the noncriminal-related background checks.[25]

The process requires gun dealers to call the number of a clearinghouse whose operators will run the purchaser's name through a state criminal database, the federal NCIC, an outstanding warrant database, and several other state databases. Possibly the most important factor in making the background check system work is ensuring that the electronic records are as accurate as possible and are updated as needed.[26]

✧ THE CAMCORDER ERA

As discussed earlier, since the Rodney King incident in 1991, videotape technology has had an impact on all above areas of policing and its administration. The use of videotaping by the general public after that incident and the benefits of utilizing camcorders as tools for police activities were recognized by police administrators, many of whom now equip their agency's patrol vehicles with videocameras.

A recent study found that one-third of all police and sheriff's departments serving populations of 50,000 or more in the United States are also videotaping at least some interrogations. Furthermore, police videos have been particularly useful in drunk-driving arrests and at crime-scene and traffic accident investigations. Videocameras are also used to record eyewitness testimony and in-progress events, such as robberies and building checks. With little investment in money or personnel, police can make in-house tapes for roll-call training, public relations, and programs in areas such as drinking and driving.[27]

✧ HI-TECH GUN CONTROL: "SMART GUNS" CAN SAVE LIVES

From 1985 to 1994, 89 police officers were slain with their own guns. Furthermore, nearly 500 children and adolescents are killed in firearms accidents each year, and some 1,400 youngsters commit suicide with guns.[28]

In the face of these horrifying facts, efforts are under way to create "smart" (or personalized) guns that can be fired only by their rightful owners and a few other authorized users. Technological options are being explored in several areas; for example, radio signals that enable a weapon to recognize and respond to a transponder worn by the authorized user are being developed. The transponder's range is only a few inches, so the gun would not work for a stranger who steals it. A gun could be designed to recognize up to 50 transponders so a number of officers could fire the weapon if necessary. Although such a system could increase the price of a standard service pistol from $600 to about $900, the development of this system is gaining political momentum; states and localities are drafting laws that could require the use of personalized guns.[29]

✧ THE SEARCH FOR THE CONSUMMATE LESS-THAN-LETHAL WEAPON

For several decades, police administrators and inventors around the world have endeavored to find the "perfect" weapon to use against rioters and other offenders. Many of these items were developed when little if any policy or training was available to guide their use. We briefly examine the kinds of weapons that have been attempted and, for the most part, put back on the shelf by administrators because of their inherent problems.

Until the 1960s international policing witnessed only one major addition to the small array of less-than-lethal police tools: chemical weapons. Invented in 1869, CN gas was the first tear gas that produced a burning sensation in the throat, eyes, and nose. CN gas became available in aerosol cans in 1965; Chemical Mace was the most well-known variety.[30] The 1960s brought the age of rioting in the United States and abroad, and numerous presidential commissions as well as citizens on the street were debating the degree and types of force that should be exerted by the police against rioters. Mace seemed to be manna from heaven and Mace-squirting nightsticks were developed. Wooden rounds, rubber bullets, the British riot police watercannons, the Sound Curdler (consisting of amplified speakers that produce loud, shrieking noises at irregular intervals) were all developed.[31]

In 1970 another unique less-than-lethal weapon—a gun that shot beanbags rather than bullets—was introduced. The Photic Driver produced a strobe effect whose light caused giddiness, fainting, and nausea. Other inventions of this decade included an electrified water jet, a baton that carried a 6,000 volt shock, shotgun shells filled with plastic pellets, plastic bubbles that immobilized rioters, a chemical that created slippery street surfaces for combatting rioters, and an instant "cocoon" that, when sprayed over crowds, made people stick together.[32] The side-handle baton remains popular among police officers today.

Two new types of projectiles were developed in the mid-1970s: the plastic bullet, and the TASER, which shot two tiny darts into its victim and delivered a 50,000-volt electrical shock that could knock down a person at a distance of 15 feet. Also introduced in the mid-1970s, the stun gun, shaped like an electric razor, delivered a 50,000 volt shock when its two electrodes were pressed directly against the body.

During the 1980s, flashlights that had stun capacity or contained chemical agents were marketed. The entanglement net and the action chain control device required four officers to operate, in what seems today much like a Keystone Cops scenario. An expandable baton (from 6 to 16 inches "with a flick of the wrist") and a 6-inch steel whip that, when opened to its 13-inch length, projected three steel coils and was transformed into something resembling the Medieval "cat-o-nine-tails" were also available.

Pepper spray, or oleoresin capsicum (OC), introduced in the early 1990s, is now believed to hold much promise as a less-than-lethal police tool, reducing injuries and complaints about force. Although OC has been used in situations in which the suspects later died, a review by the International Association of Chiefs of Police found no evidence linking OC to such deaths.[33] The use of OC has spread across the country, even in many prisons, but a number of police agencies believe that it is not a panacea and have discontinued its use in the aftermath of these reported in-custody deaths.

Another possible solution to the ongoing search for a perfect less-than-lethal weapon, now being peddled to police agencies for use against criminals, uses two very strange types of foam. One is supersticky; intruders would be drenched in a substance that, exposed to the air, turns into taffylike glue. The other creates an avalanche of very dense soap bubbles that leave offenders unable to see or move but able to breathe. Other chemical compounds, known as *slick'ems and stick'ems,* make pavements either too sticky or too slippery for vehicles to move.[34]

✦ COURT TECHNOLOGIES THAT INCREASE EFFICIENCY

"Courts *are* their records." This adage captures the essence of the important role played by the courts in serving as the primary repository for the records of a community's arrests, convictions, births, deaths, marriages, divorces, and so on. But in so doing, lawyers, judges, and society daily create a blizzard of paper documents, all of which require filing, sorting, and indexing for later retrieval. Most courthouses have file cabinets occupying every inch of wall space, as well as basements filled with boxes of decaying records.

The justice system is sagging under the weight of its paper at a time when few resources exist to deal with massive volumes of complaints, briefs, and motions. About 50 percent of the cost of running the court is attributed to moving paper. The magnitude of this problem was demonstrated when one consulting firm estimated that if 80 percent of 19 million lawsuits in one year had been filed electronically, attorneys and their clients could have saved $646 million.[35]

In this section we briefly examine two developments that exist to greatly reduce this deluge of paperwork in the courts: electronic filing and document imaging. Then we look at videoconferencing, a system that greatly reduces staff time spent in transporting prisoners and security risks in courthouses. We also present a futuristic view of a court that has been created to showcase technological products for the 21st century.

✦ Electronic Filing

Electronic filing is an exciting advancement for courts that wish to streamline their expanding caseloads. The proliferation of computers, local area networks (LANS), and electronic mail technologies present a unique opportunity to cost effectively organize court procedures.

Various methods are available to file documents electronically. The first is the transfer of word-processing files from one computer to another through a file transfer program. This method has some drawbacks, however. Most file transfer programs require some technical knowledge by the user, and the multiplicity of formats increases the chance that information will be lost or altered. The second method for filing documents electronically is the use of E-mail-enabled electronic forms with fields, or blank spaces, on which users place specific information that is stored in a database. Users send completed forms to the court via a modem, a mail service, or a diskette. Benefits of this system include the friendly graphical user interfaces of most software packages; the ability of users to send E-mail information simultaneously to multiple parties 24 hours a day; and the reduction of photocopy and postal charges, resulting in cost savings.[36]

In summary, using electronic forms offers many benefits for the courts. Automatic entry of information into case management systems reduces entry time and eliminates errors. The ability to control the information entered in a form is important. With an electronic form, one can prevent incorrect, inappropriate, or incomplete information from being entered and can place data in required formats automatically. This procedure saves the space that would be taken by paper forms and reduces time and costs of transferring information to appellate courts. The purchase and maintenance of equipment and software by which to complete electronic forms and the training for personnel are more costly than paper forms, however.[37]

Courts are realizing that computer filing and retrieval of documents can be faster and less expensive and more accurate and secure than the traditional method; furthermore, computerized documents require far less space to store than paper.

✦ Document Imaging

Another promising solution to the courts' record-keeping problem is document imaging, which can provide better control of document tracking and distribution as well as reduced costs and greater efficiency because higher volumes of work can be handled rapidly and accurately, requiring less paper and office space. Imaging offers significant, exponentially growing advantages for high-volume, paper-intensive, service-oriented operations such as courts. Next is a list of some of the advantages of document imaging for the courts.

◊ Courts enter information into case processing systems from numerous sources. Some documents submitted directly to the administrator's or clerk's office could be scanned into the imaging system locally. Other documents come from external sources such as attorneys, police and probation agencies, and community services. These documents could be scanned into the system remotely or faxed directly into it.

◊ Imaged documents may be part of an integrated court information system that consists of case processing and word processing. An integrated system would enable court clerks and administrators to switch between display screens containing document images, case processing data, and word processing text.

◊ Many official documents produced by courts contain signatures, seals, letterheads, and other inscriptions. These documents can be stored as images with blank spaces for data and text to be supplied later by technicians using case processing and word processing systems.

◊ Judges may need customized case folders containing documents arranged in a particular order or only those documents pertaining to a certain part of the case. These types of functions can be accomplished easily with electronic case folders containing imaged documents.[38]

As with any system, imaging has its disadvantages, including its initial cost; difficulty of system implementation (for integration with other systems) and of reading lengthy imaged documents on a computer screen; the impossibility of modifying, manipulating, or copying text in imaged documents; the potential need for additional staff; and the potential for the entire operation to be immobilized by system failures.[39] Figure 16.2 shows a sample page of document imaging.

✦ VIDEOCONFERENCING

Videoconferencing has evolved using relatively simple technology because of the increased awareness of security risks and costs of transporting prisoners between jail and court buildings. For these reasons, videoconferencing is becoming one of the most demanded systems in today's court systems; judges and court administrators everywhere would do well to investigate the cost and feasibility of this technology for their respective courts. First used with videophone bail hearings in 1972, the primary components of a simple videoconferencing system are television cameras, monitors, microphones, speakers, and a communications network; the latter can be as simple as a pair of coaxial cables running between the court and the jail or as complicated as a satellite transmission and reception facilities.[40]

One step in the criminal justice process that can be addressed without hindering a fair hearing and eventual trial is the arraignment during which the defendant enters a plea. Defendants usually are transported from jails to the courtroom, which requires transportation and security. The arraignment process in

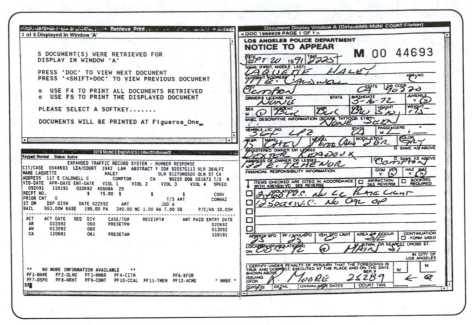

Figure 16.2 Document imaging screen. (*Source:* National Center for State Courts, *Court Technology Reports,* Vol. 4. Williamsburg, Va.: Author, p. 15. Copyright 1992. Used with permission.)

particular needs an injection of technology and streamlining.[41] Although each state has different statutes governing the use of technology, courts in at least 30 states use video arraignment for first appearance felonies and misdemeanors,[42] which represent about three-fourths of 12 million new criminal cases each year. Approximately 200 video arraignment sites exist in state court systems today. Thus, it is evident that this technology is becoming established as an accepted criminal justice practice. As video technology becomes even more affordable, interest in video arraignment should increase.

Video arraignment provides several benefits including reduced security risks associated with transporting and handling inmates, reduced overcrowding of courthouse holding facilities, improved custody conditions for defendants while they await arraignment, improvements in the overall efficiency of court proceedings, reduced tension levels among guards and prisoners, minimized delays, and the prevention of commingling of first-time offenders with hardened offenders.[43] Criticisms of video arraignments commonly come from defense attorneys, who believe that such technology interferes with the defendant's right to adequate defense representation; in addition, some judges believe that this procedure does not afford them the same control over the courtroom environment or guarantee confidential communication between defendant and counsel.[44]

Overall, video technology provides better public service at a reduced cost. In addition to arraignments, videoconferencing can enhance other court processes as well; travel and waiting time can be eliminated when attorneys can meet with judges from their own offices. Videoconferencing can also be used for bond hearings, probation revocation hearings, and child support hearings.[45] In addition, court reporters can transcribe these hearings.

One of the most exciting occurrences in U.S. courts centers on technology. Rapid advances in computer technology, particularly in available software, have allowed some courts to become more effective, efficient, and customer oriented. For example, some states now have electronic kiosks installed in public places and shopping malls. These kiosks have an interactive screen that allows citizens to pay traffic fines with their ATM card and obtain information about contesting traffic citations, attending traffic school, or setting court dates. Some electronic kiosks provide citizens information on small-claims court (in both Spanish and English). These devices are obviously convenient for consumers, comparatively inexpensive to operate, and free court clerks to handle more serious problems and inquiries.

✦ COURTROOM 21

Recently, the College of William and Mary and the National Center for State Courts unveiled Courtroom 21, the most technologically advanced courtroom in the United States. All of its technology should be available soon after the arrival of the 21st century. This project demonstrates how technology can enrich the legal process by assisting judges, court administrators, counsel, jurors, court reporters, and other staff. Courtroom 21 includes the following integrated capabilities:[46]

◊ *Automatic video recording of proceedings using ceiling-mounted cameras with voice activation.* Courtroom 21 has five ceiling television cameras in the courtroom. When someone in the courtroom speaks, the microphone and camera closest to that person are activated. With cameras properly aimed, the entire courtroom is visible via small video windows; the person speaking is visible through a large video window. (Such video record is viewed as superior to a written transcript because appellate judges can observe the demeanor of witnesses and their voice inflections, facial expressions, and gestures.)

◊ *Recorded televised evidence display with analog optical disk storage.* Evidence can be prerecorded on small analog disks for later use at trial. Counsel may present documentary or real evidence to judge and jury via television display. Trial evidence and events also may be preserved on disk for later trial use or for appeals.

◊ *Remote, two-way television arraignment.* Video arraignment (i.e., teleconferencing, described earlier) is possible between the bench and some remote site. Audio and video signals are received by the control center and then are sent to the several courtroom computer monitors.

◊ *Jury box computers.* Courtroom 21's jury box contains computers for information display. Each monitor can display documents, real evidence, live or recorded video, transcription, and the usual graphics (charts, diagrams, pictures).

◊ *LEXIS legal research.* Judges and counsel are provided immediate access to legal resources through the LEXIS on-line legal database. If an unanticipated legal question arises during trial, judges and counsel can use the computers to consult the database.

◊ *Video deposition playback facilities.* Because more depositions are being video recorded by attorneys in preparation for trial, Courtroom 21 has video deposition playback. To impeach a witness or present expert witness testimony, video depositions can be played on court monitors.

✦ COURT REPORTERS AND TECHNOLOGY

It is not uncommon for a court reporter who spends three or four days working on one case, sits in court in one place, and works without breaks to develop a variety of physical ailments because of the intense nature of their work.

Now a system that can afford relief to reporters is available. A unique digital audio transcription system that changes the way court reporters do their work is slowly being implemented in courtrooms across the country. The system digitally captures the spoken word on ultrasensitive condenser microphones located at specific points in the courtroom, including the witness stand, judge's bench, and counsel tables. Audio is transmitted to a central control room where it is digitized by system audio servers and stored on a hard disk and tape.[47]

Instead of sitting in the courtroom, court reporters monitor proceedings from the control room. For every four courtrooms, one reporter is required to sit and monitor all of the activities; thus, the system allows one reporter to do the work of four. The initial investment of the system is about $15,000, versus paying about $50,000 per year for each reporter. Therefore, the court realizes a heavy return on its investment. Accuracy is enhanced by taking the human factor out of the recording process. It is easy to tell who is speaking in the courtroom, and voices can be isolated as well.

✦ OTHER USES OF TECHNOLOGY

Courts around the country have devised other technological innovations, such as the following:

◊ The Los Angeles County Municipal Court has a traffic records imaging system that has eliminated 90 percent of all manual tasks involved in handling traffic citations.

◊ A Florida circuit court has developed an Automated Telephone Calendaring System that diverts hundreds of calls a month from judicial assistants; attorneys interact directly with the scheduling computer by telephone to schedule civil hearings. Figure 16.3 is the concise, one-page instruction sheet that serves as a reference for attorneys using the system.

◊ New York's Automated Budget System (ABS) has databases and spreadsheets that have replaced a paper-driven budgetary process, resulting in significant savings for budget preparers and reviewers. Figure 16.4 shows a sample screen for worksheet navigation through this system.

◊ Washington state's Information Strategy Plan is a planning resource for judicial information systems development and has broad implications for judicial electronic data interchange.

◊ Oregon's Financial Information and Accounting System tracks all financial transactions of a case, integrating financial and case management. Figure 16.5 shows a sample case financial history screen.

◊ Arkansas' Supreme Court has a CD-ROM legal research database that saves time and increases the effectiveness of legal research in state appellate courts.[48] Figure 16.6 is a sample computer screen for a case search.

These technologies indicate what can be done in the courts for greater efficiency and effectiveness. Much room for development still exists because the courts are far behind in technological advances. Certainly funding is one major factor. In addition, an attorney has observed that lawyers are generally technophobic. They took courses in English and history, not electronics, mathematics, and computers. They resist computer education. Computer-literate people have been stunned by the extremely low level of computer literacy among lawyers. As the attorney stated, "We need to . . . get down to the business of running this process efficiently."[49]

✦ TECHNOLOGY IN CORRECTIONS FACILITIES

In Chapter 12 we discussed two types of electronic monitoring devices that have been used since the mid-1980s as part of intensive supervision programs in corrections facilities. Indeed, computers have been used extensively in corrections work for many years. In state-of-the-art prisons, automated systems control access gates and doors, individual cell doors, and the climate in cells and other areas of the prison. Corrections agencies have also used computers to manage inmate records, conduct presentence investigations, supervise offenders in the community, provide instruction to inmates, and train correctional personnel. With computer assistance, jail administrators receive daily reports on court schedules, inmate rosters, time served, statistical information, maintenance costs, and other data.

Technological advancement in the corrections field has been adapted to a

```
AUTOMATED COURT SCHEDULING REFERENCE SHEET

Attorney Name: _____     Bar No: _____

┌─────────────────────────────────────┬──────────────────────────────┐
│     Caller Supplied Information:     │  System Generated Responses: │
├──────────┬─────────┬────────────────┼──────────────┬──────┬────────┤
│   CASE   │ LENGTH  │ TYPE (Request Code)│ DAY-DATE  │ TIME │CONFIRM #│
├──────────┼─────────┼────────────────┼──────────────┼──────┼────────┤
│          │         │                │              │      │        │
│          │         │                │              │      │        │
│          │         │                │              │      │        │
└──────────┴─────────┴────────────────┴──────────────┴──────┴────────┘
```

DIVISION A: 951-5742
 DIVISION D: 364-4685
 	
 TO ACCESS THE SYSTEM:
 	
 1) Dial the phone number given above
 When you hear the greeting, press
 the appropriate response on your phone.
 	
 2) After you have choosen to use the
 automated scheduler, the system will
 ask for the Attorney Bar no.
 Enter the 7-digit Bar no.
 	
 (All Bar #'s are 7 digits long!
 If necessary, add leading 0's
 until the Bar no. is 7 digits long.)
 	
 TO SCHEDULE A HEARING TIME:
 	
 3) Press 7 - (S)chedule if the court
 appearance will be in person;
 Press 8 - (T)elephone Appearance if
 the appearance will be by telephone.
 4) Enter the 6-digit numeric portion of
 the case no. when asked to do so.
 5) Enter the 2-digit Request Code using
 the table to the right as a guideline.
 6) A list of time choices will be played;
 press a no. (1-4) which represents
 the amount of time you are requesting.
 7) If the date and time are OK, press 9
 (Y)es; otherwise, press 6 for (N)o.
 8) Once you have accepted a hearing time,
 it will be repeated; write it down.
 9) The system will give you a special
 confirmation #. You should write it
 down! This number provides a secure
 and convenient way for you to cancel
 the hearing if it is necessary.
 	
 TO CANCEL A HEARING TIME:
 	
 3) Press 2 - (C)ancel when prompted.
 4) Enter the 4-digit special confirmation #
 when you asked to do so.
 5) System will inform you if the hearing
 was successfully cancelled.
	Hearing Request Codes:
	
	 01 - DISMISS
	 02 - STRIKE
	 03 - COMPEL
	 04 - CONTINUE
	 05 - QUASH
	 06 - SUMMARY JUDGEMENT
	 07 - FINAL DEFAULT JUDGEMENT
	 08 - VACATE
	 09 - INTERVENE
	 10 - TAX FEES/COSTS
	 11 - ABATE
	 12 - AMEND
	 13 - DEFAULT
	 14 - SEVER
	 15 - CONSOLIDATE
	 16 - LIMINE
	 17 - PROTECTIVE ORDER
	 18 - CONTEMPT
	 19 - WITHDRAW
	 20 - STAY
	 21 - SANCTIONS
	 22 - SET ASIDE
	 23 - DEFICIENCY JUDGEMENT
	 24 - EXTEND TIME
	 25 - FINAL HEARING
	 26 - QUIET TITLE
	 27 - OBJECTION TO INTERROG.
	 28 - ORDER TO SHOW CAUSE
	 29 - OBJECTION TO REQUEST FOR
	      PRODUCTION
	 30 - ANY OTHER SINGLE MOTION
	 31 - ALL PENDING MOTIONS OR
	      MULTIPLE MOTIONS
	 32 - NEW TRIAL
	 33 - TEMPORARY INJUNCTION
	
	 TO LIST ALL OF YOUR HEARINGS:
	
	 3) Press 5 - (L)ist to play
	 a list of the hearings
	 you have auto-scheduled.
	
	 TO DISCONTINUE A CALL:
	
	 3) Press 4 - (H)angup

Figure 16.3 Automated court scheduling reference sheet.
(*Source:* National Center for State Courts, *Court Technology
Reports,* Vol. 4. Williamsburg, Va.: Author, p. 62. Copyright 1992.
Used with permission.)

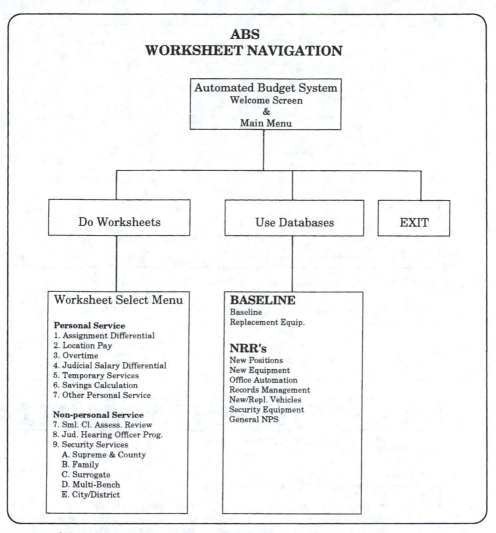

Figure 16.4 Automated budget system worksheet navigation. (*Source:* National Center for State Courts, *Court Technology Reports,* Vol. 4. Williamsburg, Va.: Author, p. 46. Copyright 1992. Used with permission.)

much greater advantage than by courts and police agencies. We next discuss some of these other uses of technology in prisons, jails, and probation and parole agencies.

✧ TRACKING PRISON INMATES IN CALIFORNIA

The California Department of Corrections (CDC) is one of the largest criminal justice agencies in the world. It tracks more than 120,000 inmates in 27 state

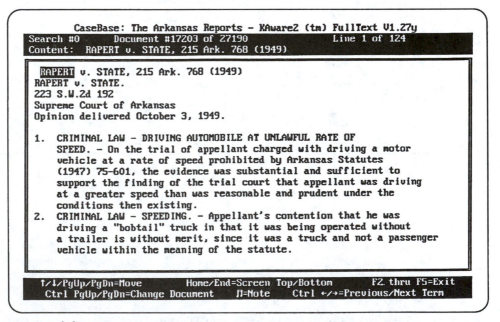

```
                                                         AEH  5/14/92 10:09 AM
 Financial History.... Clackamas County Circuit Court      Status Open     VBL
 Case#......    UNAS16 Oregon State Of/Doe John
_____Offense_Misdemeanor_-_Comm_Weight/Measure_Viola_-_U/MIS_
 Trust                          Received        Disbursed        Balance
    A/R Payment                 1,300.00        -1,300.00           0.00
    Restitution                   500.00          -500.00           0.00
 Trust Balance                                                      0.00
 ---------------------------------------------------------------------------
 Accounts Receivable            Deferred          Applied         Balance
    A/R Payment                     0.00             0.00            0.00
    Fine                        1,000.00          -725.00          275.00
    Restitution                   500.00          -500.00            0.00
    Unitary Assessment             75.00           -75.00            0.00
 Accounts Rcv Balance          1,575.00        -1,300.00          275.00
 ---------------------------------------------------------------------------
    4/30/92 VBL  100786 Due:  4/30/92 Distribution: S REST          500.00
            IMP     1 CRD Mr Measure It
            SNT     1
 ---------------------------------------------------------------------------  +


 CF05-DSPPMT    CF07-DSPTRSLGR  CF08-DSPVBLLGR  CF10-BROWSE FWD CF11-BROWSE BCK
```

Figure 16.5 Computer-assisted case financial history. (*Source:* National Center for State Courts, *Court Technology Reports,* Vol. 4. Williamsburg, Va.: Author, p. 95. Copyright 1992. Used with permission.)

```
          CaseBase: The Arkansas Reports - KAware2 (tm) FullText V1.27y
 Search #0       Document #17203 of 27190                    Line 1 of 124
 Content:  RAPERT v. STATE, 215 Ark. 768 (1949)

   RAPERT v. STATE, 215 Ark. 768 (1949)
   RAPERT v. STATE.
   223 S.W.2d 192
   Supreme Court of Arkansas
   Opinion delivered October 3, 1949.

   1.  CRIMINAL LAW - DRIVING AUTOMOBILE AT UNLAWFUL RATE OF
       SPEED. - On the trial of appellant charged with driving a motor
       vehicle at a rate of speed prohibited by Arkansas Statutes
       (1947) 75-601, the evidence was substantial and sufficient to
       support the finding of the trial court that appellant was driving
       at a greater speed than was reasonable and prudent under the
       conditions then existing.
   2.  CRIMINAL LAW - SPEEDING. - Appellant's contention that he was
       driving a "bobtail" truck in that it was being operated without
       a trailer is without merit, since it was a truck and not a passenger
       vehicle within the meaning of the statute.


   ↑/↓/PgUp/PgDn=Move      Home/End=Screen Top/Bottom      F2 thru F5=Exit
   Ctrl PgUp/PgDn=Change Document     ∫]=Note    Ctrl ←/→=Previous/Next Term
```

Figure 16.6 Computer-assisted legal research system. (*Source:* National Center for State Courts, *Court Technology Reports,* Vol. 4. Williamsburg, Va.: Author, p. 122. Copyright 1992.)

institutions and 38 camps during and after incarceration. This Herculean task includes monitoring their movements, medical histories, visitors, restitution fines, and job assignments.[50]

The foundation of the CDC's inmate tracking program is an integrated information sharing system with at least one computer located at each institution. Pertinent data are entered by custody staff each day and are transmitted via a wide area network to the central office in Sacramento. When entering a prison, a new inmate is assigned a unique CDC number; this number helps the staff track the inmate's movements and status at all times. A complex data file that consists of information ranging from medical problems and cell assignment to previous escape history is maintained for each inmate. CDC also accounts for the money an inmate may have arrived with, any money sent to him or her through the mail, and amounts deducted to pay court-ordered restitution fines.[51]

✧ AUTOMATED DIRECT SUPERVISION IN JAILS

Direct supervision jails are springing up across the country, eschewing typical jail cells with steel bars. Some of these facilities—such as those in Knox County, Tennessee, Forsythe County, North Carolina, and Pima County, Arizona—are replacing the bars with bar-coded wristbands and state-of-the-art computerized information management systems. As one data communications engineer stated, "Everything from the toilets to the telephones is fully computerized" in these facilities.[52]

The information technology package used in these facilities includes live-scan fingerprinting, an automated fingerprint identification system, digitized mug shots, and computerized inmate and records management. Each inmate's wristband is keyed into the central computer system, which contains his or her name, physical description, picture, and prisoner number; it is used to track each inmate's location, visitations, library use, medical treatment, and court appointments. The $6.5 million system is expected to reduce costs, provide an unheard of level of records integrity, and increase the safety of both officers and inmates by allowing the administrators to develop a completely cashless inmate society. Without cash and with limits set on how much an inmate can spend each week, correctional officers hope to curtail contraband problems. This cashless system virtually eliminates the illicit transactions that once were common because the administration can regulate and monitor the flow of cash.[53]

✧ KIOSK CHECK-IN FOR PROBATIONERS

Several problems plague probation agencies in the United States. With more police officers and therefore more arrests, probation caseloads continue to rise while taxpayers resolutely refuse to give more money to anything that smacks of rehabilitation or coddling offenders. Many probation practitioners believe that something had to be done to alleviate their overworked and understaffed condition and are turning to automated means of doing so.

A new computer system allows probationers who pose little or no public risk and need very little personal supervision to check in from a remote location rather than making a trip to the probation officer's office and then waiting and wasting time while the officer finishes other work. The probationers simply push a few buttons at an electronic kiosk to show they have not left town and perhaps breathe into a breathalyzer if abstention from alcohol is a condition of probation. The system is user friendly, very accessible, and works without invading privacy.[54]

The kiosks are strategically located and linked to a network of personal computers in the probation department. During the initial meeting with a probation officer, a probationer's biometric keys (fingerprints, voice, retina scan, signature, hand structure) and digital photo of the face are captured electronically. They are entered, along with case-specific information, into the database. The system's server can be programmed to expect check-ins from several times a day to weekly, monthly, or longer intervals. Specific questions can be written for each client. A probationer may check in at any kiosk, where a biometric sample is taken via scanner and compared to the one collected during enrollment. Once identification is established, the probationer may check in. When the session is complete, the probationer is given a receipt for his or her records. The kiosk operates every day, serving a maximum of 180 people per day.

Evaluations of the system by academics give it high marks for its efficiency in computerized record keeping and for giving probation officers more time to deal with their more serious offenders.[55]

An excellent new resource is a must-read for both criminal justice practitioners and students wishing to travel the information superhighway. *Internet Investigations in Criminal Justice* by Cynthia B. Leshin[56] includes discussion and hands-on practice in the use of the Internet, finding information and resources, using criminal justice web sites, and employing cyberspace to find a job. Furthermore, persons wishing to access new developments in technology may find the following World Wide Web address useful:

http://www.govtech.net

This resource provides information about new products, solutions to problems, jobs, training resources, and conferences. For Internet access to the National Criminal Justice Reference Service Online, use Telnet to access ncjrsbbs.aspensys.com or Gopher to access ncjrs.aspensys.com 71. UNOJUST, the United Nations Online Justice Information System, may be reached at http://ncjrs.org/unojust.

Summary

This chapter has reviewed several exciting technological developments that are in use by or available to police, courts, and correction organizations. Readers, especially present and future administrators, managers, and supervisors, are encouraged to stay tuned in this area because the age of computer technology makes almost anything possible. Computer-assisted systems can be economical.

Questions for Review

1. What can technology do to help the police answer calls? Investigate traffic accidents?
2. Which technologies described in this chapter have the primary benefit of making the environment safer for employees and clients? Which are primarily advantageous in their cost savings?
3. What are some of the major technological capabilities now in use in the nation's courts? What are some of the futuristic technological items or methods found in the 21st century courtroom?
4. What technologies are available to help all agencies of criminal justice to become paperless?
5. Try to conceive of areas in which computer hardware and software could provide additional assistance in criminal justice. What cost issues come into play with these technologies?

Notes

1. George Nicholson and Jeffrey Hogge, "Retooling Criminal Justice: Interbranch Cooperation Needed," *Government Technology* (February 1996): 32.
2. *Ibid.*
3. Tod Newcombe, "Bandwidth Blues," *Government Technology* (August 1996): 1, 52.
4. Kaveh Ghaemian, "Small-Town Cops Wield Big-City Data," *Government Technology* (September 1996): 38.
5. Meghan Cotter, "Will Integrated Public Safety and Criminal Justice Become a Reality?" *Government Technology* (December 1995): 52.
6. Justine Kavanaugh, "Community Oriented Policing and Technology," *Government Technology* (March 1996): 14.
7. *Ibid.*
8. Bill McGarigle, "Electronic Mapping Speeds Crime and Traffic Investigations," *Government Technology* (February 1996): 20–21.
9. Justine Kavanaugh, "Drunk Drivers Get a Shot of Technology," *Government Technology* (March 1996): 26.
10. Tod Newcombe, "Imaged Processing Sharpens Crime Video," *Government Technology* (March 1996): 22.

11. Tod Newcombe, "Imaged Prints Go Online, Cops Return to Streets," *Government Technology* (April 1996): 1, 31.

12. U.S. Department of Justice, National Institute of Justice Research in Action, "The Use of Computerized Mapping in Crime Control and Prevention Programs" (July 1995): 1.

13. U.S. Department of Justice, National Institute of Justice Program Focus, "The Chicago Police Department's Information Collection for Automated Mapping (ICAM) Program" (July 1996): 2.

14. U.S. Department of Justice, National Institute of Justice Research in Action, "The Use of Computerized Mapping in Crime Control and Prevention Programs," p. 2.

15. Tod Newcombe, "Adding a New Dimension to Crime Reconstruction," *Government Technology* (August 1996): 32.

16. Justine Kavanaugh, "Locator System Targets Shooters," *Government Technology* (June 1996): 14–15.

17. Patrick Joyce, "Firearms Training: As Close to Real as It Gets," *Government Technology* (July 1995): 14–15.

18. Justine Kavanaugh, "Gang Data Systems Help Close Cases," *Government Technology* (December 1995): 12.

19. Ray Dussault, "Dispatchers Provide Information Age Kevlar," *Government Technology* (January 1996): 14–15.

20. Brian Miller, "Spent Cartridges Nail Shooters," *Government Technology* (October 1996): 15.

21. Milford H. Sprecher, "States Gearing Up for NCIC 2000," *Government Technology* (January 1995): 12.

22. Newcombe, "Bandwidth Blues," p. 52.

23. *Ibid.*

24. *Ibid.,* p. 13.

25. Brian Miller, "Implementing Brady Background Check," *Government Technology* (May 1996): 36.

26. *Ibid.*

27. U.S. Department of Justice, National Institute of Justice Research in Brief, *Videotaping Interrogations and Confessions* (Washington, D.C.: Author, March 1993), p. 2.

28. Ted Gest, "Can 'Smart' Guns Save Many Lives?" *U.S. News and World Report* (December 2, 1996): 37.

29. *Ibid.,* p. 38.

30. Ken Peak, "The Quest for Alternatives to Lethal Force: A Heuristic View," *Journal of Contemporary Criminal Justice* (1990): 8–22.

31. *Ibid.*

32. Sarah Manwaring-White, *The Policing Revolution: Police Technology, Democracy, and Liberty in Britain* (Brighton, Sussex: The Harvester Press, 1983).

33. "IACP 'Acquits' OC Spray in 22 In-Custody Deaths," *Law Enforcement News* (April 30, 1994): 1.

34. John Barry and Tom Morganthau, "Soon, 'Phasers on Stun,' " *Newsweek* (February 7, 1994): 24–25.

35. James Evans, "JusticeLINK: Maryland's Electronic Court Test," *Government Technology* (July 1995): 34.

36. David J. Egar, "Electronic Filing," paper presented at the Fourth National Court Technology Conference, National Center for State Courts, Nashville, Tennessee, October 1994, p. 3.

37. *Ibid.,* pp. 3–4.

38. Carter C. Cowles, National Center for State Courts, "Document Imaging," *Court Technology Reports* (1992): 26–27.

39. Carter C. Cowles, "Document Imaging," *Court Technology Bulletin* (September/October 1995): 5.

40. National Center for State Courts Court Technology Briefing Paper, "Videoconferencing," 1995, p. 1.

41. Meghan Cotter, "Video Arraignment Improves Public Safety," *Government Technology* (December 1995): 24.

42. *Ibid.*

43. *Ibid.,* pp. 24–25.

44. *Ibid.,* p. 25.

45. *Ibid.*

46. Fredric I. Lederer, "Courtroom 21: A Model Courtroom of the 21st Century," *Court Technology Bulletin* (January/February 1994): 1, 5.

47. Michelle Gamble-Risley, "A Smart Tool for Modern Courtrooms," *Government Technology* (October 1996): 32.

48. National Center for State Courts, *Court Technology Report,* (1991): iii.

49. Richard Power, "Technology in the Criminal Appellate Process," *Government Technology* (August 1995): 35.

50. Dona Snow, "Stretching Corrections Resources With Project Management," *Government Technology* (January 1995): 78.

51. *Ibid.*

52. Raymond Dussault, "Direct Supervision and Records Automation," *Government Technology* (August 1995): 36.

53. *Ibid.,* p. 37.

54. James Evans, "Kiosk Check In for Probationers," *Government Technology* (May 1995): 42.

55. *Ibid.,* pp. 42, 44.

56. Cynthia B. Leshin, *Internet Investigations in Criminal Justice* (Upper Saddle River, NJ: Prentice Hall, 1997).

Chapter 17

Peeking Over the Rim: What Lies Ahead?

I like the dreams of the future better than the history of the past.
—Patrick Henry

The trouble with our times is that the future is not what it used to be.
—Paul Valery

✦ INTRODUCTION

Internal combustion engines twice as fuel efficient but only half as environmentally harmful; virtually free telephone calls; accurate long-term weather forecasts; machines that automatically translate printed text into different languages; the emergence of virtual universities, which students attend by videoteleconferencing; a 40 percent reduction in crime because buildings and public spaces are designed for better security; the use of electronic cash in most homes. These developments are not projected to occur 100, 50, or even 25 years in the future; the first-ever United Kingdom Technology Foresight Program predicts that they will all occur by the year 2005.[1] Clearly, the future is now.

We all have probably wished at some time that we could gaze into a crystal ball and have what former President George Bush termed "the vision thing." Criminal justice students—our administrators of tomorrow—must listen to what the prognosticators tell us about the future and understand their methods. Like current justice administrators, these future administrators must take the time today to peek over the rim to anticipate the future and plan for it.

This final chapter examines some of the things that futurists see that the future holds. We also look at what appears imminent with respect to demographics and crime in the United States. We consider what the experts predict in terms of police methods for coping with crime as well as forecasted changes in courts and corrections. We also examine the methods of police, courts, and corrections in the future. Some areas for which reforms are needed are identified. We close the chapter with a general discussion of the necessary steps administrators need to take to reinvent their agencies, specifically whether they can bring about changes in governance to become more customer oriented and streamline and enhance many of their operations by joining the information technology revolution.

✦ HOW TO PREDICT THE FUTURE

Many variables can affect justice agencies; one of the most important is money. In the future, the economy will be the driving force for major changes in justice agencies.

Contemporary futures research involves environmental scanning and scenario writing. Environmental scanning is an effort to put a social problem under a microscope and to predict its future. We may consult experts, such as demographers, social scientists, technologists, and economists. A Delphi process may be used to assist in gathering data from experts, looking at all possible factors, and getting an idea of what will happen in the future. Thus, environmental scanning permits us to identify, track, and assess changes in the environment.[2]

Through scanning, we can examine the factors that seem likely to "drive" the environment. *Drivers* are factors or variables—economic conditions, demographic shifts, governmental policies, social attitudes, technological advances, and so on—that will have a bearing on future conditions. Three categories of drivers will serve to identify possible trends and impacts on the U.S. criminal justice system beyond the year 2000: (1) social conditions (e.g., size and age of the population, immigration patterns, nature of employment, and lifestyle characteristics); (2) shifts in the amounts and types of crimes (including the potential for new types of criminality and for technological advances that might be used for illegal behavior); and (3) possible developments in the criminal justice system itself (e.g., changes in the way the police, courts, and corrections subsystems operate and important innovations).[3]

Scenario writing is simply the application of drivers to primary situations or elements. In the context of our discussion, three scenarios are public tolerance for crime, amount of crime, and the capacity of the criminal justice system to deal with crime. An important consideration is whether each will occur in high or low degrees. For example, drivers may be analyzed in a scenario of *low* public tolerance for crime, a *high* amount of crime, and a *high* capacity of the criminal justice system to deal with crime. Conversely, a scenario may include a view of the future in which a *high* tolerance for crime, a *low* amount of crime, a *low* capacity for the system to cope with crime, and so on exist.

✦ THE CHANGING FACE OF AMERICA

In 1996 the first wave of "baby boomers" turned 50; by 2010 one in every four Americans will be 55 or older. By the year 2000, an estimated 34.9 million elderly people will constitute 13 percent of the population. The minority population is increasing rapidly; by the year 2000 an estimated 34 percent of U.S. children will be Hispanic, African-American, or Asian. More than 25 million women headed their own households in 1990, 28 percent of the nation's 91 million households. Two-thirds of African-American and Hispanic households are headed by women. If present trends continue, one-half of all marriages occurring today will end in divorce within a decade.[4]

In our postindustrial society, the number of blue-collar jobs has decreased and white-collar jobs increased. Jobs that are declining in number are those that could be filled by individuals with fewer skills. The fastest-growing jobs are those requiring more language, math, and reasoning skills. For the first decade of the 21st century, 90 percent of all new jobs will be in the service sector—fields that often require high levels of education and skill. In 1987, 77 percent of all jobs required some type of generating, processing, retrieving, or distribution of information; by the year 2000, this will increase to 95 percent of all jobs. Statistics indicate that the United States is becoming a bifurcated society, with more wealth and poverty and a shrinking middle class. The gap between the "haves" and "have nots" is widening. An underclass of people who are chronically poor and live outside society's rules is growing. Between 1970 and 1980 the underclass tripled.[5]

The influence of immigration to the United States and the growth of minority-group populations in general cannot be overstated. The United States now accepts nearly a million newcomers per year, which equates to about 10 million new residents each decade, excluding their offspring, even if immigration rates do not rise. Shortly after the turn of the 21st century, Asians are expected to reach 10 million; the 18 million legal and illegal Hispanics at the end of the century may well double by then. In less than 100 years we can expect white dominance of the United States to end as the growing number of African-Americans, Hispanics, and Asians together become the new majority.

History has shown that when newcomers cluster together in poor neighborhoods with high crime rates, the criminal justice system is soon involved. When these various minority groups are forced to compete for increasingly scarce, low-paying service jobs, intergroup relations are strained and can become combative, as has occurred recently in major cities.[6]

✦ THE CHANGING NATURE OF CRIME

Three important drivers contribute to the changing nature of crime in the West: (1) the advent of high technology, (2) the distribution and use of narcotics, and (3) a declining population in the 15- to 24-year-old segment.[7]

The nature of crime is rapidly changing. The new crimes of data manipulation, software piracy, bank card counterfeiting, and embezzlement via computer are here to stay. The traditionally illegal means of obtaining funds—robbery and burglary—will be used less frequently. These new crimes will require the development of new investigative techniques, specialized training for police investigators, and the employment of people with specialized, highly technological backgrounds.

The abuse of narcotics is increasing throughout various social classes and continues to demand an ever-increasing amount of police time and resources. The true solution to the drug problem is for people to stop demanding a supply; however, this is probably an impossible goal.

The decrease in the number of the 15- to 24-year-old segment, the crime-prone youth of our society, has significantly affected crime rates: the frequency of several types of crime is declining. As we see the increase in the graying of America, however, young criminals will prey more and more on the elderly and flourish. The increasing numbers of crime-prone youths in our metropolitan areas virtually ensure that high crime rates will continue in the inner cities.

The nation's shift in demographic makeup has implications for future criminal justice recruiting efforts. A change toward older workers, fewer entry-level workers, and more women, minorities, and immigrants in the population will force criminal justice agencies and private industry to become more flexible to compete for qualified applicants. With the aging of the United States, justice agencies that recruit only recent high school graduates will probably face a shortage of qualified workers. Agencies must devise new strategies to attract 21- to 35-year-olds, an age group that will be at a premium over the next 10 years, a trend that will continue well into the middle of the next century. Criminal justice will also need to offer better wage and benefits packages (such as day care, flexible hours, and paid maternity leave) to compete with private businesses.[8]

✦ POLICING METHODS OF THE FUTURE

The technological revolution discussed in Chapter 16 will result in new weapons for both criminals and the police. Some futurists believe that traditional old methods and equipment for doing police work will be replaced. Electric and methane-fueled scooters and bubble-topped tricycles will be used in densely populated areas; police in rural and suburban areas will employ steamwagons and diesel superchargers; and methane-filled helium dirigibles, equipped with infrared night goggles and sophisticated communications and lighting devices will assist in setting traps for high-speed drivers and in performing search and rescue operations.[9]

Patrol officers in this scenario will type in the facts of a crime and receive a list of suspects. With a bit more analysis and data, the computer will give a probability that various suspects committed the particular crime at that particular place. All homes and businesses will be linked to a central dispatch system in a police-approved, computer-based remote linkage system that will combine burglar and fire alarms. Community policing teams will be assigned by zone, the officers wearing blazers or other dress instead of paramilitary uniforms. Basic police training will last a minimum of 10 months and will be designed so that the lower one-third of the class will not succeed.[10]

Others see the future of policing differently. The 21st century cop may patrol by means of jet backpack flight equipment, and officers will be able to tie in to "language banks" of translators via their wrist radios. Holographic, or three-dimensional, photography may be used for mug photos, and satellite photography will probably be used to assist in criminal investigations. Police vehicles will have electronic equipment built in, and private vehicles will have a factory-installed "kill switch" that can be activated by pressing a button in a nearby patrol vehicle, thus preventing high-speed pursuits.[11]

Obviously, police administrators need to assign some of their best thinkers to the task of probing the future. What should the agency's budget be? How should police personnel be trained? What skills will be needed? What new technologies will be available to the police? How should forces be deployed?

An area of concern among futurists is policing's organization structure. Increasing numbers of police executives are beginning to question whether the pyramid-shaped police bureaucracy will be effective in the future; indeed, the spread of community policing and problem solving (discussed in Chapter 4) has allowed many police executives to flatten their organizations. As we discussed in Chapter 2, communication within the pyramid structure is often stymied by many barriers and frustrated by the levels of bureaucracy; perhaps the organization structure, the argument goes, could be changed to a more horizontal design to facilitate the flow of information and ideas.

Personnel and labor/management problems will continue to loom large in the future. Because opportunities for police graft and corruption will not decline, police administrators must be sure to develop personnel policies that will protect the integrity of the profession. Mandatory drug testing and the use of the polygraph to safeguard the organizations are currently being debated. Such matters as age discrimination, employment misconduct, sexism, racism, new employee attitudes, and poor work habits will not be resolved in the near future.

✦ FUTURE CHANGES IN THE COURTS

✧ SHIFTS IN PHILOSOPHY AND PRACTICES

Futurists have also been considering the future of the courts as their caseloads expand, society demands greater assistance from them in addressing its social ills, and technology continues to advance. Futurist Clement Bezold offered some interesting court-related speculations for the early 21st century:

1. Private businesses offering adjudication, arbitration, and mediation services will increasingly compete with public courts to resolve disputes more quickly and fairly.
2. The adversary system, which is slow, costly, and fraught with unfairness, will die.
3. The vast majority of judicial decision making (in such areas as small claims courts, traffic courts, and status offenses) will be by nonlawyer, citizen pro-tempore judges.
4. Courts will be depoliticized. Appointed professional managers will become the norm, and the merit selection of judges will become more commonplace.
5. Courts will increasingly be called on to resolve social problems involving drugs, poverty, and domestic violence, but with little success.
6. Court programs will become increasingly decentralized and closer to client groups.
7. Court organization structures will become more informal, with less reliance on hierarchical, bureaucratic structures, and shared leadership.[12]

Certainly not to be overlooked in the courts' future is the impact of high technology on their internal operations. Next we examine the technological advances that are now developing.

✧ HELP ON THE HORIZON WITH TECHNOLOGY

On a Tuesday evening, in the suburbs of a large, traffic-choked city, Smith is in court to contest a speeding ticket. Instead of getting into his car and driving into the city for night court, Smith strolls a few blocks to a public library and enters a small, enclosed booth and interacts with a computer screen that displays a menu of functions and colorful icons. He touches the symbol of a courthouse and then the one indicating traffic court. A pleasant voice instructs him to insert his driver's license into a slot on the monitor. Seconds later he sees the date, time, and nature of the charged offense. Smith is told that his case will be called in two minutes. Soon the monitor shows a black-robed figure who addresses Smith and asks how he pleads ("not guilty"). The testimony of Smith and the arresting officer, who appears on another monitor, are then given to the judge, who also calls up and views Smith's DMV record on the monitor. After the case is resolved, Smith pays any fine assessed and he removes his driver's license from the monitor and exits the booth to go home.[13]

Many problems must be solved before this scenario can become a reality; however, virtually none of the problems are technological ones. In Chapter 16 we discussed document imaging, electronic filing, and other high technology developments that are either already available or are on the horizon. With the assimilation of these developments, the courts have the fundamental tools to create this scenario. The tough issues involve the way we view the judicial process. Artificial intelligence, or "AI" (where computers are programmed to exhibit characteristics of human intelligence), expert systems (AI programs that capture the knowledge of experts for use with new situations), virtual reality (AI that combines computers and sensory apparatus to create simulated, controlled environments and experiences), robotics (using computers to accomplish a useful action), speech recognition (the interface between people and computers), and high technology access systems for court security are some of the tools that can be implemented in the courts to ease their burden provided that the public will accept their use.

✦ CORRECTIONS AND THE FUTURE

✧ CONTINUING THE BOOM INDUSTRY

Probably the most difficult area in the justice system to make future projections is the corrections area. The most ominous problems for corrections will continue to be those we have concentrated on already and that are the most difficult to predict, crowding and its related costs.

Many attempts have been made in the past to estimate future state prison populations. Mathematical models were used to extrapolate crime, incarceration, and demographic patterns.[14] Reality has a way of outstripping forecasts and mathematical models, however, especially in corrections. Forecasters cannot anticipate changes in sentencing policy or capture adequately the subtle and possibly changing interactions among age, race, crime, and criminal justice processing. For example, the baby boom never really stopped in the black and Hispanic communities, and these groups will constitute an increasingly large proportion of the young male cohort in the coming decades—a cohort that has high arrest and incarceration rates.

Even more ominous are predictions that the U.S. prison population might double in the next 10 years; the current rates of growth point in that direction.[15] If the prison population doubles, governments will rapidly have to construct as many cells as now exist to handle the demand in addition to replacing currently substandard facilities. The cost of this construction, which is based on a cost of approximately $100,000 per bed, will be astronomical.

The situation will be more severe in those states having high incarceration rates, few plans for alternatives to incarceration, and higher levels of poverty (with, by extension, weaker tax bases). Most states in the south are so characterized. Local governments maintaining jails will fare even worse than state governments because their revenue bases are narrower.[16]

✧ FUTURE NEEDS OF CORRECTIONAL MANAGERS

With all of the issues and problems affecting corrections (discussed in this chapter and in more depth in Chapter 13), it is clear that more than ever the effective correctional administrator is one who, in the words of Alvin Cohn, "not only recognizes the inevitability of change, but tries to harness and direct the change process."[17] Cohn suggested that the pedestrian correctional manager reacts to crises, fails to plan, views his or her position as one of a sinecurist (requiring little or no work), and otherwise fails to lead the organization. Conversely, the progressive correctional manager is proactive, views the organization as a system, and plans for and attempts to control its future.[18]

Three significant developments in the fields of business and industry can be transferred to correctional practice. First is *technology*. At the end of the 20th century, more information can be recorded and processed in ways that are faster, more complete, and accurate than ever before. The second major development is *total quality management,* which is a philosophy that practices participative management and moves attention away from clients to customers. The third development is *reinventing government,* or finding ways to reduce both the size and complexity of government operations. Each of these developments has critical impact on government but is not always employed by correctional administrators to affect current and projected programs and services.[19]

Cohn believes that the traditional role of correctional managers—much of which revolves around information gathering and case reviewing—may be unnecessary with today's technology; if middle managers and supervisors can be recycled to demonstrate a willingness to change from traditional ways of doing business and incorporate these developments into their work, restructuring today's correctional agencies will be an easier process.[20]

✧ PRISONS: TO REFORM OR NOT TO REFORM

Given the extent of corrections' responsibility and problems throughout its history, it is not surprising that many people have called for its reform. The story of penal reform in the United States is an old and discouraging one. From the development of the penitentiary in the late 18th and early 19th centuries to the determinate sentencing movement of the last two decades, penal "reforms" in this country have led to few real improvements in the practice of punishment. Even if the reforms alleviated problems, in so doing they often created new ones, requiring new reforms, which led to further problems, and so on.[21] Now that we are ending the current reform cycle of determinate sentencing, however, it is timely and perhaps even necessary to consider why reforms fail and whether anything will work. According to Samuel Pillsbury,

> Reform begins with the proposal of a scheme for penal improvement. In most instances it is suggested by an idealist who links the proposed penal reform to a view of the ideal society prominent at the time. The idealist promotes a penal ideology which emphasizes the rightness or goodness of the proposed change in terms of society's relation to the offender.[22]

George Bernard Shaw warned against penal reform more than a half century ago. He urged persons interested in pursuing penal reform for benevolent purposes:

> to put it down and go about some other business. It is just such reformers who have in the past made the neglect, oppression, corruption, and physical torture of the common gaol the pretext for transforming it into that diabolical den of torment, mischief, and damnation, the modern prison.[23]

Many have sought, both within the system as well as without, to make prisons better places. Internally initiated reform has from time to time been sought by inmates through rioting; although this method is not the most effective way to express inmate grievances, it has focused attention on prison problems and helped pave the way for inmate councils, grievance procedures, conflict resolution, and the position of ombudspersons.

Another means of attempting internal reform is changing the internal administration. Normally, internally initiated reform by the staff is short-lived; either the familiar routine returns or the reforms settle into a new but equally sterile routine. Unless real reform occurs at all levels, little incentive for initiating new programs exists. The most lasting reforms appear to be those that have been initiated by external sources or with the knowledge and support of the outside community and public leaders.[24]

At the state level, externally induced reform is usually brought by legislative or executive action. A state's criminal code may be revised to allow such benefits as educational and home furloughs. The executive branch of government can enact executive orders. At the federal level, the most active reformer has been the Supreme Court. As noted previously, a number of major court decisions have effected prisoners' rights and the ability to file writs of habeas corpus in death penalty cases. External pressure is also brought to bear by private organizations, such as The John Howard Association, the American Correctional Association, and the National Council on Crime and Delinquency. All seek reform through prison certification visits and suggestions to correctional administrators. Organizations of former offenders who work with prisoners, such as the Seventh Step Foundation, Man-to-Man, and the Fortune Society, also seek correctional reform.[25] An official of the California school system provided some food for thought for simple prison reform, saying

> You want to know where prison reform starts? I'll tell you. It's the third grade. We know the high risk groups who will drop out of school. We know individuals from these groups make up a disproportionate share of prison inmates. Give me part of the $20,000 a year we now spend on these kids as adults [in prison], give it to me now, and we can make sure they won't wind up in prison, costing the state money not only to lock them up, but for the crimes they've committed, and for the welfare payments if they have a family.[26]

According to prison expert John DiIulio, Jr., prison officials could take three steps to help create better prisons in the short and long terms:

1. Provide continuity in the commissioner's office (and, it should be added, in the warden's office; both have an average tenure that is often less than five years). The current situation of high turnover for the past 15 years fosters a power vacuum at many levels of management.
2. Adopt the practice of unit management (the concept described earlier in this chapter) as a means of reducing prison violence. In addition to its potential for calming the institution and its residents, there are fewer staff rotations, allowing management to measure performance better. Officers are given more authority, act more as professionals, and morale is boosted.
3. Allow products manufactured by inmates in state prisons to be sold to the federal government. This would eliminate the presently endless hours of idleness for inmates. The federal system has a large and ready market for its products.[27]

✦ BUILDING MORE PRISONS: LARGE, SMALL, OR NONE AT ALL?

No issue has brought criminal justice more to the forefront of public policy—and into the living rooms of America—than that of corrections costs. In fact, state spending for corrections throughout the nation grew by more than 50 percent during the 1980s—the largest increase of any state-funded service.[28] Furthermore, from 1975 to 1985, the cost of operating corrections in the country rose by nearly 240 percent.[29] Americans now spend $13 billion to confine adult offenders.

As discussed earlier, legal reforms have expanded the use of determinate and mandatory sentences and thus enlarged the correctional population. With the annual cost of incarceration running in some states now more than $50,000 per inmate, concern over the cost of incarcerating such large numbers of offenders and crowding in general is increasing. As a result, a variety of proposals has surfaced to cope with the problem of population and to save money. As presented previously, one purported cost-saving mechanism is privatization, by which correctional institutions are run by for-profit enterprises. Others include marginally credible ideas ranging from that of a New York City mayor, who suggested using old tugboats to hold prisoners,[30] to politically volatile solutions such as early-release programs,[31] to electronic surveillance home-detention programs.

Although it is clear that the concern among legislators, correctional administrators, and the public over the cost of corrections is justified, the public is sending mixed messages. For example, legislative changes to penal codes in the late 1980s in the form of mandatory prison terms for drunk drivers and for those who commit gun crimes and calls for the abolition of parole boards, seemed to indicate a popular sentiment for adding prison space. More recently, however, the public seems to be gradually reversing itself, balking at the prospect of spending more than $50 million every few years to construct a new prison to house offenders (especially when schools, highways, health care, and social services are suffering). Thus, we now see a movement toward early release and other types of programs designed to reduce the overload and divert offenders from incarceration.

Douglas McDonald determined that larger prisons are less expensive on a per prisoner basis than smaller ones. In addition, the average per capita cost of operating maximum security prisons is lower than the cost of minimum security camps, which in turn were less expensive than medium security facilities. These cost differences resulted largely from variations in the way each type of facility was staffed. Maximum security prisons were larger, on average, and had fewer staff persons per inmate than did other facilities. "As the staff/inmate ratio increased, so did cost."[32]

All is not gloom and doom in the area of corrections costs, however. Construction and financing costs can make building prisons seem overwhelmingly expensive. According to the National Institute of Justice (NIJ), however, when these charges are amortized over the useful life of a facility, they become quite modest. The NIJ also noted that other unintended costs of imprisonment for a community exist. Imprisoning breadwinners may force their families into welfare dependency. If an inmate were unemployed at the time of imprisonment, however, the state would actually gain by paying less unemployment compensation.[33]

One estimate is that society loses an average of $408 in taxes and $84 in welfare payments per year of imprisonment. Assuming a total social loss of $5,000 per year, the NIJ concluded that a year in prison implies confinement costs of roughly $20,000, for a total social cost of about $25,000. Carrying this analysis a bit further and adding a new twist by combining crime costs and offense rates, NIJ found that a typical inmate (found in a survey to commit 187 crimes per year) is responsible for $430,000 in crime costs. Sentencing 1,000 more offenders to prison would obligate correctional systems to an additional $25 million per year, but about 187,000 felonies would be averted in the process of incapacitation. *These crimes represent about $430 million in social costs.*[34]

In addition to being sensitive to the high cost of imprisonment and the political sensitivity of this issue, correctional administrators must be adept at determining the best approach to keeping abreast of the structural needs of their criminal population. Timing can be a hidden yet important variable because the public is not always amenable to new, normally expensive construction proposals. Legislative enactments (such as those concerning mandatory sentencing or early release proposals) also weigh into the prison construction decision. Alternatives to imprisonment (such as those discussed in Chapter 12) must also be considered.

✦ CAN ADMINISTRATORS "REINVENT" CRIMINAL JUSTICE?

✧ CASTING OFF OLD WAYS

Reinventing Government, the book that swept the country and was on the bookshelves of many governors, city managers, and criminal justice administrators, provided ideas about how government can and should work as efficiently and productively as the best-run private businesses. It uses myriad examples of government agencies that have slashed red tape, begun focusing on the "customer," cut costs tremendously, revamped the budget-expenditure process to provide incentives for saving money, abandoned archaic civil service systems, decentralized authority, and empowered their employees. The book showed how these agencies can become more entrepreneurial and "steer" rather than "row," be driven by missions rather than by rules, encourage competition over monopoly, and invest in prevention rather than cure. The reason for the book's widespread popularity is that it demonstrated what can be accomplished when government leaders decide to "break the mold" and try new methods.

The authors of *Reinventing Government,* David Osborne and Ted Gaebler, went beyond the five principles of total quality management, espoused by W. Edwards Deming in 1950, which focused on results, customers, decentralization, prevention, and a market (or systems) approach. Osborne and Gaebler found that most entrepreneurial governments focused on promoting *competition* between service providers; they *empower* citizens by pushing control out of the bureaucracy and into the community; and they measure the performance of their agencies, focusing not on inputs but on *outcomes*. They are driven by their goals—their *missions*—rather than by rules and regulations. They redefine their clients as *customers* and offer them choices between levels of involvement, training programs, and so on. They *prevent* problems before they emerge rather than simply offer services afterward. They *decentralize* authority, embracing participatory management. They prefer *market* mechanisms to bureaucratic mechanisms. They focus not simply on providing public services but also on *catalyzing* all sectors—public, private, and voluntary—into action to solve their community's problems.[35]

✦ A Shift in Governance

Unfortunately, the great majority of our federal, state, and local government agencies do not operate as entrepreneurs. Instead, they reward failure and enhance bureaucracies rather than create incentives to save money or serve customers. When the crime rates increase, justice agencies are given more money; if they continue to fail, they are given even more. As police departments became professional, they began focusing on chasing criminals, not on solving community problems. This approach encourages agencies to ignore the root causes of crime and not to consider possible solutions to problems.

What Osborne and Gaebler call for is nothing less than a shift in the basic model of governance used in America—a shift that is already under way, doubtless largely because of the recent recession and demands on government agencies to "do more with less." It is now essential that justice administrators engage in strategic planning, looking beyond tomorrow and anticipating the future. Some police administrators have begun coping with recent revenue shortfalls in some new and unique—if not always popular—ways: as noted earlier, charging fees for traditionally free public services, such as unlocking vehicles and responding to false alarms.

It will become increasingly important for justice administrators to think of revenue-enhancing possibilities and ways to save money. They must also listen more to one of their greatest resources—the rank and file—although a revamped or "inverted" pyramidal organization structure may be necessary for accomplishing this goal. Increased collaboration with the public is also needed; the police must insist that private citizens, institutions, and organizations within their communities shoulder increased responsibility for assisting in crime control. Some examples of excellent collaborative efforts are DARE, MADD, Neighborhood Watch, and Court Watch.

In sum, justice administrators and members of society must rethink their approach to crime. They must play a catalytic role rather than merely reducing services or, as in the past, throwing money and personnel at ongoing problems. They must steer rather than row with a clear map in hand. In short, they need a new vision of government.

✦ Computer Applications

Although we discussed the uses of technology in criminal justice thoroughly in Chapter 16, this subject should be discussed again here in brief because computers are a major component of our future perspective.

Advances in computer technology have revolutionized many organizational and operational aspects of administration. We are clearly witnessing an "information technology revolution."[36] When a police officer investigates a crime, a probation officer prepares a presentence report, a court schedules a case for trial, a victim calls the district attorney's office to learn the status of his case, or a parole board tracks an inmate's parole eligibility date, information is collected, analyzed, and stored for future use. Computers allow justice administrators to engage in *planning* at a level never before possible. As we saw earlier in this chapter, strategic planning and forecasting are essential for developing and implementing policy within the limitations of present knowledge and decision making within political and economic realities.[37]

Mainframe computer systems are designed to store, retrieve, manipulate, and analyze massive amounts of information. The three well-known mainframe data bases in criminal justice are (1) the National Crime Information Center (NCIC), which contains detailed arrest and intelligence information on known and wanted offenders; (2) the *Uniform Crime Reports (UCR),* published annually by the FBI, which compiles, summarizes, and reports national crime data on a quarterly and annual basis; (3) the *Sourcebook of Criminal Justice Statistics,* published by the federal Bureau of Justice Statistics, which includes a comprehensive summary of justice activities across the country. Mainframe data-based management systems are also used extensively in criminal justice at all levels of government in functions ranging from developing psychological profiles of terrorists and kidnappers to registering automobiles and preparing descriptions and sketches of criminal subjects. Computers are also used as investigative tools in crime laboratories across the country.[38]

Our ability to use computer technology for additional purposes is limited only by our imagination and available funds. Clearly, today's criminal justice students and practitioners must become knowledgeable about computer applications, particularly word processing, the Internet, and use of modems. The future is high technology. Criminal justice cannot drive into the future looking into the rearview mirror as far as technology is concerned.

Summary

This chapter has discussed how the future may be predicted, the changing face of America and its crime problem, and future changes that are anticipated in police, courts, and corrections organizations. Emphasis was also placed on shifts in governance and computer applications.

For criminal justice organizations to implement innovation successfully, administrators and their staffs must have an abiding commitment to change and must motivate personnel for supporting innovations. Criminal justice agencies must become proactive.

Questions for Review

1. What are the primary methods for justice administrators to use in predicting the future? Discuss each.

2. What are some of the country's major demographic changes in the future? Which of them is/are most significant for criminal justice?

3. What does the future hold concerning crime? What criminal justice technology will be developed? How must justice agencies adapt to change?

4. What are some of the issues involved in the construction of new correctional institutions?

5. What are specific means by which government—and justice administrators in particular—can "reinvent" their operations? Why do many people believe they must do so?

6. How has computer technology changed criminal justice? In what ways will it continue to change justice administration in the future?

Notes

1. "The World in 2005," *U.S. News and World Report* (January 22, 1996): 15.

2. Kenneth J. Peak, *Policing America: Methods, Issues, Challenges* (2d ed.) (Upper Saddle River, N.J.: Prentice Hall, 1997), p. 390.

3. *Ibid.*

4. *Ibid.*, p. 392.

5. *Ibid.*

6. *Ibid.*

7. *Ibid.*

8. Rob McCord and Elaine Wicker, "Tomorrow's America: Law Enforcement's Coming Challenge," *FBI Law Enforcement Bulletin* 59 (January 1990): 31.

9. Edward A. Thibault, "Proactive Police Futures," in Gene Stephens (ed.), *The Future of Criminal Justice* (Cincinnati, Ohio: Anderson, 1982), pp. 67–85.

10. *Ibid.*, pp. 73–77.

11. Clyde L. Cronkhite, "21st Century Cop," *The National Centurion* (April 1984): 26–29, 47–48.

12. Adapted from Clement Bezold, "On Futures Thinking and the Courts," *The Court Manager* 6 (Summer 1991): 4–11.

13. Adapted from Lawrence P. Webster, James E. McMillan, J. Douglas Walker, and Barbara C. Kelly, "What's New in Court Technology: An Overview," *Judges' Journal* 32 (Summer 1993): 11, 73.

14. See, for example, Thomas F. Rich and Arnold I. Barnett, "Model-Based U.S. Prison Population Projections," *Public Administration Review* 45 (November 1985): 780–789.

15. Douglas C. McDonald, "The Cost of Corrections: In Search of the Bottom Line," in Joan Petersilia (ed.), *Research in Corrections* 2 (February 1989): 23.

16. *Ibid.*, pp. 23–24.

17. Alvin W. Cohn, "The Failure of Correctional Management: Recycling the Middle Manager," *Federal Probation* 59 (June 1995): 10.

18. *Ibid.*

19. *Ibid.*

20. *Ibid.*, p. 15.

21. Samuel H. Pillsbury, "Understanding Penal Reform: The Dynamic of Change," *The Journal of Criminal Law and Criminology* 80 (1989): 726–780.

22. *Ibid.*, pp. 726–727.

23. George Bernard Shaw, *The Crime of Imprisonment* 13 (1922).

24. Harry E. Allen and Clifford E. Simonsen, *Corrections in America: An Introduction* (5th ed.) (New York: Macmillan, 1989), p. 66.

25. *Ibid.*, p. 71.

26. Quoted in Jim Bencivenga, "State Prisons: Crucibles for Justice," *The Christian Science Monitor* (July 28, 1988): 14–15.

27. *Ibid.*

28. National Institute of Corrections, "Editor's Note," *Research in Corrections* 2 (February 1989).

29. *Ibid.*, p. 1.

30. *New York Times* (October 14, 1986).

31. *Gainesville Sun* (April 21, 1988): 3B.

32. McDonald, "The Cost of Corrections," p. 19.

33. U.S. Department of Justice, National Institute of Justice Research in Brief, *Making Confinement Decisions* (Washington, D.C.: Author, 1987), pp. 2–3.

34. *Ibid.*, p. 4.

35. David Osborne and Ted Gaebler, *Reinventing Government: How the Entrepreneurial Spirit Is Transforming the Public Sector* (Reading, Mass.: Addison-Wesley, 1992), pp. 19–20.

36. William G. Archambeault and Betty J. Archambeault, *Computers in Criminal Justice Administration and Management: Introduction to Emerging Issues and Applications* (2d ed.) (Cincinnati, Ohio: Anderson, 1989), pp. 1, 3.

37. William G. Archambeault and Betty J. Archambeault, *Correctional Supervisory Management: Principles of Organization, Policy, and Law* (Englewood Cliffs, N.J.: Prentice Hall), p. 10.

38. Archambeault and Archambeault, *Computers in Criminal Justice Administration and Management,* p. 63.

Index

Decision-maker role of police chief, 108
Declaration of Independence, 12
Defense attorneys, 158, 256
Definition, principle of, 26
Delay in processing cases, dilemma of,
    193–95
Del Carmen, Rolando, 275
Delegating style of management, 109
Demassing, 43
Deming, W. Edwards, 415
Democratic leadership (management) style,
    38–39, 109, 267, 268
Demographic trends, 406, 407
Detention facilities, liability and design of, 338
Detention jail officers, 254
de Tocqueville, Alexis, 161–62
Dickens, Charles, 193
Digital audio transcription system, 394
DiIulio, John J., Jr., 230, 239, 240, 413
Dilbert principle, 21–22
Disabilities, people with, 334–35
Disasters, major, 138
Discipline and discharge
    employee rights and, 320–22
    political affiliations and, 326
Discovery, process of, 167
Discrimination
    age, 314, 317, 323
    disparate treatment and, 315–17
    legislation against employment, 313–14
    religious, 329
    reverse, 317–18
Disparate impact, 315
Disparate treatment, 315–17
Dispatch systems, technologically enhanced,
    385
Dissemination tasks of CEO, 107
Disturbance handler, CEO as, 108
Diversification, 43
Division of labor, 23, 25, 83–84
Document imaging, 390–91, 392
Downward communication, 31
Drivers in environmental scanning, 405
Driving under the influence (DUI) arrests, expe-
    diting, 380–81
Drucker, Peter, 28, 117
Drug courts, 193
Drugfire network, 385–86
Drug interdiction and treatment in prisons,
    287–88
    drug addiction, treatment for, 221
    drug deterrence programs, 272
Drugs in workplace, 332–34
Drug testing, 333–34
Due deference doctrine, 218
Due process. 251
    court interpreters and, 200
    crime control through, 14–15
    discipline and discharge and, 321
    property interest in employment and, 319,
        320

Due process clause
    of Fifth Amendment, 318
    of Fourteenth Amendment, 324
DUI arrests, technology for expediting, 380–81
Durham, Alexis, 295

E

Education
    of chief of police, 113
    of correctional officers, 251
EEOC v. *Wyoming*, 317
Effectiveness/efficiency, specialization and in-
    creased, 84
Eighth Amendment to Constitution, 218
Electronic filing, 390
Electronic kiosks, 393
Electronic monitoring, 271, 274–75
Electronics. *See* Technology
Elmira, prison at, 69
Emerson, Ralph Waldo, 163
Empathy, 42
Employee rights and responsibilities, 312–43
    Americans with Disabilities Act (ADA) and,
        314, 334–35
    civil liability in justice administration, 335–38
    constitutional rights, 324–34
        alcohol and drugs in workplace, 332–34
        free speech, 324–27
        misuse of firearms, 331–32
        moonlighting, 331
        religious practices, 328–29
        residency requirements, 330–31
        searches and seizures, 327–28
        self-incrimination, 328
        sexual misconduct, 329–30
    employment relationship and, 315–24
        affirmative action and, 317–18
        age discrimination, 314, 317, 323
        discipline and discharge, 320–22
        disparate treatment, 315–17
        pay and benefits, 322–23
        property rights in employment, 318–20
        workplace safety, 323–24
    legislation on, 313–14
Employer model of prison industries, 223
Endispute, Inc., 167
Entrepreneur, CEO as, 108
Environment, sociotechnical, 266
Environmental scanning, 405
Equal Employment Opportunity Commission
    (EEOC), 317
Equal opportunity law, 315
Equal Pay Act, 34, 323
Esprit de corps, group, 84
Estelle, W.J., 72, 73
Estelle v. *Gamble*, 73
Ethics, medical, 198–99
Ethnic inmate self-help groups, 249
Etzioni, Amitai, 21